Aesthetics: the Big Questions

Philosophy: The Big Questions

Series Editor: James P. Sterba, University of Notre Dame, Indiana

Designed to elicit a philosophical response in the mind of the student, this distinctive series of anthologies provides essential classical and contemporary readings that serve to make the central questions of philosophy come alive for today's students. It presents complete coverage of the Anglo-American tradition of philosophy as well as the kinds of questions and challenges that it confronts today, both from other cultural traditions and from theoretical movements such as feminism and postmodernism.

Aesthetics: The Big Questions
Edited by Carolyn Korsmeyer

Epistemology: The Big Questions
Edited by Linda Martín Alcoff

Ethics: The Big Questions
Edited by James P. Sterba

Metaphysics: The Big Questions
Edited by Peter van Inwagen and Dean W. Zimmerman

Philosophy of Language: The Big Questions
Edited by Andrea Nye

Philosophy of Religion: The Big Questions
Edited by Eleonore Stump and Michael J. Murray

Race, Class, Gender, and Sexuality: The Big Questions
Edited by Naomi Zack, Laurie Shrage, and Crispin Sartwell

Philosophy: The Big Questions
Edited by Ruth J. Sample, Charles W. Mills, and James P. Sterba

AESTHETICS:

The Big Questions

EDITED BY CAROLYN KORSMEYER

Blackwell
Publishing

© 1998 by Blackwell Publishing Ltd

BLACKWELL PUBLISHING
350 Main Street, Malden, MA 02148-5020, USA
9600 Garsington Road, Oxford OX4 2DQ, UK
550 Swanston Street, Carlton, Victoria 3053, Australia

First published 1998

10   2008

Library of Congress Cataloging-in-Publication Data

Aesthetics : the big questions / edited by Carolyn Korsmeyer
    p.   cm. — (Philosophy, the big questions; 2)
  Includes bibliographical references and index.
  ISBN 978-0-631-20593-7 (hbk); ISBN 978-0-631-20594-4 (pbk.)
  1. Aesthetics. I. Korsmeyer, Carolyn. II. Series.
BH39.A297   1998
111'.85—dc21   97–47399
                                                          CIP

A catalogue record for this title is available from the British Library.

Set in 10 ½ on 12 ½ pt Galliard
by Ace Filmsetting Ltd, Frome, Somerset

The publisher's policy is to use permanent paper from mills that operate a sustainable forestry policy, and which has been manufactured from pulp processed using acid-free and elementary chlorine-free practices. Furthermore, the publisher ensures that the text paper and cover board used have met acceptable environmental accreditation standards.

For further information on
Blackwell Publishing, visit our website:
www.blackwellpublishing.com

CONTENTS

CONTENTS

PLATES

ACKNOWLEDGMENTS

I would like to thank Ruth Kelly for her invaluable help tracking down and obtaining permissions to reprint materials in this book. Four other assistants were also generous with their time and energy in helping to assemble this manuscript, and I thank them as well for contributing several of the Prefaces. Jason Adsit wrote the Preface for Part Six; David Kaspar wrote the Preface for Part Three; and Jennifer McMahon Railey and Sarah Worth jointly composed the Prefaces to Parts Two and Five.

The editor and publishers gratefully acknowledge the following for permission to reprint copyright material:

Anderson, Richard, from *Calliope's Sisters* (Prentice-Hall Inc., Upper Saddle River, N.J. © 1990), pp. 1, 4–5, 34–7, 40–54, 238–40. Reprinted by permission of Prentice-Hall Inc., Upper Saddle River, NJ.
Aristotle, from *The Poetics of Aristotle*, translated by Stephen Halliwell. Copyright © 1987 by Stephen Halliwell. Used by permission of the publisher.
Battersby, Christine, from *Gender and Genius: Towards a Feminist Aesthetics*, pp. 23, 71–8, 103–5, 156–7, first published in Great Britain by The Women's Press Ltd, 1989, 34 Great Sutton Street, London EC1V 0DX, used by permission of The Women's Press Ltd.
Baxandall, Michael, "Truth and Other Cultures" from *Patterns of Intention* (Yale University Press, New Haven, 1985), pp. 105–11.
Bourdieu, Pierre, from *Distinction*, Introduction reprinted by permission of the publisher Harvard University Press, Cambridge, Mass. Copyright © 1984 by Routledge and Kegan Paul Ltd, L'Editions de Minuit, Paris, and by the President and Fellows of Harvard College.
Burke, Edmund, from *A Philosophical Enquiry into the Origin of Our Ideas of the Sublime and Beautiful* (Boulton, J. T. [ed.]) (Routlege and Kegan Paul, London, 1958), pp. 32–3, 38–40, 44–8, 67–78, 124–5, 134–5. Reprinted by kind permission of Professor J. T. Boulton.
Carroll, Noël, from *The Philosophy of Horror* (Routledge, New York, 1990), pp. 14–19, 26–7, 157–8, 182–8. Reprinted by kind permission of Professor Noël Carroll.

Cohen, Ted, "High and Low Thinking About High and Low Art" from *Journal of Aesthetics and Art Criticism* 51:2 (Spring 1993), and by kind permission of Professor Ted Cohen.

Danto, Arthur C., "The Artworld" from *The Journal of Philosophy* LXI, 19 (October 15, 1964). Reprinted by kind permission of the *Journal of Philosophy* and Professor Arthur Danto.

Danto, Arthur C., "The Vietnam Veterans Memorial" from *The Nation* (August 31, 1985) reprinted with permission from the August 31 issue of *The Nation* magazine.

Dewey, John, "The Live Creature" from *Art As Experience,* from *John Dewey, The Later Works, 1925–1953,* vol. 10: 1934, ed. Jo Ann Boydston (Carbondale, Illinois: Southern Illinois University Press, 1987), reprinted with the permission of the Center for Dewey Studies, Southern Illinois University at Carbondale.

Duncan, Carol, "The MoMA's Hot Mamas" from *Art Journal,* 48, Summer 1989. Reprinted by permission of the College Art Association. Article reprinted from Duncan, Carol, *The Aesthetics of Power: Essays in the Critical History of Art* (Cambridge University Press, New York, 1993), by permission of Carol Duncan.

Eaton, Marcia Muelder, from *Aesthetics and the Good Life* (Fairleigh Dickinson University Press, Rutherford, Madison/Teaneck, New Jersey 1989), pp. 28–36.

Feagin, Susan L., "Paintings and Their Places" from *Australasian Journal of Philosophy,* vol. 73, no. 2 (June 1995).

Foucault, Michel, reprinted with changes from *Language, Counter-Memory, Practice: Selected Essays and Interviews,* pp. 113–38. Edited, with an Introduction, by Donald F. Bouchard. Copyright © 1977 by Cornell University. Used by permission of the publisher, Cornell University Press.

Freeland, Cynthia, "Realist Horror" from *Philosophy and Film* (Routledge, New York, 1995).

Gadamer, Hans-Georg, from *Truth and Method,* pp. 85–6, 97–8, 101–5, 109–16, English translation copyright © 1975 by Sheed and Ward Ltd., second revised edition Copyright © 1989 by The Crossroad Publishing Company. Reprinted with permission of The Continuum Publishing Company, New York.

Hanson, Karen, "Dressing Down Dressing Up" from *Hypatia,* 5:2 (Summer, 1990) (Indiana University Press, 1990).

Hume, David, "Of the Standard of Taste" from *Essays, Moral, Political, and Literary,* ed. Eugene F. Miller (Liberty Fund Inc., 8335 Allison Pointe Trail, #300, Indianapolis, IN 46250-1687). Used by permission.

Kant, Immanuel, from *Critique of Judgment* (Pluhar, Werner, S. [trans]) (Hackett Publishing Co. Inc., Indianapolis, 1987).

Murdoch, Iris, from *The Sovereignty of Good* (Routledge and Kegan Paul, London, 1991).

Nettl, Bruno, "Musical Thinking and Thinking about Music in Ethnomusicology" from *Journal of Aesthetics and Art Criticism,* 52:1 (Winter, 1994), and by kind permission of Bruno Nettl.

Nietzsche, Friedrich, from *The Birth of Tragedy and the Case of Wagner,* translated by Walter Kaufmann, pp. 33–8, 40–3, 143–4. Copyright © 1966 by Random House, Inc. Reprinted by permission of Random House Inc.

Nochlin, Linda, "Why Are There No Great Women Artists?" reprinted by kind permission of the author.

Norman, Michael, "Carnage and Glory, Legends and Lies" from *The New York Times*, July 7, 1996. By permission of *The New York Times*.

Nussbaum, Martha, "Form and Content, Philosophy and Literature" from *Love's Knowledge: Essays on Philosophy and Literature* (Oxford University Press, New York, 1990), pp. 3–5, 17–18, 23–4, 27, 40–2, 47–8, 53. Reprinted by permission of Oxford University Press.

Parker, Rozsika and Pollock, Griselda, "Crafty Women and the Hierarchy of the Arts" from *Old Mistresses: Women, Art and Ideology* (Routledge and Kegan Paul Ltd., London, 1981), pp. 50–1, 54, 58–62, 66–71, 75, 78, 80.

Plato, from *The Republic* (Grube, G. M. S. [trans.], Reeve, C. D. C. [revised]) (Hackett Publishing Company. All rights reserved.)

Poe, Edgar Allan, from *The Complete Tales and Poems of Edgar Allan Poe* (Vintage Books, New York 1975).

Sophocles, "Oedipus at Colonus" from *Three Theban Plays*, translated by Robert Fagles. Translation copyright © 1982 by Robert Fagles. Used by permission of Viking Penguin, a division of Penguin Books USA Inc.

Stolnitz, Jerome, "The Aesthetic Attitude" from *Aesthetics and Philosophy of Art Criticism, A Critical Introduction* (Houghton Mifflin Co., Boston, 1960). Reprinted by kind permission of Dr Jerome Stolnitz.

Suzuki, Daisetz, "Zen and the Art of Tea" from *Zen and Japanese Culture* (copyright © 1959 by Princeton University Press, revised in 1987. Reprinted by permission of Princeton University Press), pp. 271–8, 313–14.

The publishers apologize for any errors or omissions in the above list, and would be grateful to be notified of any corrections that should be incorporated in the next edition or reprint of this book.

Philosophical theories can be considered extended answers to certain kinds of questions. Questions about human conduct and the nature of obligation, for example, generate ethical theories; inquiries about the limits and grounds for knowledge give rise to epistemology, and so on. This anthology is intended to introduce students to the area of philosophy known as aesthetics and philosophy of art. The collection is organized into six sections, each of which contains entries addressing a central question about the nature of art, of artists, and of aesthetic response and appreciation. The entries combine classic pieces from the history of philosophy, contemporary essays that carry on that heritage, and challenges that depart from the assumptions and conceptual frameworks commonly adopted by philosophers in the western intellectual tradition. Some of these challenges come from other cultural traditions such as those developed in Africa and Asia; these implicitly offer alternative ways to understand aesthetic values and art. Other sorts of challenge emerge within the framework of the western tradition, such as the feminist entries included here, which examine aesthetic concepts through the lens of gender.

The questions that define the first two sections address what are sometimes seen as the most basic issues of aesthetics. Part One advances the question, "What is Art?" What we call "art" includes artifacts and events produced and organized with a certain conceptual framework in mind. Art is often categorized as something especially valuable and fine, and in recognition of this works of visual art often command high prices; ticket sales to events such as symphonies and operas may also be beyond the means of many. These facts may seem to imply that art is set apart from ordinary life, that it is captured and saved in galleries and museums and special venues of this nature. But we also need to remember that art is an activity that produces many forms, including popular entertainment such as movies and television series, pop concerts and radio broadcasts. How far ought the concept of art be extended? To clothing and fashion? Tattoos? Eating and drinking? Furniture, embroidery, and artifacts of use? The issue of the boundaries of art generates additional questions regarding the viability of a distinction between "fine art" and "craft," between "high" and "low" or "popular" art, as well as between that which is art and that which simply is something else. Can we speak of art in the same terms across cultures and history? Would what we call art today be recognizable to peoples of the past or to those who occupy dramatically different societies? The answers that theorists present to such questions differ widely. Some believe that art is too varied and disparate a phenomenon to admit of any single definition at all; others believe that there is a common creative impulse that produces artifacts in all societies, and that despite differences they bear enough similarities all to merit the label "art."

Part One presents a selection of entries that range from a focus on contemporary art movements and their theoretical foundations, to the social contexts in which art and artists are produced and identified. John Dewey's classic statement from *Art as Experience* asserts that art needs to be understood as an outgrowth of the kinds of aesthetic experience we appreciate in everyday life. Arts from vastly different cultures pique consideration of what may be common to art, or perhaps what remains irreconcilably different. Richard Anderson examines the art of several societies to identify a common, unifying trait. Considering contemporary art movements and their departure from past traditions, Arthur Danto stresses the context of theory that is necessary in order for us even to recognize artworks. The categories of fine art and craft are analyzed by Rozsika Parker and Griselda Pollock, who discover gender roles at work in the classification and evaluation of the arts. A description of the Japanese tea ceremony by D. T. Suzuki offers for comparison and contrast an activity that is not considered an art in the western tradition; and Karen Hanson ponders what might be lost from aesthetic consideration by philosophy's customary neglect of fashion.

Part Two, "Experience and Appreciation: How Do We Encounter Art?" is divided into two segments. The first contains entries on the nature of what is generally termed "aesthetic experience," that is to say, the experience of noticing and appreciating the qualities presented by objects that we are moved to find "beautiful" or aesthetically pleasing in other ways. Among the three representatives of this topic, the reader will note an important division in the ways that the nature of the aesthetic is considered, for two authors (Jerome Stolnitz and Marcia Eaton) consider the aesthetic to be a particular kind of enjoyment, and the third (Hans-Georg Gadamer) considers it to be a particular mode of knowledge. This difference marks an important division in the history of aesthetics. Aesthetics is often interpreted as having its beginnings in the Enlightenment philosophy of the eighteenth century, a period that came to be dominated by "philosophies of taste" that attempted to articulate what is special about aesthetic pleasure. The majority conclusion was that beauty and other aesthetic values are pleasures that are definable in contrast to the practical values of morals, science, and functional necessity. As a result, some aesthetic theory tends to divorce aesthetic value from cognitive values such as understanding and insight. (Of particular influence here is Immanuel Kant's *Critique of Judgment*, to which several authors in this volume refer.) However, there is a competing concept of the aesthetic that rejects the idea that aesthetic value is detachable from the insight and understanding for which we value art. Hans-Georg Gadamer, a contemporary German philosopher, is a vociferous advocate of the idea that aesthetic experience is a mode of understanding. Theorists who stress the cognitive significance of art also appear in Part Four, "Can We Learn From Art?" and in the discussions of tragedy, sublimity, and horror included in Part Five.

The second part of Part Two turns to another aspect of the experience of art and aesthetic value, namely, the conditions under which many of us encounter works of art. Our education in art may be formal or implicit, and we may feel at home or alien in the world of fine art. How does this come about, and what consequences does it have for our appreciation of what others value as the finest products of our times? What is the role of institutions in the development of our appreciation of art, institutions such as schools and museums? When we do encounter art, how is it presented to us? Such questions reflect on both the subject of art's identity discussed in the first section, and upon the social expectations and contexts that influence our appreciation, for our enjoyment of art is shaped by the way it is presented by conventions and histories of display. Two of the entries in this discussion, those by Kevin Melchionne and Hilde Hein, consider the general question of art education and museum spaces, and two others focus on specific types of art. Carol Duncan analyzes one of the icons of modern painting, Pablo Picasso, in a way that reveals the continuity between the presentation of female bodies in art and in pornography. Arthur Danto discusses the frequently visited Vietnam Veterans Memorial and demonstrates how art works influence and perpetuate private memories and experiences of political events. These latter two pieces make us aware that who we are and our own particular histories can influence how we appreciate art. This leads to the questions of evaluation and assessment addressed next.

Any discussion of art and aesthetic appreciation will sooner or later confront controversy over value. Part Three, "Aesthetic Evaluation: Who Decides?" contains a set of essays that consider taste and its varieties and the questions of how we adjudicate among competing assessments of art. This section includes one of the classic positions regarding the standards that taste might admit, that of the eighteenth-century empiricist philosopher David Hume, as well as a statement from one of the vociferous skeptics about grounds for standards of taste of our own time, the sociologist Pierre Bourdieu. Is there an optimum approach to art that ideally reveals its value to all? Is there a viable distinction between good and bad taste? Are we limited by our own interests not only as to what we prefer, but also what we can appreciate at all? Can we appreciate art works if we are put off or disgusted by the message they apparently convey? The influence of interest over appreciation is further explored by Peggy Zeglin Brand, who focuses on some contemporary art that is particularly difficult to confront because of its explicitly political content. Questions of taste naturally lead to consideration of the types of experiences we enjoy. Many of us are aware that we are supposed to value the high art of our culture, such as the works of Shakespeare, Milton, Goethe, Wagner. Yet we spend our time watching television or reading mystery novels, seeming by our actions to prefer "low" or "popular" art over fine art. We may wonder whether people who prefer popular art have worse taste than others, though Ted Cohen suggests another way to approach the large and small communities of those who appreciate different kinds of art.

It was mentioned above that approaches to aesthetic value fall into two large groups, those that conceive of aesthetic value as a type of delight or pleasure, and those that regard it as a species of insight or cognition. The latter approach is implicit in the discussions of Part Four, "Can We Learn from Art?" The terms of the debate over this question were actually set long ago, and we have here one of the first discussions of the subject, that of Plato from the *Republic*. Plato is famous (or infamous) for his censorship of poetry, which he considered a poor source of knowledge and more apt to be dangerous than enlightening. He does art the honor of crediting it with considerable psychological and political power in his recommendation that stories be carefully controlled. (His contemporary, Aristotle, argued that poetry and all *mimesis* (imitation) could be a source for learning. A selection from his *Poetics* is included in the next section and can be read along with Plato in Part Four as well.) Despite Plato's concerns, many other philosophers are more inclined to credit art with the ability to enlighten and inform, as the subsequent entries in this section attest. Iris Murdoch, herself a contemporary platonist, argues that experiences of beauty and of art open the mind to truths of the world and divert us from our customary self-interest. Art can thereby be a force for moral education. Literature in particular is often regarded as a source of insight about human life and values, and Martha Nussbaum argues that certain narratives ought to be considered supplements to standard philosophy. Movies and paintings are also included in this debate by two writers, Michael Norman and Susan Feagin, who are somewhat more cautious about assigning art an educational role.

Aesthetic experience is not always pleasant. Indeed, some of the most powerful and revered examples of art deliver downright painful emotions. Three categories of difficult aesthetic experience are the tragic, the sublime, and the horrible, which are discussed in Part Five, "Why Do We Enjoy Painful Experience in Art?" Why do we seek out stories about death, murder, loss, and madness, when these are the very events that we would flee were we confronted with them in our own actual lives? This question has piqued philosophers since the days of the ancient Greeks, who invented the tragic theatre and wondered themselves why such painful stories could be so appreciated, even revered. Two classic statements about what is gained through tragedy are included in this section, those of Aristotle and of Friedrich Nietzsche.

Another extreme experience that seems to participate as much in pain as in pleasure is the encounter with the sublime. Sublime experience was a matter of particular interest among eighteenth-century theorists, who were intrigued by aesthetic encounters that strain the limits of human endurance and understanding. These might be tested by experiences of the might and danger of nature or by art that teases the boundaries of human control and understanding. There are three entries on the sublime here. Two philosophers, Edmund Burke and Immanuel Kant, both speculate about the source of pleasure in the sublime. A short story by Edgar Allan Poe describes a fictional encounter with a powerful force of nature, an actual whirlpool off the coast of Norway, during which the narrator undergoes experiences the description of which aptly combines with Burke and Kant to suggest further ideas about sublime experience.

The horror story is a genre of art which has gained a special popularity in movies. Accounting for the enjoyment of horror is even more perplexing than for the tragic and the sublime, for it seems to be an even more perverse search for one of the emotional experiences we most avoid in real life: fear. Yet it is an increasingly popular form of art, and the last two essays of this section by Noël Carroll and Cynthia Freeland speculate about the nature of horror, its role as art, and our continuing attraction to it.

The final section of the volume addresses the relationship between the artist and the work of art. How and under what conditions is art created and recognized? What social and personal factors enter into creativity? Once a work is finished, whether it be a piece of music, a novel, a poem, a painting, need we refer back to the actual artist in order to know what it means or how to assess it? Questions of genius, creativity, tradition, innovation, and interpretation are addressed by the essays of Part Six, "Where is the Artist in the Work of Art?" The first part of this section focuses on the notion of creative genius, beginning with Kant's influential statement praising the artistic genius. Kant and other promoters of genius are criticized by Christine Battersby, who argues that the concept is exclusionary, especially to women, because rather than generally identifying individuals of unique talent, the idea of genius selects only from males of certain segments of society. The social determinants of training in the arts are discussed broadly by Linda Nochlin, who focuses on the traditional training of painters that excluded all but a few women.

The latter two essays and several in earlier sections prepare us to consider the influence of social context over how we identify and evaluate artists. This is directly addressed in the second segment of Part Six, in which four essays foreground the context within which art is created and achieves its meaning. Michel Foucault considers the phenomenon of identifying an "author" within a "work," and his discussion considers literature in particular. W. Msosa Mwale examines the role of individual master dancers in perpetuating and changing one traditional African dance form. The problem of determining the meaning of a painting and of discovering what the artist intended to convey is addressed by Michael Baxandall through the case of the artist Piero della Francesca. Bruno Nettl discusses the social and cultural traditions of the music of three societies that illuminate the identification and evaluation of composers.

For those who wish to read beyond the authors here included, each section concludes with a list of suggested further reading.

None of these sections is devoted to any particular genre of art, nor is the distinction among the different art forms or their definitional parameters addressed by the book. However, the questions that organize the essays pertain to many forms of art, and most of the major recognized arts are discussed in the book as a whole. Painting, for example, is treated in the essays by Rozsika Parker and Griselda Pollock, Susan Feagin, Linda Nochlin, and Michael Baxandall. Literature is the chief topic of interest for Martha Nussbaum, Iris Murdoch, Friedrich Nietzsche, Aristotle, and Michel Foucault. Music is the topic of the essay by Bruno Nettl, and it is also discussed by Nietzsche and by W. Msosa

Mwale; the latter's essay chiefly discusses dance. Movies are the subject of the pieces on horror by Noël Carroll and Cynthia Freeland, and Michael Norman's discussion of war. Ted Cohen also considers movies in the course of his discussion of high and low art. What are sometimes called "crafts" are discussed by Parker and Pollock and by Richard Anderson, and fashion is the subject of the essay by Karen Hanson. Art of cultures that do not share the same traditions affords a cross-cultural comparison of how these questions may be considered in different contexts. This opportunity is furnished by the contributions by Richard Anderson, D. T. Suzuki, Hilde Hein, W. Msosa Mwale, and Bruno Nettl.

This collection is assembled so that one who reads the selections in the order of their presentation will gradually move towards material that refers increasingly to previous selections. In this way the influence and continuity of tradition, as well as the challenges mounted to that tradition emerge. However, no field is presentable in only one manner, and there are numerous other ways to group this material thematically. If one wishes to focus on the feminist analyses, for example, the essays by Parker and Pollock, Hanson, Brand, Freeland, Battersby, and Nochlin address questions about gender and art, artistic point of view and evaluation, and creativity and genius from feminist critical perspectives. The concept of the aesthetic is addressed not only by the entries in the first part of Part Two, but also by Hume, Brand, and Nietzsche. The historical roots of aesthetics and philosophy of art may be traced chronologically by reading the entries from Plato, Aristotle, Hume, Burke, Kant, Nietzsche, and Dewey. Political questions concerning art, ideology, and power are the central focus of Bourdieu and Freeland, and are also addressed by Brand and Mwale. Aesthetic experience and everyday life is considered by Dewey, Hanson, Melchionne, Suzuki, Anderson, and Cohen.

Whether read in the order of presentation or organized into different clusters, these essays together participate in the continuing discussion of central questions raised by art and aesthetic encounters.

PART ONE

WHAT IS ART?

Preface

One of the basic questions in the philosophy of art concerns the concept of art itself. So many different objects, events, and activities are designated "art" that one may wonder just what characteristic they all have in common that merits the shared label. The question is complicated even further when we consider artifacts produced in various societies. Different cultures have different artistic traditions, and what is considered art changes over time even within a single society. Rather than anticipating the limited suggestions of a dictionary definition, "what is art?" is a question that probes the conceptual frameworks employed when considering the social functions of art, the role of the creator in producing art, and the sorts of values that art offers its audiences and participants.

In the western intellectual tradition, the first reigning concept of art held that art is *mimesis*, that is, that it is in some sense or other an "imitation" of reality. From the ancient Greeks through early modern European theory, mimetic concepts of art held sway, even though the types of art produced in that long historical period varied enormously. With the rise of Romanticism in the late eighteenth century and an increased focus on the imagination of the creative artist, the concept of *expression* came to play a more central role in concepts of art, and for a time many philosophers crafted definitions that refined the idea of expression so that it would pertain to all works of art and to only works of art. Other theorists explored the difference between art and the reality that so often comprises the subject of art, concluding that what makes art distinctive is its *form*. Formalist theories, which are particularly suitable for visual arts and music, emphasize the composition, arrangement, line, color, and harmony of the art work, and pay less attention to the content or subject matter of art.

The problem with all of these options is that in selecting one or even several features of art works as defining characteristics, there remain large numbers of objects and practices that one might want to consider art but that do not fit the definition very aptly. Craft objects are one such case, for they do not imitate, and their practical functions limit the degree of expression permissible. Perhaps they qualify in terms of form, but one may doubt that their formal features exhaust the valuable artistic qualities of such functional objects. Moreover, mimetic, expressionist, and formalist definitions of art all emerge from a western philosophical tradition, and while some may be applicable to objects developed in other cultural contexts, one suspects that those definitions may not reach the intent of their originators, and hence that they miss what is most important about such objects.

So difficult is the task of arriving at a single definition of art that some philosophers of the mid-twentieth century abandoned the search altogether. Following the idea of Ludwig Wittgenstein that certain concepts are not definable because their meaning shifts and emerges in context and use, these theorists argued that the general question "what is art?" is misleading because it presumes there is an answer when in fact there is not. Two of the entries in this section, those by Richard Anderson and Arthur Danto, directly address this issue. The essays in this section by no means deal with all of the definitions of art that have been proposed, nor do they exhaust the examples of art that one needs to consider if the question "what is art?" is to be answered thoroughly. But they approach the question in different ways and invite continued exploration of the idea of art and of the objects and events that are considered art, as well as the social conditions that produce art and identify certain people as artists.

The opening piece is by John Dewey, an American philosopher of the mid-twentieth century known for his development of a concept of art from the perspective of pragmatist philosophy. Dewey complains that art objects of the "high" or "fine" art tradition have become so venerated that they are virtually detached from the circumstances in which art develops, and thus they have become remote from our daily experience and understanding. Dewey recommends that we return to the very concept of *experience* of art and to the sorts of aesthetic experience that make up our everyday lives. Dewey draws our attention to the very foundation of the urge to create works of art: the aesthetic enjoyment of life itself.

Richard Anderson is aware that philosophical concepts of art have chiefly arisen within a Euro-American cultural tradition, and he seeks to avoid such narrowness by considering the common characteristics of art that can be discovered by looking at art produced by a number of very different societies. (The section of his work reprinted here focuses on art of the traditional Inuits or Eskimos.) Anderson takes on the challenge mentioned above of those philosophers who came to the conclusion that art is the sort of phenomenon that does not admit of a definition, that it is an "open concept," and its objects do not share any common important characteristic. Anderson believes that art does manifest common traits, and he proposes a definition that he thinks serves to characterize artistic activity across all cultures and traditions.

The contemporary philosopher Arthur Danto approaches art by taking seriously the problem of defining art works in all their bewildering variety. He too addresses the challenge of the claim that art is indefinable, arguing that the characteristics linking all and only works of art are themselves theoretical, not discernible properties that one can discover upon inspection of a representative sample of art. His route to this position is Dada and Pop Art, both of which produced objects that are visually indiscernible from "real things." These phenomena, argues Danto, force the definition of art by bringing it to the surface of our awareness. He proposes that it is the very concept of art, its theoretical basis, which – though evolving through history – constitutes the essential characteristic of art. Though Anderson and Danto both conclude that art requires and offers a unified conceptual treatment, their approaches and their characterizations of the concept of art differ greatly. The artworks they examine in arriving at their conclusions are also quite different, for Anderson takes a sweeping look at artifacts produced world wide, and Danto delves deeply into changes in the concept of art in the western tradition.

Feminist art historians Rozsika Parker and Griselda Pollock offer us yet another approach to the concept of art by examining the exclusion of certain creations from the category of "fine" or "high" art. Why, they ask, has the work of so few women appeared in the canon of great art? Women's creative activity, which traditionally included still-life painting, needlework, and other domestic crafts, is almost invariably classified as "minor" or "decorative" or "craft," labels that contrast to the notion of fine art. Parker and Pollock trace the history of certain types of craft to show how they in fact are used conceptually to shore up the notion of fine art, just as the notion of "feminine" sharpens and supports the notion of "masculine." They offer a perspective on the development of the concept of art that draws attention to the social function of such concepts, observing that categories such as art depend for their meaning on what they exclude as well as what they include.

The final two essays in the section do not address the concept of art directly. Rather, they present two sorts of activities and objects that do not ordinarily come to mind when one thinks of art, though perhaps they should. These essays thus indirectly challenge our ideas about art and aesthetic activity by broadening consideration of artistically important phenomena. D. T. Suzuki, a Japanese philosopher of Zen Buddhism who introduced many western readers to Zen in the earlier part of the twentieth century, describes the Japanese tea ceremony. The "art of tea" is a practice that manifests the Zen values of simplicity, harmony, and tranquility. The tea ceremony is an important artistic practice of Japanese traditional culture, and one may ponder the degree to which it conforms to the ideas advanced by the first three essays. Certainly the experience it induces seems to fit Dewey's notion that one should begin to investigate art by first considering the experience that affords aesthetic attention.

Fashion is the focus of Karen Hanson's essay. Clothing, while often considered part of the "craft" of a culture (note that Anderson's essay includes Eskimo ceremonial clothing among its examples), is usually scorned by philosophers as of little importance. In this way, traditional western philosophy shares certain values with contemporary feminism. Hanson suspects that both philosophers and feminists have been uneasy about the fact that clothing reminds us of the fact that we are mortal, physical objects as well as minds. Rather than rejecting the "objecthood" that embodiment requires, as well as the fickle trends of fashion or standards of beauty, perhaps we ought to take clothing more seriously as something to be enjoyed in our everyday lives as well as something that reveals the inevitable impermanence of life.

While by no means exhaustive, the approaches of these six essays to the concept of art and objects of artistic value invite the reader to extended consideration of the question, What is art'?

1   The Live Creature

John Dewey

By one of the ironic perversities that often attend the course of affairs, the existence of the works of art upon which formation of aesthetic theory depends has become an obstruction to theory about them. For one reason, these works are products that exist externally and physically. In common conception, the work of art is often identified with the building, book, painting, or statue in its existence apart from human experience. Since the actual work of art is what the product does with and in experience, the result is not favorable to understanding. In addition, the very perfection of some of these products, the prestige they possess because of a long history of unquestioned admiration, creates conventions that get in the way of fresh insight. When an art product once attains classic status, it somehow becomes isolated from the human conditions under which it was brought into being and from the human consequences it engenders in actual life-experience.

When artistic objects are separated from both conditions of origin and operation in experience, a wall is built around them that renders almost opaque their general significance, with which aesthetic theory deals. Art is remitted to a separate realm, where it is cut off from that association with the materials and aims of every other form of human effort, undergoing, and achievement. A primary task is thus imposed upon one who undertakes to write upon the philosophy of the fine arts. This task is to restore continuity between the refined and intensified forms of experience that are works of art and the everyday events, doings, and sufferings that are universally recognized to constitute experience. Mountain peaks do not float unsupported; they do not even just rest upon the earth. They *are* the earth in one of its manifest operations. It is the business of those who are concerned with the theory of the earth, geographers and geologists, to make this fact evident in its various implications. The theorist who would deal philosophically with fine art has a like task to accomplish.

If one is willing to grant this position, even if only by way of temporary experiment, he will see that there follows a conclusion at first sight surprising. In order to understand the meaning of artistic products, we have to forget them for a time, to turn aside from them and have recourse to the ordinary forces and conditions of experience that we do not usually regard as aesthetic. We must arrive at the theory of art by means of a detour. For theory is concerned with understanding, insight, not without exclamations of admiration, and stimulation of that emotional outburst often called appreciation. It is quite possible to enjoy flowers in their colored form and delicate fragrance without knowing anything about plants theoretically. But if one sets out to *understand* the flowering of plants, he is committed to finding out something about the interactions of soil, air, water and sunlight that condition the growth of plants.

By common consent, the Parthenon is a great work of art. Yet it has aesthetic standing only as the work becomes an experience for a human being. And, if one is to go beyond personal enjoyment into the formation of a theory about that large republic of art of which the building is one member, one has to be willing at some point in his reflections to turn from it to the bustling, arguing, acutely sensitive Athenian citizens, with civic sense identified with a civic religion, of whose experience the temple was an expression, and who built it not as a work of art but as a civic commemoration. The turning to them is as human beings who had needs that were a demand for the building and that were carried to fulfillment in it; it is not an examination such as might be carried on by a sociologist in search for material relevant to his purpose. The one who sets out to theorize about the aesthetic experience embodied in the Parthenon must realize in thought what the people into whose lives it entered had in common, as creators and as those who were satisfied with it, with people in our own homes and on our own streets.

In order to *understand* the aesthetic in its ultimate and approved forms, one must begin with it in the raw; in the events and scenes that hold the attentive eye and ear of man, arousing his interest and affording him enjoyment as he looks and listens: the sights that hold the crowd – the fire-engine rushing by; the machines excavating enormous holes in the earth; the human-fly climbing the steeple-side; the men perched high in air on girders, throwing and catching red-hot bolts. The sources of art in human experience will be learned by him who sees how the tense grace of the ball-player infects the onlooking crowd; who notes the delight of the housewife in tending her plants, and the intent interest of her good man in tending the patch of green in front of the house; the zest of the spectator in poking the wood burning on the hearth and in watching the darting flames and crumbling coals. These people, if questioned as to the reason for their actions, would doubtless return reasonable answers. The man who poked the sticks of burning wood would say he did it to make the fire burn better; but he is nonetheless fascinated by the colorful drama of change enacted before his eyes and imaginatively partakes in it. He does not remain a cold spectator. What Coleridge said of the reader of poetry is true in its way of all who are happily absorbed in their activities of mind and body: "The reader should be carried forward, not merely or chiefly by the mechanical impulse of curiosity, not by a restless desire to arrive at the final solution, but by the pleasurable activity of the journey itself."

The intelligent mechanic engaged in his job, interested in doing well and finding satisfaction in his handiwork, caring for his materials and tools with genuine affection, is artistically engaged. The difference between such a worker and the inept and careless bungler is as great in the shop as it is in the studio. Oftentimes the product may not appeal to the aesthetic sense of those who use the product. The fault, however, is oftentimes not so much with the worker as with the conditions of the market for which his product is designed. Were conditions and opportunities different, things as significant to the eye as those produced by earlier craftsmen would be made.

So extensive and subtly pervasive are the ideas that set Art upon a remote pedestal, that many a person would be repelled rather than pleased if told that he enjoyed his casual recreations, in part at least, because of their aesthetic quality. The arts which today have most vitality for the average person are things he does not take to be arts: for instance, the movie, jazzed music, the comic strip, and, too frequently, newspaper accounts of love-nests, murders, and exploits of bandits. For, when what he knows as art is relegated to the museum and gallery, the unconquerable impulse towards experiences enjoyable in themselves finds such outlet as the daily environment provides. Many a person who protests against the museum conception of art, still shares the fallacy from which that conception springs. For the popular notion comes from a separation of art from the objects and scenes of ordinary experience that many theorists and critics pride themselves upon holding and even elaborating. The times when select and distinguished objects are closely connected with the products of usual vocations are the times when appreciation of the former is most rife and most keen. When, because of their remoteness, the objects acknowledged by the cultivated to be works of fine art seem anemic to the mass of people, aesthetic hunger is likely to seek the cheap and the vulgar.

The factors that have glorified fine art by setting it upon a far-off pedestal did not arise within the realm of art nor is their influence confined to the arts. For many persons an aura of mingled awe and unreality encompasses the "spiritual" and the "ideal" while "matter" has become by contrast a term of depreciation, something to be explained away or apologized for. The forces at work are those that have removed religion as well as fine art from the scope of the common or community life. These forces have historically produced so many of the dislocations and divisions of modern life and thought that art could not escape their influence. We do not have to travel to the ends of the earth nor return many millennia in time to find peoples for whom everything that intensifies the sense of immediate living is an object of intense admiration. Bodily scarification, waving feathers, gaudy robes, shining ornaments of gold and silver, of emerald and jade, formed the contents of aesthetic arts, and, presumably, without the vulgarity of class exhibitionism that attends their analogues today. Domestic utensils, furnishings of tent and house, rugs, mats, jars, pots, bows, spears, were wrought with such delighted care that today we hunt them out and give them places of honor in our art museums. Yet in their own time and place, such things were enhancements of the processes of everyday life. Instead of being elevated to a niche apart, they belonged to display of prowess, the manifestation of group and clan membership, worship of gods, feasting and fasting, fighting, hunting, and all the rhythmic crises that punctuate the stream of living.

Dancing and pantomime, the sources of the art of the theater, flourished as part of religious rites and celebrations. Musical art abounded in the fingering of the stretched string, the beating of the taut skin, the blowing with reeds. Even in the caves, human habitations were adorned with colored pictures that kept alive to the senses experiences with the animals that were so closely bound with the lives of humans. Structures that housed their gods and the instrumentalities that facilitated commerce with the higher powers were wrought with especial fineness. But the arts of the drama, music, painting, and architecture thus exemplified had no peculiar connection with theaters, galleries, museums. They were part of the significant life of an organized community.

The collective life that was manifested in war, worship, the forum, knew no division between what was characteristic of these places and operations, and the arts that brought color, grace, and dignity, into them. Painting and sculpture were organically one with architecture, as that was one with the social purpose that buildings served. Music and song were intimate parts of the rites and ceremonies in which the meaning of group life was consummated. Drama was a vital reenactment of the legends and history of group life. Not even in Athens can such arts be torn loose from this setting in direct experience and yet retain their significant character. Athletic sports, as well as drama, celebrated and enforced traditions of race and group, instructing the people, commemorating glories, and strengthening their civic pride.

Under such conditions, it is not surprising that the Athenian Greeks, when they came to reflect upon art, formed the idea that it is an act of reproduction, or imitation. There are many objections to this conception. But the vogue of the theory is testimony to the close connection of the fine arts with daily life; the idea would not have occurred to any one had art been remote from the interests of life. For the doctrine did not signify that art was a literal copying of objects, but that it reflected the emotions and ideas that are associated with the chief institutions of social life. Plato felt this connection so strongly that it led him to his idea of the necessity of censorship of poets, dramatists, and musicians. Perhaps he exaggerated when he said that a change from the Doric to the Lydian mode in music would be the sure precursor of civic degeneration. But no contemporary would have doubted that music was an integral part of the ethos and the institutions of the community. The idea of "art for art's sake" would not have been even understood.

There must then be historic reasons for the rise of the compartmental conception of fine art. Our present museums and galleries to which works of fine art are removed and stored illustrate some of the causes that have operated to segregate art instead of finding it an attendant of temple, forum, and other forms of associated life. An instructive history of modern art could be written in terms of the formation of the distinctively modern institutions of museum and exhibition gallery. I may point to a few outstanding facts. Most European museums are, among other things, memorials of the rise of nationalism and imperialism. Every capital must have its own museum of painting, sculpture, etc., devoted in part to exhibiting the greatness of its artistic past, and, in other part, to exhibiting the loot gathered by its monarchs in conquest of other nations; for instance, the accumulations of the spoils of Napoleon that are in the Louvre. They testify to the connection between the modern segregation of art and nationalism and militarism. Doubtless this connection has served at times a useful purpose, as in the case of Japan, who, when she was in the process of westernization, saved much of her art treasures by nationalizing the temples that contained them.

The growth of capitalism has been a powerful influence in the development of the museum as the proper home for works of art, and in the promotion of the idea that they are apart from the common life. The *nouveaux riches*, who are an important by-product of the capitalist system, have felt especially bound to surround themselves with works of fine art which, being rare, are also costly. Generally speaking, the typical collector is the typical capitalist. For evidence of good standing in the realm of higher culture, he amasses paintings, statuary, and artistic *bijoux*, as his stocks and bonds certify to his standing in the economic world.

Not merely individuals, but communities and nations, put their cultural good taste in evidence by building opera houses, galleries, and museums. These show that a community is not wholly absorbed in material wealth, because it is willing to spend its gains in patronage of art. It erects these buildings and collects their contents as it now builds a cathedral. These things reflect and establish superior cultural status, while their segregation from the common life reflects the fact that they are not part of a native and spontaneous culture. They are a kind of counterpart of a holier-than-thou attitude, exhibited not toward persons as such but toward the interests and occupations that absorb most of the community's time and energy.

Modern industry and commerce have an international scope. The contents of galleries and museums testify to the growth of economic cosmopolitanism. The mobility of trade and of populations, due to the economic system, has weakened or destroyed the connection between works of art and the *genius loci* of which they were once the natural expression. As works of art have lost their indigenous status, they have acquired a new one – that of being specimens of fine art and nothing else. Moreover, works of art are now produced, like other articles, for sale in the market. Economic patronage by wealthy and powerful individuals has at many times played a part in the encouragement of artistic production. Probably many a savage tribe had its Maecenas. But now even that much of intimate social connection is lost in the impersonality of a world market. Objects that were in the past valid and significant because of their place in the life of a community now function in isolation from the conditions of their origin. By that fact they are also set apart from common experience, and serve as insignia of taste and certificates of special culture.

Because of changes in industrial conditions the artist has been pushed to one side from the main streams of active interest. Industry has been mechanized and an artist cannot work mechanically for mass production. He is less integrated than formerly in the normal flow of social services. A peculiar aesthetic "individualism" results. Artists find it incumbent upon them to betake themselves to their work as an isolated means of "self-expression." In order not to cater to the trend of economic forces, they often feel obliged to exaggerate their separateness to the point of eccentricity. Consequently artistic products take on to a still greater degree the air of something independent and esoteric.

Put the action of all such forces together, and the conditions that create the gulf which exists generally between producer and consumer in modern society operate to create also a chasm between ordinary and aesthetic experience. Finally we have, as the record of this chasm, accepted as if it were normal, the philosophies of art that locate it in a region inhabited by no other creature, and that emphasize beyond all reason the merely contemplative character of the aesthetic. Confusion of values enters in to accentuate the separation. Adventitious matters, like the pleasure of collecting, of exhibiting, of ownership and display, simulate aesthetic values. Criticism is affected. There is much applause for the wonders of appreciation and the glories of the transcendent beauty of art indulged in without much regard to capacity for aesthetic perception in the concrete.

My purpose, however, is not to engage in an economic interpretation of the history of the arts, much less to argue that economic conditions are either invariably or directly relevant to perception and enjoyment, or even to interpretation of individual works of art. It is to indicate that *theories* which isolate art and its appreciation by placing them in a realm of their own, disconnected from other modes of experiencing, are not inherent in the subject matter but arise because of specifiable extraneous conditions. Embedded as they are in institutions and in habits of life, these conditions operate effectively because they work so unconsciously. Then the theorist assumes they are embedded in the nature of things. Nevertheless, the influence of these conditions is not confined to theory. As I have already indicated, it deeply affects the practice of living, driving away aesthetic perceptions that are necessary ingredients of happiness, or reducing them to the level of compensating transient pleasurable excitations.

Even to readers who are adversely inclined to what has been said, the implications of the statements that have been made may be useful in defining the nature of the problem: that of recovering the continuity of aesthetic experience with normal processes of living. The understanding of art and of its role in civilization is not furthered by setting out with eulogies of it nor by occupying ourselves exclusively at the outset with great works of art recognized as such. The comprehension which theory essays will be arrived at by a detour; by going back to experience of the common or mill run of things to discover the aesthetic quality such experience possesses. Theory can start with and from acknowledged works of art only when the aesthetic is already compartmentalized, or only when works of art are set in a niche apart instead of being celebrations, recognized as such, of the things of ordinary experience. Even a crude experience, if authentically an experience, is more fit to give a clue to the intrinsic nature of aesthetic experience than is an object already set apart from any other mode of experience. Following this clue we can discover how the work of art develops and accentuates what is characteristically valuable in things of everyday enjoyment. The art product will then be seen to issue from the latter, when the full meaning of ordinary experience is expressed, as dyes come out of coal tar products when they receive special treatment.

Many theories about art already exist. If there is justification for proposing yet another philosophy of the aesthetic, it must be found in a new mode of approach. Combinations and permutations among existing theories can easily be brought forth by those so inclined. But, to my mind, the trouble with existing theories is that they start from a ready-made compartmentalization, or from a conception of art that "spiritualizes" it out of connection with the objects of concrete experience. The alternative, however, to such spiritualization is not a degrading and Philistinish materialization of works of fine art, but a conception that discloses the way in which these works idealize qualities found in common experience. Were works of art placed in a directly human context in popular esteem, they would have a much wider appeal than they can have when pigeon-hole theories of art win general acceptance.

A conception of fine art that sets out from its connection with discovered qualities of ordinary experience will be able to indicate the factors and forces that favor the normal development of common human activities into matters of artistic value. It will also be able to point out those conditions that arrest its normal growth. Writers on aesthetic theory often raise the question of whether aesthetic philosophy can aid in cultivation of aesthetic appreciation. The question is a branch of the general theory of criticism, which, it seems to me, fails to accomplish its full office if it does not indicate what to look for and what to find in concrete aesthetic objects. But, in any case, it is safe to say that a philosophy of art is sterilized unless it makes us aware of the function of art in relation to other modes of experience, and unless it indicates why this function is so inadequately realized, and unless it suggests the conditions under which the office would be successfully performed.

The comparison of the emergence of works of art out of ordinary experiences to the refining of raw materials into valuable products may seem to some unworthy, if not an actual attempt to reduce works of art to the status of articles manufactured for commercial purposes. The point, however, is that no amount of ecstatic eulogy of finished works can of itself assist the understanding or the generation of such works. Flowers can be enjoyed without knowing about the interactions of soil, air, moisture, and seeds of which they are the result. But they cannot be *understood* without taking just these interactions into account – and theory is a matter of understanding. Theory is concerned with discovering the nature of the production of works of art and of their enjoyment in perception. How is it that the everyday making of things grows into that form of making which is genuinely artistic? How is it that our everyday enjoyment of scenes and situations develops into the peculiar satisfaction that attends the experience which is emphatically aesthetic? These are the questions theory must answer. The answers cannot be found, unless we are willing to find the germs and roots in matters of experience that we do not currently regard as aesthetic. Having discovered these active seeds, we may follow the course of their growth into the highest forms of finished and refined art.

[. . .]

2 From *Calliope's Sisters*

Richard L. Anderson

When the early Greeks speculated about the fundamental nature of art, they initially thought the matter was simple. The goddess Mnemosyne (memory) bore a daughter of the great god Zeus. The child was called Calliope. When she was grown, she gave to human beings the gift of art, a benefaction that was particularly fitting from one who joined the genius of past experience, as represented by memory, with the awesome and immediate power over the present moment that was Zeus's. But this mythical account of the origin of art soon seemed inadequate. How could a single goddess foster such diverse activities as comedy and tragedy, music and dance, sacred poetry and the lyrics of love? By the eighth century BC. Hesiod was describing Calliope's enlarged family. Now she was the foremost member of a group of nine sisters, the Muses, each associated with a specific art. Or were the nine led by a tenth Muse, Apollo, the god of light? Other accounts assigned still different duties, names, and numbers to these Olympian patrons of the arts.

But mythology's chief value lies in its ability to give humans an unambiguous understanding of their seemingly contradictory and chaotic lives. The classical poets must have realized this for Calliope's family was soon simplified again by attributing all art to "The Muse." This usage generally remains with us today, reflecting our common assumption that all art derives from a single source, that it is possessed of a unitary nature and purpose, and that it can be evaluated by a single principle of criticism. Of course, on closer reflection, most Westerners concede (as did Hesiod) that things may not be so simple; and even a passing acquaintance with non-Western art complicates the picture even further. But despite such problems, this assumption continues to inform much of our thinking about art.

Thus we still have the ancient dilemma of Calliope's sisters. Are they, and the arts they represent, distinctly different personages with no more than a slight familial resemblance to each other? Or does the Muse have a single identity; capable of donning superficially differing guises depending on time, place, and medium? [. . .]

The concerns of aesthetics

As the term is used here and in much other scholarly writing, "*aesthetics*" refers to theories about the fundamental nature and value of art. This definition is of course logically contingent upon a definition of art, a thorny matter that reflective people in the West have failed to satisfactorily resolve after 2,500 years of continual debate.

Indeed, the American philosopher Morris Weitz (1967; see also Ladd 1973: 417–21) has argued that we can never hope to isolate a single quality that is the definitive feature of all art. Rather, Weitz suggests, art can have only what Wittgenstein called an "open definition." That is, the best we can ever do is note the several traits that commonly give a "family resemblance" to those things that we currently think of as art. When we meet things with which we are unfamiliar, either because they are new or because they come from alien cultures, they are judged to be art according to the degree to which they share these familial similarities – or else the repertoire of family resemblances will itself evolve.

The tentativeness and unwieldiness of Weitz's approach to defining art may be frustrating, but I feel it to be realistic, if for no other reason than that it does not ignore a pervasive feature in the history of art, namely the unpredictability of art's evolution. The traits that seem to nicely characterize the art of one era always change as artists and their art move creatively into the future. (I have previously discussed (Anderson 1989: 8–17) the hazards of attempting to use a closed definition of art cross-culturally, especially if the proffered definitive trait is art's being non-utilitarian or prompting a qualitatively unique affective response in the percipient or person who perceives the art work.)

Aesthetics may also deal with conceptions about beauty, but inasmuch as the grotesque may also play an active role in art, aesthetics is not solely a theory of beauty. On the other hand, although natural things such as sunsets and flowers may also prompt feelings similar to those generated by art, the primary concern here is with art produced by the human mind and body. It is usually the shared beliefs and consistent behaviors of a society that most interest the anthropologist, and the present comparative study of aesthetics will likewise deal primarily with aesthetic values held by a sizable portion of the populace for a significant period of time. However, unanimity of belief is neither expected nor necessary. The aesthetic diversity that exists in all societies is both quantitative (some individuals devote more thought to art than do others) and qualitative (there are differences of opinion as to what art is and isn't).

[. . .]

[Anderson presents the art traditions of ten societies: the !Kung San, Eskimos, Australian aborigines, the Sepik of New Guinea, Navaho, Yoruba, Aztec, medieval Indian, and traditional Japanese. The following is from the chapter on Eskimo aesthetics.]

Eskimo Aesthetics: Art as Transformer of Realities

A life of moving nomadically from one location to another, accompanied by fewer than thirty relatives and friends, and providing for the material necessities of life with a technology not of iron and fossil fuels but primarily of wood, stone, and human muscle – such was the sole life way of humans for almost all our history. Only during the last 10,000 years has the primeval technique of hunting and gathering been supplanted in some locales by a sedentary existence; by clusters of population numbering hundreds, thousands, and even millions of people; and by a technology dramatically different from the flint knife and spear-thrower of the past.

Of course, compared to one person's life, 10,000 years is still a long time, so it is natural that these innovations (which were the basis for the "Neolithic Revolution") are often taken for granted and that we view as exotic cultural aberrations the few stone-age peoples that survived into the twentieth century. But we should constantly remind ourselves that such an assumption is as temptingly comfortable as it is dangerously wrong. In the true long-term picture of the human race, *we* are the aberrant ones, and nomadic hunter-gatherers are the norm.

This being the case, we are lucky that a handful of small-scale societies did survive into recent times and, wonder of wonders, that a few individuals had the foresight to study and record their cultures in detail. One such nomadic culture, well known in the ethnographic literature, is that of the Eskimos, or Inuit,[1] of the North American Arctic.

Admittedly, the Inuit of the late twentieth century differ markedly from most peoples of the pre-neolithic past. Fish and sea mammals have always been more prominent in arctic diets than in those of most hunter-gatherers, and vegetable foods have been relatively less important. Also, for many decades the effects of Western culture have been increasingly apparent, due both to the colonial policies of Western nations and to the Inuits' own appetite for Western technology.

But compared to other areas of the New World, most natives of the Arctic were still relatively unacculturated when Knut Rasmussen organised the Fifth Thule Expedition in the 1920s. Born in Greenland with Eskimo ancestry on his mother's side, Rasmussen spoke fluent Eskimo, and his and his colleagues' research led to the publication of extensive accounts of traditional Inuit "intellectual culture" (by which Rasmussen meant religion and mythology) and "material culture" (i.e., artifacts and technology). Taken together with the field reports of others, this literature gives us a good picture of traditional Eskimo life.[2]

Background: origins and art production

The first Inuits probably migrated into North America from northeast Asia between 4,000 and 6,000 years ago. By 1000 BC, they had dispersed across the entire Arctic region, living in hundreds of locations north of the treeline, from southwestern Alaska, across northern Canada, to the shores of eastern Greenland. And wherever they wandered, they took along characteristic cultural adaptations to the Arctic, many of which they shared with their near relatives in northern Siberia (Eskimos differ genetically, linguistically, and culturally from the Native American Indians living south of the treeline, peoples whose ancestors had been in the Western hemisphere for thousands of years before the arrival of the first Inuit.)

Some eras of Eskimo prehistory have produced more art than others,[3] but art of one kind or another has been made in virtually all possible media. Western collectors and museums have long prized Inuit ivory carving (Plate 1), but Eskimo men also made durable figures in bone and wood, as well as ephemeral

Plate 1   *Eskimo ring and pin game, carved ivory. Ungava Bay, Labrador, Canada. Courtesy the Smithsonian Institution Dept of Anthropology, catalogue no. 90228.*

works in snow and ice. Most such pieces were smoothly molded human and animal forms, polished to a lustrous sheen, sometimes decorated with incised patterns of lines and dots. The exigencies of a nomadic life dictated that few, if any, such items served solely decorative purposes. Some served as tools for the shaman, others as toys for children. Many utilitarian items, such as bone tubes for storing women's needles, were carved in such a way as to suggest animal forms. Masks were carved for various uses, and they ranged in size from two to twenty inches (5 to 50 centimeters).

If carving was a man's art, the leather, fur, and sinew used to make arctic clothing provided an avenue of artistic expression for Inuit women (Plate 2). The design and the amount of decoration on clothing varied from one locale to another, with especially elaborate parkas being worn for group festivities in both Alaska and Greenland. In some regions, specially decorated mittens and fans were made for use in dances. Most patterns were geometric and were created by the ingenious use of varying colors and textures of furs.

In some places, kayaks, mortuary boards, and dance drums bore painted and carved designs, but tattooing was the most widespread type of two-dimensional art. Created mostly by women, tattoo patterns were made by either rubbing ashes into pin pricks, or else a needle and thread were covered with grease and ash and then passed under the skin (Birket-Smith 1959: 119), a method that the Eskimos' counterparts in Siberia called *vyshiva*, Russian for embroidery. Cat's cradle string designs, some of which were extremely elaborate, constituted the only other pan-Arctic three-dimensional art form. Alaskan Eskimos made basketry and pottery, but these media had limited importance for aesthetic expression.

By contrast, the performing arts of dance, music, and song were quite important throughout the Arctic, both in ceremonial and recreational settings. In traditional times, at any given moment in an Inuit camp the singing of women could be heard (cf. Lutz 1978: 43). Except for the songs that were sung to accompany juggling (and whose contents are not well understood), most songs' subject matter focused on hunting, on animals and birds, and on legendary

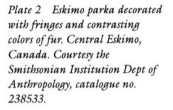

Plate 2   Eskimo parka decorated with fringes and contrasting colors of fur. Central Eskimo, Canada. Courtesy the Smithsonian Institution Dept of Anthropology, catalogue no. 238533.

beings of the mythic past. Eskimo dances ranged from highly formalized and rehearsed solos to freestyle, group performances; but even in the latter, dancers' movements came from a traditional repertoire of motions, and the best dancers were those who could combine subtlety with liveliness, not an easy feat. One field study reports that "it is remarkable to see a young dancer spring eagerly to the dance floor, spry, energetic, and enthusiastic, but give a disappointing and awkward performance, while an aging dancer who must be led to the dance floor blind and hobbling is transfigured at the first drumbeat to an angel of grace" (Luttmann and Luttmann 1985: 58). [. . .]

Eskimo aesthetics: the enhancement of present life

In the minds of traditional Inuit, one important rationale of art's existence was that it made today's life more livable. This occurred in several ways, not the least of which was the enjoyment derived from artistic creation itself. For example, one early explorer wrote, "in places where ivory is plentiful the men appeared to delight in occupying their leisure time in making carvings from that material or from bone, sometimes for use, but frequently merely for pastime, and many little images are made as toys for children" (Nelson 1899: 1996).

But Eskimos also realised that the pleasure engendered by art continues after the creative act is complete. That they savored beautiful things is proven in several ways. For one thing, although the Inuit language had no single word for art or aesthetics, there was a term, *takminaktuk*, meaning "it is good to look at or beautiful" that was applied to a wide range of referents (Graburn 1967: 28). For example, the monolingual Pitseolak, who grew up in a traditional setting but who became a successful printmaker in her later years, once reminisced about her girlhood when she had "the most beautiful drinking water, the most beautiful water I have ever had" (Eber 1979, unpaginated). Significantly, many art objects were also said to be *takminaktuk*.

Myth, too, confirms the relish that Inuit feel for sensuous beauty. A major spirit being of the Central Eskimo is a handsome, and sometimes evil, young woman named Sedna, who in one story is courted by a fulmar, or large Arctic sea bird. "Come to me," says the fulmar; "come into the land of the birds, where there is never hunger, where my tent is made of the most beautiful skins." Sedna is won over by the bird's seductive promises but later is disappointed to discover that her new home "was not built of beautiful pelts, but was covered with wretched fishskins, full of holes, that gave free entrance to wind and snow. Instead of soft reindeer skins her bed was made of hard walrus hides" (Boas 1964/1888: 175–6).

Inuit most commonly applied the concept of beauty to an individual's appearance, where one's natural features could be enhanced in various ways. Eskimos in southern Alaska could choose from lip, cheek, and ear plugs; nose pins; string of beads suspended from the lower lip; facial tattoos or paint – or they might decorate their black hair with white down. Ornaments were less profuse elsewhere, but Eskimos in most regions decorated themselves in one way or another, not for ceremony but for beauty's sake (cf. Hrdlicka 1975: 43; Boas 1964/1888: 151–3; Birket-Smith 1929: 226, 229).

The themes of personal beauty and body decoration also appear in Inuit myth. The "Tale of the Red Bear," for example, tells of the time a group of women met Ta-kú-ka, a woman they had never seen before. They

> admired [Ta-kú-ka's] face and its color, which was lighter than theirs, also several tattooed lines on her face, one up and down between her eyes and three that extended down across the chin from her lower lip; they were pleased also with the shape of her garments, which were very different from theirs. By and by one of the women said, "You are very handsome with the beautiful lines marked on your face; I would give much if you would teach me how to make my face like yours." "I shall not mind the pain,' said the woman, "for I wish to be handsome, as you are, and am ready to bear it." (Nelson 1899: 467–70)

As recounted by Nelson, the story ends with Ta-kú-ka tricking the vain woman by drowning her in a pot of hot oil, saying, "There, you will always be beautiful now!" (ibid.).

Like the woman in the myth, mortal Inuit women were willing to bear the discomforts and dangers of tattooing to appear aesthetically, perhaps even erotically, attractive. Among the Copper Eskimo, "tattooing on a woman had no religious significance; it was merely a time-honored method of adornment. . . . Just as there were no fixed rules regarding the exact time for the process [of tattooing], so there were no definite ceremonies surrounding it" (Jenness 1946: 54; see also Carpenter 1973: 160; Ray 1977: 23; Hrdlicka 1975: 45; Birket-Smith 1933: 69).

Art enhanced Inuit life by giving pleasure to the creator and by adding sensuous beauty to the visual environment. But art also lightened the cares and tedium of mundane life through its role in recreation. Children's toys, for example, were often fashioned with aesthetic considerations in mind. Most Eskimo parents openly expressed love for their children, and they indulged their youngs' wishes when possible. In areas with particularly barren environments, natural objects such as small bones had to suffice as children's toys, but elsewhere men often went to great lengths to make ingenious and entertaining playthings. For example, some time in the late nineteenth century a father in St Michael, western Alaska, constructed the object shown in Plate 3 for his son. As Nelson describes the toy, it was

> the image of a woodpecker made of wood fastened to a small wooden spatula by means of a stout quill in place of legs. The surface of the spatula is dotted over with red paint to represent food. By means of a string fastened to the point of the bird's beak and passing down through a hole in the spatula, the child is enabled to pull the bird's beak down. On releasing it, the elasticity of the quill throws it up again, thus giving a pecking motion and imitating the movements of feeding. (Nelson 1899: 341–2)

[. . .]

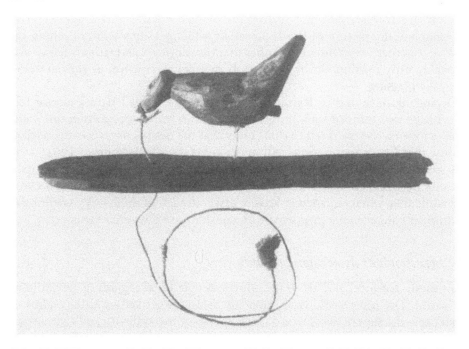

Plate 3   Eskimo toy woodpecker. Pastolik, western Alaska. Courtesy the Smithsonian Institution Dept of Anthropology, catalogue no. 33798.

The performing arts were, if anything, even more important for relieving the tedium of the long winter months. Sometimes there were formal, planned get-togethers. Rasmussen's description captures the atmosphere of such activities over half a century ago:

> The great song festivals at which I have been present during the dark season are the most original and the prettiest kind of pastime I have ever witnessed. Every man and every woman, sometimes also the children, will have his or her own songs, with appropriate melodies, which are sung in the *qag'e*, the great snow hut which is set up in every village where life and good spirits abound. (Rasmussen 1929: 228)

A more recent observer noted that in such song "there is no literary, intellectual detachment; the Eskimo is emotionally immersed in immediate experience, including musical experience, for sound is fleeting" (Johnston 1976: 6). Like music, there is good evidence that dance also gives great pleasure and enjoyment (Luttmann and Luttmann 1985: 57).

Traditionally, impromptu opportunities for song were also common. Rasmussen again:

> Where all are well, and have meat enough, everyone is cheerful and always ready to sing, consequently there is nearly always singing in every hut of an evening, before the family retires to rest. . . . While one of the younger members takes the drum and beats time, all the rest then hum the meolodies and try to fix the words in their minds. (Rasmussen 1929: 228)

To complete the picture of the Inuit family whiling away a winter evening by singing together, we should remember that the mother's and father's hands are enjoyably busy making clothes and tools that are as practical as they are aesthetically pleasing.

Orpingalik once said to Rasmussen, "How many songs I have I cannot tell you. I keep no count of such things. There are so many occasions in one's life when a joy or a sorrow is felt in such a way that the desire comes to sing, and so I know that I have many songs. All my being is song" (Rasmussen 1931: 16). The spontaneous satisfaction of artistic creation; the sensuous pleasure of experiencing beautiful things, actions, and people; and the enjoyment felt by child and adult alike when engaged in artistic play – in each of these ways, traditional Eskimo art enhanced life in an environment that gave few other pleasures. [. . .]

The transcendent dimension of Eskimo art

Inuit myth, folklore, and art usage convey deeper ideas regarding art's role in the world. The Inuit world view implicitly distinguishes among three realms of existence – the supernatural world, with its out-of-the-ordinary and awe-inspiring qualities; the social world of day-to-day human interaction; and the natural world of animals, plants, and inanimate objects. Many peoples tacitly accept the existence of these three worlds but ignore the problem of how they are related to each other. How can cold, lifeless elements become warm, living human flesh; and how can the spirit that lives within the flesh transcend its mortal habitation and touch the divine? There is considerable evidence that Eskimos conceptualize art as a sort of cultural "philosopher's stone" that makes such transformations possible.

Consider, for example, a creation myth recorded in the late nineteenth century in which First Man, having emerged spontaneously from a pea pod, encounters Raven. Seeing Man, Raven "raised one of its wings, pushed up its beak, like a mask, to the top of its head, and changed at once into a man" (Nelson 1899: 451). The superhuman raven/man was astonished to see in First Man a living creature who looked so much like himself. Raven then set about creating the things of the world. For example,

> Raven made two animals of clay which he endowed with life . . . but as they were dry only in spots when they were given life, they remained brown and white, and so originated the tame reindeer with mottled coat. . . .
>
> [Finally, Raven] went to a spot some distance from where he had made the animals, and, looking now and then at Man, made an image very much like him. Then he fastened a lot of fine water grass on the back of the head for hair, and after the image had dried in his hand, he waved his wings over it as before and a beautiful young woman arose and stood beside Man.   (Nelson 1899: 454)

Aside from the fact that the myth has males coming spontaneously into existence whereas females are a product of male manufacture, the interesting point in this story is the way transitions occur between the natural, human, and supernatural worlds. First, Raven, a creature with miraculous abilities, removes an art work – a mask – from his face and is thereby transformed into something resembling Man himself. Then, through another act of artistic creativity, the modeling of clay, Raven transforms inert earth into living animals and, ultimately, into Man's companion, Woman. [. . .]

Besides providing symbolic bridges between an Eskimo, the material world below, and the spiritual world above, art also helps define social relationships between one Eskimo and another. Compared to other societies, Eskimo culture is relatively homogeneous, with all families relying on the same subsistence techniques and living nomadic lives that prohibit the accumulation of many luxuries. Nevertheless, there are at least a few distinct social roles in Eskimo society: Men and women hold noticeably different positions in the culture, as do boys and girls from an early age; and art, in the form of body decoration and clothing, displays these statuses in a highly visible fashion (cf. Ray 1977: 23).

In addition to these statuses, Eskimo shamans were also somewhat set apart, and this too was reflected in art, at least in some communities. When a young man attained the status of shaman in the central Canadian Arctic, he put on a special belt. His friends and relatives gave him small, carved figures of humans, fishes, and harpoons which he wore hanging from the belt. These figures insured his control over powerful spirits (Rasmussen 1929: 114).

In a few Inuit groups, art also disseminated noteworthy information by recording the events of the past. The human and animal figures engraved on ivory tools in Alaska – especially on bow drills – related to hunts and other activities the carver had engaged in (cf. Ray 1961: 22–23, 1977: 25; Mason 1927: 253, 279). Such subject matter was also recorded in song and thereby handed down from one generation to the next.

Given its sociological attributes and the harshness of the environment in which it exists, one might not expect Eskimo culture to be the site of significant art production and serious aesthetic thought. But traditional Eskimos produced items that have been held in high aesthetic esteem not only by Western art collectors but by Inuit themselves.

There is clear evidence that Eskimos recognised the difference between ordinary, run-of-the-mill productions versus things that stand out for their special artistic merit. Subtle ivory carvings are reported to have been "tests of the skill of the worker" (Martijn 1964: 556); and Carpenter (1973: 203), probably inspired by a remark by Leach (1961: 29), has compared carving among Inuit to handwriting among members of literate societies. In both instances, most adults possess the skill in question, but a few individuals – called "sculptors" and "calligraphers," respectively – are recognized for their superior abilities.

Our perception of Eskimo ideas about aesthetic excellence is obscured somewhat by a native ethos that discourages competitiveness and that seldom overtly rewards an outstanding performance in any endeavor. But the consummate Inuit artist does sometimes get his or her due. Recall, for example, that a woman's well-made tattoos provide a pathway to a superior life after death whereas poorly made tattoos destined the wearer to a dreary eternity of subsisting on butterflies. Also, it has been pointed out that

> through dance an adolescent could demonstrate acquired knowledge and capabilities in the roles to be played in life, a significant outlet in a culture which censured any form of overt bragging or self-congratulation. . . . [Thus,] a young marriageable woman could demonstrate her desirability as a spouse by miming her talents in dance. (Luttmann and Luttmann 1985: 55)

Traditional dress, too, provided a domain for critical evaluation. The aging Pitseolak recalled, "I tried hard to learn how to sew because I envied the women who could sew nicely" (Eber 1979). And it has been said that in contemporary Northwest Alaska where almost all men make carvings, only a small fraction are considered to be experts, and every man knows his level of competence relative to all the other carvers (Ray 1961–133).[4]

Eskimos not only create art, but they make it for purposes that are important and profound. Again, the situation is obscured by a trait of Eskimo culture, namely the absence of a specific word for art: Some of the objects we have just discussed are simply said to be *sulijuk* (i.e., true or honest), but many others are indicated by the suffix, -*nguaq*, which connotes "diminutive-likeness-imitation-model-play" (Swinton 1978: 81).

But although the Eskimo vocabulary for discussing art may seem cumbersome, we must admit that the traditional Inuit philosophy of art was complex and subtle. In the first place, Eskimos appreciated the immediate pleasure that artistic production can give to artist and audience alike. The satisfactions of the creative process itself, the sensuous pleasure afforded by artistic beauty, and the enjoyment found in recreations that use artistic paraphernalia – all of these were recognised in traditional Eskimo culture. Moreover, Inuit were convinced that art has the power to influence the course of future events, bringing such desirable and important effects as health, food, and fertility.

The belief that art can do these things rests upon a fundamental conception of art that is as profound as any produced by the philosophers of the East and West. Eskimos recognise the frightening chasms that separate humans from, on the one hand, the cold, unresponsive material world that surrounds us, and, on the other hand, the transcendent realm of the supernatural and eternal that we conceive to be beyond us. Surely reflective people everywhere agonize over these alienating gulfs, instinctively feeling that something should bridge them – but what? The Inuit answer to the dilemma is that a link does indeed exist, and that it is art. (This notion is not altogether foreign to the Western student of art who firmly believes, say, that a masterpiece painting is far more than mere pigment and canvas.) Eskimos know that through art mortals can influence events in the other wise indifferent realm of nature, and that art touches the spirits that stand above both humans and the natural world.

Phrased in these terms, it is easy to see the importance of art's role in Eskimo culture and little wonder that the Inuit, despite the simplicity of their material means and the hardships necessitated by their environment, produce art with such conviction. [. . .]

Defining Art

Many philosophers have given up the search for an absolute and eternal definition of art. In a particularly influential article, Morris Weitz (1967/1957) has argued that although there may be agreement on art's definition at any particular place and time, even a cursory look at the history of intellectual thought reveals that people have held quite different views at other periods and in different places. Perhaps, said Weitz, the only constant lies in art's always being creative, always evolving in style, in purpose, and, significantly, in definition. This being the case, art can only have an "open" definition that specifies several traits that are *usually* present in those things commonly designated as art, even though no single trait is definitively present in *all* art. Using a line of reasoning developed by Wittgenstein, Weitz claimed that art is like a large family, the members of which share a genuine resemblance with one another even though no single trait is found in every individual.

Having surveyed aesthetic systems in ten largely independent and highly diverse societies, we can now ask whether or not any open definition can subsume art cross-culturally. The answer, I believe, is yes; and I propose the following open, cross-culturally applicable definition of art: *Art is culturally significant meaning, skillfully encoded in an affecting, sensuous medium.* Although this definition reads syntactically as a sentence, it is in fact a list of qualities – "culturally significant meaning," "skill," "code," and "affecting, sensuous medium" – and I believe it can be shown that each one of the diverse congeries of "arts" that [I have] described have most or all of these qualities. Furthermore, these traits are notably present in those things that we commonly consider to be art from other times and places.[5]

Granted, art traditions and individual art works vary in the relative emphasis placed upon each of these qualities. Australian Aborigines, for example, think of their *tjurungas* as embodying the deepest of spiritual meanings, whereas the manual skill of the *tjurunga* maker may be no greater than those of most other men in his tribe. Or to cite another case, the sensuousness of most types of San and Inuit body decorations is paramount in native thought, whereas the cultural significance of the decorations is limited to notions about social status and personal beauty, values that may be somewhat superficial to the cores of the cultures involved. But despite such variations (which, after all, are inevitably present in an open definition), most or all of these qualities seem inevitably to be present in those things that we consider to be art.

Moreover, those things not commonly considered to be art rarely have all of the qualities listed above. (That is to say, the traits specified in the definition are not only *necessarily* present in art, but their absence is *sufficient* to set non-art apart from art.) Thus although Western religion embodies cultural meaning of great significance and the execution of religious ritual typically requires the skills of a specialist, only those things that are executed in such a way as to capitalize on the affecting qualities of a sensuous medium are considered to be religious "art." For example, a passage from the Bible is not generally considered to be art unless its aural delivery is enhanced by setting it to music or its literary qualities are heightened by poetic techniques, such as those found in the *Psalms* or the *Song of Songs*.

Although the majority of things can unequivocally be classed as either "art" or "non-art" by the definition proposed above, some things fall in an indeterminate area between the two categories. The traits that make up the definition obviously do not lend themselves to quantification; and we will probably never be able to specify precisely *how much* of the traits qualify something as being art. Such a situation is inelegant and aesthetically unpleasing, but it reflects disagreements in the real world, where consensus sometimes gives way to heated debate about whether a particular thing is "really" art or not. [. . .]

In keeping with the nature of an open definition, we must be prepared to see Calliope take on differing guises in varied cultural contexts; and there is every likelihood that she, like art works themselves, will evolve creatively with the passage of time.

Notes

1   People in some regions of the Arctic wish to be called "Inuit," their name for themselves in their own language, and others prefer "Eskimo." The issue is important, involving as it does the self-image of a sizable population. In the absence of a con-

sensus among the people involved, I have chosen to use the two terms interchange-ably.

2   In addition to the rich literature our appreciation of Inuit art and culture is aided by numerous excellent films. Of particular interest is a series made by Asen Balikci under the auspices of the National Film Board of Canada that document the annual migratory cycle of the Netsilik of the Pelly Bay area.

3   Robert McGhee (1976) has examined variations in the quantity of art produced in the Arctic from one time and place to another. Interestingly, he found that art pro-duction is not correlated with the availability of leisure time, nor was there a gradual increase in the amount of art with the passage of time. Variations were only weakly correlated with the duration and size of settlements, factors thought to be important in promoting art production elsewhere. In a more recent study, Taçon (1983) found that art production was particularly prolific during the Late Dorset period, 800–1500 AD, and he speculated that this development may have been a result of stress due to adverse changes in the environment or the in-migration from Alaska of Eski-mos bearing the new Thule culture.

4   Interestingly, those who are considered to be "experts" by other Eskimo carvers are also the ones judged to be "artists" by Western buyers (Ray 1961: 32). But before we conclude that Inuit and Western notions of "expertness" are identical we should take into account the following anecdote recorded by Rasmussen:

> I shall never forget [the Iglulik poet] Ivaluardjuk's astonishment and confusion when I tried to explain to him that in our country, there were people who devoted themselves exclusively to the production of poems and melodies. His first attempt at an explanation of this incon-ceivable suggestion was that such persons must be great shamans who had perhaps attained to some intimate relationship with the spirits, these then inspiring them continually with utterances of spiritual force. But as soon as he was informed that our poets were not shamans, merely people who handled words, thoughts, and feelings according to the technique of a particular art, the problem appeared altogether beyond him.   (Rasmussen 1929: 223–34)

5   Weitz's tentative definition is that art implies "there being present some sort of artifact, made by human skill ingenuity and imagination, which embodies in its sen-suous, public medium . . . certain distinguishable elements and relations" (1967: 9). If my proposed definition bears a "family resemblance" itself to that of Weitz, this may, of course, be because I read Weitz's definition some time before I began the present study. However, it was *after* I had formulated the above definition that I found one that Clifford Geertz proposed: "If there is a commonality in art it lies in the fact that certain activities everywhere seem specifically designed to demonstrate that ideas are visible, audible, and – one needs to make up a word here – tactible, that they can be cast in form where the senses, and through the senses the emotions, can reflectively address them" (Geertz 1983: 120), Osborne (1974) and Cohen (1983/1962) have discussed similar issues.

References

Anderson, Richard L., 1989: *Art in Small-Scale Societies* (second edition of *Art in Primi-tive Societies*). Englewood Cliffs, NJ: Prentice-Hall.

Birket-Smith, Kaj, 1929: *The Caribou Eskimos*. Copenhagen: Gyldendal.

——, 1933: *The Chugach Eskimo*. Copenhagen: National-museets Skrifter, Etnografisk Raekhe, 6 København, Nationalmuseets Publikationsfond.

——1959: *The Eskimos*. Second edition. London: Methuen.

Boas, Franz, 1964: [orig. 1888] *The Central Eskimo*. Lincoln: University of Nebraska

Press. Originally published as Report of the Bureau of Ethnology 1884–5. Washington: Smithsonian Institution, 399–669

Carpenter, Edmund, 1973: *Eskimo Realities*. New York: Holt, Rinehart and Winston.

Cohen, Marshall, 1983: [orig. 1962] "Aesthetic Essence." In Earle J. Coleman, ed., *Varieties of Aesthetic Experience*. Lanham, MD.: University Press of America, 235–54. orig. in Max Black, ed., *Philosophy in America*. Ithaca, NY: Cornell University Press.

Eber, Dorothy, ed., 1979: *Pitseolak: Pictures out of my Life*. Seattle: University of Washington Press.

Geertz, Clifford, 1983: *Local Knowledge: Further Essays in Interpretive Anthropology*. New York: Basic Books.

Graburn, Nelson H. H., 1967: "The Eskimo and 'Airport Art.'" *Trans-Action* 4(10): 28–33.

Hrdlicka, Aleš, 1975: *The Anthropology of Kodiak Island*. New York: AMS Press.

Jenness, Diamond, 1946: *Material Culture of the Copper Eskimo*. Canadian Artic Expedition 1913–18, Ottawa: King's Printer.

Johnston, Thomas F., 1976: *Eskimo Music by Region: A Comparative Circumpolar Study*. Ottawa: National Museum of Man.

Ladd, John, 1973: "Conceptual Problems Relating to the Comparative Study of Art." In Warren L. d'Azevedo, ed., *The Traditional Artist in African Societies*. Bloomington: Ind. University Press, 417–24.

Leach, Edmund R., 1961: "Aesthetics." In E. E. Evans-Pritchard et al., eds, *The Institutions of Primitive Society*. Glencoe, Ill.: The Free Press, 25–38.

Luttmann, Gail and Rick Luttman, 1985: "Aesthetics of Eskimo Dance: A Comparison Methodology." In Betty True Jones, ed., *Dance as Cultural Heritage*, Vol. 2. Council on Dance Research: Dance Research Annual XV, 53–61.

Lutz, Maija M., 1978: *The Effects of Acculturation on Eskimo Music of Cumberland Peninsula*. Canadian Ethnology Service, Paper No. 41, a Diamond Jenness Memorial Volume. Ottawa: National Museums of Canada.

Martijn, Charles A., 1964: "Canadian Eskimo Carving in Historical Perspective." *Anthropos* 59: 546–96.

Mason, J. Alden, 1927: "Eskimo Pictoral Art." *The Museum Journal* 18(3): 248–83. Philadelphia: Museum of the University of Pennsylvania.

McGhee, Robert, 1976: "Differential Artistic Productivity in the Eskimo Cultural Tradition." *Current Anthropology* 17(2): 203–20.

Nelson, Edward, 1899: *The Eskimo about Bering Strait*. Washington, DC: 18th Annual Report – Bureau of American Ethnology.

Osborne, Harold, 1974: "Primitive Art and Society: Review Article." *British Journal of Aesthetics* 14(4): 290:303.

Rasmussen, Knut, 1929: "Intellectual Culture of the Iglulik Eskimos." *Fifth Thule*, Vol. 7(1). New York: AMS Press.

——1931: "The Netsilik Eskimos: Social Life and Spiritual Culture." *Fifth Thule*, Vol. 8. New York: AMS Press.

Ray, Dorothy Jean, 1961: *Artists of the Tundra and Sea*. Seattle: University of Washington Press.

——1977: *Eskimo Art: Tradition and Innovation in North Alaska*. Seattle: University of Washington Press.

Swinton, George, 1978: "Touch and the Real: Contemporary Inuit Aesthetics – Theory, Usage, and Relevance." In Michael Greenhalgh and Vincent Megaw, eds, *Art in Society*. New York: St. Martins, 71–88.

Taçon, Paul S. C., 1983: "Dorset Art in Relation to Prehistoric Culture Stress." *Etudes Inuit/Inuit Studies* 7(1): 41–65.

Weitz, Morris, 1967: [orig. 1957] "The Role of Theory in Aesthetics." In Monroe C. Beardsley and Herbert M. Schueller, eds, *Aesthetic Inquiry*. Belmont, Calif.: Dickenson, 3–11.

3   The Artworld

Arthur C. Danto

> HAMLET: *Do you see nothing there?*
> THE QUEEN: *Nothing at all; yet all that is I see.*
>
> Shakespeare: *Hamlet*, Act III, Scene IV

Hamlet and Socrates, though in praise and deprecation respectively, spoke of art as a mirror held up to nature. As with many disagreements in attitude, this one has a factual basis. Socrates saw mirrors as but reflecting what we can already see; so art, insofar as mirrorlike, yields idle accurate duplications of the appearances of things, and is of no cognitive benefit whatever. Hamlet, more acutely, recognised a remarkable feature of reflecting surfaces, namely that they show us what we could not otherwise perceive – our own face and form – and so art, insofar as it is mirrorlike, reveals us to ourselves, and is, even by Socratic criteria, of some cognitive utility after all. As a philosopher, however, I find Socrates' discussion defective on other, perhaps less profound grounds than these. If a mirror image of *o* is indeed an imitation of *o*, then, if art is imitation, mirror-images are art. But in fact mirroring objects no more is art than returning weapons to a madman is justice; and reference to mirrorings would be just the sly sort of counterinstance we would expect Socrates to bring forward in rebuttal of the theory he instead uses them to illustrate. If that theory requires us to class *these* as art, it thereby shows its inadequacy: "is an imitation" will not do as a sufficient condition for "is art." Yet, perhaps because artists *were* engaged in imitation, in Socrates' time and after, the insufficiency of the theory was not noticed until the invention of photography. Once rejected as a sufficient condition, mimesis was quickly discarded as even a necessary one; and since the achievement of Kandinsky, mimetic features have been relegated to the periphery of critical concern, so much so that some works survive in spite of possessing those virtues, excellence in which was once celebrated as the essence of art, narrowly escaping demotion to mere illustrations.

It is, of course, indispensable in socratic discussion that all participants be masters of the concept up for analysis, since the aim is to match a real defining expression to a term in active use, and the test for adequacy presumably consists in showing that the former analyzes and applies to all and only those things of which the latter is true. The popular disclaimer notwithstanding, then, Socrates' auditors purportedly knew what art was as well as what they liked; and a theory of art, regarded here as a real definition of 'Art,' is accordingly not to be of great use in helping men to recognize instances of its application. Their antecedent ability to do this is precisely what the adequacy of the theory is to be tested against, the problem being only to make explicit what they already know. It is our use of the term that the theory allegedly means to capture, but we are supposed able, in the words of a recent writer, "to separate those objects which are works of art from those which are not, because . . . we know how correctly to use the word 'art' and to apply the phrase 'work of art'." Theories, on this account, are somewhat like mirror-images on Socrates' account, showing forth what we already know, wordy reflections of the actual linguistic practice we are masters in.

But telling artworks from other things is not so simple a matter, even for native speakers, and these days one might not be aware he was on artistic terrain without an artistic theory to tell him so. And part of the reason for this lies in the fact that terrain is constituted artistic in virtue of artistic theories, so that one use of theories, in addition to helping us discriminate art from the rest, consists in making art possible. Glaucon and the others could hardly have known what was art and what not: otherwise they would never have been taken in by mirror-images.

I

Suppose one thinks of the discovery of a whole new class of artworks as something analogous to the discovery of a whole new class of facts anywhere, viz., as something for theoreticians to explain. In science, as elsewhere, we often accommodate new facts to old theories via auxiliary hypotheses, a pardonable enough conservatism when the theory in question is deemed too valuable to be jettisoned all at once. Now the Imitation Theory of Art (IT) is, if one but thinks it through, an exceedingly powerful theory, explaining a great many phenomena connected with the causation and evaluation of artworks, bringing a surprising unity into a complex domain. Moreover, it is a simple matter to shore it up against many purported counterinstances by such auxiliary hypotheses as that the artist who deviates from mimeticity is perverse, inept, or mad. Ineptitude, chicanery, or folly are, in fact, testable predications. Suppose, then, tests reveal that these hypotheses fail to hold, that the theory, now beyond repair, must be replaced. And a new theory is worked out, capturing what it can of the old theory's competence, together with the heretofore recalcitrant facts. One might, thinking along these lines, represent certain episodes in the history of art as not dissimilar to certain episodes in the history of science, where a conceptual revolution is being effected and where refusal to countenance certain facts, while in part due to prejudice, inertia, and self-interest, is due also to the fact that a well-established, or at least widely credited theory is being threatened in such a way that all coherence goes.

Some such episode transpired with the advent of post-impressionist paintings. In terms of the prevailing artistic theory (IT), it was impossible to accept these as art unless inept art: otherwise they could be discounted as hoaxes, self-advertisements, or the visual counterparts of madmen's ravings. So to get them accepted *as* art, on a footing with the *Transfiguration* (not to speak of a Landseer stag), required not so much a revolution in taste as a theoretical revision of rather considerable proportions, involving not only the artistic enfranchisement of these objects, but an emphasis upon newly significant features of accepted artworks, so that quite different accounts of their status as artworks would now have to be given. As a result of the new theory's acceptance, not only were post-impressionist paintings taken up as art, but numbers of objects (masks, weapons, etc.) were transferred from anthropological museums (and heterogeneous other places) to *musées des beaux arts*, though, as we would expect from the fact that a criterion for the acceptance of a new theory is that it account for whatever the older one did, nothing had to be transferred out of the *musées des beaux arts* – even if there were internal rearrangements as between storage rooms and exhibition space. Countless native speakers hung upon suburban mantelpieces innumerable replicas of paradigm cases for teaching the expression 'work of art' that would have sent their Edwardian forebears into linguistic apoplexy.

To be sure, I distort by speaking of a theory: historically, there were several, all, interestingly enough, more or less defined in terms of the IT. Art-historical complexities must yield before the exigencies of logical exposition, and I shall speak as though there were one replacing theory, partially compensating for historical falsity by choosing one which was actually enunciated. According to it, the artists in question were to be understood not as unsuccessfully imitating real forms but as successfully creating new ones, quite as real as the forms which the older art had been thought, in its best examples, to be creditably imitating. Art, after all, had long since been thought of as creative (Vasari says that God was the first artist), and the post-impressionists were to be explained as genuinely creative, aiming, in Roger Fry's words, "not at illusion but reality." This theory (RT) furnished a whole new mode of looking at painting, old and new. Indeed, one might almost interpret the crude drawing in Van Gogh and Cézanne, the dislocation of form from contour in Rouault and Dufy, the arbitrary use of color planes in Gauguin and the Fauves, as so many ways of drawing attention to the fact that these were *non-imitations*, specifically intended not to deceive. Logically, this would be roughly like printing "Not Legal Tender" across a brilliantly counterfeited dollar bill, the resulting object (counterfeit *cum* inscription) rendered incapable of deceiving anyone. It is not an illusory dollar bill, but then, just because it is non-illusory it does not automatically become a real dollar bill either. It rather occupies a freshly opened area between real objects and real facsimiles of real objects: it is a non-facsimile, if one requires a word, and a new contribution to the world. Thus, Van Gogh's *Potato Eaters*, as a consequence of certain unmistakable distortions, turns out to be a non-facsimile of real-life potato eaters; and inasmuch as these are not facsimiles of potato eaters, Van Gogh's picture, as a non-imitation, had as much right to be called a real object as did its putative subjects. By means of this theory (RT), artworks re-entered the thick of things from which socratic theory (IT) had sought to evict them: if no *more* real than what carpenters wrought, they were at least no *less* real. The Post-Impressionist won a victory in ontology.

It is in terms of RT that we must understand the artworks around us today. Thus Roy Lichtenstein paints comic-strip panels, though ten or twelve feet high. These are reasonably faithful projections onto a gigantesque scale of the homely frames from the daily tabloid, but it is precisely the scale that counts. A skilled engraver might incise *The Virgin and the Chancellor Rollin* on a pinhead, and it would be recognizable as such to the keen of sight, but an engraving of a Barnett Newman on a similar scale would be a blob, disappearing in the reduction. A *photograph* of a Lichtenstein is indiscernible from a photograph of a counterpart panel from *Steve Canyon*; but the photograph fails to capture the scale, and hence is as inaccurate a reproduction as a black-and-white engraving of Botticelli, scale being essential here as color there. Lichtensteins, then, are not imitations but *new entities*, as giant whelks would be. Jasper Johns, by contrast, paints objects with respect to which questions of scale are irrelevant. Yet his objects cannot be imitations, for they have the remarkable property that any intended copy of a member of this class of objects is automatically a member of the class itself, so that these objects are logically inimitable. Thus, a copy of a numeral just *is* that numeral: a painting of 3 is a 3 made of paint. Johns, in addition, paints targets, flags, and maps. Finally, in what I hope are not unwitting footnotes to Plato, two of our pioneers – Robert Rauschenberg and Claes Oldenburg – have made genuine beds.

Rauschenberg's bed hangs on a wall, and is streaked with some desultory housepaint. Oldenburg's bed is a rhomboid, narrower at one end than the other, with what one might speak of as a built-in perspective: ideal for small bedrooms. As beds, these sell at singularly inflated prices, but one *could* sleep in either of them: Rauschenberg has expressed the fear that someone might just climb into his bed and fall asleep. Imagine, now, a certain Testadura – a plain speaker and noted philistine – who is not aware that these are art, and who takes them to be reality simple and pure. He attributes the paintstreaks on Rauschenberg's bed to the slovenliness of the owner, and the bias in the Oldenburg bed to the ineptitude of the builder or the whimsy, perhaps, of whoever had it "custom-made." These would be mistakes, but mistakes of rather an odd kind, and not terribly different from that made by the stunned birds who pecked the sham grapes of Zeuxis. They mistook art for reality, and so has Testadura. But it was meant to *be* reality, according to RT. Can one have mistaken reality for reality? How shall we describe Testadura's error? What, after all, prevents Oldenburg's creation from being a misshapen bed? This is equivalent to asking what makes it art, and with this query we enter a domain of conceptual inquiry where native speaker are poor guides: *they* are lost themselves.

II

To mistake an artwork for a real object is no great feat when an artwork is the real object one mistakes it for. The problem is how to avoid such errors, or to remove them once they are made. The artwork is a bed, and not a bed-illusion; so there is nothing like the traumatic encounter against a flat surface that brought it home to the birds of Zeuxis that they had been duped. Except for the guard cautioning Testadura not to sleep on the artworks, he might never have discovered that this was an artwork and not a bed; and since, after all, one cannot discover that a bed is not a bed, how is Testadura to realize that he has made an error? A certain sort of explanation is required, for the error here is a curiously philosophical one, rather like, if we may assume as correct some well-known views of P. F. Strawson, mistaking a person for a material body when the truth is that a person *is* a material body in the sense that a whole class of predicates, sensibly applicable to material bodies, are sensibly, and by appeal to no different criteria, applicable to persons. So you cannot *discover* that a person is not a material body.

We begin by explaining, perhaps, that the paintstreaks are not to be explained away, that they are *part* of the object, so the object is not a mere bed with – as it happens – streaks of paint spilled over it, but a complex object fabricated out of a bed and some paintstreaks: a paint-bed. Similarly, a person is not a material body with – as it happens – some thoughts superadded, but is a complex entity made up of a body and some conscious states: a conscious-body. Persons, like artworks, must then be taken as irreducible to *parts* of themselves, and are in that sense primitive. Or, more accurately, the paintstreaks are not part of the real object – the bed – which happens to be part of the artwork, but are, like the bed, part of the artwork as such. And this might be generalized into a rough characterization of artworks that happen to contain real objects as parts of themselves: not every part of an artwork *A* is part of a real object *R* when *R* is part of *A* and can, moreover, be detached from *A* and seen merely as *R*. The mistake thus far will have been to mistake *A* for *part* of itself, namely *R*, even though it would not be incorrect to say that *A* is *R*, that the artwork is a bed. It is the 'is' which requires clarification here.

There is an *is* that figures prominently in statements concerning artworks which is not the *is* of either identity or predication; nor is it the *is* of existence, of identification, or some special is made up to serve a philosophic end. Nevertheless, it is in common usage, and is readily mastered by children. It is the sense of *is* in accordance with which a child, shown a circle and a triangle and asked which is him and which his sister, will point to the triangle saying "That is me"; or, in response to my question, the person next to me points to the man in purple and says "That one is Lear"; or in the gallery I point, for my companion's benefit, to a spot in the painting before us and say "That white dab is Icarus." We do not mean, in these instances, that whatever is pointed to stands for, or represents, what it is said to be, for the *word* 'Icarus' stands for or represents Icarus: yet I would not in the same sense of *is* point to the word and say

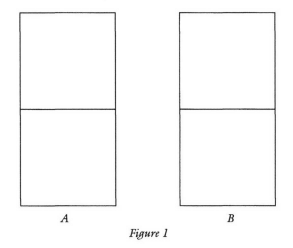

A   *B*

Figure 1

"That is Icarus." The sentence "That *a* is *b*" is perfectly compatible with "That *a* is not *b*" when the first employs this sense of *is* and the second employs some other, though *a* and *b* are used non-ambiguously throughout. Often, indeed, the truth of the first *requires* the truth of the second. The first, in fact, is incompatible with "That *a* is not *b*" only when the *is* is used non-ambiguously throughout. For want of a word I shall designate this the *is of artistic identification*; in each case in which it is used, the *a* stands for some specific physical property of, or physical part of, an object; and, finally, it is a necessary condition for something to be an artwork that some part or property of it be designable by the subject of a sentence that employs this special *is*. It is an *is*, incidentally, which has near-relatives in marginal and mythical pronouncements. (Thus, one *is* Quetzalcoatl; those *are* the Pillars of Hercules.)

Let me illustrate. Two painters are asked to decorate the east and west walls of a science library with frescoes to be respectively called *Newton's First Law* and *Newton's Third Law*. These paintings, when finally unveiled, look, scale apart, as in Figure 1. As objects I shall suppose the works to be indiscernible: a black, horizontal line on a white ground, equally large in each dimension and element. *B* explains his work as follows: a mass, pressing downward, is met by a mass pressing upward: the lower mass reacts equally and oppositely to the upper one. *A* explains his work as follows: the line through the space is the path of an isolated particle. The path goes from edge to edge, to give the sense of its *going beyond*. If it ended or began within the space, the line would be curved: and it is parallel to the top and bottom edges, for if it were closer to one than to another, there would have to be a force accounting for it, and this is inconsistent with its being the path of an *isolated* particle.

Much follows from these artistic identifications. To regard the middle line as an edge (mass meeting mass) imposes the need to identify the top and bottom half of the picture as rectangles, and as two distinct parts (not necessarily as two masses, for the line could be the edge of *one* mass jutting up – or down – into empty space). If it is an edge, we cannot thus take the entire area of the painting as a single space: it is rather composed of two forms, or one form and a non-form. We could take the entire area as a single space only by taking the middle horizontal as a line which is not an edge. But this almost requires a three-dimensional identification of the whole picture: the area can be a flat surface which the line is above (*Jet-flight*), or below (*Submarine-path*), or *on* (*Line*), or *in* (*Fissure*), or *through* (*Newton's First Law*) – though in this last case the area is not a flat surface but a transparent cross section of absolute space. We could make all these prepositional qualifications clear by imagining perpendicular cross sections to the picture plane. Then, depending upon the applicable preposi-tional clause, the area is (artistically) interrupted or not by the horizontal ele-ment. If we take the line as *through* space, the edges of the picture are not really the edges of the space: the space goes beyond the picture if the line itself does; and we are in the same space as the line is. As *B*, the edges of the picture can be part of the picture in case the masses go right to the edges, so that the edges of the picture are *their* edges. In that case, the vertices of the picture would be the vertices of the masses, except that the masses have four vertices more than the picture itself does: here four vertices would be part of the art work which were not part of the real object. Again, the faces of the masses could be the face of the picture, and in looking at the picture, we are looking at these faces: but *space* has no face, and on the reading of *A* the work has to be read as faceless, and the face of the physical object would not be part of the artwork. Notice here how one artistic identification engenders another artistic identification, and how, consistently with a given identification, we are *required* to give others and *pre-cluded* from still others: indeed, a given identification determines how many elements the work is to contain. These different identifications are incompat-ible with one another, or generally so, and each might be said to make a differ-ent artwork, even though each artwork contains the identical real object as part of itself – or at least parts of the identical real object as parts of itself. There are, of course, senseless identifications: no one could, I think, sensibly read the mid-dle horizontal as *Love's Labour's Lost* or *The Ascendency of St Erasmus*. Finally, notice how acceptance of one identification rather than another is in effect to exchange one *world* for another. We could, indeed, enter a quiet poetic world by identifying the upper area with a clear and cloudless sky, reflected in the still surface of the water below, whiteness kept from whiteness only by the unreal boundary of the horizon.

And now Testadura, having hovered in the wings throughout this discussion, protests that *all he sees is paint*: a white painted oblong with a black line painted across it. And how right he really is: that is all he sees or that anybody can, we aesthetes included. So, if he asks us to show him what there is further to see, to demonstrate through pointing that this is an artwork (*Sea and Sky*), we cannot comply, for he has overlooked nothing (and it would be absurd to suppose he had, that there was something tiny we could point to and he, peering closely, say "So it is! A work of art after all!"). We cannot help him until he has mastered the *is of artistic identification* and so *constitutes* it a work of art. If he cannot achieve this, he will never look upon artworks: he will be like a child who sees sticks as sticks.

But what about pure abstractions, say something that looks just like *A* but is entitled No. 7? The 10th Street abstractionist blankly insists that there is nothing here but white paint and black, and none of our literary identifications need apply. What then distinguishes him from Testadura, whose philistine utterances are indiscernible from his? And how can it be an artwork for him and not for Testadura, when they agree that there is nothing that does not meet the eye? The answer, unpopular as it is likely to be to purists of every variety, lies in the fact that this artist has returned to the physicality of paint through an atmosphere compounded of artistic theories and the history of recent and remote painting, elements of which he is trying to refine out of his own work; and as a consequence of this his work belongs in this atmosphere and is part of this history. He has achieved abstraction through rejection of artistic identifications, returning to the real world from which such identifications remove us (he thinks),' somewhat in the mode of Ch'ing Yuan, who wrote:

> Before I had studied Zen for thirty years, I saw mountains as mountains and waters as waters. When I arrived at a more intimate knowledge, I came to the point where I saw that mountains are not mountains, and waters are not waters. But now that I have got the very substance I am at rest. For it is just that I see mountains once again as mountains, and waters once again as waters.

His identification of what he has made is logically dependent upon the theories and history he rejects. The difference between his utterance and Testadura's "This is black paint and white paint and nothing more" lies in the fact that he is still using the *is* of artistic identification, so that his use of "That black paint is black paint" is not a tautology. Testadura is not at that stage. To see something as art requires something the eye cannot descry – an atmosphere of artistic theory, a knowledge of the history of art: an artworld.

III

Mr Andy Warhol, the Pop artist, displays facsimiles of Brillo cartons, piled high, in neat stacks, as in the stockroom of the supermarket. They happen to be of wood, painted to look like cardboard, and why not? To paraphrase the critic of the *Times*, if one may make the facsimile of a human being out of bronze, why not the facsimile of a Brillo carton out of plywood? The cost of these boxes happens to be 2×10^3 that of their homely counterparts in real life – a differential hardly ascribable to their advantage in durability. In fact the Brillo people might, at some slight increase in cost, make their boxes out of plywood without these becoming artworks, and Warhol might make *his* out of cardboard without their ceasing to be art. So we may forget questions of intrinsic value, and ask why the Brillo people cannot manufacture art and why Warhol cannot *but* make artworks. Well, his are made by hand, to be sure. Which is like an insane reversal of Picasso's strategy in pasting the label from a bottle of Suze onto a drawing, saying as it were that the academic artist, concerned with exact imitation, must always fall short of the real thing: so why not just *use* the real thing? The Pop artist laboriously reproduces machine-made objects by hand, e.g., painting the labels on coffee cans (one can hear the familiar commendation "Entirely made by hand" falling painfully out of the guide's vocabulary when confronted by these objects). But the difference cannot consist in craft: a man who carved pebbles out of stones and carefully constructed a work called *Gravel Pile* might invoke the labor theory of value to account for the price he demands; but the question is, What makes it art? And why need Warhol *make* these things anyway? Why not just scrawl his signature across one? Or crush one up and display it as *Crushed Brillo Box* ("A protest against mechanization . . .") or simply display a Brillo carton as *Uncrushed Brillo Box* ("A bold affirmation of the plastic authenticity of industrial . . .")? Is this man a kind of Midas, turning whatever he touches into the gold of pure art? And the whole world consisting of latent artworks waiting, like the bread and wine of reality, to be transfigured, through some dark mystery, into the indiscernible flesh and blood of the sacrament? Never mind that the Brillo box may not be good, much less great art. The impressive thing is that it is art at all. But if it is, why are not the indiscernible Brillo boxes that are in the stockroom? Or has the whole distinction between art and reality broken down?

Suppose a man collects objects (ready-mades), including a Brillo carton; we praise the exhibit for variety, ingenuity, what you will. Next he exhibits nothing but Brillo cartons, and we criticize it as dull, repetitive, self-plagiarizing – or (more profoundly) claim that he is obsessed by regularity and repetition, as in *Marienbad*. Or he piles them high, leaving a narrow path; we tread our way through the smooth opaque stacks and find it an unsettling experience, and write it up as the closing in of consumer products, confining us as prisoners: or we say he is a modern pyramid builder. True, we don't say these things about the stockboy. But then a stockroom is not an art gallery, and we cannot readily separate the Brillo cartons from the gallery they are in, any more than we can separate the Rauschenberg bed from the paint upon it. Outside the gallery, they are pasteboard cartons. But then, scoured clean of paint, Rauschenberg's bed is a bed, just what it was before it was transformed into art. But then if we think this matter through, we discover that the artist has failed, really and of necessity, to produce a mere real object. He has produced an artwork, his use of real Brillo cartons being but an expansion of the resources available to artists, a contribution to *artists' materials*, as oil paint was, or *tuche*.

What in the end makes the difference between a Brillo box and a work of art consisting of a Brillo Box is a certain theory of art. It is the theory that takes it up into the world of art, and keeps it from collapsing into the real object which it is (in a sense of *is* other than that of artistic identification). Of course, without the theory, one is unlikely to see it as art, and in order to see it as part of the artworld, one must have mastered a good deal of artistic theory as well as a considerable amount of the history of recent New York painting. It could not have been art fifty years ago. But then there could not have been, everything being equal, flight insurance in the Middle Ages, or Etruscan typewriter erasers. The world has to be ready for certain things, the artworld no less than the real one. It is the role of artistic theories, these days as always, to make the artworld, and art, possible. It would, I should think, never have occurred to the painters of Lascaux that they were producing *art* on those walls. Not unless there were neolithic aestheticians.

IV

The artworld stands to the real world in something like the relationship in which the City of God stands to the Earthly City. Certain objects, like certain individuals, enjoy a double citizenship, but there remains, the RT notwithstanding, a fundamental contrast between artworks and real objects. Perhaps this was already dimly sensed by the early framers of the IT who, inchoately realizing the non-reality of art, were perhaps limited only in supposing that the sole way objects had of being other than real is to be sham, so that artworks necessarily had to be imitations of real objects. This was too narrow. So Yeats saw in writing "Once out of nature I shall never take/My bodily form from any natural thing." It is but a matter of choice: and the Brillo box of the artworld may be just the Brillo box of the real one, separated and united by the *is* of artistic identification. But I should like to say some final words about the theories that make artworks possible, and their relationship to one another. In so doing, I shall beg some of the hardest philosophical questions I know.

I shall now think of pairs of predicates related to each other as "opposites," conceding straight off the vagueness of this *démodé* term. Contradictory predicates are not opposites, since one of each of them must apply to every object in the universe, and neither of a pair of opposites need apply to some objects in the universe. An object must first be of a certain kind before either of a pair of opposites applies to it, and then at most and at least one of the opposites must apply to it. So opposites are not contraries, for contraries may both be false of some objects in the universe, but opposites cannot both be false; for of some objects, neither of a pair of opposites *sensibly* applies, unless the object is of the right sort. Then, if the object is of the required kind, the opposites behave as contradictories. If F and non-F are opposites, an object o must be of a certain kind K before either of these sensibly applies; but if o is a member of K, then o either is F or non-F, to the exclusion of the other. The class of pairs of opposites that sensibly apply to the $(ô)Ko$ I shall designate as the class of *K-relevant predicates*. And a necessary condition for an object to be of a kind K is that at least one pair of K-relevant opposites be sensibly applicable to it. But, in fact, if an object is of kind K, at least and at most one of each K-relevant pair of opposites applies to it.

I am now interested in the K-relevant predicates for the class K of artworks. And let F and non-F be an opposite pair of such predicates. Now it might happen that, throughout an entire period of time, every artwork is non-F. But since nothing thus far is both an artwork and F, it might never occur to anyone that non-F is an artistically relevant predicate. The non-F-ness of artworks goes unmarked. By contrast, all works up to a given time might be G, it never occurring to anyone until that time that something might both be an artwork and non-*G*; indeed, it might have been thought that *G* was a *defining trait* of artworks when in fact something might first have to be an artwork before *G* is sensibly predicable of it – in which case non-*G* might also be predicable of artworks, and *G* itself then could not have been a defining trait of this class.

Let *G* be 'is representational' and let *F* be 'is expressionist.' At a given time, these and their opposites are perhaps the only art-relevant predicates in critical use. Now letting '+' stand for a given predicate *P* and '−' for its opposite non-*P*, we may construct a style matrix more or less as follows:

F	*G*
+	+
+	−
−	+
−	−

The rows determine available styles, given the active critical vocabulary: representational expressionistic (e.g., Fauvism); representational non-expressionistic (Ingres); non-representational expressionistic (Abstract Expressionism); non-representational non-expressionist (hard-edge abstraction). Plainly, as we add art-relevant predicates, we increase the number of available styles at the rate of 2^n. It is, of course, not easy to see in advance which predicates are going to be added or replaced by their opposites, but suppose an artist determines that *H* shall henceforth be artistically relevant for his paintings. Then, in fact, both *H* and non-*H* become artistically relevant for *all* painting, and if his is the first and only painting that is *H*, every other painting in existence becomes non-*H*, and the entire community of paintings is enriched, together with a doubling of the available style opportunities. It is this retroactive enrichment of the entities in the artworld that makes it possible to discuss Raphael and De Kooning together, or Lichtenstein and Michelangelo. The greater the variety of artistically relevant predicates, the more complex the individual members of the artworld become; and the more one knows of the entire population of the artworld, the richer one's experience with any of its members.

In this regard, notice that, if there are *m* artistically relevant predicates, there is always a bottom row with *m* minuses. This row is apt to be occupied by purists. Having scoured their canvases clear of what they regard as inessential, they credit themselves with having distilled out the essence of art. But this is just their fallacy: exactly as many artistically relevant predicates stand true of their square monochromes as stand true of any member of the Artworld, and they can exist as artworks only insofar as "impure" paintings exist. Strictly speaking, a black square by Reinhardt is artistically as rich as Titian's *Sacred and Profane Love*. This explains how less is more.

Fashion, as it happens, favors certain rows of the style matrix: museums, connoisseurs, and others are makeweights in the Artworld. To insist, or seek to, that all artists become representational, perhaps to gain entry into a specially prestigious exhibition, cuts the available style matrix in half: there are then

$2^n/2$ ways of satisfying the requirement, and museums then can exhibit all these "approaches" to the topic they have set. But this is a matter of almost purely sociological interest: one row in the matrix is as legitimate as another. An artistic breakthrough consists, I suppose, in adding the possibility of a column to the matrix. Artists then, with greater or less alacrity, occupy the positions thus opened up: this is a remarkable feature of contemporary art, and for those unfamiliar with the matrix, it is hard, and perhaps impossible, to recognize certain positions as occupied by artworks. Nor would these things be artworks without the theories and the histories of the Artworld.

Brillo boxes enter the artworld with that same tonic incongruity the *commedia dell'arte* characters bring into *Ariadne auf Naxos*. Whatever is the artistically relevant predicate in virtue of which they gain their entry, the rest of the Artworld becomes that much the richer in having the opposite predicate available and applicable to its members. And, to return to the views of Hamlet with which we began this discussion, Brillo boxes may reveal us to ourselves as well as anything might: as a mirror held up to nature, they might serve to catch the conscience of our kings.

---

4 Crafty Women and the Hierarchy of the Arts

Rozsika Parker and Griselda Pollock

The sex of the artist matters. It conditions the way art is seen and discussed. This is indisputable. But precisely how does it matter? Art history views the art of the past from certain perspectives and organizes art into categories and classifications based on a stratified system of values, which leads to a hierarchy of art forms. In this hierarchy the arts of painting and sculpture enjoy an elevated status while other arts that adorn people, homes or utensils are relegated to a lesser cultural sphere under such terms as 'applied', 'decorative' or 'lesser' arts. This hierarchy is maintained by attributing to the decorative arts a lesser degree of intellectual effort or appeal and a greater concern with manual skill and utility.

The clear division of art forms into fine arts and decorative arts, or more simply the arts and crafts, emerged in the Renaissance and is reflected in changes of art education from craft-based workshops to academies and in the theories of art produced by those academies. By the mid-nineteenth century the complete divorce of 'high art' and craft was a cause of considerable concern to Jane Morris's husband, William Morris, who looked back to the Middle Ages when this damaging division was not so absolute. He also warned of the immediate dangers, to all forms of art, from this hierarchy:

I shall not meddle much with the great art of Architecture, and still less with the great arts commonly called Sculpture and Painting, yet I cannot in my own mind quite sever them from those lesser, so called Decorative Arts, which I have to speak about: it is only in latter times and under the most intricate conditions of life, that they have fallen apart from one another; and I hold that, when they are so parted, it is ill for the Arts altogether: the lesser ones become trivial, mechanical, unintelligent, incapable of resisting the changes pressed upon them by fashion or dishonesty; while the greater, however they may be practised for a while by men of great minds and wonder-working hands ... are sure to lose their dignity of popular arts, and become nothing but dull adjuncts to unmeaning pomp, or ingenious toys for a few rich or idle men. (*William Morris, Selected Writings and Designs*, ed. Asa Briggs, 1962, p. 84)

The art and craft division can undoubtedly be read on class lines, with an economic and social system dictating new definitions of the artist as opposed to the artisan. However, there is an important connection between the new hierarchy of the arts and sexual categorization, male–female. [...]

An example from the development of the stratification in the fine arts themselves, the history of flower painting, provides the necessary link between sex and status. It shows how the presence of women in large numbers in a particular kind of art changed its status and the way it was seen. Flower painting originated as a branch of still-life painting all over Europe in the sixteenth and early seventeenth centuries, becoming a major genre in Holland during the seventeenth century and continuing to attract a substantial number of practitioners well into the twentieth century. [...]

By the late eighteenth century flower painting had become a common genre for women artists. The characterization of flower painting as petty, painstaking, pretty, requiring only dedication and dexterity is related to the sex of a large proportion of its practitioners, for as the following comment by the late nineteenth-century writer Lèon Legrange shows, the social definition of femininity affects the evaluation of what women do to the extent that the artists and their subjects become virtually synonymous: 'Let women occupy themselves with those kinds of art they have always preferred ... the paintings of flowers, those prodigies of grace and freshness which alone can compete with the grace and freshness of women themselves' ('Du rang des femmes dans l'art', *Gazette des Beaux-Arts*, 1860). One can hardly imagine a serious art historian attempting to explain Michelangelo's *David* by equating its lithe, athletic vigour with the temperament and physique of the artist himself. The historical process by which women came to specialize in certain kinds of art and the symbolism of still-life and flower painting have been obscured by the tendency to identify women with nature. Paintings of flowers and the women who painted them became mere reflections of each other. Fused into the prevailing notion of femininity, the painting becomes solely an extension of womanliness and the artist becomes a woman only fulfilling her nature. This effectively removes the paintings and the artists from the field of fine arts. Descriptions of flower paintings by nineteenth-century critics and modern art historians employ exactly the same terms that are used to justify the secondary status accorded to crafts, which are similarly described as manually dexterous, decorative and intellectually undemanding.

Feminist historians have reacted to the hierarchical classification of art by asserting the value of women's work in the crafts. Some have hailed embroidery and other forms of needlework as women's 'true cultural heritage':

> Women have always made art. But for women the arts most highly valued by male society have been closed to them for just that reason. They have put their creativity instead into needlework arts which exist in a fantastic variety wherever there are women, and which in fact are a universal female art form transcending race, class and national borders. Needlework is the one art in which women controlled the education of their daughters and the production of art, and were also the critics and audience . . . it is our cultural heritage. (Patricia Mainardi, 'Quilts: The Great American Art', *Feminist Art Journal*, Winter 1973, p. 1)

While women can justifiably take pride in these areas, asserting their value in the face of male prejudice does not displace the hierarchy of values in art history. By simply celebrating a separate heritage we risk losing sight of one of the most important aspects of the history of women and art, the intersection in the eighteenth and nineteenth centuries of the development of an ideology of femininity, that is, a social definition of women and their role, with the emergence of a clearly defined separation of art and craft.

The history of English embroidery shows how a medieval art became a 'feminine' craft. Embroidery may well be considered one of women's richest contributions to culture, but simply to glorify its history and to defend its value as a cultural product, leads us into the sentimental trap which ensnared Victorian historians of needlework. They were, for very different reasons, equally dedicated to claiming needlework as an *art*. Numerous nineteenth-century women wrote on embroidery, beginning with Elizabeth Stone, whose *Art of Needlework* was published in 1840. She insisted that there was an indissoluble, God-given link between her sex and the craft and provided needlework with a long, pious history to sanction the hours upper- and middle-class women spent at their 'work'. Even in the Wilderness, she wrote, the daughters of Israel were never without their needles:

> With proud and pleased humility did the fair images of these tents, the most accomplished of Israel's daughters, display to their illustrious visitors the 'fine needlework' to which their time and talents had been for a long season devoted. (Elizabeth Stone (ed. Viscountess Wilton), *Art of Needlework*, 1840, p. 29)

Not all historians of embroidery went so far as to transport the Victorian drawing-room into the desert, but all effected a complete identification between women and the craft. 'Of one thing we may be sure – that it is inherent in the nature of English-women to employ their fingers' (Lady Marion Alford, *Needlework as Art*, 1886). Today we live with a legacy of Alford's certainty. Some art schools teach embroidery, but the vast majority, if not all, the students are women, and stitchery is commonly disparaged as 'women's work'.

The earliest references to British embroidery workers, however, dispel the notion that embroidery has always been an exclusively female craft. In pre-twelfth-century Britain, needlework was practised both by monks and nuns in religious houses and by independent professionals. It was also common for royal and noble households to have their own workshops. Some of the most famous pieces of Anglo-Saxon and Norman embroidery that have survived were made by queens and their household workshops. This association conferred on the practice a particular status in later periods. Embroidery was one of a number of arts and crafts which all served the same function, the glorification of the ruling institutions, church, monarchy and the nobility. Individuals of both sexes prac-tised in all the arts. Monks and nuns, for example, both illuminated manuscripts and embroidered so that the two media display the same styles and design.

But crucial changes took place in British needlework production during the thirteenth and fourteenth centuries which affected both men's and women's relationship to the craft. Medieval embroidery culminated in a style known as Opus Anglicanum, with its silver-gilt thread, seed pearls, semi-precious stones and fine silk embroidery in split stitch which delineated the most subtle nuance of feature and gesture. Greatly in demand, it was exported all over Europe and the mode of production changed to meet the needs of the expanding market. Whereas the commercial production of embroidery had previously been in the hands of individuals, often women, scattered around the country, it came to be produced in tightly organized, male-controlled guild workshops, centred on London. [. . .]

So long as family industry survived, men and women collaborated in embroi-dery production. It was only with the social and economic changes beginning in the Elizabethan era that women's relationship to embroidery altered. The Reformation brought the large-scale production of ecclesiastical embroidery to an end, while greater national prosperity led to enormously increased demand for domestic embroidery. Tighter regulations and quality control were placed on embroidery production and the Broderers Guild was reconstituted as a com-pany in 1568. All the officials were men. Simultaneously a much sharper divi-sion developed between amateur and professional work and the numbers of amateurs increased rapidly. They were all women.

[. . .] Embroidery, however, with its aristocratic connections, was a perfect proof of gentility, providing concrete evidence that a man was able to support a leisured woman, so that by the eighteenth century 'women's work', as it was called, played a crucial part in maintaining the class position of the household. It conveyed class connotations on several levels. Women were encouraged to ornament every conceivable surface because decoration in itself suggested a refined, tasteful life-style. And at the same time, the act of embroidering, the hours a woman spent sitting stitching for love of home and family, symbolized the domestic virtues of tireless industry, selfless service and praiseworthy thrift. 'It is as scandalous for a woman not to know how to use a needle as for a man not to know how to use a sword', wrote Lady Mary Wortley Montague in 1753. Thus, the delicate flowers patterning an eighteenth-century gentleman's waistcoat displayed both the value of his wife and the quality of his economic circumstances.

Needlework began to embody and maintain a feminine stereotype. The status of the craft plummetted and became prey to satirical attacks from men such as Addison who began a debate on women's devotion to needlework:

> What a delightful entertainment must it be to the fair sex, when their native modesty, and tenderness of men towards them, exempts them from public business, to pass their time in imitating fruit and flowers. . . . Another argument for busying good women in works of fancy is because it takes them off scandal, the usual attendant of tea-tables and all unactive scenes of life. (*Spectator*, No. 606, 1712)

[. . .]

Women too questioned their sex's preoccupation with embroidery, but not to ridicule it. They tried to explain why women dedicated so many hours to their work. One reason was that it made a considerable contribution to the domestic economy. Women did indeed furnish and clothe their households. Their needlework had both a decorative and utilitarian function. Anne Sherley's will of 1622, for example, listed items she embroidered including ten carpets, four long cushions and six chairs. Opponents of embroidery attacked such industry as misplaced economy. The *Ladies Magazine* of March 1810 printed an article 'On Female Education' blaming women's general ignorance on the time spent on their sewing and suggesting that they should buy rather than sew their embroidery:

> Twenty pounds paid for needlework would give a whole family leisure to acquire a fund of real knowledge. They are kept with nimble fingers and vacant understanding, till the season for improvement is utterly passed away.

Yet in the same issue of the magazine there were the usual needlework patterns and the enthusiastic descriptions, stitch by stitch, of the embroidery worn by ladies at Court. Clearly thrift was only one of a number of factors behind women's compulsive needleworking. [. . .]

[W]omen had a slightly ambivalent relationship towards embroidery for by the late eighteenth century it had become synonymous with femininity. Its practice was marked by the constraints it imposed on women's lives and it acted as a restraining force. Samplers are a good example of this. With the increase in amateur embroiders during the Renaissance, women began to make and exchange embroidery which provided examples of designs and stitches. These 'exemplers', from the old French *examplaire* or *essamplaire*, were carefully preserved and bequeathed in wills, but the arrival of pattern books, first published in 1523, replaced them. Instead the sampler became an educative exercise for young girls. [. . .]

Compared to the virtuosity of earlier samplers, those of the late eighteenth century were naive and technically limited. To work a sampler was no longer an exercise of skill, it had become instead a display of 'femininity'. The act of embroidering both embodied and maintained the feminine stereotype. It still carried overtones of aristocratic status, but the domestic qualities wanted in a good

wife were impressed upon girls by the verses they stitched on their samplers.
[...]

As objects, samplers are often beautiful, and we rightly admire the use of colour, texture, the designs of stitches and the distinction of motifs. But they also represent a female childhood structured around the acquisition of pre-scribed feminine characteristics. Patience, submissiveness, service, obedience and modesty were taught both by the concentrated technical exercises as well as by the pious, self-denying verses and prayers which the samplers carried. [...]

Today, however, samplers are not generally seen as expressive art forms, and if they are valued at all it is for nostalgic reasons or for the manual dexterity they display. Despite the assertions to the contrary by Victorian needlework histori-ans and contemporary feminists, it is highly significant that embroidery was only acknowledged as an art form when it copied fine art prints and oil paint-ings. In the eighteenth century Mary Linwood was the best known of the 'needlepainters'. In 1798 an exhibition of over one hundred of her glazed, framed, embroidered pictures, copies of Old Master paintings, opened at the Hanover Square Rooms in London and subsequently toured the country. A critic commented approvingly:

> The ladies of Great Britain may boast in the person of Miss Linwood an example of the force and energy of the female mind, free from any of those ungraceful manners which have in some cases accompanied strength of genius in a woman. Miss Linwood has awakened from its long sleep the art which gave birth to paint-ing. (*Library of Anecdote*, quoted in Jourdain, 1910, pp. 171–2)

Mary Linwood's needlepictures translated oil paintings into the medium of em-broidery, the skill of a woman's fingers serving and subservient to fine art. For this she was praised, though misguidedly. That embroidery has a history is ig-nored by this critic, for whom it only 'awakens' and wins recognition when it apes painting and moves outside the domestic sphere to be exhibited publicly as framed pictures. It is also suggested by this critic that embroidery is an earlier form of art – it 'gave birth to painting', a choice of words that subtly implicates it with women's reproductive role while placing both at a less advanced stage of development.

In one text on prehistoric art this implicit suggestion is made explicit and prehistoric forms of craft are identified with the feminine spirit in art:

> The geometric style is primarily a feminine style. The geometric ornament seems more suited to the *domestic*, pedantically tidy and at the same time superstitiously careful spirit of woman than that of man. It is, considered purely aesthetically, a petty, lifeless and, despite all its luxuriousness of colour, a strictly limited mode of art. *But within its limits*, healthy and efficient, pleasing by reason of the *industry* displayed and its *external decorativeness* – the expression of the feminine spirit in art. (H. Hoernes and O. Menghin, *Urgeschichte der bildenden Kunst*, 1925, p. 574, our italics)

This passage runs the gamut of the now familiar package of derogatory definitions: limitedness, decorativeness, industriousness and pettiness. However, in
the wake of developments in contemporary abstract art certain 'geometric crafts'
have invited comparison with fine art forms because of their non-representational and colourful forms on large two-dimensional surfaces. In order to justify
a change of status for such crafts and to move them from the antique trade or
folk museum on to the fine art circuit, they have to undergo a particularly revealing transformation. Woven blankets by American Navaho Indian women,
for example, have been exhibited in major museums of art in Los Angeles (1972),
London (1974) and Amsterdam (1975). Some writers who reviewed the exhibitions provided anthropological accounts of the blankets and the people who
made them, but those who wished to see them as art works had to expunge all
traces of craft association. Ralph Pomeroy introduced his appreciative, formalist
critique of the London exhibition with this highly revealing statement:

> I am going to forget, *in order to really see them*, that a group of Navajo blankets are
> not only that. In order to consider them, as I feel they ought to be considered – as
> Art with a capital 'A' – I am going to look at them as paintings – created with dye
> instead of pigment, on unstretched fabric instead of canvas – by *several nameless
> masters of abstract art*. ('Navaho Abstraction', *Art and Artists*, 1974, p. 30, our
> italics)

Several manoeuvres are necessary in order to see these works as art. The geometric becomes abstract, woven blankets become paintings and women weav-
ers become nameless masters. This term is crucial. In art history the status of an
art work is inextricably tied to the status of the maker. The most common form
of art historical writing is the monograph on a named artist, often supported by
a *catalogue raisonné* of all the paintings and drawings so that a group of works
is given coherence because it is seen to issue from the hand of an individual. In
other words, the way a work of art is viewed depends on who made it. By
contrast, books on craft history are more concerned with the objects themselves, in relation to how they were made, their purpose and function; the maker
is of secondary importance. Thus in order to give the final stamp of approval to
Navaho products as art, Pomeroy conjures up 'nameless masters', a phrase which
echoes that used by modern historians to create an artistic identity for an artist
whose name has become lost to history. He does not call them 'nameless mistresses', nor even the neutral term 'nameless artists'; he calls them 'masters'.
This indicates once again that in modern art history the fine artist is synonymous with the male artist. These blankets can be appreciated aesthetically and
formally by critics such as Pomeroy only by creating a new status for the maker
which includes not only a change of terminology but also of sex and, implicitly,
of race.

The treatment of Navaho women at the hands of critics shows how much the
status of the maker matters in the evaluation of art, and that status depends on
sex, not because it biologically predetermines the kind of work produced but as
a result of a more significant aspect of the sexual division in our society. The

two historians of Neolithic art quoted above, Hoernes and Menghin, provided a clue, for the feminine spirit in art is also linked with the domestic sphere.

But why would women's activities in the home be given a lower status than men's outside the home? Using the theories and analyses of structural anthropology, developed in the work of Claude Lévi-Strauss, feminist anthropologists have tried to confront the problem of women's secondary status. Lévi-Strauss's analyses of myths and belief systems of many cultures have shown how differences in the status of objects, practices, customs and indeed groups of people depend on the place they are given on a symbolic scale from Nature to Culture. This scale provides one of the most important structures of differentiation by which human society represents, defines and evaluates its activities. For one of the most distinctive features of human society is that people, unlike animals, produce their own means of subsistence. They transform raw materials into tools, houses, clothes and utensils. Human society distinguishes itself because it works over raw materials to produce cultural artefacts. In an article, 'Is Female to Male as Nature is to Culture?', Sherry Ortner argues that one possible way of accounting for women's secondary status is that their roles are perceived as occupying an intermediate position on the symbolic and structuring scale from Nature to Culture. On the one hand, because of women's role in bearing and initially nursing children, women could be considered closer to Nature. But at the same time, the complementary roles, cooking for children and initiating their education and socialization, are obviously cultural and social. Yet these roles are performed in a particular place, the home. She gives the example of cooking, one of the most common transformations of nature to culture:

> In the overwhelming majority of societies cooking is women's work. No doubt this stems from practical considerations – since the woman has to stay at home with the baby, it is convenient for her to perform chores centred in the home. But if it is true, as Lévi-Strauss has argued, that transforming the raw into the cooked may represent, in many systems of thought, the transition from nature to culture, then here we have women aligned with this important culturising process, which could easily place her in the category of culture, triumphing over nature. Yet it is interesting to note that when a culture (e.g. France or China) develops a tradition of *haute cuisine* –'real' cooking as opposed to trivial, ordinary, domestic cooking – the high chefs are almost always men. Thus the pattern replicates that in the area of socialisation – women perform lower level conversions from nature to culture, but when culture distinguishes a higher level of the same functions, the higher level is restricted to men. (In *Women, Culture and Society*, ed. Rosaldo and Lamphere, 1974, p. 80)

Women's work is inevitably in the sphere of culture as opposed to nature and women often perform tasks similar to those of men, but their work is awarded a secondary status because of the different place the tasks are performed. The structures of difference are between private and public activities, domestic and professional work.

This provides an important insight into the structure of sexual division in art hierarchies. For in fact what distinguishes art from craft in the hierarchy is not so much different methods, practices and objects but also where these things are made, often in the home, and for whom they are made, often for the family. The fine arts are a public, professional activity. What women make, which is usually defined as 'craft', could in fact be defined as 'domestic art'. The conditions of production and audience for this kind of art are different from those of the art made in a studio and art school, for the market and gallery. It is out of these different conditions that the hierarchical division between art and craft has been constructed; it has nothing to do with the inherent qualities of the object nor the gender of the maker.

The example of the Navaho blankets shows what has to be changed in order to effect the transformation of Indian weaving into accepted definitions of Fine Art. The recent critical acclaim of American patchwork quilts which also led to exhibitions in art galleries shows, more interestingly, what has to be left out.

In the expensively produced, richly illustrated books and adulatory essays on patchwork quilts that have accompanied their appearance in art galleries and on the walls of dealers' showrooms the fact that women made the quilts is not easily overlooked. Yet, characteristically, the role of the maker is rendered less significant. One exhibition in 1972, at the Whitney Museum of Modern Art in New York, was entitled 'Abstract Design *in* American Quilts' (our italics), emphasizing the formal elements in the quilts as their reason for new found recognition as art. The creators of abstract forms are oddly acknowledged in the introductory essay of the exhibition catalogue and indeed the exhibition was dedicated to 'the anonymous women whose skilled hands and eyes created the American quilt'. This separates the makers from the objects, dedicating the exhibition to them suggests that they are not present, that they are not represented by the work they made. It is practically inconceivable that an exhibition devoted to the works of, say, van Gogh, would also be dedicated to him. Moreover the women are reduced to skilled hands and eyes as if quilt-making bypasses the mind, feeling, thought or intention. Quilts were not even made anonymously. They were frequently signed and dated, exhibited proudly at county fairs and recorded in wills. We owe their very existence in this century to the value placed on them by the families who treasured them and passed them on from generation to generation or to the admirers who collected and carefully preserved fine examples of that art.

The patchwork quilts are rightly celebrated as objects of great beauty. Made from thousands of pieces of shaped and coloured fabric, sewn into elaborate and intricate patterns, they produced rich colouristic effects and contained symbolic meanings. They were given a variety of suggestive titles, 'Mariner's Compass', 'Jacob's Ladder', 'Star of Bethlehem' and 'Sunburst', the last superbly conveying the effect of the radiating beams of the sun and the beneficence of its golden light. But some of these names, rather than being specific titles of quilts, refer instead to categories of basic methods of putting the fabrics together. This has often, erroneously, led to a dismissal of quilt-making as mere repetitious use of pattern. But, individual quilt-makers used the basic patterns to dramatically different effect by choice of colours, size of pieces, optical illusion and intended meaning.

One such type, 'Log Cabin', is made from thin rectangles of material sewn in squares in a manner that recalls and records the dwellings of American settlers from which it derives its name. However, the hundreds of quilts based on this method are so remarkably varied and different from one another, largely because of the more important role of the compositional use of colour and the playing-off of figure against ground. This decisive role of the individual quilt-maker is completely effaced in typical histories of the craft as the following passage indicates:

> In these geometrical creations, every seam is a straight line. Any person who could thread a needle and sew could learn to make an even stitch in a straight line. In this way she assembled her countless dozens of pre-cut pieces. . . . The fabrics that were available in country towns *had a way of creating their own patterns.* (Carlton L. Safford and Robert Bishop, *America's Quilts and Coverlets*, 1972, p. 86, our italics)

The revaluation of the quilts which has led to their exhibition in museums and to lavish illustration quickly disposes of the notion that a so-called utilitarian art form such as the quilt is inherently less aesthetically significant than painting. However, the very fact that this recognition of quilts as art has been achieved by spotlighting the finished objects in isolation as a valuable commodity and by dissociating them from the means of their production shows how important the particular place and ways of making are to the definition of art. The role of the maker has had to be reduced and the processes of production either sentimentalized or suppressed entirely because their connections with the traditional notions of craft might get in the way of an interpretation of quilts as art.

The contradictions of significant omissions by commentators on quilts are highly revealing for it is precisely the particular history and conditions of production of the quilts which provide the basis for a radical critique of art history. The implications of this have not been examined fully either by feminists in their attempt to valorize women's separate cultural heritage or by collectors and dealers in search of higher prices for their now more valuable commodities.

Patchwork and quilting have a very long history, but these practices became a distinctive feature of American society in the eighteenth and nineteenth centuries, and they played an important role in the communities that settled the continent. The names of many quilt types commemorate the pioneer life and the great movements of people, for instance, 'Log Cabin', 'Barn Raising', 'Prairie Lily' and 'The Road to California'. The significance of needlework in the education and preparation of women for marriage was carried over from Europe with the pioneer women. Responding to specific socio-economic and cultural needs of the new communities, women's needlework made an important contribution to their society on many levels. Quilting and other forms of needlework were used to provide the necessary warm bedding. In a cold Massachussetts winter at least five quilts could be needed by each member of the family. [. . .]

Personal, political, religious and social meanings were sewn into these quilts in abstract forms by means of colour and symbolic compositions. Free from the pressures of the dominant conventions of contemporary painting, perspective, illusionism and narrative subject matter, the quilt-makers evolved an abstract language to signify and communicate their joys and sorrows, their personal and social histories. It is this exploration of abstract forms and colours which invited the reconsideration of quilts in recent times because they thus compare with contemporary forms of modern art. But when the quilts are appreciated as decorative wall hangings or examples of abstract *design* rather than as structures of abstract symbols, it is this specific language that is suppressed and denied.

Furthermore, skill with one's needle was necessary for full membership in the community. [. . .] The quilting bee was the occasion on which women in the community came together to sew the quilt-tops, designed and made by individual women, onto the backing and stuffing. This is the procedure that is, strictly speaking, quilting, since by means of patterns of tiny stitches the quilt-top and other layers were secured and given their final appearance. This collective part of the process has been used wrongly to argue that quilts are not artistically significant because they are made by many unknown hands. However, the actual quilt-top was always the work of one person. But, since the quilting meant working over another woman's work, it behoved all women to be expert with their needles or else be left out of this activity. Exclusion from a quilting bee amounted to social exclusion since the occasion was not only a gathering of women but a place of meeting, matchmaking and communication for the whole community. At one such occasion, for instance, women in Cleveland, Ohio, heard the first speech in support of women's suffrage made in that state by the later famous feminist campaigner and writer, Susan B. Anthony.

Patchwork quilt-making was a domestic art and therefore different from painting or sculpture. Because of the place quilts were made, at home by women in the fulfilment of domestic duties, they are a distinctive form of art with different kinds of relations between maker and object and between object and viewer or user which, as William Morris foresaw, are in some ways richer than the relations of making, using and reception customary in high art. Usefulness and aesthetic sensibility coincide, work and art come together, individual and group collaborate. It is precisely the specific history of women and their artwork that is effaced when art historical discourse categorizes this kind of art practice as decorative, dexterous, industrious, geometric and 'the expression of the feminine spirit in art'.

However, the use of these terms which maintains the hierarchy and establishes distinctions between art and craft represents an underlying value system. Any association with the traditions and practices of needlework and domestic art can be dangerous for an artist, especially when that artist is a woman. [. . .]

Our discussion of women's art is therefore not concerned with a feminine sensibility, natural preference and inclination in subject matter, nor with separate spheres and hidden heritages. Women artists have always existed. The important questions concern women artists' relationship to an ideology of sexual difference in which the notions of masculine and feminine are meaningful only in relation to each other. What accounts for the endless assertion of a feminine stereotype, a feminine sensibility, a feminine art in criticism and art history? Precisely the necessity to provide an opposite against which male art and the male artist find meaning and sustain their dominance. That there are Old Masters and not Old Mistresses and that all women's art is seen homogeneously as inevitably feminine in painting and sculpture as much as in the crafts is the effect of this ideology. We never speak of masculine art or man artist, we say simply art and artist. But the art of men can only maintain its dominance and privilege on the pages of art history by having a negative to its positive, a feminine to its unacknowledged masculine.

Ideology is not a conscious process, its effects are manifest but it works unconsciously, reproducing the values and systems of belief of the dominant group it serves. As we have shown the current ideology of male dominance has a history. It was adumbrated in the Renaissance, expanded in the eighteenth century, fully articulated in the nineteenth century and finally totally naturalized with the result that in twentieth-century art history it is so taken for granted as part of the natural order it need not be mentioned. This ideology is reproduced not only in the way art is discussed, the discipline of art history, but in works of art themselves. It operates through images and styles in art, the ways of seeing the world and representing our position in the world that art presents. It is inscribed into the very language of art. [. . .]

---

5   Zen and the Art of Tea

Daisetz T. Suzuki

What is common to Zen and the art of tea is the constant attempt both make at simplification. The elimination of the unnecessary is achieved by Zen in its intuitive grasp of final reality; by the art of tea, in the way of living typified by serving tea in the tearoom. The art of tea is the aestheticism of primitive simplicity. Its ideal, to come closer to Nature, is realized by sheltering oneself under a thatched roof in a room which is hardly ten feet square but which must be artistically constructed and furnished. Zen also aims at stripping off all the artificial wrappings humanity has devised, supposedly for its own solemnization. Zen first of all combats the intellect; for, in spite of its practical usefulness, the intellect goes against our effort to delve into the depths of being. Philosophy may propose all kinds of questions for intellectual solution, but it never claims to give us the spiritual satisfaction which must be accessible to every one of us, however intellectually undeveloped he may be. Philosophy is accessible only to those who are intellectually equipped, and thus it cannot be a discipline of universal appreciation. Zen – or, more broadly speaking, religion – is to cast off all one thinks he posesses, even life, and to get back to the ultimate state of being, the "Original Abode," one's own father or mother. This can be done by everyone of us, for we are what we are because of it or him or her, and without it or him or her we are nothing. This is to be called the last stage of simplification, since things cannot be reduced to any simpler terms. The art of tea symbolizes simplification, first of all, by an inconspicuous, solitary, thatched hut erected, perhaps, under an old pine tree, as if the hut were part of nature and not specially constructed by human hands. When form is thus once for all symbolized it allows itself to be artistically treated. It goes without saying that the principle of treatment is to be in perfect conformity with the original idea which prompted it, that is, the elimination of unnecessaries.

[. . .]

I have often thought of the art of tea in connection with Buddhist life, which seems to partake so much of the characteristics of the art. Tea keeps the mind fresh and vigilant, but it does not intoxicate. It has qualities naturally to be appreciated by scholars snd monks. It is in the nature of things that tea came to be extensively used in the Buddhist monasteries and that its first introduction to Japan came through the monks. If tea symbolizes Buddhism, can we not say that wine stands for Christianity? Wine is used extensively by the Christians. It is used in the church as the symbol of Christ's blood, which, according to the Christian tradition, was shed for sinful humanity. Probably for this reason the medieval monks kept wine-cellars in their monasteries. They look jovial and happy, surrounding the cask and holding up the wine cups. Wine first excites and then inebriates. In many ways it contrasts with tea, and this contrast is also that between Buddhism and Christianity.

We can see now that the art of tea is most intimately connected with Zen not only in its practical development but principally in the observance of the spirit that runs through the ceremony itself. The spirit in terms of feeling consists of "harmony" (*wa*), "reverence" (*kei*), "purity" (*sei*), and "tranquility" (*jaku*). These four elements are needed to bring the art to a successful end; they are all the essential constituents of a brotherly and orderly life, which is no other than the life of the Zen monastery. [. . .]

The character for "harmony" also reads "gentleness of spirit" (*yawaragi*), and to my mind "gentleness of spirit" seems to describe better the spirit governing the whole procedure of the art of tea. Harmony refers more to form, while gentleness is suggestive of an inward feeling. The general atmosphere of the tea-room tends to create this kind of gentleness all around – gentleness of touch, gentleness of odor, gentleness of light, and gentleness of sound. You take up a teacup, handmade and irregularly shaped, the glaze probably not uniformly overlaid, but in spite of this primitiveness the little utensil has a peculiar charm of gentleness, quietness, and unobtrusiveness. The incense burning is never strong and stimulating, but gentle and pervading. The windows and screens are another source of a gentle prevailing charm, for the light admitted into the room is always soft and restful and conducive to a meditative mood. The breeze passing through the needles of the old pine tree harmoniously blends with the sizzling of the iron kettle over the fire. The entire environment thus reflects the personality of the one who has created it. [. . .]

When Dōgen (1200–1253) came back from China after some years of study of Zen there, he was asked what he had learned. He said, "Not much except soft-heartedness (*nyūnan-shin*)." "Soft-heartedness" is "tender-mindedness" and in this case means "gentleness of spirit." Generally we are too egotistic, too full of hard, resisting spirit. We are individualistic, unable to accept things as they are or as they come to us. Resistance means friction, friction is the source of all trouble. When there is no self, the heart is soft and offers no resistance to outside influences. This does not necessarily mean the absence of all sensitivities or emotionalities. They are controlled in the totality of a spiritual outlook on life. And in this aspect I am sure that Christians and Buddhists alike know how to follow Dōgen in the appreciation of the significance of selflessness or "soft-heartedness." In the art of tea the "gentleness of spirit" is spoken of in the same spirit enjoined by Prince Shōtoku. Indeed, "gentleness of spirit" or "soft-heartedness" is the foundation of our life on earth. If the art of tea purports to establish a Buddha-land in its small group, it has to start with gentleness of spirit. To illustrate this point further, let us quote the Zen Master Takuan (1573–1645).

TAKUAN ON THE ART OF TEA (*CHA-NO-YU*)

The principle of *cha-no-yu* is the spirit of harmonious blending of Heaven and Earth and provides the means for establishing universal peace. People of the present time have turned it into a mere occasion for meeting friends, tasking of worldly affairs, and indulging in palatable food and drink; besides, they are proud of their elegantly furnished tearooms, where, surrounded by rare objects of art, they would serve tea in a most accomplished manner, and deride those who are not so skillful as themselves. This is, however, far from being the original intention of *cha-no-yu*.

Let us then construct a small room in a bamboo grove or under trees, arrange streams and rocks and plant trees and bushes, while [inside the room] let us pile up charcoal, set a kettle, arrange flowers, and arrange in order the necessary tea utensils. And let all this be carried out in accordance with the idea that in this room we can enjoy the streams and rocks as we do the rivers and mountains in Nature, and appreciate the various moods and sentiments suggested by the snow, the moon, and the trees and flowers, as they go through the transformation of seasons, appearing and disappearing, blooming and withering. As visitors are greeted here with due reverence, we listen quietly to the boiling water in the kettle, which sounds like a breeze passing through the pine needles, and become oblivious of all worldly woes and worries; we then pour out a dipperful of water from the kettle, reminding us of the mountain stream, and thereby our mental dust is wiped off. This is truly a world of recluses, saints on earth.

The principle of propriety is reverence, which in practical life functions as harmonious relationship. This is the statement made by Confucius when he defines the use of propriety, and is also the mental attitude one should cultivate as *cha-no-yu*. For instance, when a man is associated with persons of high social rank his conduct is simple and natural, and there is no cringing self-deprecation on his part. When he sits in the company of people socially below him he retains a respectful attitude toward them, being entirely free from the feeling of self-importance. This is due to the presence of something pervading the entire tearoom, which results in the harmonious relationship of all who come here. However long the association, there is always the persisting sense of reverence. The spirit of the smiling Kāśyapa and the nodding Tsêng-tzǔ must be said to be moving here; this spirit, in words, is the mysterious Suchness that is beyond all comprehension.

For this reason, the principle animating the tearoom, from its first construction down to the choice of the tea utensils, the technique of service, the cooking of food, wearing apparel, etc., is to be sought in the avoidance of complicated ritual and mere ostentation. The implements may be old, but the mind can be invigorated therewith so that it is ever fresh and ready to respond to the changing seasons and the varying views resulting therefrom; it never curries favor, it is never covetous, never inclined to extravagance, but always watchful and considerate for others. The owner of such a mind is naturally gentle-mannered and always sincere – this is *cha-no-yu*.

The way of *cha-no-yu*, therefore, is to appreciate the spirit of a naturally harmonious blending of Heaven and Earth, to see the pervading presence of the five elements (*wu-hsing*) by one's fireside, where the mountains, rivers, rocks, and trees are found as they are in Nature, to draw the refreshing water from the well of Nature, to taste with one's own mouth the flavor supplied by Nature. How grand this enjoyment of the harmonious blending of Heaven and Earth!

[. . .] Some of my readers may blame me for making a mountain of a molehill: "Tea-drinking is a matter of insignificant importance; to develop it into something of the highest thought that engages the human mind is altogether out of proportion; if we have to take up every little incident of life in this fashion, we will not have anything enjoyable, free from perplexing and wearing thoughts. What has tea-drinking, after all, to do with metaphysics of a most annoying sort? Tea is tea and cannot be anything else. When we are thirsty we have a cup of it, and that is enough. What is the use of making a strange art out of it? Oriental people are too fussy. We of the West have no time for such trivialities." Now let me ask: Is a funeral ceremony a more significant event than tea drinking? Has a wedding a more moral or metaphysical meaning than tea-drinking? From the point of view of "God's *is*ness" or "a flea's *is*ness," death is what inevitably follows from birth; there is nothing ominous about it. So with marriage. Why then do we make so much of it? If we wanted to, it could be reduced easily to the level of eating a morning meal or going to one's business office. We turn it into a grand ceremony because we just want it so. When we think life is too monotonous, we break it into several occasions and get sometimes excited, sometimes depressed. [. . .]

As far as life itself is concerned, time and space are not of much consequence, though they are the mediums whereby life (expresses itself from our human point of view. Our senses and intellect are so constructed as to interpret objectivity along the line of space and time. For this reason, we are really interested in quantitative estimates. We think eternity is something beyond our sensuous measurements, but from the innerness of life one minute or one second is just as long, just as important, as one thousand years. The morning-glory lasting only a few hours of the summer morning is of the same significance as the pine tree whose gnarled trunk defies wintry frost. The microscopic creatures are just as much manifestations of life as the elephant or the lion. In fact, they have more vitality, for even if all the other living forms vanish from the surface of the earth, the microbes will be found continuing their existence. Who would then deny that when I am sipping tea in my tearoom I am swallowing the whole universe with it and that this very moment of my lifting the bowl to my lips is eternity itself transcending time and space? The art of tea really teaches us far more than the harmony of things, or keeping them free from contamination, or just sinking down into a state of contemplative tranquility. [. . .]

6   Dressing Down Dressing Up: The Philosophic Fear of Fashion

Karen Hanson

Thoughtful feminists can find themselves concerned about matters of dress and appearance, provoked to attend to and theorize about the causes and conse- quences of fashion. This reflection may begin with a sunny spirit of analytical confidence and interest, or it may be undertaken with a glum sense of the press- ing need to reexamine all aspects of women's lives. Whatever the original mood, however, the enlistment of traditional philosophy as an ally in the exploration of this topic is likely to produce a sour and anxious state.

Feminism may suppose it shares with traditional philosophy an initial distrust of fashion, but this could prove poor ground for fellowship. Philosophy does indeed manifest sustained scorn for attention to personal appearance and fash- ionable dress, but there is a risk that a sympathetic response to that scorn may simply mean attachment to an unattractive and sometimes abusive partner. What is the character of the philosophic attitude? Whence the philosopher's hostility to fashionable dress?

Beautiful clothes, up to the minute in style, carefully made and proudly worn, do tend more often than not to arouse the philosopher's contempt. But why should this be? Santayana claimed:

> Beauty is a value, . . . it is an emotion, an affection of our volitional and apprecative nature. . . . [And] this value is positive, it is the sense of the presence of something good, or (in the case of ugliness) of its absence. It is . . . never a negative value.   (1961: 43)

And yet the changing modes of dress which *are* a source of pleasure to many, *are* appreciated and desired by most, are often seen by the philosopher as worse than worthless: for *this* serious thinker, fashionable beauty – whether of men or of women – does seem a negative value. Is there any justification for the philosopher's opposition?

There may be moral, socioeconomic, and political concerns that can be ranged against the demands and effects of fashion. Some may object to the use of animals – their pelts in luxurious garments, for example, their oils and their living tissues in the formulations and the testing of cosmetics. The conditions of clothing production in the industrial age – the exploitation of workers, the potential for misallocation of limited agricultural resources, the prospects for economic colonialism – all can contribute to the sense that the beauty of fashion is a false front covering ugly human misery and economic abuse. Fashion can be seen to mark and help maintain class differences, to promote and enforce repellent social distinctions based on wealth, heritage, and gender. New operations of imperialism may be discerned as the changing standards of Western fashion are disseminated globally, asserting a peculiar cultural hegemony as they abruptly displace traditional clothing, the indigenous styles presumably better suited to local climate and surely more expressive of native craft and culture.

But are considerations of these sorts really at the heart of the philosopher's hostility? The political and social issues connected with textile and apparel manufacturing and merchandising can, after all, be directly addressed, addressed *as* political and economic problems. That there is room for moral improvement in this area of commerce does not distinguish the fashion business from any other sphere of human activity, and neither does the fact that individuals, in their concern for fashionable adornment, can demonstrate a great range of vices and irresponsibilities. The prospects for profligacy and unfairness are probably no wider in matters of clothing than they are in matters of food and shelter. Yet some philosophers seem to reserve a special disapprobation for fashionable dress, even while they enjoy a well-furnished and spacious dwelling, even while they relish a meal of veal and baby vegetables, kiwi soufflé and cognac to follow. What could account for this? In complex and relatively affluent societies, choices among alternative styles and types of dress become available. Choices are here not only possible but nearly inevitable. Why should *this* exercise of taste so often provoke disgust?

Fashion is inherently associated with change, and the instability of the fashionable choice may seem to some a proof of the emptiness and confusion of this sort of discrimination. If there is a philosophic conviction that the desirable cannot be identified with the desired, it is a conviction perversely supported by adversion to the vagaries of desire; so that suspicion of fashion is almost immediate: what real value can there possibly be in something virtually defined by *changing* desire? Still, there is little reason to charge the fashion plate with confusion or ignorance about the nature of the relevant choices: fashion knows it lives on change. Why must some philosophy – since Plato – deny the propriety of such a life?

The search for lasting truths and enduring values is a noble activity, but it has sometimes engendered a flight from ordinary, common experience, the experience of growth and decay, coming-to-be and passing away. The Platonic version of this flight is both uniquely thrilling and persistently representative. Philosophy again and again finds itself in pursuit of the real truth hidden behind the merely apparent, taking thought to discover what *is* as opposed to what merely *seems* to be the case, and confident that the wisdom worth loving will endure. Philosophy may, then, take itself to have a natural antagonism to fashion, as well as a perfect antipathy to any interest in clothes – those wrappings of the wrappings of the mind – those superficial goods situated at least two removes from reality, from the philosopher's perdurable realm of ideas.

If some notice *must* be made of clothes, however, the attraction to permanence can still be made plain. "The healthy state" that Socrates describes in Book II of the *Republic* has citizens in "summer for the most part unclad and unshod and in the winter clothed and shod sufficiently"; and this community remains content with simple garb, with a simple life, as they "hand on a like life to their offspring" (Plato 618–19). Glaucon's goading of course leads Socrates to consideration of the "luxurious city," the "fevered state," and it is only then that mention must be made of "embroidery" and "the manufacture of all kinds of articles . . . that have to do with women's adornment"; there is suddenly the need for "beauty-shop ladies" and "barbers" (Plato 619).

Utopian visions do typically focus on some version of stable simplicity: Thomas More's good island folk: all wear work clothes of durable leather. Most of their public occasions call for a covering cloak, but all citizens wear the same style, the same color ("the color of natural wool") (More 43). Everyone puts on white for church, but with these few outfits every closet is complete, from season to season, year upon year. Temptations to personal adornment are said to have been extinguished long ago by making jewels the playthings of children, gold and silver the material of chamber pots, slaves' chains, and criminals' uniforms.

If there is in such utopian tales a recognition that a wide range of political practices can influence and be influenced by sartorial desires, and that these desires can be socially molded, there is still the assumption that a *right* way of dressing can be found and, once found, sustained. Historical dress reform movements have tended to share this assumption, and have formed themselves around discoveries that prevailing fashions are unhealthy, dysfunctional, unnatural, and irrational. But is there a style of clothing that will promote human health? What functions do we expect our clothes to perform, to assist, to advance? What is natural in the way of dress? And what has reason to do with raiment? If rationality involves appropriate adjustments of means to ends, rational dress will serve the final aims of clothing. But what are those aims? Can we suppose that, behind the flux of time, place, culture, and individual history, clothing has a permanent *point*?

The intuition may prevail that clothing is in some very a necessity of life, while the apprehension remains that some forms of attention to this necessity constitute serious mistakes in the conduct of a life worth living. Uneasiness persists on the matters of appearance and change. Thoreau's famous caution – "beware of all enterprises that require new clothes" – may typically be taken as a warning about the vanities of an unperfected society and its distracting demands, and it is true that Thoreau has harsh words to say about fashion and its requirements of novelty. But Thoreau welcomes the new – even, emblematically, new clothes – so long as it is substance – human character – and not just appearance that is transformed:

> I say, beware of all enterprises that require new clothes, and not rather a new wearer of clothes. If there is not a new man, how can the new clothes be made to fit? . . . Perhaps we should never procure a new suit, however ragged and dirty the old, until we have so conducted, so enterprised or sailed in some way, that we feel like new men in the old, and that to retain it would be like keeping new wine in old bottles. Our moulting season, like that of the fowl, must be a crisis in our lives. (15)

Clothing may still seem to figure only the surface, so that change in it, driven only by fashion, is inherently superficial, and on that ground despicable The change in appearance that is condemned, however, is now a specific type – the merely superficial, the unbecoming illusion of the changed man. And if appearances in general continue to bear deceptive possibilities, and thus remain suspect, appearances can also be celebrated, be themselves celebrations, if the substantial affairs of life are at the same time put right.

If we would follow the spirit of Thoreau's admonition, then, we would not measure our integrity by the shabbiness of our old clothes; we would rather find fitting occasions for the new. If we, too, wish to live deliberately, we, too, might think about clothing; but we might also go on to weigh differently the distinction between personal appearance and reality, judge differently the suitability of a particular desire for change.

Conscientious advocates of superficial change will want to recast the distinction between appearance and substance, and they may make oblique assaults upon the fortress of the functional, the useful, and the natural, as those latter are erected against the artificial, the deceptive, and the irrational forces of culture. Baudelaire is a prime instance of this sort of argumentative championing of the ephemeral surface, the short-lived societal overlay. He insists upon a "historical theory of beauty," a claim that beauty is composed of not only "an eternal, invariable element" but also a "relative, circumstantial" one – "the age, its fashions, its morals, its emotions" (3). "*Particular* beauty, the beauty of circumstance," is a function of its being fugitive, transitory: just as art of the past may have not only a general beauty, but also a specific historical value or interest; so, Baudelaire claims, that which conveys the present can give us pleasure in "its essential quality of being present" (1). Particular beauty throughout the ages has a common source, but its substance is ineluctably indexed by time – it is the "mysterious beauty" contributed "accidently" by *human life* (13). If part of the truth of beauty is a contribution of the momentary, then perhaps fashion, even if – indeed just because – it shadows the ever changing present, is not to be scorned.

Baudelaire also defends cosmetics, seeing in makeup not the workings of a lie but something more like a poem. According to Baudelaire, our natural state is neither good nor true; he takes seriously the problem of original sin. Moral reformation now positively requires an improvement of our natural condition. (Indeed, we might remember that when Adam and Eve ate the forbidden fruit, and their eyes were opened, the first thing they did was sew fig leaves, to make themselves aprons. God must have approved of this adornment, for even as he curses the couple, he pauses – at Genesis 3:21 – to make them "coats of skins," to clothe them.) Baudelaire claims that if we fairly scrutinise the natural – "all the actions and desires of the purely natural man" – we

> will find nothing but frightfulness. Everything beautiful and noble is the result of reason and calculation. . . . Virtue . . . is artificial, supernatural. . . . Good is always the product of some art. (32)

Good looks are evidently no exception. Baudelaire pleads for the powder that tames the blemishes left by beastly nature, and he praises black eyeliner and bright rouge for their effect of surpassing, not imitating, nature or youth. This artifice can "represent life, a supernatural and excessive life," and it ought to "display itself," not hide, announce its transfiguration of nature "with frankness and honesty" (34).

This way of breaking the tie between the plain and the honest, this mode of opposing the natural and the good, may relieve an ancient philosophic suspicion of change; but it may also breathe new life into a certain Platonic aspiration. A peculiar disdain for the body may paradoxically lie beneath these recommendations for attention to it. Painstaking adornment of the natural figure and face are appropriate not because these features of the human being are worthy of the veneration such a preoccupation might imply. It is rather that the ordinary human body must be overcome – face powder is "to create an abstract unity in the color and texture of the skin," to "[approximate] the human being to the statue, that is to something superior and divine (Baudelaire 33) – so that the truly worthy element – the soul – may be expressed. Baudelaire's interest in the transformed surface is backed by this conviction about the underlying structure of values, so that he is "led to regard external finery as one of the signs of the primitive nobility of the human soul":

> Fashion should thus be considered as a symptom of the taste for the ideal which floats on the surface of all the crude, terrestrial and loathsome bric-à-brac that natural life accumulates in the human brain: . . . every fashion is . . . a new and more or less happy effort in the direction of Beauty, some kind of approximation to an ideal for which the restless human mind feels a constant titillating hunger. (32)

Thorstein Veblen conveys a very different moral tone in his remarks on clothing, but he, too, aligns an interest in fashion with the strivings of the soul: "It is by no means . . . uncommon . . . , in an inclement climate, for people to go ill clad in order to appear well dressed. . . . The need of dress is eminently a 'higher' or spiritual need" (1899: 168). And Clive Bell, in endorsing and extending

Veblen's view, asks us to verify from our own experience clothing's claim to spirituality, its disdain for the constraints of the material world: "Who does not appreciate the expense, the inconvenience, perhaps even the discomfort of that which they feel themselves compelled to wear?" (1947: 12). This compulsion is really, Bell suggests, "the categorical imperative of fashion," and he hazards a connection between this imperative and another, a tie to our deepest rules of behavior:

> [I]t is difficult in praising clothes not to use such adjectives as "right," "good," "correct," "unimpeachable," or "faultless," . . . while in discussing moral short-comings we tend very naturally to fall into the language of dress and speak of a person's behaviour as being shabby, shoddy, threadbare, down at the heel, botched, or slipshod. (12)

As a straight defense of fashion, this approach is inherently liable to lapse into sarcastic irony. If we would truly seek the spiritual, should we take so long getting dressed? How can we take ourselves to be approaching a deeper reality, or higher ideals, by repeatedly changing our clothes and our faces? The bulging closet and the cluttered makeup table seem to instantiate, not to surmount, "the crude, terrestrial and loathsome bric-à-brac" that the sublime soul would prefer to ignore.

And philosophers do tend to cast their lots with the sublime soul and its superior interests. Even Santayana, whose remark about beauty helped to set this puzzle about the philosopher's scorn for beautiful clothes, in fact contrasts merely physical pleasures with the pleasures intrinsic to the sense of beauty, claiming that the "greater dignity and range of aesthetic pleasure" must be attributed to its dissociation from the body (43). All pleasures may require a functioning body, but the pleasures called physical "call attention" to some part of the body, whereas aesthetic pleasures are "transparent." The sense organs that condition aesthetic pleasure do not "intercept our attention," and this is what makes the sense of beauty especially valuable:

> The soul is glad, as it were, to forget its connection with the body. . . . [The] illusion of disembodiment is very exhilarating, while immersion in the flesh and confinement to some organ gives a tone of grossness and selfishness to our consciousness. (36)

Fashion, however, calls attention to illusions grounded on embodiment. The last thing it would let the soul forget is its connection to the body, and it is certainly conceivable that these reminders are a source of historic resentment. There is no general philosophic indignation about otherwise comparable cultural artifacts: intricately worked cloth hanging on the wall as a tapestry or lying on the floor as a carpet, metal and stones cast into utilitarian or votive vessels – these can be straightforwardly admired, with no apology. But attention to dress is inseparable from attention to the body – when cloth, metal, and stones are used in clothing, their aesthetic characteristics are at least partly a matter of their relation to the body – and philosophers may begin to feel a kind of rudeness in the appreciative stare.

Some feminists have inflected this stare with gender, complaining of the male gaze.[1] A grievance filed on this score may thus seem to elicit the support of traditional philosophy, but the implications of accepting such chivalrous assistance must be carefully considered. Women may have a keen sense of the threat to identity posed by the gaze that turns its own limitation into the other's liability, but resentment at being regarded as a mere object should not drive the feminist into the comforting arms of traditional philosophy. Philosophy may share certain anxieties about things, may want to insist that we must get beyond the surfaces of things, beyond the merely superficial.[2] But philosophy's drive to get past what it takes to be the inessential has usually been linked with a denial or devaluation of what it has typically associated with the woman. Thus, even when traditional philosophy turns to aesthetics, and, for once, interest can focus unashamedly on appearances, an opportunity is still sought to disparage the body. A tradition that displays this sort of embarrassment about carnality, a repressive tradition, may not be the most agreeable companion on the quest to reassert and revalue women's lives and feminine experience.

The tradition wants to claim that aesthetic judgments are disinterested. But if, as Kant says, the satisfaction determined by the beautiful is unrelated to inclination, then one who would judge some fashionable dress beautiful will clearly have to cope with some difficult problems of desire. These are general philosophic problems; this uneasiness about desire is not simply a function of trying carefully to follow Kant's aesthetics. Jean-Paul Sartre piously claims that "great beauty in a woman kills the desire for her":

> we cannot simultaneously place ourselves on the plane of the aesthetic and on the realistic plane of physical possession. To desire her we must forget she is beautiful, because desire is a plunge into the heart of existence, into what is most contingent and most absurd. (1972: 225)

Socrates' insistence on the philosopher's distance from physical desire – estrangement from an interest not only in sexual pleasures but also in "other attentions . . . to our bodies," "smart clothes and shoes and other bodily ornaments" (Plato 47) – is a constraining legacy; his deathbed testament that the true philosopher lives for death, practices dying – freeing the soul from the body – constitutes an inheritance philosophers seem to find difficult either to ignore or to accept They are, after all, only human.

If they were pure mind, spirits, the issue of clothing wouldn't arise. But they are *not* disembodied thinking things, they are in fact neither angels nor brutes, so there is a need for clothes; and that need may stand as irritating proof of some fatal failures. Most obviously, there is the failure to achieve the ideal philosophic death sought from ancient to modern times – the separation of the soul from the body. And as our clothing is testimony to our embodiment, it can whisper of the actual material death that, as humans, we may rather seek, in vain, *to avoid*. The uncanny quality of empty clothes may quietly speak of the intensity of the fact of our embodiment and thus at once murmur the truth of our *real* mortality.

Thoreau says that we may laugh at the clothing of dead kings and queens, but our laughter simply expresses our eerie sense of the mysterious relation between dress and the life of human beings:

> All costume off a man is pitiful or grotesque. It is only the serious eye peering from and the sincere life passed within it, which restrain laughter and consecrate the costume of any people. (17)

In his own way, Baudelaire agrees:

> If one wants to appreciate them properly, fashions should never be considered as dead things; you might just as well admire the tattered old rags hung up, as slack and lifeless as the skin of St. Bartholomew, in an old-clothes dealer's cupboard. Rather they should be thought of as vitalised and animated by the beautiful women who wore them. (33)

The idea that clothing apart from the animated body is dead is given a more lascivious treatment in a short story by Guy de Maupassant:

> O dear friend, do you know more precious moments in life than those in which we watch the woman as she allows each garment in turn to fall with a slight rustle to her feet. . . . And what can be more charming than [women's] movements in removing these soft garments which drop limply as if they had been touched by death . . . (1908: 116–17)

But if clothes detached from a lively human presence seem touched by death, if costumes beheld disconnected from a wearer are pitiful, grotesque, as disturbing as the sight of skin removed from a martyr, then a strong interest in clothes seems once again a sort of perversion of the human mind. Clothes, in their intrinsic and yet always breakable relation to our embodied life, can seem a *memento mori*. It is then no wonder if some may turn their faces from a notice of dress.

If the thought of clothes can produce this sort of dejection, the appearance of fashionable dress might lead to complete despair. Fashion, defined by *changing* desire, may cover the changing, always aging human body, but may also – in its very transitoriness – uncover, or underscore, the fact of mortality. Fashions are born and die; they may sometimes be revived, but – just as we feared – the revivals are never quite the same as the originals.

Freud connects a failure to appreciate transient beauty with a revolt against mourning. According to Freud, the mysterious pain of mourning occurs as love clings to objects destroyed or forever lost. Given our instinctive recoil from anything painful, a protective anticipation of the inevitable necessity of mourn-ing may work to block a wholehearted investment of love or admiration when we recognise the fragility, the perishability, of the prospective love object. Freud recounts a desperate walk "through a smiling countryside," in the company of a young poet. The scenery was undeniably beautiful, but the poet felt no joy in it. He was disturbed by the thought that all this beauty was fated to extinction, that it would vanish when winter came, like all human beauty and all the beauty and splendor that men have created or may create. All that he would otherwise have loved and admired seemed to him to be shorn of its worth by the transience which was its doom. (79)

Freud argued with the unhappy poet. He insisted to the contrary that the transience of the beautiful increases its worth:

> Transience value is scarcity value in time. Limitation in the possibility of an enjoyment raises the value of the enjoyment. . . . The beauty of the human form and face vanish forever in the course of our own lives, but their evanescence only lends them a fresh charm. A flower that blossoms only for a single night does not seem to us on that account less lovely. (80)

Freud found his own considerations "incontestable," but he noticed they "made no impression" upon the poet; so he concluded that "some powerful emotional factor was at work which was disturbing [the poet's] judgment." The problem, again, was the revolt against mourning: the thought that all this beauty would fade had given that sensitive soul "a foretaste of mourning" over the inevitable decease; and an aversion to the pain or grief then interfered with an immersion in the pleasure of beauty.

If this can happen with the beauties of Nature, which, as Freud points out, are so recurrent that "in relation to the length of our lives" they can in fact be regarded as eternal," how much more likely is despair over clothes, which not only *wear* out but *go* out. The new look becomes old, and what was young and fresh last season may now seem tired and old; by next year it will be dead. Couldn't this trouble the sensitive soul?

Some tough philosophers will declare that this is not their problem. They do not, they are certain, suffer from a sort of fearful love of beautiful new clothes, or hold back their appreciation of fashionable dress because it occasions an unhappy apprehension of human transience. The spiritually hearty assurance returns if there is a vision of death in the sight of the fashion plate, it is from the appearance that truly vital values have been extinguished, submerged by superficial concerns. Death by this sort of drowning is the fate of fashion followers, for they are the narcissists: they spend a dangerously inordinate amount of time gazing into their mirrors. And the good life, these philosophers say, is lost.

The story of Narcissus is an appropriate cautionary tale, but its moral may not be fully understood. That beautiful boy is made to fix on his own reflection precisely because of his failure to respond to the glances of others. Narcissus spurns all lovers; he cares not at all about the feelings his appearance seems to inspire. When the gods hear the prayers of one wounded by Narcissus' indifference, and the youth who loved no one is doomed to love himself, it is clear that Narcissus' flaw is not his beauty but his hard heart. Narcissus tells the nymphs who pursue him, who want his love, "You shall have no power over me," and he seems oblivious to the powerful effects of his own good looks on those around him. Unwilling to let others have power over him, uninterested in his power over others, Narcissus is socially disconnected, and it is that disconnection which prefigures his fate. When Narcissus is captivated by his own image in the pool, and he pines away for his own reflection, his problem is not new: he was always too self-absorbed.

The dangers and the appeal of social disconnection are as real as the dangers and the appeal of social conformity. Philosophers may want to view themselves as critical outsiders, sufficiently alienated to find a perspective on the world and distanced enough to offer accurate assessments. One who would be fashionable, however, must attend to the choices of others and let his or her own choices be somehow, somewhat, influenced by the dynamics of others' desires. William Hazlitt expresses contempt for such an enterprise by describing fashion as a

> continual struggle between "the great vulgar and the small" to get the start of, or keep up with each other in the race of appearances. . . . To look like nobody else is a sufficiently mortifying reflection; to be in danger of being mistaken for one of the rabble is worse. Fashion constantly begins and ends in the two things it abhors most, singularity and vulgarity. (Quoted in Bell 1947: 68)

But if a "race of appearances" seems pointless, and if it seems not only ignoble but even incoherent to worry about both being odd and being common, the insistence on a position on the sidelines can also be ill-grounded.

It is not merely that, as Marx almost said, philosophers have tried to interpret the world, while the point is rather to refashion it. The greater mistake is to suppose that a place can really be found outside the reach of social judgment and influence. The philosopher who denies or decries the force of social norms of dress can put one in mind of Molière's misanthrope, Alceste, that unhappy advocate of plain speech – "the naked truth" – and plain dress. When Alceste's friend, Philinte, suggests that politeness, courtesy, decrees a certain outward show, Alceste rails,

> No, no, this formula you'd have me follow,
> However fashionable, is false and hollow. (17)

Alceste's rage about a world of false fronts is understandable, and his disgust with social disguises is not an altogether discreditable reaction. He says he prizes sincerity, and he presents his bilious mood as a simple result of his devotion to honesty and truth. His bad temper is also tiresome, however, and requires the unsolicited indulgence of his friends. Philinte gently combats Alceste's outburst:

> This philosophic rage is a bit extreme;
> You've no idea how comical you seem. . . . (17)

Alceste indeed does not know how he seems. He might want to borrow Hamlet's line and swear that he *is*, that he knows not "seems"; but this might not always work as an oath of authenticity. It could instead attest to failures of tact and self-awareness.

Alceste's resolute refusal to modify his behavior through some anticipatory thought of how it might he perceived by or affect others, his inability to discern any but the basest motives in all acts of social courtesy – these suggest a zeal for incivility that is neither defensible nor uplifting. Alceste does not escape the mores of this world; he just fails to find or give pleasure. When Thoreau warns us that new clothes will not fit unless we, too, are new, we might remember that in fitting into society, in taking a proper place and working through the adjustments that may be required on both sides, reciprocally, we may be made new – and so may society – and this is not inevitably for the worse. Alceste's unwillingness to see this leaves him with the option he continually proposes but cannot really achieve – fleeing the world. His demented dream of being honest in isolation, apart from all people, is obviously incoherent; but Alceste's failures extend beneath the logical to the personal.

When he sarcastically derides judgments and affections resting on matters of dress, we may sympathize –

> Because of what high merits do you deem
> Him worthy of the honor of your esteem?
> Are you in love with his embroidered hose?
> Do you adore his ribbons and his bows?
> Or is it that this paragon bewitches
> Your tasteful eye with his vast German breeches? (50)

But Alceste is the man who wears "green ribbons" (143), and we can see that his grudges against society spring from jealousy as well as from devotion to truth and disgust with superficiality. His failure to acknowledge his own mixed motivations shows he is not wholly honest, even to himself; and thus the problem of not knowing how he "seems" is joined to the problem of not knowing how, what, he *is*.

Self-consciousness, it must be remembered, is generally an epistemological *advance*. One would need a special argument to show that the self-consciousness connected with an awareness of and interest in one's appearance is inherently retrograde. Even the Western myth that most clearly promotes nostalgia for the Eden before self-consciousness deserves a different reading by committed philosophers. When Adam and Eve eat from the tree of knowledge, their eyes *are* opened. They know they are naked, so they sew together the fig leaves and make aprons. When God subsequently adds to their wardrobe, making the coats of skins, his act of clothing them is treated as – it *is* – a ceremony of investiture: accompanying the robing are God's solemn words, "Behold, the man is become as one of us, to know good and evil" (Genesis 3:22).[3]

Clothing is a part of our difficult, post-Edenic lives; and dress, stationed at a boundary between self and other, marking a distinction between private and public, individual and social, is likely to be vexed by the forces of border wars.[4] Philosophers, those who believe that the life worth living is the examined life, should find that willful ignorance of these matters ill suits them. Could something else be disturbing their thought of fashion?

Philosophers define themselves as the lovers of wisdom, not the beloved. They are the cognizers, and their purest professional aim is to know, not to be known, to think, not to be thought about. A personal interest in dress and open responsiveness to the changing whims of fashion depend upon a recognition that one is *seen*, that one is – among other things – an *object* of others' sight, others' cognition. The activity of philosophy may engender a deep antipathy to the acknowledgment of personal passivity, an acknowledgment required for this recognition.[5] And yet we humans *are* seen – no one is really just a seer. There is a passive phase in the human being, and philosophy is wrong to deny or to berate it.

A correction on this point may be classified as a feminine task: the tradition takes the active/passive distinction to sort with the masculine/feminine. And if feminism sometimes wants to break down these distinctions altogether, it also wants to assert the value – the beauty, the truth, the importance – of what has traditionally been labled feminine. Feminists may appropriately offer instruction on the neglected character of passivity in human experience, without thereby contributing to the idea that women alone suffer this fate, that women alone are, in particular, natural objects of sight. Although feminism may have genuine complaints about "the male gaze," an angry refusal to grant the sight of oneself may do little to overcome a world of limited vision. Indeed, there is the worrisome possibility that some feminist refusals of the gaze may not reform but instead simply partake of philosophy's dread of passivity and its devaluation of the body.[6]

But feminism could rather teach philosophy some lessons. Eve helped bring Adam to self consciousness, to a realisation that he was seen, and even God admitted this was an increase in knowledge. So if philosophy – with the help of feminism – could be brought to terms with our embodiment, could work to find an appropriate stance on the relation between the individual and social norms, could come to admit that each of us is, in part, an object to others, then philosophy might just change its attitude toward fashionable dress. Philosophers – wisdom-loving women and men – might then learn how to participate happily, deriving appropriate if ephemeral satisfactions, in fashion's fickle embrace.[7]

Notes

1   I thank Hilde Hein for pressing me to be more explicit on this subject and for providing detailed and useful reactions to a number of other points in this paper.
2   I owe the suggestion to Stanley Cavell, who, in a set of helpful comments on a first draft of this paper, asked whether feminism – "or one strand of feminism" – might be understood "to represent or create a new phase in the philosophical rage against the inessential."
3   Genesis 3:22. This reading of the clothing of Adam and Eve is suggested in a large reexamination of their story proposed by Dennis M. Senchuk (1985: 6–24).
4   For some discussion of this issue of ambiguous boundaries, see Elizabeth Wilson (1985, ch. 1 and ch. 6).
5   Cf. my "Being Doubted, Being Assured."
6   This formulation and line of thought are also due to Stanley Cavell's generous comments on a first draft.

7 An earlier version of this paper was read in Vancouver, B.C., at the 1988 meeting of the American Society for Aesthetics. I am grateful to Julius Moravscik, and the ASA Program Committee he chaired, for the invitation to give a paper on a topic connected with fashion and dress, and I profited from the comments of those colleagues and others in attendance at the ASA meeting.

References

Baudelaire, Charles. 1964. *The Painter of Modern Life and Other Essays*. Jonathan Mayne, trans. and ed. London: Phaidon Press.
Bell, Clive. 1947. *On Human Finery*. London: The Hogarth Press.
De Maupassant, Guy. 1908. *L'Inconnue. Oeuvres Complètes*. v.mo. Paris: L. Conard. (Also in *The Novels and Tales of Guy de Maupassant*. 1928. London: Alfred A. Knopf.)
Freud, Sigmund. 1959. *On Transience*. Vol. 5 of *Collected Papers*. James Strachey, ed. New York: Basic Books.
Hanson, Karen. 1987. Being doubted, being assured. In *Images in Our Souls*. Vol. 10 of *Psychiatry and the Humanities*. Joseph Smith and William Kerrigan, eds. Baltimore: Johns Hopkins University Press.
Molière, Jean. 1965. *The Misanthrope*. Richard Wilbur, trans. New York: Harcourt Brace Jovanovich.
More, Thomas. 1975. *Utopia*. Robert M. Adams, trans. New York: Norton.
Plato. 1963. *Phaedo*. In *The Collected Dialogues*. Hugh Tredennick, trans. Edith Hamilton and Huntington Cairns, eds. New York: Bollingen.
Plato. 1963. *Republic*. In *The Collected Dialogues*. Paul Shorey, trans. Edith Hamilton and Huntington Cairns, eds. New York: Bollingen.
Santayana, George. [1896] 1961. *The Sense of Beauty*. New York: Collier Books.
Sartre, Jean-Paul. 1972. *The Psychology of Imagination*. London: Methuen.
Senchuk, Dennis M. 1985. Innocence and education. *Philosophical Studies in Education*: 6–24.
Thoreau, Henry David. 1966. *Walden and Civil Disobedience*. Owen Thomas, ed. New York: Norton.
Veblen, Thorstein. 1899. *The Theory of the Leisure Class*. New York: Macmillan.
Wilson, Elizabeth. 1985. *Adorned in Dreams*. Berkeley: University of California Press.

Suggestions for Further Reading

Bell, Clive. *Art*. London: Chatto and Windus, 1914.
Collingwood, Robin. *Principles of Art*. Oxford: Clarendon Press, 1938.
Danto, Arthur. *The Transfiguration of the Commonplace*. Cambridge, MA: Harvard University Press, 1981.
Davies, Stephen. *Definitions of Art*. Ithaca: Cornell University Press, 1991.
Dickie, George. *Art and the Aesthetic*. Ithaca: Cornell University Press, 1974.
Goodman, Nelson. *Languages of Art*. Second edition. Indianapolis: Hackett Publishing Co., 1976.

Kennick, William. "Does Traditional Aesthetics Rest on a Mistake?" *Mind* 67 (1958).

Kristeller, Paul Oskar. "The Modem System of the Arts," in *Renaissance Thought and the Arts*. Princeton: Princeton: University Press, 1980.

Langer, Susanne. *Feeling and Form*. New York: Scribner's, 1953.

Margolis, Joseph. *Art and Philosophy*. Brighton, Sussex: 1980.

Rosenberg, Harold. *The De-Definition of Art: Action Art to Pop to Earthworks*. New York: Horizon Press, 1972.

Sparshott, Francis. *The Theory of the Arts*. Princeton: Princeton University Press, 1982.

Stecker, Robert. *Artworks: Definition, Meaning, Value*. University Park: Pennsylvania State University Press, 1997.

Tolstoy, Leo. *What Is Art?* [1986] Trans. Aylmer Maude. Indianapolis: Bobbs-Merrill, 1960.

Weitz, Morris, "The Role of Theory in Aesthetics," *Journal of Aesthetics and Art Criticism* 15 (1956).

Wollheim, Richard. *Art and Its Objects*. Second edition. Cambridge: Cambridge University Press, 1980.

PART TWO

EXPERIENCE AND APPRECIATION:
HOW DO WE ENCOUNTER ART?

Preface

We began with the question of the nature of art. However, in order to offer an adequate analysis of aesthetic experience, it is necessary not only to determine what counts as a work of art but also to investigate the way we experience and appreciate aesthetic objects. In short, we must address the question What is the aesthetic? What does it mean to speak of aesthetic appreciation? In the previous section, we came to understand the difficulty of arriving at any consensus about what constitutes a work of art. The project of articulating the meaning of the term "aesthetic" is equally problematic.

Some of the questions we must address concern the nature of aesthetic value and whether our encounters with objects of aesthetic appreciation differ from our encounters with other sorts of objects; whether the quality of aesthetic experience differs from individual to individual and culture to culture; and how aesthetic experience is affected by the manner of an object's presentation. For example, when we view a painting we must consider how things like imagination and experiential context affect our aesthetic perception, and whether the quality of our experience of the painting would differ if it were hung in a private home or a fast food restaurant as opposed to a museum.

The first part of this section focuses primarily on the question "What is the aesthetic?" In the first reading, Jerome Stolnitz addresses the issue of aesthetic perception. He argues that anything can be viewed aesthetically when the viewer takes an aesthetic attitude toward the object. Stolnitz maintains that determination of the aesthetic depends on the attitude taken towards an object. He recommends a "disinterested" attitude in order to suppress our concerns with non-aesthetic matters such as morals and practical values so that the presentational qualities of an object emerge and can be appreciated for their own intrinsic qualities.

Marcia Eaton continues the consideration of how we understand the term "aesthetic," especially given the fact that what is valued as aesthetically pleasing varies over time and across cultures. Eaton locates the aesthetic in the way that works of art affect us rather than in certain features of those objects. Specifically, Eaton considers "aesthetic" those things that serve to arouse feelings of delight. While other theories struggle to explain how things can fall in and out of aesthetic favor, by locating the aesthetic in the capacity a work has to affect individuals rather than in specific properties, Eaton's view can accommodate temporal and cultural fluctuations in what is considered aesthetic. As she explains, "what is aesthetic remains constant even though specific features pointed to as aesthetically valuable may change."

Like Eaton and Stolnitz, Hans-Georg Gadamer focuses his discussion of the aesthetic on the dynamic relation between the spectator and the work of art itself. Gadamer gives the audience a decidedly active role by characterizing the relationship between the perceiver and the work of art as one of "play." He maintains that the concept of play more adequately illustrates our experience of works of art because it overcomes the division between perceiver and object of perception and captures the way we become absorbed in art objects. What is more, Gadamer disputes the idea that the aesthetic is chiefly important as a type of pleasure. He emphasizes the cognitive value of aesthetic experience, maintaining that art affords insight and knowledge of the world and of ourselves.

The readings in the second part of this section direct our attention to how art is presented to the public and how we encounter it in schools, museums, galleries, and other social spaces. In his discussion of art education, Kevin Melchionne advocates the idea of "aesthetic health" to remedy the problem of the "artistic dropout." He explains that a person who is aesthetically healthy is one who appreciates not just what is put in front of him or her, but one who has learned to put together many different aspects of the aesthetic presentation and has developed confidence as well as flexibility in his or her preferences. Melchionne asserts that aesthetic health can be seen to be "the capacity to be sensitive to and express one's own aesthetic pleasures and preferences." Just as an appreciator of cuisine seeks out new and interesting combinations of spices and foods, the aesthetically healthy person seeks out and refines new aesthetic interests.

Hilde Hein discusses changes in the nature of our experiences of art and other valued objects that have come about due to technological advances of various kinds that affect museums. Museums, which once were places that simply arranged and displayed objects, are moving toward more interactive and environmentally sensitive presentations. They now often rely on computer technology to replace large and cumbersome displays and digitized images that substitute for fragile, rare, and inaccessible artifacts. With these sorts of changes, our experiences of museums are also changing. We are asked to be more involved with the presentations, and yet at the same time we are more removed from the objects of our attention. Because the value of our encounters with art is not only to be found in the works of art themselves but in our overall experience, Hein observes, museums need to be as discriminating with the experiences they foster as the displays they choose to present. Ultimately, the experiences will be more influential than the objects hanging on the wall.

The final two readings in the section examine how works of art, either in their form or content or in their manner of presentation, express and perpetuate prevailing cultural beliefs and public attitudes. Both readings explore the intimate connection between art and social values. Though various theories of art have argued that the aesthetic can – and in some cases should – be determined apart from all other practical considerations, Carol Duncan argues that in reality works of art serve various cultural and political purposes. Duncan maintains that through their selection of works of art and their careful manipulation of the opportunities we have for viewing these works, "museums are powerful and prestigious engines of ideology." She focuses her attention specifically on the issue of gender through her examination of several premier pieces of the collection of New York's Museum of Modern Art, in particular Pablo Picasso's *Les Demoiselles D'Avignon*, which she compares both to ancient depictions of women and to modern pornography. She maintains that the continued elevation of works of art that objectify or demean women and typify the artistic quest as an exclusively male venture perpetuates some very old and persistent ways of regarding women.

Arthur Danto also explores the power art has to convey cultural attitudes and to express and mold public sentiment. The genre of art Danto examines is the war memorial, and through this topic he raises questions about the way society uses art to acknowledge significant political events. Monuments and memorials help society acknowledge both its victories and its defeats. Attending specifically to the Vietnam Veterans Memorial, he discusses how its various formal components function together with its spatial placement to affect the public psyche and express certain emotions regarding the Vietnam war. Danto's rumination on different types of monuments and memorials prompts consideration of how art helps us to remember and reminds us not to forget our connection to events of the past.

Even if there is a way to characterize aesthetic experience in general, it is evident that the different ways that art is encountered greatly affect its meaning and the significance it holds for individuals and for societies.

Jennifer McMahon Railey and Sarah Worth

A Contested Term: What is "Aesthetic"?

7 The Aesthetic Attitude

Jerome Stolnitz

Aesthetic perception will be explained in terms of the aesthetic attitude. It is the attitude we take which determines how we perceive the world. An attitude is a way of directing and controlling our perception. We never see or hear everything in our environment indiscriminately. Rather, we "pay attention" to some things, whereas we apprehend others only dimly or hardly at all. Thus attention is selective – it concentrates on some features of our surroundings and ignores others. Once we recognize this, we realize the inadequacy of the old notion that human beings are simply passive receptors for any and all external stimuli. Furthermore, what we single out for attention is dictated by the purposes we have at the time. Our actions are generally pointed toward some goal. In order to achieve its goal, the organism watches keenly to learn what in the environment will help and what will be detrimental. Obviously, when individuals have different purposes they will perceive the world differently, one emphasizing certain things which another will ignore. The Indian scout gives close attention to markings and clues which the person who is simply strolling through the woods will pass over.

Thus an attitude or, as it is sometimes called, a "set," guides our attention in those directions relevant to our purposes. It gives direction to our behavior in still another way. It prepares us to respond to what we perceive, to act in a way we think will be most effective for achieving our goals. By the same token, we suppress or inhibit those responses which get in the way of our efforts. A man intent on winning a chess game readies himself to answer his opponent's moves and thinks ahead how best to do this. He also keeps his attention from being diverted by distractions.

Finally, to have an attitude is to be favorably or unfavorably oriented. One can welcome and rejoice in what he sees, or he can be hostile and cold toward it. The Anglophobe is a person whose attitude toward all things British is negative, so that when he meets someone with a British accent or hears "Rule Brittania," we expect him to say something disparaging or cynical. When one's attitude toward a thing is positive, he will try to sustain the object's existence and continue to perceive it; when negative, he will try to destroy it or avert his attention from it.

To sum up, an attitude organises and directs our awareness of the world. Now the aesthetic attitude is not the attitude which people usually adopt. The attitude which we customarily take can be called the attitude of "practical" perception.

We usually see the things in our world in terms of their usefulness for promoting or hindering our purposes. If ever we put into words our ordinary attitude toward an object, it would take the form of the question, "What can I do with it, and what can it do to me?" I see the pen as something I can write with, I see the oncoming automobile as something to avoid; I do not concentrate my attention upon the object itself. Rather, it is of concern to me only so far as it can help me to achieve some future goal. Indeed, from the standpoint of fulfilling one's purposes it would be stupid and wasteful to become absorbed in the object itself. The workman who never gets beyond looking at his tools, never gets his job done. Similarly, objects which function as "signs," such as the dinner bell or traffic light, are significant only as guides to future behavior. Thus when our attitude is "practical," we perceive things only as means to some goal which lies beyond the experience of perceiving them.

Therefore our perception of a thing is usually limited and fragmentary. We see only those of its features which are relevant to our purposes, and as long as it is useful we pay little attention to it. Usually perception is merely a rapid and momentary identification of the kind of thing it is and its uses. Whereas the child has to learn laboriously what things are, what they are called, and what they can be used for, the adult does not. His perception has become economised by habit, so that he can recognize the thing and its usefulness almost at once. If I intend to write, I do not hesitate about picking up the pen rather than a paper clip or the cigarette lighter. It is only the pen's usefulness-for-writing-with, not its distinctive color or shape, that I care about. [. . .]

If we stop to think about it, it is astonishing how little of the world we really *see*. We "read the labels" on things to know how to act with regard to them, but we hardly see the things themselves. As I have said, it is indispensable to getting on with the "work of the world" that we should do this. However, we should not assume that perception is always habitually "practical," as it probably is in our culture. Other societies differ from our own, in this respect.

But nowhere is perception exclusively "practical." On occasion we pay attention to a thing simply for the sake of enjoying the way it looks or sounds or feels. This is the "aesthetic" attitude of perception. It is found wherever people become interested in a play or a novel or listen closely to a piece of music. It occurs even in the midst of "practical" perception, in "casual truant glances at our surroundings when the pressing occupations of practical effort either tire us or leave us for a moment to our own devices, as when in the absorbing business of driving at forty or fifty miles an hour along a highway to get to a destination, the tourist on his holiday glances at the trees or the hills or the ocean."[1]

It will forward our discussion of the aesthetic attitude to have a definition of it. But you should remember that a definition, here or in any other study, is only a point of departure for further inquiry. Only the unwary or intellectually lazy student will rest content with the words of the definition alone, without seeing how it helps us to understand our experience and how it can be employed to carry on the study of aesthetics. With this word of caution, I will define "the aesthetic attitude" as "disinterested and sympathetic attention to and contemplation of any object of awareness whatever, for its own sake alone." Let us now take up in turn each of the ideas in this definition and see what they mean precisely. Since this will be a piecemeal analysis, the truth of the account must be found in the total analysis and not in any single part of it

The first word, "disinterested," is a crucially important one. It means that we do not look at the object out of concern for any ulterior purpose which it may serve. We are not trying to use or manipulate the object. There is no purpose governing the experience other than the purpose of just *having* the experience. Our interest comes to rest upon the object alone, so that it is not taken as a sign of some future event, like the dinner bed, or as a cue to future activity, like the traffic light.

Many sorts of "interest" are excluded from the aesthetic. One of them is the interest in owning a world of art for the sake of pride or prestige. A book collector, upon seeing an old manuscript, is often interested only in its rarity or its purchase price, not its value as a work of literature. (There are some book collectors who have never *read* the books that they own!) Another non-aesthetic interest is the "cognitive," i.e., the interest in gaining knowledge about an object. A meteorologist is concerned, not with the visual appearance of a smoking cloud formation, but with the causes which led to it. Similarly, the interest which the sociologist or historian takes in a work of art [...] is cognitive. Further, where the person who perceives the object, the "percipient,"[2] has the purpose of passing judgment upon it, his attitude is not aesthetic. This should be kept in mind, for, as we shall see later, the attitude of the art critic is significantly different from the aesthetic attitude.

We may say of all these non-aesthetic interests, and of "practical" perception generally, that the object is apprehended with an eye to its origins and consequences, its interrelations with other things. By contrast, the aesthetic attitude "isolates" the object and focuses upon it—the "look" of the rocks, the sound of the ocean, the colors in the painting. Hence the object is not seen in a fragmentary or passing manner, as it is in "practical" perception, e.g., in using a pen for writing. Its whole nature and character are dwelt upon. One who buys a painting merely to cover a stain on the wall paper does not see the painting as a delightful pattern of colors and forms.

For the aesthetic attitude, things are not to be classified or studied or judged. They are in themselves pleasant or exciting to look at. It should, then, be clear that being "disinterested" is very far from being "*un*-interested." Rather, as all of us know, we can become intensely absorbed in a book or a moving picture, so that we become much more "interested" than we usually are in the course of our "practical" activity.

The word "sympathetic" in the definition of "aesthetic attitude" refers to the way in which we prepare ourselves to respond to the object. When we apprehend an object aesthetically, we do so in order to relish its individual quality, whether the object be charming, stirring, vivid, or all of these. If we are to appreciate it, we must accept the object "on its own terms." We must make ourselves receptive to the object and "set" ourselves to accept whatever it may offer to perception. We must therefore inhibit any responses which are "unsympathetic" to the object, which alienate us from it or are hostile to it. [. . .] [A]ny of us might reject a novel because it seems to conflict with our moral beliefs or our "way of thinking." When we do so, we should be clear as to what we are doing. We have not read the book aesthetically, for we have interposed moral or other responses of our own which are alien to it. This disrupts the aesthetic attitude. We cannot then say that the novel is *aesthetically* bad, for we have not permitted ourselves to consider it aesthetically. To maintain the aesthetic attitude, we must follow the lead of the object and respond in concert with it.

This is not always easy, for all of us have deep-seated values as well as prejudices. They may be ethical or religious, or they may involve some bias against the artist or even against his native country. (During the First World War, many American symphony orchestras refused to play the works of German composers.) The problem is especially acute in the case of contemporary works of art, which may treat of disputes and loyalties in which we are deeply engaged. When they do so, we might remind ourselves that works of art often lose their topical significance with the passing of time and then come to be esteemed as great works of art by later generations. Milton's sonnet "On the Late Massacre in Piedmont" is a ringing protest called forth by an event which occurred shortly before the writing of the poem. But the heated questions of religion and politics which enter into it seem very remote to us now. People sometimes remonstrate with a friend who seems to reject offhand works of art of which they are fond, "You don't even give it a chance." To be "sympathetic" in aesthetic experience means to give the object the "chance" to show how it can be interesting to perception.

We come now to the word "attention" in our definition of "aesthetic attitude." As has been pointed out, any attitude whatever directs attention to certain features of the world. But the element of attention must be especially underscored in speaking of aesthetic perception. For, as a former teacher of mine used to say, aesthetic perception is frequently thought to be a "blank, cow-like stare." It is easy to fall into this mistake when we find aesthetic perception described as "just looking," without any activity or practical interest. From this it is inferred that we simply expose ourselves to the work of art and permit it to inundate us in waves of sound or color.

But this is surely a distortion of the facts of experience. When we listen to a rhythmically exciting piece of music which absorbs us with its energy and movement, or when we read a novel which creates great suspense, we give our earnest attention to it to the exclusion of almost everything else in our surroundings. To be "sitting on the edge of the chair" is anything but passive. In taking the aesthetic attitude, we want to make the value of the object come fully alive in our experience. Therefore we focus our attention upon the object and "key up" our capacities of imagination and emotion to respond to it. [. . .] Attention is always a matter of *degree*, and in different instances of aesthetic perception, attention is more or less intense. A color, briefly seen, or a little melody, may be apprehended on the "fringe" of consciousness, whereas a drama will absorb us wholly. But to whatever extent it does so, experience is aesthetic only when an object "holds" our attention.

Furthermore, aesthetic attention is accompanied by activity. This is not the activity of practical experience, which seeks an ulterior goal. Rather it is activity which is either evoked by disinterested perception of the object, or else is required for it. The former includes all muscular, nervous, and "motor" responses such as feelings of tension or rhythmic movement. Contrary to what some snobs would have us believe there is nothing inherently unaesthetic about tapping one's foot in time to the music. The theory of *empathy* points out that we "feel into" the object our muscular and bodily adjustments. We brace ourselves and our muscles become taut in the face of a sculptured figure which is tall, vigorous and upright. This does not occur in aesthetic experience alone, and it does not occur in all aesthetic experience, but when it does, it exemplifies the kind of activity which may be aroused in aesthetic perception. The direction of attention itself may not improperly be called "activity." But even overt bodily movement and effort may be required for aesthetic perception. We usually have to walk round all sides of a sculpture, or through a cathedral, before we can appreciate it. We would often reach out and touch sculptured figures if only museum guards would permit us to do so.

But focusing upon the object and "acting" in regard to it, is not all that is meant by aesthetic "attention." To savor fully the distinctive value of the object, we must be attentive to its frequently complex and subtle details. Acute awareness of these details is discrimination. People often miss a good deal in the experience of art, not only because their attention lapses, but because they fail to "see" all that is of significance in the work. Indeed, their attention frequently lapses for just this reason. They miss the individuality of the work, so that one symphony sounds like any other piece of "long-hair" music, and one lyric poem is indistinguishable from another, and all are equally boring. If you have had the good fortune to study literature with an able teacher, you know how a play or novel can become vital and engaging when you learn to look for details to which you were previously insensitive. But awareness of this kind is not always easily come by. It often requires knowledge about allusions or symbols which occur in the work, repeated experience of the work, and even, sometimes, technical training in the art-form.

As we develop discriminating attention, the work comes alive to us. If we can keep in mind the chief themes in the movement of a symphony, see how they are developed and altered in the course of the movement, and appreciate how they are played off against each other, then there is a great gain in our experience. The experience has greater richness and unity. Without such discrimination it is thin, for the listener responds only to scattered passages or to a patch of striking orchestral color. And it is disorganized, for he is not aware of the structure which binds the work together. His experience may be said to be intermittently and to a limited degree aesthetic, but it is not nearly as rewarding as it might be. Everybody knows how easy it is to start thinking of other things while the music is playing, so that we are really aware of it only now and again. All the more reason, then, why we should develop the capacities for appreciating its richness and profundity. Only so can we keep our experience from becoming, in Santayana's famous phrase, "a drowsy revery relieved by nervous thrills."[4]

If you now understand how aesthetic attention is alert and vigorous, then it is safe to use a word which has often been applied to aesthetic experience – "contemplation." Otherwise, there is the great danger that this word will suggest an aloof, unexcited gaze which, we have seen, is untrue to the facts of aesthetic experience. Actually, "contemplation" does not so much add something new to our definition as it sums up ideas which we have already discussed. It means that perception is directed to the object in its own right and that the spectator is not concerned to analyze it or to ask questions about it. Also, the word connotes thoroughgoing absorption and interest, as when we speak of being "lost in contemplation." Most things are hardly noticed by us, whereas the object of aesthetic perception stands out from its environment and rivets our interest.

The aesthetic attitude can be adopted toward "any object of awareness whatever." This phrase need not, strictly speaking, be included in our definition. We could understand the aesthetic attitude as the kind of perceptual attention we have been talking about, without adding that "any object whatever" may be its object. But definitions are flexible to an extent. We can choose to include in them even what is not strictly necessary to identify the term being defined. The great and even limitless scope of aesthetic experience is one of the most interesting and important things about it.

The definition permits us to say that any object at all can be apprehended aesthetically, i.e., no object is inherently unaesthetic. [. . .]

Notes

1 D. W. Prall, *Aesthetic Judgment* (New York: Crowell, 1929), p. 31.
2 This is a clumsy and largely outmoded word, but it is more convenient for our purpose then words of more limited meaning such as "spectator," "observer," "listener," and is accordingly used here and elsewhere in the text.
3 Cf. Herbert S. Langfeld, *The Aesthetic Attitude* (New York: Harcourt, Brace, 1920), chaps. V–VI; Vernon Lee, "Empathy," in Melvin Rader, ed., *A Modern Book of Esthetics*, rev. ed. (New York: Holt, 1952), pp. 460–5.
4 George Santayana, *Reason in Art* (New York: Scribner's, 1946), p. 51.

8   Locating the Aesthetic

Marcia Muelder Eaton

One of the characteristics of art that strikes both experts and non-experts is not simply that tastes and preferences differ between individuals, but that works valued almost universally in one place or time lose their status when moved spatially or temporally. Everybody is familiar with stories of works that have not come to be appreciated until long after their creators could benefit from the adulation. The story of the artist who lives "ahead of" his or her time is common. There are also art forms that go in and out of fashion. Alan Tormey and Judith Farr Tormey have described the incredible popularity of intarsia – wood inlay – in fifteenth-century Florence, where masters were kept busy in no less than eighty-four workshops. Today we have very few of these, and such workers would more likely be called "craftspeople" than "artists."[1]

In our own period we are witnessing marked changes in what is valued – in what is considered suitable for aesthetic appreciation. It is not just that we value more and different things (quilts and other *women's art*, for example). Ideas about which properties matter aesthetically are changing as well. For much of the twentieth century, critics argued that formal properties such as shape or color or rhythmic or harmonic structures were the sole vehicles of aesthetic value. References to subject matter (love or autumn or a crucifixion) or to the artist's life, to a work's history or political repercussions, for example, were denigrated to such an extent that they achieved the status of "fallacy." The text or the canvas or the score was not merely thought to be central to aesthetic experience; attention to anything extrinsic was viewed as likely to pollute that experience.

> Ours has been a formalist century, interested more in [the analysis of light, fluid brushwork, pure hues, and so on] than in subject matter, content, and personal motivation.[2]

There are still plenty of critics who are dismayed by what they contemptuously call "literary" discussions of painting – remarks about content or subject matter. Some postmodernists have rejected any relation between art and the world. In a very interesting – and sometimes upsetting – article, "The Death of Character," Elinor Fuchs describes avant-garde theater as so self-conscious as to be self-contained.

> Writers and directors working at the edge of theatre seem to perceive that they are in a new kind of world in which there is no longer anything "out there" or anyone "in here" to imitate or to represent.[3]

And in explaining how photography achieved artistic status, Alan Trochtenburg asserts,

> The suppression of what is denoted . . . [signified] the coming-of-age of photography within an already existing system of discourse. Photography earned its place within that system by showing itself capable of a process similar to that implied by abstract and cubist composition. . . .[4]

But suppression of subject matter and refusal to talk about connections between art and what is "out there" or "in here" are no longer characteristic of all, or even most, critics. Even Impressionist works, which for many years were discussed primarily as studies of light, are studied as products of individuals who were interested in what was beautiful and in how the world should be interpreted. No longer are we told to concentrate only on color and light; it has become possible "to read Impressionist painting as we have read earlier painting, with an interest in subject matter and the personality of the artist, and in wider sociological, economic, and philosophical terms," asserts one author of a catalog for a recently successful exhibit.[5]

One of the leaders of the move away from purely formalistic discussion of art works is John Berger. Like formalists, Berger believes that the medium is aesthetically important, but for ideological or social reasons, not simply because of the way it reflects light. He insists, for example, that oil allowed painters to depict the lavishness of possessions, and this was what patrons often desired and enjoyed aesthetically during the seventeenth century.[6] [. . .] Berger himself is extremely interested in subject matter, and writes about it in a way that has inspired others to take it seriously aesthetically.

> In 1645 Hals painted a portrait of a man in black looking over the back of a chair. Probably the sitter was a friend. His expression is another one that Hals was the first to record. It is the look of a man who does not believe in the life he witnesses, yet can see no other alternative. He has considered, quite impersonally, the possibility that life may be absurd. He is by no means desperate. He is interested. But his intelligence isolates him from the current purpose of men and the supposed purpose of God.[7]

After years of being urged to attend only to formal properties, it is often a great relief to be able to talk openly about subject matter and characters and artists' intentions and social context – to speak, that is, as if there were something out there and in here that art deals with. Even in the heyday of formalism these topics have always found their way into ordinary people's discussions of art and have been valued as partially responsible for aesthetic delight. Surely using such topics is the easiest way to engage students. Berger's descriptions are more interesting to most people than discussions limited exclusively to receding planes and patches of grey. Throughout history there has been much discussion of subject matter, which I believe is a truly aesthetic property. I offer it as an example of a feature that theorists have considered an aesthetic property in some periods but not in others. It is worth attention because we are witnessing for ourselves its return to favor. There are many other examples of such fluctuations.

Such changes might lead one to believe that 'aesthetic' cannot be defined because no necessary or sufficient conditions seem to exist that will serve to tie together what counts aesthetically or to distinguish the aesthetic from the non-aesthetic. This is what I want to deny. What is *aesthetic* remains constant even though specific features pointed to as aesthetically valuable may change. This becomes apparent, I think, when we look further at examples of changes in aesthetic values.

Among other places, these can be found in histories of art and culture. Some scholars try to explain changes in taste or attitude. Raymond Williams, for instance, places heavy emphasis on the changes effected on our cultural history when masses of people learned to read.[8] Joseph Epstein has discussed the way acceptance of Freudian psychoanalytic theories altered the nature of literary biography.[9] Obviously, when such social changes occur there are corresponding changes in conceptions of art and the aesthetic. An outstanding study of the way in which culture affects art is Arnold Hauser's *The Social History of Art and Literature*. Speaking of the early Middle Ages he says,

> When the forms of property, the organisations of labour, the sources of education, and the methods of instruction remained practically unchanged, it would have been remarkable had any sudden change occurred in the current conception of art.[10]

Another historian who traces the history of art within the larger cultural and social context is William Fleming. Like Hauser's book, Fleming's *Art and Ideas* has many examples of ways in which cultures other than our own took interest in quite different properties of the objects they believed to carry artistic and aesthetic value. The Romans, wanting grandeur in their ceremonies, made musical instruments bigger. Quintillian wrote,

> And what else is the function of the horns and trumpets attached to our legion? The louder the concert of their notes, the greater is the glorious supremacy of our arms over all the nations of earth.[11]

Being *big* and *loud* were a source of delight; and they mattered for Quintillian and his contemporaries aesthetically as well as militarily.

But how can we know if the Romans actually experienced these instruments aesthetically? Do we have any reason for thinking that people in other times had experiences like those we identify as aesthetic? When they pick out quite different things for praise, can we say theirs was aesthetic appreciation? Our ability to do just that points us toward locating the aesthetic generally, I believe.

Consider this description of a wedding feast in Normandy at the beginning of the eleventh century.

> Everyone performed at his best and the noise of the instruments and the voices of the narrators made a considerable uproar in the hall.[12]

"Considerable uproar" might not, in isolation, be taken initially as naming an aesthetic property, but in this context, where best performance is also considered, it is clearly deserves to be described this way. The phrase "performed at his best" signals the presence of *delight taken in features in the performance.*

In the visual arts we also find unexpected features pointed out in periods removed from our own:

> Of all subjects, the most congenial to Veronese's art was festivity. Painted with the primary object of delighting the eye, his canvases nevertheless capture an important aspect of Venetian life – the conviviality of large social gatherings and the love of sumptuous surroundings embellished with fruits, followers, furniture, draperies, and jesters in bizare costumes.[13]

On the back of one painting is this note:

> If I ever have time . . . I want to represent a sumptuous banquet in a superb hall, at which will be present the Virgin, the Saviour, and St Joseph. They will be served by the most brilliant retinue of angels which one can imagine, busied in offering them the daintiest viands and an abundance of splendid fruit in dishes of silver and gold. Other angels will hand them precious wines in transparent crystal glasses and gilded goblets, in order to show with what zeal blessed spirits serve the Lord.[14]

How surprising it would be to find such a note on the back of a twentieth-century canvas!

In seventeenth-century Holland, church services were simplified and churches were less and less decorated so that worshippers might not be distracted (aesthetically) from their (religious) purposes. Thus, art was found more and more in personal residences. Artists came to conceive their work differently. Patrons wanted to find in the paintings they owned indications of their worldly possessions. "The room shows my rug" would then have been part of a positive aesthetic description. Even religious paintings exemplify significant changes. The rather rebellious Protestant Rembrandt "was under no compulsion to conform to the usual iconographical tradition of Madonnas and Child, [or] Crucifixions."[15] Therefore pointing out a lack of standard icons would describe a feature in his paintings worth attending to.

These few examples, which could be multiplied indefinitely, are sufficient for my purpose here – to suggest what is special about the aesthetic.

What do these changes in the concept of art have to do with the aesthetic? My contention is this: The particular features pointed to – whether a thing is big or loud or shows Christ or a rug – may vary dramatically throughout space and time. However, what we do when our experience is aesthetic retains a common element. We attend to intrinsic features in the belief that this attention will be rewarded by delight. Thus, delight in what resides intrinsically in something is a mark of the aesthetic generally.

The Relevance of Artists

We certainly delight in the creative skills of artists. Those who cannot do what artists do – from lack of talent or training (and those who lack the skill never believe that mere training will provide it) – feel a special wonder. Aristotle asserted that human beings naturally delight in imitation, and although this does not imply that imitation is the only source of delight, we do appreciate others' ability to turn words and shapes almost magically into recognizable and coherent forms. According to Ernst Kris and Otto Kurz, respect has given artists even legendary and mythic status.[16] [. . .]

Kris and Kurz demonstrate that "the myth of the artist" reflects the fact that people value special creative talent. This is one reason that discussions about works of art are not limited to manifest or directly observable properties. We value not only *what* we see or hear but also *how* it came to be – aspects of cause as well as effect. Yet without the *what*, the value and importance of the *how* disappear. My claim is not that aesthetic experience demands attention to only intrinsic properties. A legitimate part of what we value often lies beyond the created object itself. An appreciation of artistry is often present. But when response is aesthetic, appreciation of the artist is directed *back* to features of the object. If we did not value intrinsic properties, we would not aesthetically care how they got there.

It is both interesting and instructive to note that sometimes conflicting claims are advanced to certify an artist's genius. One composition, we are told, was "done in a week." Of another we are assured that the artist "labored over a single word for months." Although at first these descriptions seem to imply inconsistent theories of aesthetic value, what they in fact do is draw attention to particular properties of particular objects. So they are not inconsistent. We value things done quickly *and* things done meticulously, although we rarely find both qualities in the same work.

Usually we are given such information when the work described seems otherwise – it looks as though it was done quickly (a Mondrian, for instance) or as though it required a great deal of time (a symphony, for instance) – and we are told that just the opposite is actually true. Told that a Mondrian was done in two hours, some observers might respond contemptuously that they could have guessed it. But told that he labored over lines and colors for months, viewers look more carefully – to see what about the painting could account for such prolonged care. Only this second look yields aesthetic appreciation of the work.

Kris and Kurz give examples of other claims made so typically about artists that they have become legendary or mythic. (Such tales function in heroic biographies generally; they are not unique to books about artists.) It is common to tell stories that show that an artist's abilities had become apparent in childhood, that he or she was marked for success from the beginning. But just as often it is said that fate made the difference – the artist was in the right place at the right time and the right person just happened to appear. Sometimes lucky accidents play a significant role in artistic achievement. Pliny told a story about Protogenes' attempt to depict a dog foaming at the mouth. When he couldn't get the foam right, he threw a sponge at the painting—and got just what he wanted.

The particular legend in ascendancy at any time reflects cultural interests and preoccupations. Such stories "work" only when they tell the audience something about an artist that it wants to hear and something that connects what the artist did with what is valued in the artwork and in the artworld. If we valued only what is put carefully, precisely, and intentionally on the canvas, then the sponge throwing incident would detract from the artist's contribution. But it does not. Kris and Kurz attribute this to the growing role of and emphasis upon imagination or "invention" in the history of art (an example of the sort of "changing value" that we looked at in the last section).[17]

This view is supported by David Summers in *Michelangelo and the Language of Art*.

> The Cinquecento no longer regarded the imitation of nature as the acme of artistic achievement, but rather viewed "invention" as its foremost aim.[18]

Thus, what in a work of art was worth attending to and reflecting upon became what was considered a product of imagination. It was simply not enough that the object resulted from technique, dexterity, or intense labor. New appreciation of *il furore dell'arte* (artistic ecstasy) resulted in looking for and then, and only then, finding one set of worthwhile properties rather than another. As Aretino said,

> This point of view also decisively influenced the evaluation of the work of art itself. . . . Soon . . . the unfinished was highly appreciated in its own right; and the strange statement found in guidebooks to Florence, that Michelangelo's unfinished slaves in the grotto of the Boboli Gardens are in that state more beautiful and more impressive than if the master had completed them, is nothing but a reflection of the same aesthetic that has continued to exert its influence to this day. This is in complete contrast to what was valued in the Middle Ages which used as the aesthetic yardstick the degree to which a work was finished in the sense of craftsmanship.[19]

If imagination (in both artistic production and experience) is valued, then *unfinishedness* as an intrinsic property is worthy of attention and reflection; if craftsmanship is valued, then *finishedness* is what rewards our attention and reflection.

Both terms (*finished* and *unfinished*) become "aesthetic" only within a context of a special sort – one that assumes valuing or taking delight as the goal. Both "done in two hours" and "took a lifetime" may be "aesthetic" remarks if they invite attention to something with the promise of a satisfying perception. The appropriateness of *finished* and *unfinished* will depend upon particular aesthetic features that are being referred to.

The legends and myths about artists reflect the milieu of the viewer, and this will be made apparent in the sorts of things that he or she chooses to tell us about the object being discussed. Stories emphasising long years of practice are not likely to emerge when the role of imagination and invention is foregrounded. In such contexts the more likely stories are those in which artists are born, not made.

The dichotomy between artist as faithful copier of nature and artist as surpasser of nature parallels the dichotomy between imagination and craftsmanship and the accompanying legends and divergence in properties to which attention is directed when first one and then the other is dominant. The latter provides the background for such famous stories as that told of Zeuxis, whose painting of grapes was so realistic that birds attempted to eat them. When this kind of artistic production is valued, viewers of the product will be expected to point to lifelike, naturalistic, deceptive, and illusionistic qualities. These will not support a positive assessment when an artist is supposed to go beyond the real to some ideal. This difference accounts for the following comment:

> Zeuxis is said to have raised the question why the birds pecked away at the picture of the grapes which a boy was carrying and why the picture of the boy did not frighten them away. Two different explanations were proposed: One, found in Pliny, suggested that the boy was "not so well" painted as the grapes; the other, by Seneca, maintained that this very incident showed that as an idealised portrait the painting of the boy was superior to that of the grapes.[20]

Whether the boy or the birds is judged to be superior depends on what one supposes the artist was trying to do. And the *value* of what the artist was trying to do will differ from period to period. What remains constant is that the stories we choose to tell and be told are tied to the features in the works that we find delightful.

Notes

1   Alan Tormey and Judith Farr Tormey, "Renaissance Intarsia: The Art of Geometry," *Scientific American*, vol. 247, no. 1, July 1982, pp. 136–43.
2   Linnea S. Dietrich, "The Subjective Vision of French Impressionism," catalog for show by same name (Tampa: The Tampa Museum, 1981) p. 8.
3   Elinor Fuchs, "The Death of Character," *Theatre Communications*, no. 2 (March 1983): p. 1.
4   Alan Trochtenburg, "Camera Work, Notes Toward an Investigation," *Massachusetts Review* (1978): pp. 838–9.
5   Richard Brettell et al., *A Day in the Country: Impressionism and the French Landscape* Exhibition Catalog (Los Angeles: Los Angeles County Museum of Art, 1984), p. 21.
6   John Berger, *Ways of Seeing* (London: Penguin Books, 1972), p. 166.
7   Ibid., p.166.
8   Raymond Williams, *The Long Revolution* (New York: Columbia University Press,1961) pp. 156–72.
9   Joseph Epstein, "Literary Biography," *New Criterion*, vol. 1, no. 9 (Massachusetts 1983): p. 27.
10 Arnold Hauser, *The Social History of Art and Literature* (New York: Vintage Books, 1951), p. 11.

11 William Fleming, *Art and Ideas* (New York: Holt, Rinehart and Winston, 1974), p. 74.

12 Ibid., p. 119.

13 Ibid., p. 210.

14 Ibid., p. 211.

15 Ibid., p. 262.

16 *Legend, Myth, and Magic in the Image of the Artist* (New Haven: Yale University Press, 1979), p. xii.

17 Ibid., p. 48.

18 David Summers, *Michelangelo and the Language of Art* (Princeton: Princeton University Press, 1981) p. 47.

19 Ibid., p. 48.

20 J. Overbeck, *Die Antiken Schriftquellen zur Geschicte der bildenen Kunste bei den Breichen*, quoted in Kris and Kurz, p. 82.

---

9 From *Truth and Method*

Hans-Georg Gadamer

What we call a world of art and experience (*erleben*) aesthetically depends on a process of abstraction. By disregarding everything in which a work is rooted (its original context of life, and the religious or secular function that gave it significance), it becomes visible as the "pure work of art." In performing this abstraction, aesthetic consciousness performs a task that is positive in itself. It shows what a pure work of art is, and allows it to exist in its own right. I call this "aesthetic differentiation."

Whereas a definite taste differentiates – i.e., selects and rejects – on the basis of some content, aesthetic differentiation is an abstraction that selects only on the basis of aesthetic quality as such. It is performed in the self-consciousness of "aesthetic experiences." Aesthetic experience (*Erlebnis*) is directed towards what is supposed to be the work proper – what it ignores are the extra-aesthetic elements that cling to it, such as purpose, function, the significance of its content. These elements may be significant enough inasmuch as they situate the work in its world and thus determine the whole meaningfulness that it originally possessed. But as art the work must be distinguished from all that. It practically defines aesthetic consciousness to say that it differentiates what is aesthetically intended from everything that is outside the aesthetic sphere. It abstracts from all the conditions of a work's accessibility. Thus this is a specifically aesthetic kind of differentiation. It distinguishes the aesthetic quality of a work from all the elements of content that induce us to take up a moral or religious stance towards it, and presents it solely by itself in its aesthetic being. Similarly, in the performing arts it differentiates between the original (play or musical composition) and its performance, and in such a way that both the original (in contrast to the reproduction) and the reproduction in itself (in contrast to the original or other possible interpretations) can be posited as what is aesthetic. The sovereignty of aesthetic consciousness consists in its capacity to make this aesthetic differentiation everywhere and to see everything "aesthetically." [. . .]

The pantheon of art is not a timeless present that presents itself to a pure aesthetic consciousness, but the act of a mind and spirit that has collected and gathered itself historically. Our experience of the aesthetic too is a mode of self-understanding. Self-understanding always occurs through understanding something other than the self, and includes the unity and integrity of the other. Since we meet the artwork in the world and encounter a world in the individual artwork, the work of art is not some alien universe into which we are magically transported for a time. Rather, we learn to understand ourselves in and through it, and this means that we sublate (*aufheben*) the discontinuity and atomism of isolated experiences in the continuity of our own existence. For this reason, we must adopt a standpoint in relation to art and the beautiful that does not pretend to immediacy but corresponds to the historical nature of the human condition. The appeal to immediacy, to the instantaneous dash of genius, to the significance of "experiences" (*Erlebnisse*), cannot withstand the claim of human existence to continuity and unity of self-understanding. The binding quality of the experience (*Erfahrung*) of art must not be disintegrated by aesthetic consciousness.

This negative insight, positively expressed, is that art is knowledge and experiencing an artwork means sharing in that knowledge.

This raises the question of how one can do justice to the truth of aesthetic experience (*Erfahrung*) and overcome the radical subjectivization of the aesthetic that began with Kant's *Critique of Aesthetic Judgment*. We have shown that it was a methodological abstraction corresponding to a quite particular transcendental task of laying foundations which led Kant to relate aesthetic judgment entirely to the condition of the subject. If, however, this aesthetic abstraction was subsequently understood as a content and was changed into the demand that art be understood "purely aesthetically," we can now see how this demand for abstraction ran into indissoluble contradiction with the true experience of art.

Is there to be no knowledge in art? Does not the experience of art contain a claim to truth which is certainly different from that of science, but just as certainly is not inferior to it? And is not the task of aesthetics precisely to ground the fact that the experience (*Erfahrung*) of art is a mode of knowledge of a unique kind, certainly different from that sensory knowledge which provides science with the ultimate data from which it constructs the knowledge of nature, and certainly different from all moral rational knowledge, and indeed from all conceptual knowledge – but still knowledge, i.e., conveying truth?

This can hardly be recognised if, with Kant, one measures the truth of knowledge by the scientific concept of knowledge and the scientific concept of reality. It is necessary to take the concept of experience (*Erfahrung*) more broadly than Kant did, so that the experience of the work of art can be understood as experience. For this we can appeal to Hegel's admirable lectures on aesthetics. Here the truth that lies in every artistic experience is recognised and at the same time mediated with historical consciousness. Hence aesthetics becomes a history of worldviews – i.e., a history of truth, as it is manifested in the mirror of art. It is also a fundamental recognition of the task that I formulated thus: to legitimate the knowledge of truth that occurs in the experience of art itself. [. . .]

For my starting point I select an idea that has played a major role in aesthetics: the concept of *play*. I wish to free this concept of the subjective meaning that it has in Kant and Schiller and that dominates the whole of modern aesthetics and philosophy of man. When we speak of play in reference to the experience of art, this means neither the orientation nor even the state of mind of the creator or of those enjoying the work of art, nor the freedom of a subjectivity engaged in play, but the mode of being of the work of art itself. In analysing aesthetic consciousness we recognised that conceiving aesthetic consciousness as something that confronts an object does not do justice to the real situation. This is why the concept of play is important in my exposition.

We can certainly distinguish between play and the behavior of the player, which, as such, belongs with the other kinds of subjective behavior. Thus it can be said that for the player play is not serious: that is why he plays. We can try to define the concept of play from this point of view. What is merely play is not serious. Play has a special relation to what is serious. It is not only that the latter gives it its "purpose": we play "for the sake of recreation," Aristotle says. More important, play itself contains its own, even sacred, seriousness. Yet, in playing, all those purposive relations that determine active and caring existence have not simply disappeared, but are curiously suspended. The player himself knows that play is only play and that it exists in a world determined by the seriousness of purposes. But he does not know this in such a way that, as a player, he actually *intends* this relation to seriousness. Play fulfills its purpose only if the player loses himself in play. Seriousness is not merely something that calls us away from play; rather, seriousness in playing is necessary to make the play wholly play. Someone who doesn't take the game seriously is a spoilsport. The mode of being of play does not allow the player to behave toward play as if toward an object. The player knows very well what play is, and that what he is doing is "only a game"; but he does not know what exactly he "knows" in knowing that.

Our question concerning the nature of play itself cannot, therefore, find an answer if we look for it in the player's subjective reflection. Instead, we are inquiring into the mode of being of play as such. We have seen that it is not aesthetic consciousness but the experience (*Erfahrung*) of art and thus the question of the mode of being of the work of art that must be the object of our examination. But this was precisely the experience of the work of art that I maintained in opposition to the leveling process of aesthetic consciousness: namely that the work of art is not an object that stands over against a subject for itself. Instead the work of art has its true being in the fact that it becomes an experience that changes the person who experiences it. The "subject" of the experience of art, that which remains and endures, is not the subjectivity of the person who experiences it but the work itself. This is the point at which the mode of being of play becomes significant. For play has its own essence, independent of the consciousness of those who play. Play – indeed, play proper – also exists when the thematic horizon is not limited by any being-for-itself of subjectivity, and where there are no subjects who are behaving "playfully."

If we examine how the word "play" is used and concentrate on its so-called metaphorical senses, we find talk of the play of light, the play of the waves, the play of gears or parts of machinery, the interplay of limbs, the play of forces, the play of gnats, even a play on words. In each case what is intended is to-and-fro movement that is not tied to any goal that would bring it to an end. Correlatively, the word "Spiel" originally meant "dance," and is still found in many word forms (e.g., in *Spielmann*, jongleur). The movement of playing has no goal that brings it to an end; rather, it renews itself in constant repetition. The movement backward and forward is obviously so central to the definition of play that it makes no difference who or what performs this movement. The movement of play as such has, as it were, no substrate. It is the game that is played – it is irrelevant whether or not there is a subject who plays it. The play is the occurrence of the movement as such. Thus we speak of the play of colors and do not mean only that one color plays against another, but that there is one process or sight displaying a changing variety of colors.

Hence the mode of being of play is not such that, for the game to be played, there must be a subject who is behaving playfully. Rather, the primordial sense of playing is the medial one. Thus we say that something is "playing" (*spielt*) somewhere or at some time, that something is going on (*im Spiele ist*) or that something is happening (*sich abspielt*).

This linguistic observation seems to me an indirect indication that play is not to be understood as something a person does. As far as language is concerned, the actual subject of play is obviously not the subjectivity of an individual who, among other activities, also plays but is instead the play itself. But we are so accustomed to relating phenomena such as playing to the sphere of subjectivity and the ways it acts that we remain closed to these indications from the spirit of language. [. . .]

Here the *primacy of play over the consciousness of the player* is fundamentally acknowledged and, in fact, even the experiences of play that psychologists and anthropologists describe are illuminated afresh if one starts from the medial sense of the word "playing." Play clearly represents an order in which the to-and-fro motion of play follows of itself. It is part of play that the movement is not only without goal or purpose but also without effort. It happens, as it were, by itself. The ease of play – which naturally does not mean that there is any real absence of effort but refers phenomenologically only to the absence of strain – is experienced subjectively as relaxation. The structure of play absorbs the player into itself, and thus frees him from the burden of taking the initiative, which constitutes the actual strain of existence. This is also seen in the spontaneous tendency to repetition that emerges in the player and in the constant self-renewal of play, which affects its form (e.g., the refrain). [. . .]

This point shows the importance of defining play as a process that takes place "in between." We have seen that play does not have its being in the player's consciousness or attitude, but on the contrary play draws him into its dominion and fills him with its spirit. The player experiences the game as a reality that surpasses him. This is all the more the case where the game is itself "intended" as such a reality – for instance, the play which appears as *presentation for an audience.*

Even a play remains a game – i.e., it has the structure of a game, which is that of a closed world. But however much a religious or profane play represents a world wholly closed within itself, it is as if open toward the spectator, in whom it achieves its whole significance. The players play their roles as in any game, and thus play is represented, but the play itself is the whole, comprising players and spectators. In fact, it is experienced properly by, and presents itself (as it is "meant") to, one who is not acting in the play but watching it. In him the game is raised, as it were, to its ideality.

For the players this means that they do not simply fulfill their roles as in any game – rather, they play their roles, they represent them for the audience. The way they participate in the game is no longer determined by the fact that they are completely absorbed in it, but by the fact that they play their role in relation and regard to the whole of the play, in which not they but the audience is to become absorbed. A complete change takes place when play as such becomes a play. It puts the spectator in the place of the player. He – and not the player – is the person for and in whom the play is played. Of course this does not mean that the player is not able to experience the significance of the whole in which he plays his representing role. The spectator has only methodological precedence: in that the play is presented for him, it becomes apparent that the play bears within itself a meaning to be understood and that can therefore be detached from the behavior of the player. Basically the difference between the player and the spectator is here superseded. The requirement that the play itself be intended in its meaningfulness is the same for both.

This is still the case even when the play community is sealed off against all spectators, either because it opposes the social institutionalization of artistic life, as in so-called chamber music, which seeks to be more authentic music-making in being performed for the players themselves and not for an audience. If someone performs music in this way, he is also in fact trying to make the music "sound good," but that means that it would really be there for any listener. Artistic presentation, by its nature, exists for someone, even if there is no one there who merely listens or watches. [. . .]

I call this change, in which human play comes to its true consummation in being art, *transformation into structure.* Only through this change does play achieve ideality, so that it can be intended and understood as play. Only now does it emerge as detached from the representing activity of the players and consist in the pure appearance (*Erscheinung*) of what they are playing. As such, the play – even the unforeseen elements of improvisation – is in principle repeatable and hence permanent. It has the character of a work, of an ergon and not only of energeia. In this sense I call it a structure (*Gebilde*).

What can be thus dissociated from the representing activity of the player is still linked to representation. This linkage does not mean dependence in the sense that the play acquires a definite meaning only through the particular persons representing it, nor even through the originator of the work, its real creator, the artist. Rather, in relation to them all, the play has an absolute autonomy, and that is what is suggested by the concept of transformation.

What this implies about defining the nature of art emerges when one takes the sense of transformation seriously. Transformation is not alteration, even an alteration that is especially far-reaching. Alteration always means that what is altered also remains the same and is maintained. However totally it may change, something changes in it. In terms of the categories, all alteration (*alloiosis*) belongs in the sphere of quality – i.e., of an accident of substance. But transformation means that something is suddenly and as a whole something else, that this other transformed thing that it has become is its true being, in comparison with which its earlier being is nil. When we find someone transformed we mean precisely this, that he has become another person, as it were. There cannot here be any gradual transition leading from one to the other, since the one is the denial of the other. Thus transformation into structure means that what existed previously exists no longer. But also that what now exists, what represents itself in the play of art, is the lasting and true.

It is clear that to start from subjectivity here is to miss the point. What no longer exists is the players – with the poet or the composer being considered as one of the players. None of them has his own existence for himself, which he retains so that his acting would mean that he "is only acting." If we describe from the point of view of the actor what his acting is, then obviously it is not transformation but disguise. A man who is disguised does not want to be recognised, but instead to appear as someone else and be taken for him. In the eyes of others he no longer wants to be himself, but to be taken for someone else. Thus he does not want to be discovered or recognised. He plays another person, but in the way that we play something in our daily intercourse with other people – i.e., that we merely pretend, act a part, and create an impression. A person who plays such a game denies, to all appearances, continuity with himself. But in truth that means that he holds on to this continuity with himself for himself and only withholds it from those before whom he is acting.

According to all that we have observed concerning the nature of play, this subjective distinction between oneself and the play implicit in putting up a show is not the true nature of play. Rather, play itself is a transformation of such a kind that the identity of the player does not continue to exist for anybody. Everybody asks instead what is supposed to be represented, what is "meant." The players (or playwright) no longer exist, only what they are playing.

But, above all, what no longer exists is the world in which we live as our own. Transformation into structure is not simply transposition into another world. Certainly the play takes place in another, closed world. But inasmuch as it is a structure, it is, so to speak, its own measure and measures itself by nothing outside it. Thus the action of a drama – in this respect it still entirely resembles the religious act – exists as something that rests absolutely within itself. It no longer permits of any comparison with reality as the secret measure of all verisimilitude. It is raised above all such comparisons – and hence also above the question of whether it is all real – because a superior truth speaks from it. Even Plato, the most radical critic of the high estimation of art in the history of philosophy, speaks of the comedy and tragedy of life on the one hand and of the stage on the other without differentiating between them. For this difference is superseded if one knows how to see the meaning of the play that unfolds before one. The pleasure of drama is the same in both cases: it is the joy of knowledge.

This gives what we called transformation into structure its full meaning. The transformation is a transformation into the true. It is not enchantment in the sense of a bewitchment that waits for the redeeming word that will transform things back to what they were; rather, it is itself redemption and transformation back into true being. In being presented in play, what is emerges. It produces and brings to light what is otherwise constantly hidden and withdrawn. [. . .]

We have established that the cognitive import of imitation lies in recognition. But what is recognition? A more exact analysis of the phenomenon will make quite clear to us the ontological import of representation, which is what we are concerned with. As we know, Aristotle emphasizes that artistic presentation even makes the unpleasant appear pleasant, and for this reason Kant defined art as the beautiful representation of something, because it can make even the ugly appear beautiful. But this obviously does not refer to artifice and artistic technique. One does not admire the skill with which something is done, as in the case of a highwire artist. This has only secondary interest, as Aristotle explicitly says. Rather, what we experience in a work of art and what invites our attention is how true it is – i.e., to what extent one knows and recognizes something and oneself.

But we do not understand what recognition is in its profoundest nature if we only regard it as knowing something again that we know already – i.e., what is familiar is recognized again. The joy of recognition is rather the joy of knowing more than is already familiar. In recognition what we know emerges, as if illuminated, from all the contingent and variable circumstances that condition it; it is grasped in its essence. It is known as something. [. . .]

My thesis, then, is that the being of art cannot be defined as an object of an aesthetic consciousness because, on the contrary, the aesthetic attitude is more than it knows of itself. It is a part of the *event of being that occurs in presentation*, and belongs essentially to play as play.

How is Art Presented to the Public?

10   Artistic Dropouts

Kevin Melchionne

Dropping Out

Sitting in a high school art class, struggling with a drawing, perhaps a still life of shiny bottles and plump oranges, the teenaged art student recognizes that her effort pales in comparison to that of the student sitting next to her. Whereas her own bottles seem lumpy and her oranges float like polka dots across the page, her classmate has captured the sparkle and transparency of the bottle, the dimpled roundness of the fruit, the flatness of the table. Faced with the unflattering comparison, our would-be artist concludes that she lacks the special gifts of her classmate and renounces art for good. She joins the chorus of students who hide frustration behind cool apathy and is relieved when she can finally put the art class behind her.

This scene is repeated every day in high schools across the country. It marks the moment when what I will term *realism anxiety* overtakes the aspiring artist. The young artist becomes increasingly aware of the distinction between her "childish scribbles" and the dominant standards of depiction in our society. She begins to substitute copying photographs for imaginative drawing, giving herself an even more uncompromising master. But unable to demonstrate competency on the terms of this realism, the student concludes she was not chosen to be an artist. She lacks that special something which we call talent, and in its extreme, genius. She assumes that artistic talent – tellingly reduced here to rendering – is innate because she has not and thinks cannot learn it. Here, the common mystification of artistic ability conspires with the intense self-criticism of the adolescent to paralyze the would-be artist, who, on top of it all, is grappling with some of the most difficult perceptual and technical problems in the visual arts.

The students who win the approval of their teachers and the admiration of their classmates through their capacity to draw realistically are the ones who go on to professional art school. But there they learn that the values of the realism that buoyed them through intermediate and secondary school are not so absolute. Even in the heroic figures of the Italian Renaissance, other artistic and cultural values are in play. If the creativity of the new art students is to remain vital, they will need to reevaluate just what makes Michelangelo or Leonardo so great. Moreover, in the art school environment, students feel the force of modernist culture with an intensity that they could not have anticipated. Most first year programs in degree-granting art schools are rooted in the Bauhaus-inspired belief that one set of skills and formal problems underlies all creative art. Three-dimensional design courses presume that the sculptor, industrial designer, and architect share common problems of spatial design. Two-dimensional design courses claim to identify the core problems of illustration, graphic design, and painting. Gray scales, color wheels, tonal studies, abstract 3-D formal constructions make up the so-called "building blocks" of all art according to the modernism which still dominates introductory college art education. But the problems students are asked to solve and the skills they are expected to develop have little in common with the popular realism that dominates the mainstream culture. Intended or not, the effect of art school is a dramatic uprooting of the budding artist. The "foundation" courses of the first year do not so much define the essential issues of art as they bring about a break with the "bad habits" of the popular realism through which the student first defined herself as an artist. This break is at the same time a leap into the "art world." Cut off from the technical standards of artistic excellence that defined her late adolescent artistic world, our proficient bottle polisher must now reflect upon and redefine her creativity. The student is now expected to understand art history and define her own project in terms of its values and problems. Naturally, many refuse to make this leap; they head off to one of the conservative academies that continue to embrace realism. Or, disillusioned, they simply drop out, making a second generation of dropouts. In any case, the sad irony remains: the criteria by which we select people to go to art school to become professional artists are the very values which are most deeply questioned in our art schools.

This is not to say that realism itself is necessarily adolescent or that nonrealistic styles are intrinsically more mature. My point is that the aspiring artist faces shifting and even contradictory standards at consecutive phases in her early development. The result is confusion and missed opportunities. Caught between, first, an over-emphasis on realism and, then, its vigorous rejection, one can only wonder with regret how many aesthetically sensitive individuals were silenced at an early age by this mixed message about artistic excellence.

But Even I Could Do That!

Each day in museums of modern art and commercial galleries, one can hear some version or another of a cry of outrage: "But even I could do that!" This remark may well be the single most common complaint heard by visitors to such institutions. One is likely to hear it in front of works which have in common only their failure to conform to traditional expectations of realism. "Even I could do that!" implies of course that the works have no value. But it is a strange way of saying so. There are other ways of making the same point. One could say that the work is boring, mindless, or simplistic. Instead of something he would but cannot do, the spectator is faced with something he can but would not do. It is as if the spectator were saying: "Since I am capable of doing work like this, rest assured that I *would* have done it, had it been worth doing." I am not interested in changing anyone's mind about contemporary fine art here. The art world is far too varied to warrant generalizations. I only wish to observe how strange it is that the knee-jerk rejection of contemporary art is usually couched in a statement about the spectator's capacity to do it. Why, of all the ways to express dissatisfaction with art, do so many people react by defining the work's worthlessness in terms of their own creativity?

Perhaps our spectator clings too tightly to this certainty of the worthlessness of art. Proud of having named the imperial nudity of the art world, he passes over the nitty-gritty questions of how and why intelligent and serious artists come to do what they do. The expectations of the spectator are not softened by the disappointment. Instead, they are hardened into self-righteous denunciation. The outrage of the spectator is couched in arrogant certainty about what art is supposed to look like. Knowing that arrogance and insecurity are usually closely linked, the smug remark "But I can do that!" can be rephrased as follows: "I am talentless and uncreative, incapable of making even competent, let alone museum-quality art. If I am capable of making this work of art, then it must be bad." The spectator is in fact another artistic dropout. The dismissal of contemporary art is linked to the dropout's rejection of an artistic side; the dropout is using his own failure as the measuring stick of the artist. In his eyes, the artist is failing, too. "Contemporary art is bad because someone like me can do it and I am considered a bad artist." The repudiation of art is coupled with the self-denigration of the detractor.

The most corrosive version of this complaint takes the form of "My child could do that!" The cruelty of this remark comes from moving the barometer of incompetence out of the parent's memory of early failure and into the life of a real child, who may still be unaware of the looming critical gauntlet. I once followed a father and daughter through several rooms of the contemporary wing of the Metropolitan Museum of Art. While he smartly peppered his criticism with this very remark, she had that I-wish-I-could-disappear-look, clearly uncomfortable at the thought of something being bad precisely because she was capable of doing it.

The artistic dropout renounces art by saying, "I can't," then, in confronting the work of those that go on to be artists, replies bitterly, "I could!" "I can't" and "I could" are two sides of the same coin. The realism anxiety that pushed the adolescent out of art returns as the standard by which he judges others. The artistic dropout's capacity to engage, let alone appreciate, new art is hampered by the fact that his aesthetic values are frozen in his adolescent experience. But the fact that I am capable of making something that resembles an existing work of art does not mean that the work is necessarily bad. "Even I could do that!" is a blanket response to works of art so diverse in aspiration and form that it makes me wonder if the detractor is really paying attention. In the end, such remarks say less about the art than about its detractor. They reveal the dropout's philistinism, the habit of rejecting all art that is not easily digestible.

The Idea of Aesthetic Health

The strict reliance on conventional realism defeats creativity, then defeats the capacity to go out and enjoy art. The rigidity of the dropout's standards becomes a barrier to exploring and appreciating the efforts of others. The dropout's interest in obtaining aesthetic satisfaction withers and so artistic failure is compounded by aesthetic undernourishment. The dropout has sunk to a state of aesthetic depression. She now lacks what I call *aesthetic health*.

The idea of aesthetic health may strike the reader as bizarre. But it is common to speak of non-physical aspects of the self in terms of health. For instance, emotional health includes the capacity to be sensitive to one's own feelings and to express them to others. It also stands for the capacity to empathize and comfort others. An emotionally unhealthy person is unaware of her feelings. She represses them or is unable to control them. Similarly, it is possible to speak of aesthetic health as the capacity to be sensitive to and express one's own aesthetic pleasures and preferences. An aesthetically healthy person reflects upon the pleasures that she has and seeks to discover their sources. Aesthetic health also means being open to sources of satisfaction encountered randomly in the world or proposed for our consideration by our friends. Another source of proposals is the artist through her artistic creations. Simply put, aesthetic health amounts to being able to appreciate a decent chunk of what is offered by the world.

Aesthetic health develops in two directions: expansion and refinement. The aesthetically healthy person is able to expand her capacity to appreciate more and more of what the world has to offer. Rather than clinging to the familiar pleasures of the past, the aesthetically expansive person seeks out new experiences or creates new variations on past successes. Seeing the world as a field of possible sources of satisfaction, she forges out in new directions. She is a gourmand, on the lookout for new spices or produce in order to concoct new recipes. In the art world, she sees a feast of visions rather than a glut of egos.

By successfully deriving satisfaction from the world, she approaches new situations with a confidence that she will be able to appreciate something about them. She is better prepared to enjoy the world. As she expands her interests to more possible sources of satisfaction, she also makes more nuanced and sophisticated distinctions between them. She is like a discriminating cook, sensitive to the subtle effects that the relative weighting of seasonings has on dishes, or the length of cooking time, or the quality of ingredients.

Without this additional capacity to refine experience, it would be impossible to develop any serious convictions about the aesthetic quality of what she encounters. She would be cast about in a sea of aesthetic possibilities, all enticing but, when taken together and without discrimination, overwhelming and nauseating. At the same time, without the thirst for new, unforeseeable experiences, her capacity to make these fine distinctions would degenerate into the pedantic quibbling of the snob. More concerned with maintaining a hierarchy of values than exploring what the world has to offer, the snob clings to the superiority of this or that Italian wine or French cheese (or even beer or potato chip) as if aesthetic health depended upon this judgment really being as clear as the snob assures us it is.

Aesthetic health doesn't depend on our recognizing that one wine is really better than another; it depends instead upon our capacity to discover which wine we ourselves enjoy more. Next, it depends upon our capacity to understand the source of that preference – dryness, sweetness, robustness, cleanness – in the wine itself. Then, it depends on our willingness to compare that satisfaction against further experiences of different wines, sharing our observations and preferences with other people. By throwing ourselves into experiences and thinking about how we respond to them, we come to develop a set of convictions called *taste*. In this way, the aesthetically healthy individual balances a capacity to appreciate with a capacity to evaluate.

With this confidence comes both a sense of adventure and higher expectations: exotic foods, complicated novels, foreign films, strange sculptural installations. An appetite for these aesthetic adventures does not rule out simpler pleasures. On the contrary, it places them in greater relief, highlighting their value as reminders of how little we need in order to be satisfied, and, at the same time, how deeply entwined aesthetic satisfaction is with the ordinary process of living. Simple pleasures clear out our aesthetic systems, bringing us back to the building blocks of more complicated experiences.

A finely honed but voracious aesthetic appetite helps us to combat the boredom and banality of everyday life: tedious jobs and arduous commutes can't be readily improved by earnest politicking. But the value of developing our everyday aesthetic perceptions, of being aesthetically healthy, lies in much more than fleeting compensation for the shortcomings in our lives. Even a life free of arbitrary bosses, petty colleagues, traffic jams, illness and loss, would stand to benefit from an enhanced capacity to appreciate the world. Aesthetic satisfactions are pleasurable in and of themselves. They cannot be replaced by anything else.

How far this picture of aesthetic health is from the complaints and distrust of the dropout! Strangely, we expect valuable art to be that which we cannot do and worthless art to be that which we can do. Sadly, rather than an empowering call to creation, the remark, "I could do that!" expresses cynicism and dismissiveness. It vindicates the apathy that has set in since that last high school art class. The dropout has received proof that she made the right choice. The proof lies in the perceived incompetence of the artist: "If this is art, then art has no value anyway." But what if we reversed the formulation and said that the most valuable art is that which we can do? What if we said that the very fact that we practice certain arts on a daily basis is exactly what makes them valuable?

Seen in this way, our well-being depends first and foremost not on the priceless museum pieces fawned over by curators, collectors and auctioneers but rather on the art that surrounds us in our everyday lives. The everyday arts are valuable simply because the everyday matters. Everyday art is the world of immediate experience upon which a good part of our overall satisfaction with life depends. When we examine this everyday artistic world more closely, we discover that the artistic dropout drops into an ordinary life full of creative possibilities. The decoration and maintenance of the home, the orchestration of daily habit, the quests for objects to fill that home, the mundane excursions across town are all art. They are ways that we arrange our lives for the enhancement of aesthetic experience. The aesthetic sensibility and creative energy of adolescents are invested in garage bands, school locker decoration, personal style, auto-customizing, and, unfortunately, graffiti. Later in life, forsaken artistic inclinations re-emerge in such diverse practices as collecting, travel, interior decoration, do-it-yourselfing, gardening, cooking, entertaining.

Almost all of us dwell someplace. Indeed, the home is the largest, most ambitious artistic project most people will ever undertake. Almost all of us go out into the world each day to work, go to school, and shop. These daily excursions put us in the position to be open to, notice, and appreciate the world. For the most part, these practices constitute the basic pattern of everyday life: most of us do most of these things on most days. When we approach these activities in such a way that we or others derive aesthetic satisfaction from them, we become artists of everyday life.

11 Museums: From Object to Experience

Hilde Hein

Imagine the following:

1) A small natural history museum, located in an environmentally conscious community, faces growing hostility toward its century-old collection of stuffed birds and mammals. Removing them from public display, it replaces the taxidermic mounts with interactive computor kiosks that provide a wealth of biological and ecological information.

2) A textile museum, cramped for exhibition space, displaces its cumbersome dioramas representing colonial home cloth-fabrication and labor intensive pre-industrial tool use with videos in which museum guides, in period costume, demonstrate how felting, spinning, and weaving were done.

3) An anthropology museum, upon discovering that sealed glass cases fail to protect certain fragile, clay, sacred figures against vermin and pollutants, exhibits in their place plastic casts that are visually indiscernible from the precious objects.

4) An art museum learns that some of the objects in its collection are of dubious provenance. It proceeds to display them in a special exhibition together with the documents that challenge and support their authenticity. The exhibition includes scholarly and curatorial correspondence, records of purchase

and sale, and other evidence pertaining to the origin of the works, their history of production and ownership, and their accession by the museum.

5) When a prize possession from an art museum's permanent collection is stolen, the museum displays a photograph of the missing item in its former place, together with printed news stories describing the theft and its impact on the artworld.

Do these anecdotes have something in common? All of them are drawn from true stories of actual displacements of historically cherished things, and the substitution for them of something conceptual. All of them invite reflection on the nature of museums, on their past purpose and function, their present audiences, and on what they do and do not characteristically include. The cases suggest an institution in transition, influenced by change in physical resources and technology as well as by cultural sensibilities and ideology. The museum is a particularly sensitive barometer of such changes. In recent decades there has been an explosion in the number of museums – estimates run as high as 25,000 world-wide and 8,000 in the United States alone – and there is growing interest in museum work as a profession.[1] By and large, however, the museum-going public has represented a small percentage of the population, generally a selection of those who are well-educated and financially secure.

Among the actual and potential changes to be contemplated is the endeavor made by museums and their supporters to expand their audience and to reach it in new ways. Correspondingly, the aim has been to make the museum enterprise more democratic and responsive at various levels to a broad-based public. This practical reconstruction entails implicit revisions of the fundamental concept of a museum, a concept that, among its earlier familiars, needed neither explanation nor reform.

Nature, Function, and History

Museums are at once very ancient and very new. Perhaps the oldest sense of "museum" refers to a Pythagorean temple of the muses, a "sylvan grove to which scholars repaired, there to conduct research, amid discourse, and with reference to books or to objects."[2] That description of a refined haven for scholarship, comparable to a contemporary "think tank," may be losing its lustre; but its immense historical power continues to be reflected in metaphorical usages of the word "museum" that evoke conflicting associations with the sacred and the barbarian, the musty and moth-eaten, the rare and precious, the strange and exotic, the desiccated and embalmed, the treasury and the trash bin, the orderly assemblage, and the chaotic accumulation. The word is commonly understood to denote a collection of entities, each having some intrinsic worth, but whose value is greatly augmented by the act of gathering together and preserving the discrete items as a totality.[3] As museum workers point out, however, the collection of rarities is worthless without additional documentation, a condition that tends to be under-appreciated by the general public.[4] Typically, museums carry out research involving individual objects, but feature collections which are aggregates of objects assembled in terms of some categoreal or value system.

A standard definition conceived for legal and professional purposes is that agreed upon in 1974 by the International Council of Museums (ICOM):

> . . . a non-profit making, permanent institution in the service of society and of its development, and open to the public, which acquires, conserves, researches, communicates, and exhibits, for purposes of study, education, and enjoyment, material evidence of man and his environment.[5]

Similar definitions have been implemented in the United States by the American Association of Museums and under the Museum Services Act of 1977.[6]

Notwithstanding their formal declaration and frequent invocation, every element of these definitions is constantly under attack from within the museum profession, and for the general public no single feature is an essential museum ingredient. Currently there is a great deal of disagreement over their true nature and even as to what sorts of entities are properly to count as museums. While the public is surprised to find zoos, aquaria, and botanical gardens, as well as libraries included among museums in the professional and touristic literature, museum workers are horrified that visitors do not distinguish between museums, commercial demonstrations centers (such as SONY's New York center), and theme parks.

While differing in their choice of priorities, those who venture to define museums typically concentrate on certain characteristic functions and behaviors. These include *collection, preservation, study, exhibition* and *education*. Nothing has seemed more central and essential to the very being of a museum than its collection, which is assumed to consist of material objects that can be identified and classified in light of their accrued taxonomic or aesthetic or historical significance.

> Whether we excavate, purchase at auction, send out expeditions, receive gifts, ferret in attics, or are the beneficiaries of bequests, we gather the objects of interest and importance to our particular discipline.[7]

After the acquisition of objects, the next order of business is conventionally held to be preservation:

> It is pointless to gather objects of great beauty, rarity and value and then allow them to deteriorate due to inadequate protection, preservation and restoration.[8]

But there is little agreement as to which objects found in museums are rare, beautiful, or valuable – or even material. Neither is it obvious what is the optimal state in which an object should be kept. Is it the condition in which its original owner(s) acquired or maintained it, or that in which it reached the museum? Most objects that now are found there were never intended to be put in museums. Many would have been destroyed under conditions of normal use. Moreover, if the cost of their keep is excessive, alternatives to the preservation of objects have been perfected that are less expensive, less labor intensive, require less space, and are, arguably, as effective educationally.

Arguments such as these prevailed in the substitutions recounted in my opening examples. They have proven convincing in the case of dinosaur exhibitions. The public is fascinated by these prehistoric creatures; but if numbers are an indicator, more thirst for knowledge is gratified by cleverly engineered models that roar and move, as in the "Dynamation" shows of the early 1990s and the 1993 film "Jurassic Park," than in the laboriously preserved paleobiological specimens of conventional natural history museums.[9]

Ironically, just as the pre-eminent status of the original is in jeopardy, restoration and conservation are enjoying a renaissance thanks to new technologies, and to the growth of environmental consciousness.[10] But philosophical questions linking the preservative impulse with the primary value of collection remain, and these threaten to unravel the historic understanding of museums. If museums are not to be thought of as storehouses for the protection of cherished objects, much less for ranked numbers of them, innovative museum uses and activities may come to the fore. Even the commitment to *study* and *research*, initially restricted to scholars and specialists, may be modified and mingled with programs to satisfy more populist educational demands. Likewise, the obligation to interpret objects and to disseminate research in academic presentations may yield to new needs for popular publication. The museum's educational role is being recast and differently performed, addressed to diverse audiences with a variety of cognitive styles.

Education in museums is merging with public programming and, further combining formerly distinct museum functions, is converging with exhibition strategy. The expanding significance attributed to "outreach" is evident from the fact that exhibition teams no longer carry out the exclusive plan of curators, but include educators, designers, publicists and marketing professionals in their composition. As a result, exhibitions are becoming more public-oriented, more theatrical, and more self-consciously rhetorical. Aesthetically focused to deliver an experience, they underline the museum's unique capacity to teach by *showing*.

Purportedly they show *objects*, and this has been their historic mission. The logic of exhibition puts objects "on view" for inspection, inviting visitors to join in contemplation with epistemically privileged museum authority. But what is seen is no longer unequivocally held to be an object; for objects have been reconstituted as sites of experience. Paradoxically, the inherent subjectivity of experience casts doubt on the museum's claim to authority. Can one guarantee a single "right" way to see an object? Indeed, are they properly seen at all? Is the object one or many? Are certain experiences (of objects) more legitimate than others? What are the conditions that validate objective judgment or justify an interpretation?

To question the status of the object and its interpretation is to challenge the hierarchy of values that sanctions museums and that the visitor is presumed to share. Contemporary museums, striving to reconcile historic commitments to collection, preservation, and scholarship with a reinvigorated and self-conscious conception of education and exhibition, are examining the meaning of interpretation and dissemination, as well as questions of identity and objectivity that were traditionally left obscure. A new museological attitude, more given to asking than answering questions, contends with metaphysical puzzles: "What is an object?" and with epistemological issues: "What is truth?" Today's museums proudly accept an amplified educational mandate to stimulate and encourage inquiry. In that environment, the object placed "on view" is not an end, but a means, its function to deliver a museum experience.[11]

In America, museums have followed a somewhat different history from museums in Europe, where they originated. Most of the latter began as private collections, reflecting the taste and fortunes of their creators, and only subsequently were seized by or bequeathed to the state for the benefit of the public. The major American museums began as an ideal, often fostered by philanthropic interests and concern for the betterment of mankind. Of course there were entrepreneurs, who quickly grasping their recreational potential, made freakshows and spectacles of museums, guiding them well along the way toward today's fun centers and theme parks. Among the most famous of these was P. T. Barnum, of circus fame, who, in 1850, with Moses Kimball, purchased the failing museum founded by the Peale family and turned it into a thriving entertainment enterprise.[12]

The American museum movement began in the mid-nineteenth century when private charitable gift giving, testifying to the spirit of individual initiative, played a large part in the country's growth. Perceived as a public benefit, charitable contribution was encouraged under subsequent tax legislation, and continues to be a primary source of museum income. Most museums are thus quasi-public institutions, incorporated along with hospitals, churches, and various educational and service agencies, as non-profit organizations. In principle, this means that, unlike their nationalized European counterparts, they are nominally independent of government supervision. In this century, most non-profits have, however, received state financial assistance in the form of grants and subsidies, and this has enabled the government to impose restrictions as a condition of receiving aid. Unable to subsist on exclusively private funds, most museums, like all other non-profit organizations, have reluctantly accepted that compromise.[13]

Today's museums perform their public service by offering themselves as resources and educational institutions, but it remains a matter of debate whether the resources they offer are objects valued as cultural treasures, or, especially in the case of works of art, whether these objects are to be valued as sources of original experience. This apparently abstract and hair-splitting distinction may be the hinge on which "the museum experience" is hung. What is that experience? Is it *of* an object that may be independently identified and studied, or is it "an experience" *tout court* for which the object serves as occasional stimulus? The answer to this question determines whether we are to think of museums as "object-centered" or "story-centered." This dispute lies at the heart of many of the "culture wars" and political confrontations that currently divide the professional museum community. It profoundly affects the organization of the museum and the design of its exhibitions and programs.

Changing Directions

The museum's presumed dedication to "the real thing" – the *authentic* object that collectors formerly prized and studied – acquires a new, and politicized, significance when objects are taken as the occasion of privatized experience. If they are no longer understood as ontological givens, museum objects become constellations of assigned meanings, directly imperceptible and indeterminately interpretable. To apprehend anything as a museum object is, then, to enter a fictional space created by the museum. The viewer takes part in a cultural trans-action that does not engage physical objects as such, although the language referring to them remains. "Collection" no longer denotes an aggregation of material objects, but designates an organizational strategy that is conceptual and radically subjective.

A close look at contemporary museum practice reveals the ambiguity of the traditional commitment to collection and its consequents. Experiences are not collectibles, but are quintessentially transient and elusive. Moreover, unlike material things, experiences are unequivocally not containable in time or space. The sense of stability that clings to museum collection belongs with the idea of monumental objects and their univocal representation. But experiences, how-ever facilitated by the presence of objects, are diverse and inconstant. Their own brand of intensity bears no necessary relation to the nature or quality of what-ever engenders them.

Some aestheticians, notably in the tradition of John Dewey's idealism, hold that works of art are subjective experiences that are occasioned by artifacts pro-duced by artists for that purpose. According to this view, the work is not actu-ally realized until it is experienced and thus there are as many works of art as there are experiences of a given artifact.[14] The present museological position would similarly extend subjective identity to all museum objects, identifying their reality with a multitude of experiential encounters.

Museums have always prized the authenticity of "the real thing," and pro-fessed to find it in objects that are genuine or original instances of their kind. Used in this context, the term "real thing" designates a singular entity and has an altogether different connotation from the reality or genuineness of an expe-rience (which might well be initiated by an illusion.) The point at issue is not whether museums defraud the public by deliberately making false representa-tions (which, of course, does occasionally happen), but rather that today's mu-seums are engaged in an entirely new enterprise aimed chiefly at eliciting thoughts and experiences in the public. That objective is not exclusive of assembling collectibles, but it takes collection as a means rather than an end – and by no means the only means to that end. The end is the achievement of a certain type of experience that is genuine. What is noteworthy about such experiences is that they do not depend on mediation by an authentic object. They can be triggered by a multitude of devices, not all of which are real, or genuine, or material – and museums are busily constructing such devices.

Returning to the illustrations which initiated these reflections, we can identify a number of different pressures for change at work in different types of museums.

1) Cultural attitudes currently prescribe the removal of real objects in some contexts where their presence would be offensive. Popular disapproval of the abuse of endangered species, for example, has influenced some natural history museums not only to eliminate stuffed whole animals from dioramas, but to exclude the display even of items manufactured out of their parts – feathered baskets, cloaks, headdresses, utensils made of bone and horn, snake and alligator skin accessories, and garments of fur. In their place, interactive computer programs and video or film loops enable the public to learn about the past use of the banished items, and also explain the prohibitions against it. Where display of "real" animals or animal parts is unavoidable, museum labels sometimes assure the public that no living creatures were harmed for the purpose of collection, but that the exhibited item is a "salvage" – of a wounded animal for example, fortuitously acquired by a donor, that cannot be returned to its natural habitat. The public thus receives a double dose of didacticism, learning the original museum lesson of how the object was used, while at the same time receiving the humane, environmentally concerned message that exploitation of rare species and injury to them, even in the pursuit of knowledge, are to be avoided.

2) Space limitation, stringent health and safety restrictions, and inevitable economic pressures on museums also conspire against the operation of inefficient real things. Although the public wants information regarding technical procedures and enjoys seeing things in motion, old machinery tends to be cumbersome, noisy, sometimes dangerous, and its use requires obsolete skills. Film loops and video demonstrations that explain and illustrate the intended operations, are livelier than glass case displays of static tools, and they avoid even the hazards of scheduled "hands on" demonstrations. The new technology is comparatively inexpensive, predictable, and makes the operation of the apparatus it replaces accessible on a broad scale and in extensive detail.

3) Some anthropology and archaeological museums have withdrawn real objects from public exposure for the protection of the objects, because under adverse climate conditions or subject to environmental pollution they risk deterioration and damage.[15] Plaster casts are making a comeback for display as well as for educational purposes, as museums are finding that fifty years of automobile exhaust produces damage in excess of several thousand years of precombustion machine traffic. The sheer volume of traffic, human and vehicular, also enlarges the risk to objects of injury from friction and handling, and so, with the exception of scholars and discerning people with special permission, visitors are commonly being denied access to the oldest and most vulnerable items of museum collections. This means that ordinary people are denied exposure to an object's "aura" – its unique presence in time and space, the authentic

quality venerated by the museum world, which determined its place in history and its traditional authority.[16] The trade-off for the disappearance of the "aura" is that the replicas made by new reproductive technologies are all but indistinguishable from originals, and they are accessible. The reproductions, moreover, are amply supported by computer documentation and images that permit close-up visualization and manipulations that would be impossible with original objects.

4) Art museums are also contemplating the merits of electronic reproduction. Digitized images are useful for educational purposes, historical scholarship, conservation, security, record-keeping, and promotion. The quality of computer imaging is far superior to other reproductive means (e.g. slides, photographs), but there are obvious disadvantages. A practical risk is that museums lose control over their art to whoever has the ability to process and reproduce its images. While it is unlikely that galleries of electronic images will soon take the place of physical paintings (and sculpture), their availability raises questions about appropriation, unauthorized reproduction or other substitutions of accessible images for hard-to-transport and expensive-to-insure material works of art.[17]

Apart from the many legal and practical issues raised by reproductive procedures, philosophical queries abound. One concern is the eroding effect upon aesthetic sensibility that comes of substituting an inauthentic object for an authentic one even and *especially* where the difference in immediate aesthetic experience is insignificant. That insensibility, prolonged over a generation, could undermine the aesthetic foundation that warranted the art museum as institution in the first place.[18] A related doubt probes the identity of indiscernibles. Just as the cloned dinosaurs of Jurassic Park could not be identical with their historic predecessors (and for that very reason), a molecularly reconstructed *Mona Lisa*, made by nanotechnologists, would not be the same work that Leonardo painted. This is so whether or not their difference is directly discernible and regardless of the (genuine) experience that each might be able to inspire. A representation is a re-presentation and in virtue of that hyphenated character, differs from what it represents. Thus, accuracy and psychological persuasiveness notwithstanding, and independently of ethical considerations, an original is logically prior to its reproduction.[19]

5) A public weaned on television and computer screens has come to accept simulations as adequate indices of reality. Information *about* is routinely substitutible for the experience *of* a phenomenon, and even thought preferable where some aspects of that experience might be considered distasteful. Moreover, with attention increasingly given to interpretation and historical contextualization, the boundary between direct visual apprehension and cognitively informed recognition has virtually disappeared. We cannot distinguish between seeing and "seeing as" experientially, and contrary to the teaching of conventional empiricism, there is no breach between the intake of sensation and the process of understanding. Surrogates are able to trigger the same interpretive operations as originals. To the extent that such cognitively fortified experience is what is wanted and can be obtained under conditions of comfort

and convenience, simulations replete with information are likely to displace phenomenologically obtuse real things in museums as elsewhere.[20]

In effect, simulacra do not replace reality, but transfigure it. "Virtual reality" achieves a level of realistic precision unmatched by any prior representational endeavor, but it does not abolish the logic of representation. Minutely accurate replication in some dimensions does not efface differences in causal history. If we take the method of production into account, there can be no confusion between what appear to be similar experiences. But there is no doubt *that* experience occurs in both instances and that these experiences are real. The relation between such experiences and their causal dissimilarity is philosophically tantalizing, but museums have a more practical interest.

Having found that things are seldom what they seem, museums are fixated on the seeming – which is sufficient to generate real experiences. The preceding examples of current museum practice are typical of a dematerialization and re-reification that can be found throughout contemporary society. Philosophers have long maintained that the world is mediated by language, and the ghost of an accurately representational Ur-language persists in efforts to trace the babel of speech back to a common source. The relativization that linguistic pluralism implies haunts the quest for certainty and truth, but it is an old story. What is new is the multiplication of mediating devices, many of which are non-linguistic. As clamorous texts these devices draw attention to themselves, no longer as mere *vehicles* but as the *only* accessible reality.[21]

Museums vie with the best of textual strategists as interpreters of things. Released from their role as repositories – now vilified as "prisons for things" – museums are indeed launched in a new career as "sanctuaries of meaning." Their historical preoccupation with non-linear communication through things places them opportunely to function in a media-induced, polyvocal, and polyvalent world of multi-dimensional experience. But this bold new position demands that museums reflect upon their historic commitments. If the objectivity of their objecthood melts into textuality, museum collections cease to distinguish museums from other cultural institutions (also charged with the interpretation of texts), or even to differentiate them typologically from one another.

Traditional content-based typological distinctions are erased if the meaning of museum objects is equivocal. Things which are neither unique nor typical, neither paragons nor specimens of their kind, effectively have no existence at all.[22] "What is it?" is revealed to be an incomplete and inexhaustible question. Posing as a request for information, it demands decision. Museums have elevated to a science the common classificatory imperative that finds joy in identifying anything from bottle caps to Vermeers to lepidoptera. They have consequently rescued billions of things from temporal oblivion by bestowing meaning and value upon them and assigning them a place in an objective order. Collecting objects has been one among several ways to render the world intelligible and domesticate its buzzing, blooming confusion. So understood, museums have also played a considerable part in conferring a sense of civic identity on social congregations. Museum collection, both cultural and aesthetic, recalls social practices that deploy power and constitute value. Translating these practices into the assemblage of meanings and dispensation of experiences does not diminish their reality, but it exposes philosophical concerns that a simpler, more materialistic respect for objects did not.

The tendency that I have noted toward dematerialization is oddly incongruous in a world that appears to exalt materialistic values above all others. It extends to aesthetic judgment as much as to legal constructions, in which, for example, private ownership pertains as plausibly to one's reputation, or image, as to one's shoes or plot of land. Indeed, property is reducible to an abstract right to prohibit access to others. What happens under such conditions to the exclusionary claim that museums house authentic articles? Controversial as that expression may have been when applied to material works of art and artifacts, it is yet more obscure when the authenticity of meanings is at issue or where experience is their goal. The age and origin of physical objects can be determined fairly reliably by scientific analysis, and conventional tests exist for the historical authentication of works of art. But meanings are an altogether different matter. How are they authenticated? Meanings are not bound by the laws of physics and have no direct physical or psychological correlates. Unlike things and loosely affiliated with experience, they can occupy several places at once, and a single entity may have a surfeit of meanings.

If museums are to remain sites for gathering whatever it is that people believe worthy of collection, preservation, study, and exhibition, they must adapt to the dislocations of meaning. And so they have done, but the epithets that describe what they do have lagged behind. Still ridiculed as "mausoleums for things"[23] and romanticized as "places to wander and muse," museums are actually more creative than either alternative suggests. They profess to produce experiences, or rather to catalyze experiences in their audiences. They imply that such experiences are valuable on their own account, or that the having of experience is intrinsically valuable. These propositions are in need of further investigation.

Museums are historically reputed both to preserve valuable things and to be conservators of values somehow embedded in the things they preserve. If their stock in trade, however, is experiences (however transmitted by things), then a different standard of evaluation calibrated to experience must be articulated. Value inquiry has a long ancestry that includes the study of ethics and aesthetics, whose focus on conduct and doing distinguishes these disciplines from theoretical studies, whose chief concern is knowing and contemplation. Museums clearly contribute to both types of enterprise. Their work centers as much on cognitive (theoretical) issues as on practical activity or the production of pleasure. A full assessment of their work would appreciate their traditional service in both of these dimensions, while addressing the merits of their newly declared experiential function as well. That inquiry might reveal that experiences are not all born equal and that some are more meritorious than others. It might lead to the conclusion that the mission of public service that museums espouse remains, as ever, embedded in values. If these are not now located in the objects museums collect, then they must be implicated in the ranking of experiences. Museums must, therefore, become as discriminating in the selection of experiences they purvey as they purported to be in their collection and care of objects. There is no evading their evaluative responsibility, but this must be recast in terms of the newly defined "museum experience."

Notes

1   Susan M. Pearce, *Museums, Objects, and Collections: A Cultural Study*, Washington, DC, Smithsonian Institution Press, 1992.
2   S. Dillon Ripley, "Museums and Education," *Curator* XI/3 1968: 183–9.
3   The titles of several recent books of various genres capitalize on these associations: e.g. Donald Hall's book of poetry, *The Museum of Clear Ideas*, exhibits those ideas as jumbled artifice, reverberating the poet's past and present; John Updike's "Museums and Women," the first of a book of stories by that name, suggests tantalizing, mysterious and not quite possessible items that mutely wait, conveying a touch of prurience that is also emphasized in Jean Baudrillard's "The System of Objects." Ellen Handler Spitz's (1995) *Museums of the Mind*, a book of essays, traces a thread of meaning through a collection of occasional thoughts and aesthetic conjectures. Lydia Goehr, in a philosophical exploration, *The Imaginary Museum of Musical Works* (1992), traces the historical concept of a musical "work" with reference to repeatable musical events that can be notated and catalogued, just as objects designated "works of art" were emancipated from their functional engagement in the lived world.
4   The degree of sensitivity of this issue was highlighted by the discovery of the wreck-site of the *Titanic* in waters outside the jurisdiction of any nation and therefore subject to private salvage. An exhibition of objects salvaged from the wreck by an American company was exhibited in the US in 1997, and earlier in Europe and Britain. Within the museum community there is concern that the excavated items will be dispersed and sold before an adequate archaeological report is produced. As a member of the International Congress of Maritime Museums put it, "If nothing is done to record and collate these data now, they might as well never have been collected in the first place." *Museum News* (May/June 1997, p. 31).
5   ICOM Statutes, Sec. II, Art. 3, adopted by the 11th General Assembly, Copenhagen, 6/14/74.
6   "a public or private non-profit agency or institution organized on a permanent basis for essentially educational or esthetic purposes which, utilizing a professional staff, owns or utilizes tangible objects, cares for them, and exhibits them to the public on a regular basis" [20 U.S.C. 968(4)]. This definition corresponds also to that of the American Association of Museums (AAM), *Museum Accreditation: Professional Standards*, Washington, DC, 1973.
7   Joseph Veach Noble, "Museum Manifesto," *Museum News* 48, no. 8, April 1970, p. 16.
8   Ibid.
9   According to a private communication by the director of the Chicago Academy of Sciences, "Dynamation" stimulated a fourfold increase of visitors to that institution during the period of its installation.
10 Credit is also due to the J. Paul Getty Conservation Institute and to its well-funded training program.

11 Inevitable philosophical differences lead to pedagogic disagreements. Sherman E. Lee contrasts the populist, uplifting view of Theodore Low in *The Museum as a Social Instrument* (1945), with the more elite position of Benjamin Ives Gilman in *Museum Ideals of Purpose and Method* (1918). The second is more congruent with Lee's own view that aesthetic vision is inherently inspirational and is degraded by educational ambitions. Sherman E. Lee, "The Idea of an Art Museum," in *Past, Present, East and West* (New York: G. Braziller, 1983).

12 Neil Harris, *Humbug: The Art of P. T. Barnum*, Chicago, University of Chicago Press, 1973; Gary Kulik, "Designing the Past: History-Museum Exhibitions from Peale to the Present," in *History Museums in the United States: A Critical Assessment*, eds Warren Leon and Roy Rosenzweig, Urbana, University of Illinois Press, 1989.

13 The ambiguity of their position continues to be a source of confusion and controversy, as is evident from such recent public debacles as the Corcoran Gallery's 1989 cancellation of its planned exhibition of the work of Robert Mapplethorpe, which had been funded by NEA in other locations, and the Cincinnati Contemporary Arts Center's 1990 ordeal in consequence of having shown the same exhibition. As Stephen Weil has pointed out, direct forms of government subsidy are more vulnerable than such indirect forms as income tax deduction for charitable contribution, which is therefore an important source of revenue for the arts.

14 John Dewey, *Art As Experience* (1934).

15 Cultural objects have also been removed from public display for the very different reason of avoiding offense to the groups or persons whose culture they represent. Such removals instantiate another paradigm, essentially that represented in example no. 1, except that the offense in this case is to "other" cultures than that of the museum cohort.

16 Walter Benjamin, "The Work of Art in the Age of Mechanical Reproduction," *Illuminations*, NY, Schocken, 1969, p. 221.

17 "Image Control" by Jonath Adlai Franklin, in *Museum News*, Sept./Oct.1993, p. 37. The author points out that those museums willing to negotiate with the software developers are hopeful that the images will bring audiences in to look at the "real thing," but that remains to be seen.

18 Nelson Goodman, *Languages of Art*, Indianapolis, Hackett, 1976.

19 These questions of philosophical aesthetics go to the heart of the discipline as grounded in the eighteenth-century perceptual theory of Alexander Baumgarten, the founder of modern aesthetics. Present day theoretical explorers of the ontology of art include Nelson Goodman, Joseph Margolis, Arthur Danto, and many others. The practical choices of the museum, however, place metaphysical reflection on the identity of the art object in a sharply new and poignant context.

20 The philosopher Jean Baudrillard maintains that while *dissimulation* is a concealment of reality which implicitly affirms it, *simulation* is a substitute for a reality that comes, in time, to take its place. The original may be entirely forgotten as the simulation acquires its own history and creates a reality of its own. "The Precession of Simulacra," *Simulacra and Simulation*, Ann Arbor, University of Michigan Press, 1981.

21 Marshal McLuhan coined the phrase "the medium is the message," which brought him instant media fame. Less attention was given at the time (1960s) to the underlying metaphysical concern that this scholar from the Medieval Institute in Toronto intended to address: that the medium was in fact *erasing* the message.

22 "the truly unique object, – absolute, entirely without antecedent, incapable of be-

ing integrated into any sort of set – is unthinkable. It exists no more than does a pure sound." Jean Baudrillard, "The System of Collecting," in *The Cultures of Collecting*, ed. John Elsner and Roger Cardinal, Cambridge, Mass., Harvard University Press, 1994.

23   "Museums are like the family sepulchres of works of art." Theodor W. Adorno, *Prisms*, Cambridge, Mass., MIT Press, 1981, p. 175.

12   The MoMA's Hot Mamas

Carol Duncan

When the Museum of Modern Art [in New York] opened its newly installed and much enlarged permanent collection in 1984, critics were struck with how little things had changed. In the new installation, as in the old,[1] modern art is once again a progression of formally distinct styles. As before, certain moments in this progression are given greater importance than others: Cézanne, the first painter one sees, announces modern art's beginnings. Picasso's dramatically installed *Les Demoiselles d'Avignon* (Plate 4) signifies the coming of cubism – the first giant step twentieth-century art took and the one from which much of the history of modern art proceeds. From Cubism unfolds the other notable avant-garde movements: German Expressionism, Futurism, and so on, through Dada-Surrealism. Finally come the American Abstract Expressionists. After purifying their work of a residue of Surrealist representation, they made the final breakthrough into the realm of absolute spirit, manifested as absolute formal and nonrepresentational purity. It is in reference to their achievement that, according to the MoMA (in its large, new final gallery), all later significant art in one way or another continues to measure its ambitions and scale.

Probably more than any other institution, the MoMA has promoted this "mainstream modernism," greatly augmenting its authority and prestige through acquisitions, exhibitions, and publications. To be sure, the MoMA's managers did not independently invent the museum's strictly linear and highly formalist art-historical narrative; but they have embraced it tenaciously, and it is no accident that one can retrace that history in its galleries better and more fully than in any other collection. For some, the museum's retrospective character is a regrettable turnaround from its original role as champion of the new. But the MoMA remains enormously important for the role it plays in maintaining in the present a particular version of the art-historical past. Indeed, for much of the academic world, as for the larger art public, the kind of art history it narrates still constitutes the definitive history of modern art.

Yet, in the MoMA's permanent collection, more meets the eye than this history admits to. According to the established narrative, the history of art is made

Plate 4   Pablo Picasso, Les Demoiselles d'Avignon. *Paris (June/July 1907). Oil on canvas, 8′ × 7′8″ (243.9 × 233.7 cm). Courtesy the Museum of Modern Art, New York. Acquired through the Lillie P. Bliss Bequest. Photograph © 1997 The Museum of Modern Art, New York. © 1998 Estate of Pablo Picasso / Artists Rights Society (ARS) New York.*

up of a progression of styles and unfolds along certain irreversible lines: from style to style, it gradually emancipates itself from the imperative to represent convincingly or coherently a natural, presumably objective world. Integral to this narrative is a model of moral action, exemplified by individual artists. As they become liberated from traditional representation, they achieve greater subjectivity and hence greater artistic freedom and autonomy of spirit. As the literature of modern art portrays it, their progressive renunciation of representation, repeatedly and minutely documented in monographs, catalogues, and critical journals, is often achieved through painful or self-sacrificing searching or courageous risk-taking. The disruption of space, the denial of volume, the overthrow of traditional compositional schemes, the discovery of painting as an autonomous surface, the emancipation of color, line, or texture, the occasional transgressions and reaffirmations of the boundaries of art (as in the adaptation of junk or non-high-art materials), and so on through the liberation of painting from frame and stretcher and thence from the wall itself – all of these advances translate into moments of moral as well as artistic choice. As a consequence of his spiritual struggle, the artist finds a new realm of energy and truth beyond the material, visible world that once preoccupied art – as in Cubism's reconstruction of the "fourth dimension," as Appolinaire called the power of thought itself; Mondrian's or Kandinsky's visual analogues of abstract, universal forces; Robert Delaunay's discovery of cosmic energy; or Miro's re-creations of a limitless and potent psychic field. Ideally and to the extent to which they have assimilated this history, museum visitors reenact these artistic – and hence spiritual – struggles. In this way they ritually perform a drama of enlightenment in which freedom is won by repeatedly overcoming and moving beyond the visible, material world.

And yet, despite the meaning and value given to such transcendent realms, the history of modern art, as it is written and as it is seen in the MoMA and elsewhere, is positively crowded with images – and most of them are of women. Despite their numbers, their variety is remarkably small. Most often they are simply female bodies or parts of bodies, with no identity beyond their female anatomy – those ever-present "Women" or "Seated Women" or "Reclining Nudes". Or they are tarts, prostitutes, artist's models, or low-life entertainers – highly identifiable socially, but at the bottom of the social scale. In the MoMA's authoritative collection, Picasso's *Demoiselles d'Avignon*, Léger's *Grand Déjeuner*, Kirchner's scenes of streetwalkers, Duchamp's *Bride*, Severini's Bal Tabarin dancer, de Kooning's *Woman I*, and many other works are often monumental in scale and conspicuously placed. Most critical and art-historical writings give them comparable importance.

To be sure, modern artists have often chosen to make "big" philosophical or artistic statements via the nude. If the MoMA exaggerates this tradition or overstates some aspects of it, it is nevertheless an exaggeration or overstatement of something pervasive in modern art practice. Why then has art history not accounted for this intense preoccupation with socially and sexually available female bodies? What, if anything, do nudes and whores have to do with modern art's heroic renunciation of representation? And why is this imagery accorded such prestige and authority within art history – why is it associated with the highest artistic ambition?

In theory, museums are public spaces dedicated to the spiritual enhancement of all who visit them. In practice, however, museums are prestigious and powerful engines of ideology. They are modern ritual settings in which visitors enact complex and often deep psychic dramas about identity – dramas that the museum's stated, consciously intended programs do not and cannot acknowledge overtly. Like those of all great museums, the MoMA's ritual transmits a complex ideological signal. My concern here is with only a portion of that signal – the portion that addresses sexual identity. I shall argue that the collection's recurrent images of sexualized female bodies actively masculinize the museum as a social environment. Silently and surreptitiously, they specify the museum's ritual of spiritual quest as a male quest, just as they mark the larger project of modern art as primarily a male endeavor.

If we understand the modern art museum as a ritual of male transcendence, if we see it as organized around male fears, fantasies, and desires, then the quest for spiritual transcendence on the one hand and the obsession with a sexualized female body on the other, rather than appearing unrelated or contradictory, can be seen as parts of a larger, psychologically integrated whole. How very often images of women in modern art speak of male fears. Many of the works I just mentioned feature distorted or dangerous-looking creatures, potentially over-powering, devouring, or castrating. Indeed, the MoMA's collection of monstrous, threatening females is exceptional: Picasso's *Demoiselles* and *Seated Bather* (the latter a giant praying mantis); the frozen, metallic odalisques in Léger's *Grand Déjeuner*, several early female figures by Giacometti; sculptures by Gonzáles and Lipschitz; and Baziotes' *Dwarf*, a mean-looking creature with saw teeth, a single large eye, and a prominent, visible uterus – to name only some. (One could easily expand the category to include works by Kirchner, Severini, Rouault, and others who depicted decadent, corrupt – and therefore *morally* monstrous – women.) In different ways, each of these works testifies to a pervasive fear of and ambivalence about woman. Openly expressed on the plane of culture, this fear and ambivalence, it seems to me, makes the central moral of modern art more intelligible – whether or not it tells us anything about the individual psyches of those who produced these works.

Even work that exchews such imagery and gives itself entirely to the drive for abstract, transcendent truth may also speak of these fears, in the very act of flee-ing the realm of matter (*mater*) and biological need that is woman's traditional domain. How often modern masters have sought to make their work speak of *higher* realms that exist above a female, biological earth. Cubism, Kandinsky, Mondrian, the Futurists, Miró, the Abstract Expressionists – all drew artistic life from some non-material energy of the self or the universe. (Léger's ideal of a rational, mechanical order can also be understood as opposed to – and a defense against – the unruly world of nature that it seeks to control.) The peculiar icono-clasm of much modern art, its renunciation of representation and the material world behind it, seems at least in part based in an impulse, common among modern males, to escape not the mother in any literal sense but a psychic image of woman and her earthly domain that seems rooted in infant or childish notions of the mother. Philip Slater noted an "unusual emphasis on mobility and flight as attributes of the hero who struggles against the menacing mother."[2] In the mu-seum's ritual, the recurrent image of a menacing woman adds urgency to such flights to "higher" realms. Hence also the frequent appearance in written art history of monstrous or threatening women or, what is their obverse, powerless or vanquished women. Whether man-killer or murder victim, whether Picasso's deadly *Seated Bather* or Giacometti's *Woman with Her Throat Cut*, their pres-ence both in the museum ritual and in the written (and illustrated) mythology is necessary. In both contexts, they provide the reason for the spiritual and mental flight. Confrontation and escape from them constitute the ordeal's dark center, a darkness that gives meaning and motive to the quest for enlightenment.

Since the heroes of this ordeal are generically men, the presence of women artists in this mythology can be only an anomaly. Women artists, especially if they exceed the standard token number, tend to degender the ritual ordeal. Accordingly, in the MoMA and other museums, their numbers are kept well below the point where they might effectively dilute the masculinity. The female presence is necessary only in the form of imagery. Of course men, too, are occasionally represented. But unlike women, who are seen primarily as sexually accessible bodies, men are portrayed as physically and mentally active beings who creatively shape their world and ponder its meanings. They make music and art, they stride, work, build cities, conquer the air through flight, think and engage in sports (Cézanne, Rodin, Picasso, Matisse, Léger, La Fresnaye, Boccioni). When male sexuality is broached, it is often presented as the experience of highly self-conscious, psychologically complex beings whose sexual feelings are leavened with poetic pain, poignant frustration, heroic fear, protective irony, or the drive to make art (Picasso, de Chirico, Duchamp, Balthus, Delvaux, Bacon, Linder).

De Kooning's *Woman I* (Plate 5) and Picasso's *Demoiselles d'Avignon* are two of art history's most important female images. They are also key objects in the MoMA's collection and highly effective in maintaining the museum's masculinized environment.

The museum has always hung these works with precise attention to their strategic roles in the story of modern art. Both before and after the 1984 expansion, de Kooning's *Woman I* hung at the threshold to the spaces containing *the* big Abstract Expressionist "breakthroughs" – the New York school's final collective leap into absolutely pure, abstract, non-referential transcendence: Pollock's artistic and psychic free flights, Rothko's sojourns in the luminous depths of a universal self, Newman's heroic confrontations with the sublime, Still's lonely journeys into the back beyond of culture and consciousness, Reinhardt's solemn and sardonic negations of all that is not Art, and so on. And always seated at the doorway to these moments of ultimate freedom and purity, and literally helping to frame them, has been *Woman I*. So important is her presence just there, that when she has to go on loan, *Woman II* appears to take her place. With good reason. De Kooning's *Women* are exceptionally successful ritual artifacts, and they masculinize the museum's space with great efficiency.

The woman figure had been emerging gradually in de Kooning's work in the course of the 1940s. By 1951–2, it had fully revealed itself in *Woman I* as a big, bad mama – vulgar, sexual and dangerous. De Kooning imagines her facing us with iconic frontality – large, bulging eyes; open, toothy mouth; massive breasts. The suggestive pose is just a knee movement away from open-thighed display of the vagina, the self-exposing gesture of mainstream pornography.

These features are not unique in the history of art. They appear in ancient and tribal cultures, as well as in modern pornography and graffiti. Together, they constitute a well-known figure type.[3] The Gorgon of ancient Greek Art (Plate 6), an instance of that type, bears a striking resemblance to de Kooning's *Woman I* and, like her, simultaneously suggests and avoids the explicit act of sexual self-display that elsewhere characterizes the type. An Etruscan example

Plate 5   Willem de Kooning, Woman I. *(1950–52). Oil on canvas, 6′3⅞″ × 58″ (192.7 × 147.3 cm). Courtesy The Museum of Modern Art, New York. Purchase. Photograph © 1997 The Museum of Modern Art, New York.*

states more of its essential components as they appeared in a wide range of archaic and tribal cultures – not only the display of genitals, but also the flanking animals that point to her origins as a fertility or mother goddess.[4] Obviously, the configuration, with or without animals, carries complex symbolic possibilities and can convey many-sided, contradictory, and layered meanings. In her guise as the Gorgon witch, however, the terrible aspect of the mother goddess, her lust for blood and her deadly gaze, is emphasized. Especially today, when the myths and rituals that may have suggested other meanings have

Plate 6   Gorgon, clay relief.
Museo Archeologico, Syracuse,
Sicily, Italy. Courtesy Scala/Art
Resource, NY.

been lost – and when modern psychoanalytic ideas are likely to color any interpretation – the figure appears especially intended to conjure up infantile feelings of powerlessness before the mother and the dread of castration: in the open
jaw can be read the *vagina dentata* – the idea of a dangerous, devouring vagina,
too horrible to depict, and hence transposed to the toothy mouth.

Feelings of inadequacy and vulnerability before mature women are common
(if not always salient) phenomena in male psychic development. Such myths as
the story of Perseus and such visual images as the Gorgon can play a role in
mediating that development by extending and recreating on the cultural plane
its core psychic experience and accompanying defenses.[5] Thus objectified and
communally shared in imagery, myth and ritual, such individual fears and desires may achieve the status of higher, universal truth. In this sense, the presence
of Gorgons on Greek temples, important houses of cult worship (they also
appeared on Christian church walls)[6] – is paralleled by *Woman I*'s presence in a
high-cultural house of the modern world.

The head of de Kooning's *Woman I* is so like that of the archaic Gorgon that
the reference could well be intentional, especially since the artist and his friends
placed great store in ancient myths and primitive images and likened themselves
to archaic and tribal shamans. Writing about de Kooning's *Women*, Thomas
Hess echoed this claim in a passage comparing de Kooning's artistic ordeal to
that of Perseus, slayer of the Gorgon. Hess is arguing that de Kooning's *Women*
grasp an elusive, dangerous truth "by the throat."

And truth can be touched only by complications, ambiguities and paradox, so,
like the hero who looked for Medusa in the mirroring shield, he must study her
flat, reflected image every inch of the way.[7]

121

But then again, the image type is so ubiquitous we needn't try to assign de Kooning's *Woman I* to any particular source in ancient or primitive art. *Woman I* can call up the Medusa as easily as the other way around. Whatever de Kooning knew or sensed about the Gorgon's meanings, and however much or little he took from it, the image type is decidedly present in his work. Suffice it to say that de Kooning was aware, and indeed explicitly claimed that his *Women* could be assimilated to the long history of goddess imagery.[8] By choosing to place such figures at the center of his most ambitious artistic efforts, he secured for his work an aura of ancient mystery and authority.

The *Woman* is not only monumental and iconic. In high-heeled shoes and brassiere, she is also lewd, her pose indecently teasing. De Kooning acknowledged her oscillating character, claiming for her a likeness not only to serious art – ancient icons and high-art nudes – but also to pinups and girlie pictures of the vulgar present. He saw her as simultaneously frightening and ludicrous.[9] The ambiguity of the figure, its power to resemble an awesome mother goddess as well as a modern burlesque queen, provides a fine cultural, psychological, and artistic field in which to enact the modern myth of the artist-hero – the hero whose spiritual ordeal becomes the stuff of ritual in the public space of the museum. As a powerful and threatening woman, it is she who must be confronted and transcended – gotten past on the way to enlightenment. At the same time, her vulgarity, her "girlie" side – de Kooning called it her "silliness"[10] – renders her harmless (or is it contemptible?) and denies the terror and dread of her Medusa features. The ambiguity of the image thus gives the artist (and the viewer) both the experience of danger and a feeling of overcoming it. Meanwhile, the suggestion of pornographic self-display – more explicit in de Kooning's later work but certainly present here – specifically addresses itself to the male viewer. With it, de Kooning knowingly and assertively exercises his patriarchal privilege of objectifying male sexual fantasy as high culture. [. . .]

Of course before de Kooning created ambiguous self-displaying women, there was Picasso's *Demoiselles d'Avignon* of 1907. The work was conceived as an extraordinarily ambitious statement – it aspires to revelation – about the meaning of Woman. In it, all women belong to a universal category of being, existing across time and place. Picasso used ancient and tribal art to reveal woman's universal mystery: Egyptian and Iberian sculpture on the left, and African art on the right. The figure on the lower right looks as if it was directly inspired by some primitive or archaic deity. Picasso would have known such figures from his visits to the ethnographic art collections in the Trocadero. A study for the work in the Öffentliche Kunstsammlung in Basel (Plate 7) closely follows the type's symmetrical, self-displaying pose. Significantly, Picasso wanted her to be prominent – she is the nearest and largest of all the figures. At this stage, Picasso also planned to include a male student of the left and, in the axial center of the composition, a sailor – a figure of horniness incarnate. The self-displaying woman was to have faced him, her display of genitals turned away from the viewer.

In the finished work, the male presence has been removed from the image and relocated in the viewing space before it. What began as a depicted male-

Plate 7   Pablo Picasso, Study for Les Demoiselles d'Avignon. *1907. Pencil, pastel, 47.7 × 63.5 cm. Courtesy Öffentliche Kunstsammlung Basel, Kupferstichkabinett. Photo: Öffentliche Kunstsammlung Basel, Martin Buhler. © 1998 Estate of Pablo Picasso/ Artists Rights Society (ARS), New York.*

female confrontation thus became a confrontation between viewer and image. The relocation has pulled the lower right-hand figure completely around, so that her stare and her sexually inciting act, although not detailed and less symmetrical than before, are now directed outward. Picasso thus isolated and monumentalized the ultimate men-only situation. As restructured, the work forcefully asserts to both men and women the privileged status of male viewers – they alone are intended to experience the full impact of this most revelatory moment.[11] It also assigns women to a visitors' gallery where they may watch but not enter the central arena of high culture.

Finally, the mystery that Picasso unveils about women is also an art-historical lesson. In the finished work, the women have become stylistically differentiated so that one looks not only at present-tense whores but also back down into the ancient and primitive past, with the art of "darkest Africa" and works representing the beginnings of Western culture (Egyptian and Iberian idols) placed on a single spectrum. Thus does Picasso use art history to argue his thesis: that the awesome goddess, the terrible witch, and the lewd whore are but facets of a single many-sided creature, in turn threatening and seductive, imposing and self-abasing, dominating and powerless – and always the psychic property of a male imagination. Picasso also implies that truly great, powerful, and revelatory art has always been and must be built upon such exclusively male property.

The museum's installation amplifies the already powerful meanings of the work. Mounted on a freestanding wall in the center of the first Cubist gallery, the painting seizes your attention the moment you turn into the room – the placement of the doorway makes it appear suddenly and dramatically. Physically dominating this intimately scaled gallery, the installation dramatizes the painting's role as progenitor of the surrounding Cubist works and their subsequent art-historical issue. So central is the work to the structure of MoMA's program that recently, when the painting was on loan, the museum felt compelled to post a notice on the freestanding wall explaining the work's absence – but also

Plate 8   Bus-stop shelter on Fifty-Seventh Street, New York City, with advertisement for
Penthouse *magazine, 1988. Photo: Carol Duncan.*

invoking its presence. In a gesture unusual for the MoMA, the notice was illustrated by a tiny color reproduction of the missing monument.

The works by de Kooning [. . .] that I have discussed, along with similar works by many other modern artists, benefit from and reinforce the status won by the *Demoiselles*. They also develop its theme, drawing out different emphases. One of the elements they develop more explicitly than did Picasso is that of pornography. By way of exploring how that pornographic element works in the museum context, I want to look first at how it works outside the museum.

Last year, an advertisement for *Penthouse* magazine appeared on New York City bus-stop shelters (Plate 8). New York City bus shelters are often decorated with near-naked women and sometimes men advertising everything from underwear to real estate. But this was an ad for pornographic images as such – that is, images designed not to sell perfume or bathing suits, but to stimulate erotic desire, primarily in men. Given its provocative intent, the image generates very different and – I think for almost everyone – more charged meanings than the ads for underwear. At least one passerby had already recorded in red spray paint a terse but coherent response: "For Pigs."

Having a camera with me, I decided to take a shot of it. But as I set about focusing, I began to feel uncomfortable and self-conscious. As I realized only later, I was experiencing some prohibition in my own conditioning, activated not simply by the nature of the ad but by the act of photographing such an ad in public. Even though the anonymous inscription had made it socially safer to photograph – it placed it in a conscious and critical discourse about gender – to photograph it was still to appropriate openly a kind of image that middle-class morality says I'm not supposed to look at or have. But before I could sort that out a group of boys jumped into the frame. Plainly they intended to intervene. Did I know what I was doing? one asked me with an air I can only call stern, while another admonished me that I was photographing a *Penthouse* ad – as if I would not knowingly do such a thing.

Apparently, the same culture that had conditioned me to feel uneasy about what I was doing also made *them* uneasy about it. Boys this age know very well what's in *Penthouse*. Knowing what's in *Penthouse* is knowing something meant for men to know; therefore, knowing *Penthouse* is a way of knowing oneself to be a man, or at least a man-to-be, at precisely an age when one needs all the help one can get. I think these boys were trying to protect the capacity of the ad to empower them as men by preventing me from appropriating an image of it. For them, as for many men, the chief (if not the only) value and use of pornography is this power to confirm gender identity and, with that, gender superiority. Pornography affirms their manliness to themselves and to others and proclaims the greater social power of men. Like some ancient and primitive objects forbidden to the female gaze, the ability of pornography to give its users a feeling of superior male status depends on its being owned or controlled by men and forbidden to, shunned by, or hidden from, women. In other words, in certain situations a female gaze can *pollute* pornography. These boys, already imprinted with the rudimentary gender codes of the culture, knew an infringement when they saw one. (Perhaps they suspected me of defacing the ad.) Their harassment of me constituted an attempt at gender policing, something adult men routinely do to women on city streets.

Not so long ago, such magazines were sold only in sleazy porn stores. Today ads for them can decorate mid-town thoroughfares. Of course, the ad as well as the magazine cover cannot itself be pornography and still be legal (in practice, that tends to mean it can't show genitals), but to work as an ad it must *suggest* it. For different reasons, works of art like de Kooning's *Women* [. . .] also refer to without actually being pornography – they depend on the viewer "getting" the reference but must stop there. Given those requirements, it shouldn't surprise us that the artist's visual strategies have parallels in the ad. *Woman I* shares a number of features with the ad. Both present frontal, iconic massive figures seen close up – they fill, even overflow, the picture surface. The photograph's low camera angle and the painting's scale and composition monumentalize and elevate the figures, literally or imaginatively dwarfing the viewer. Painting and photograph alike concentrate attention on head, breasts, and torso. Arms serve to frame the body, while legs are either cropped or, in the de Kooning, under-sized and feeble. The figures thus appear powerful and powerless at the same time, with massive bodies made to rest on unstable, weakly rendered, tentatively placed legs. And with both, the viewer is positioned to see it all should the thighs open. And of course, on *Penthouse* pages, thighs do little else but open. But de Kooning's hot mama has a very different purpose and cultural status from a *Penthouse* "pet."

De Kooning's *Woman I* conveys much more complex and emotionally ambivalent meanings. The work acknowledges more openly the fear of and flight from as well as quest for the woman. Moreover de Kooning's *Woman I* is always upstaged by the artist's self-display *as an artist*. The manifest purpose of a *Penthouse* photo is, presumably, to arouse desire. If the de Kooning awakens desire in relation to the female body, it does so in order to deflate or conquer its power of attraction and escape its danger. The viewer is invited to relive a struggle in which the realm of art provides escape from the female's degraded allure. As mediated by art criticism, de Kooning's work speaks ultimately not of male fear but of the triumph of art and a self-creating spirit. In the critical literature, the *Women* figures themselves become catalysts or structural supports for the work's more significant meanings: the artist's heroic self-searching, his existentialist courage, his pursuit of a new pictorial structure or some other artistic or transcendent end.[12]

The work's pornographic moment, now subsumed to its high-cultural import, may (unlike the *Penthouse* ad) do its ideological work with unchallenged prestige and authority. In building their works on a pornographic base and triggering in both men and women deep-seated feelings about gender identity and difference, de Kooning [. . .] and other artists (most notoriously, David Salle) exercise a privilege that our society has traditionally conferred upon men only. Through their imagery, they lay claim to public space as a realm under masculine control. Transformed into art and displayed in the public space of the museum, the self-displaying poses affirm to male viewers their membership in the more powerful gender group. They also remind women that their status as members of the community, their right to its public space, their share in the common, culturally defined identity, is not quite the same – is somehow less equal – than men's. But these signals must be covert, hidden under the myth of the transcendent artist-hero. Even de Kooning's later *Women* figures, which more openly invite comparison to pornographic photography and graffiti, qualify the reference, the closer to pornography, the more overlaid they must be with unambiguously "artistic" gestures and philosophically significant impastos.

Nevertheless, what is true in the street may not be so untrue in the museum, even though different rules of decorum may make it seem so. Inside or outside, such images wield great authority, structuring and reinforcing the psychic codes that determine and differentiate the real possibilities of women and men.

Notes

1   For an analysis of the older MoMA see Carol Duncan and Alan Wallach, "The Museum of Modern Art as Late Capitalist Ritual," *Marxist Perspectives* 4 (Winter 1978), 28–51.

2   Philip Slater, *The Glory of Hera* (Boston, 1968), p. 321.

3   See Douglas Fraser, "The Heraldic Women: A Study in Diffusion, in *The Many Faces of Primitive Art*, ed. D. Fraser (Englewood Cliffs, N.J., 1966), pp 36–99, Arthur Frothingham, "Medusa, Apollo, and the Great Mother," *American Journal of Archaeology* 15 (1911), 349–77, Roman Ghirshman, *Iran: From the Earliest Times to the Islamic Conquest* (Harmondsworth, England, 1954), pp. 340–3, Bernard Goldman, "The Asiatic Ancestry of the Greek Gorgon," *Berytus* 14 (1961), 1–22; Clark Hopkins, "Assyrian Elements in the Perseus-Gorgon Story," *American Jour-*

nal of Archaeology 38 (1934), 341–58, Clark Hopkins, "The Sunny Side of the Greek Gorgon," *Berytus* 14 (1961), 25–32, and Philip Slater (cited in note 2), pp. 16–21 and 318ff.

4 More ancient than the devouring Gorgon of Greece and pointing to a root meaning of the image type, a famous Louristan bronze pin in the David Weill Collection honors an older, life-giving Mother Goddess. Flanked by animals sacred to her, she is shown giving birth to a child and holding out her breasts. Objects of this kind appear to have been the votive offerings of women (see Ghirshman (cited in note 3), pp. 102–4).

5 See Philip Slater (cited in note 2), pp. 308–36 on the Perseus myth, and pp. 449ff. on the similarities between ancient Greek and middle-class American males.

6 See Fraser, cited in note 3.

7 Thomas B. Hess, *Willem de Kooning* (New York, 1959), p. 7. See also Hess, *William de Kooning: Drawings* (New York and Greenwich, Conn., 1972), p. 27, on a de Kooning drawing of Elaine de Kooning (ca. 1942) in which the writer finds the features of Medusa – a "menacing" stare and intricate, animated "Medusa hair."

8 As he once said, "The *Women* had to do with the female painted through all the ages. . . . Painting the *Woman* is a thing in art that has been done over and over – the idol, Venus, the nude." Quoted in *Willem de Kooning: The North Atlantic Light*, 1960–1983, exh. cat., Stedelijk Museum, Amsterdam; Louisiana Museum of Modern Art, Humleback, and the Moderna Museet, Stockholm, 1983. Sally Yard, "Willem de Kooning's Women," *Arts* 53 (November 1975), 96–101, argues several sources for the *Women* paintings, including Cycladic idols, Sumerian votive figures, Byzantine icons, and Picasso's *Demoiselles*.

9 *Willem de Kooning: The North Atlantic Light* (cited note 8), p. 77. See also Hess, *Willem de Kooning*, 1959 (cited in note 8), p. 77.

10 *Willem de Kooning: The North Atlantic Light* (cited in note 8), p. 77.

11 See, for example, Leo Steinberg, "The Philosophical Brothel," *Art News*, September 1972, pp. 25–6. In Steinberg's ground-breaking reading, the act of looking at these female figures visually re-creates the act of sexually penetrating a woman. The implication is that women are anatomically unequipped to experience the work's full meaning.

12 Very little has been written about de Kooning that does not do this. For one of the most bombastic treatments, see Harold Rosenberg, *De Kooning* (New York, 1974).

13   The Vietnam Veterans Memorial

Arthur C. Danto

We erect monuments so that we shall always remember, and build memorials so that we shall never forget. Thus we have the Washington Monument but the Lincoln Memorial. Monuments commemorate the memorable and embody the myths of beginnings. Memorials ritualize remembrance and mark the reality of ends. The Washington Monument, vertical, is a celebration, like fireworks. The

Lincoln Memorial, even if on a rise, presses down and is a meditation in stone. Very few nations erect monuments to their defeats, but many set up memorials to the defeated dead. Monuments make heroes and triumphs, victories and conquests, perpetually present and part of life. The memorial is a special precinct, extruded from life, a segregated enclave where we honor the dead. With monuments we honor ourselves.

Memorials are often just lists of those killed. Herodotus describes a megalith that carried the names of all 300 Spartans slain at Thermopylae in a defeat so stunning as to elevate their leader, Leonidas, to what Ivan Morris once called the nobility of failure. Lists figure prominently in the hundreds of Civil War memorials, where the names of fallen townsmen bear the iconographic significance that those who were lost meant more than what had been won. The paradox of the Vietnam Veterans Memorial in Washington is that the men and women killed and missing would not have been memorialized had we won the war and erected a monument instead. Among the specifications for the memorial's commission was the stipulation that it show the names of all the US dead and missing (the battlestone of Thermopylae only memorialized the Spartans, not their Theoan or Thespian allies) and that it make no political statement about the war. But just being called a memorial is as eloquent as not being called a monument: not being forgotten is the thin compensation for not having participated in an event everyone wants to remember. The list of names, as a collective cenotaph, situates the memorialized war in the consciousness of the nation.

The Washington Monument is an obelisk, a monumental form with connotations of the trophy in Western art. Augustus carried obelisks to Alexandria, whence they were in time borne off to London and New York; Constantine brought one to Rome, where it was appropriated by Pope Sixtus V for San Giovanni in Laterano; Napoleon was obliged to cart an obelisk to Paris. The Lincoln Memorial is in the form of a classical temple, in which Lincoln is enthroned like a brooding god. It is a metaphor for sacrifice and a confession of the limits of human power. The Veterans Memorial carries no explicit art-historical references, though it consists of two symmetrical walls, mirror images of one another, right triangles sharing a common vertical base, which point, like a pair of long wings, east, to the obelisk of triumph, and west, to the temple of submission. Everything about it is part of a text. Even the determination to say nothing political is inscribed by the absence of a political statement. A third stipulation for the memorial was that it harmonize with its surroundings. It does more: it integrates the two structures it points to into a moral landscape. Because the two wings form an angle, the Veterans Memorial together with the Washington Monument and the Lincoln Memorial compose a large triangle, with the long reflecting pool as a segment of the base.

The memorial was dedicated on November 13, 1982 – Veterans Day – when there were only the walls and the names, each wall composed of seventy granite panels with about 58,000 names and room for several hundred more. Two years later a bronze statue of three servicemen, done in an exacting realism, was added to the site. Their backs are to the axis that connects the Monument and the Memorial, as though they are oblivious to the historical meanings to which the walls return us by pointing. Like innocents who look at the pointer rather than that to which it points, they see only rows and columns of names. They are dazed and stunned. The walls reflect their obsessed gaze, as they reflect the flag to which the servicemen's back is also turned, as they reflect the Monument and the Memorial. The gently flexed pair of walls, polished black, is like the back of Plato's cave, a reflecting surface, a dark mirror. The reflections in it of the servicemen, the flag, the Monument and the Memorial, are appearances of appearances. It also reflects us, the visitors, as it does the trees. Still, the living are in it only as appearances. Only the names of the dead, on the surface, are real.

The reflecting walls constituted the Veterans Memorial at the time of its dedication, but before they were in place a concession was made to a faction that demanded figurative realism instead of what it perceived as an abstract monument to the liberal establishment. Thus the bronze servicemen. Those walls could have stood on their own, artistically, but the bronze group could not have. As a piece of free-standing sculpture it is intrinsically banal. Its three figures belong to obligatorily distinct racial types: a black and someone vaguely ethnic – a Jew, perhaps, or some Mediterranean type – stand on either side of a Nordic figure. The central figure has a holstered pistol, but the end figures carry more powerful weapons – though not held in a position for use – and there are no empty spaces in the cartridge belts: fighting is suspended. The garb and gear of this war are precisely documented: visitors will learn how many eyelets were in G.I. boots and that soldiers carried two canteens. More realistic than the military figures that guard the honor rolls in Civil War memorials, they look too much like specimens for a military museum, at least when considered alone. But they are greatly enhanced by their relationship to the great walls. In a way, the harmonization of their presence in the triangle generated by the walls is a monument to the triumph of political compromise rather than a memorial to artistic strife. The dead are remembered in their gaze, even when there are no living to look.

The walls are the design of Maya Ying Lin, who won a competition against 1,421 contestants when she was 21 and a student at Yale University. An Asian-American from Athens, Ohio, she was a child at the time of the memorialized conflict, too young to remember the tumult and the protest, which for her are simply history, like the War of Independence or the Civil War. The bronze group was done by Frederick Hart, a Washington sculptor, who was, ironically, a demonstrator against the Vietnam War. The irony is that artistic realism was associated with patriotism and endorsement of the war in the minds of those who insisted on figuration. They regarded the walls as a symbol for peaceniks. "A wailing wall for liberals"; "a tribute to Jane Fonda"; "a degrading ditch"; "the most insulting and demeaning memorial to our experience that was possible": these were among the nasty things said. The walls are non-figurative, of course, but they are deeply representational, given the textual nature of memorial art (of all art, when it comes to that), and the question of the meaning of Lin's text was acknowledged by those who rejected what they took to be its supposed representation of reality. Its being black, for example, was loudly read as a sign of shame until a black general brought an abrupt end to that effort to pre-empt the language of color.

The winning design was the unanimous choice of a panel of eight experts, and it was accepted by the group that pushed the idea of a memorial as an expression of the feelings they wanted to have objectified. It gave a form to those feelings, as public art is supposed to do: the issues are never solely aesthetic. It was accepted by 150,000 participants at the dedication. No one has defaced it, no one has tried to blow it up, though there was a threat of this once. It has been accepted by the nation at large, which did not even know it wanted such a memorial. It is now one of the sites most visited in the capital. Still, it was wholly appropriate that the design should have been put in question when a schism opened up, that intense emotion and antagonism should have raged, that terrible and foolish things should have been said by everyone. Lin mounted the same high horse favored by artists whose work is publicly criticized and accused the critics of sexism. Even so, her design held. It was not replaced by a monument, as though the tacit rules that govern the distinction between monuments and memorials finally prevailed. Those who wanted realism finally got their mannequins, not exactly where they wanted them, with the walls to their back and a proud flag flying at the vee, but off to one side, up a gentle slope, and at a certain distance, with the flag still farther away. By a miracle of placement, Hart's shallow work has acquired a dignity and even a certain power. The complex of walls and figures reminded me of a memorial sculpture of Canova, in which a single figure sits in white silence outside a pyramidal sepulcher. A dimension is even added to the triangular walls, wonderful as they are. The entire complex is an emblem of the participation of the public in the framing of public art. It did not, to paraphrase Richard Serra, cost the government a dime. More than 275,000 Americans responded to the call for funds with contributions in small denominations – those bearing the faces of Washington and Lincoln.

Lin's instructor told her that the angle where the walls meet had to mean something, and I asked myself, when I pilgrimed down one hot Tuesday in July, what its meaning was. A writer in the "Talk of the Town" section of *The New Yorker* described it as "a long open hinge, it leaves cut vertically into the ground, which descends very gradually toward the vertex." The hinge is a powerful symbol – we speak of "the hinge of fate" – and it has the mysterious property of opening and closing at once. Still, that is something of a misdescription. A hinge 140 feet long sounds too much like Claes Oldenburg, who might, consistent with his *oeuvre*, have submitted the Vietnam Veterans Memorial Hinge had he entered the competition. The *New Yorker* writer does better on a nearer approach: "a little like facing a huge open book with black pages." The book lies open now that the episode is closed and all or nearly all the dead are known. A book of the dead. And that would fit with their being listed in chronological order, from the first one killed in 1959 to the last one killed in 1975, when the remaining Americans were evacuated from Saigon as the Republic of Vietnam surrendered, on April 30.

This brings me to my chief criticism of Lin's work, which concerns an incongruity between narrative and form. An effort has been made to make the slight angle meaningful by having the narrative begin and end there: RICHARD VANDE GEER is at the bottom right of the west panel and DALE R. BUIS is at the top left of the east panel on either side of the joint. As though a circle were closed, and after the end is the beginning. But a circle has the wrong moral geometry for a linear conflict: the end of a war does not mean, one hopes, the beginning of a war. As it stands now, we read from the middle to the end, then return to the other end and read again our way to the middle. This means that the terminal panels, architecturally the most important, carry one name each but the end points of the walls are not the end points of the list. If the first were first, we would read through to the last, from left to right. The panels grow larger, which is to say the space in which the walls are set grows deeper, as we approach the center. So there are more names on the central panels than on the rest. But that exactly reflects the shape of the war itself, our involvement being greatest in the late 1960s. So the angle could represent a high point and a turning point. And you would leave with the Monument before you, as you entered with the Memorial behind you, and the whole complex would acquire the direction of time and perhaps, hope.

You can read a chronicle of the making of this singular work in *To Heal a Nation*, by Jan C. Scruggs and Joel L. Swerdlow (Harper & Row). The memorial would not exist without Scruggs, a veteran of that terrible war and a man of great vision. I like to think that the voice of the book, optimistic, enthusiastic, conciliatory, is his, whoever did the writing. It also contains some photographs, but there is really no way to imagine the memorial from them, or from any pictures I have seen. For that you must make a visit. If you know someone who was killed, an attendant from the National Parks Service will help you locate his or her name. They are all listed alphabetically in directories near the site.

Be prepared to weep. Tears are the universal experience even if you don't know any of the dead. I watched reverent little groups count down the rows of a panel and then across to the name they sought. Some place a poignant, hopeless offering underneath: a birthday card, a flag, a ribbon, a flower. Some leave little notes. Most photograph the name, but many take rubbings of it on pamphlets handed out by the Parks Service. You can borrow a ladder to reach the top names. The highest panels are about ten feet high – or, more accurately, their bottom edges are about ten feet below ground level. Someday, I suppose, visiting it will be like standing before a memorial from the Civil War, where the bearers of the names really have been forgotten and, since the theory is that the meaning of name is its denotation, the names themselves will have lost their meaning. They will merely remain powerful as names, and there will only be the idea of death to be moved by. Now, however, we are all moved by the reality of death, or moved by the fact that many who stand beside us are moved by its reality. I copied down two of the names of which rubbings were made:

EDWARD H. FOX
WILBUR J. MILLER

Suggestions for Further Reading

Adorno, Theodor, *Aesthetic Theory,* trans. C. Lenhardt. London: Routledge and Kegan Paul, 1984.

Arnheim, Rudolf, *Toward a Psychology of Art.* Berkeley and Los Angeles: University of California Press, 1972.

Benjamin, Walter, *Illuminations,* trans. Harry Zohn. New York: Shocken, 1968.

Berger, John, *Ways of Seeing.* London: Penguin, 1972.

Berleant, Arnold, *Art and Engagement.* Philadelphia: Temple University Press, 1991.

Bullough, Edward, " 'Psychical Distance' as a Factor in Art and an Aesthetic Principle," *British Journal of Psychology* V, (1912). [Widely reprinted.]

Crimp, Douglas, *On the Museum's Ruins.* Cambridge Mass.: MIT Press, 1993.

Devereaux, Mary, "Oppressive Texts, Resisting Readers, and the Gendered Spectator," in *Feminism and Tradition in Aesthetics,* ed. Peggy Zeglin Brand and Carolyn Korsmeyer. University Park: Pennsylvania State University Press, 1995

Hein, Hilde, *The Exploratorium: The Museum as Laboratory.* Washington, DC: Smithsonian Institution Press, 1990.

Hooper-Greenhill, Eilean, *Museums and the Shaping of Knowledge.* London: Routledge, 1992.

Kant, Immanual, *The Critique of Judgment* [1790], trans. Werner Pluhar. Indianapolis: Hackett Publishing Co.,

Karp, Ivan and Steven D. Lavine, *Exhibiting Cultures: The Poetics and Politics of Museum Display.* Washington, DC: Smithsonian Institution, 1991.

Macquet, Jacques, *The Aesthetic Experience: An Anthropologist Looks at the Visual Arts.* New Haven: Yale University Press, 1986.

PART THREE

AESTHETIC EVALUATION:
WHO DECIDES?

Preface

It is a common experience in nearly any discussion of values to reach a point where someone asks, "Who is to say? We are talking about subjective reactions, and there is no way to decide whose opinion is right." The case is no different when it comes to issues of aesthetic value. There are many aspects of aesthetic evaluation that give rise to important questions about the subjectivity or objectivity of the perspective brought to judgment. For instance, is it possible that one person's judgment on works of art may be of greater worth than another's? And if there is such a person, what qualities would he or she have to possess in order to have the advantage in making aesthetic assessments? Is there a preferred approach or attitude to take to art that maximizes the possibilities of appreciation? We commonly employ a distinction between high art and low art. Is this distinction a valid or an artificial one? Finally, what connection is there between our appreciation of some kind of art and our social background – our social class, historical position, or gender? The articles in this section pose some answers to these questions about aesthetic value and the process of evaluation.

David Hume (1711–76), the Scottish empiricist philosopher, wrote his essay "Of the Standard of Taste" (1757) at a time when modern aesthetic theory was developing; philosophers of the time were preoccupied with the attempt to establish standards for subjective responses to beauty. Hume notes that when it comes to deciding the value of a particular work of art, disagreement is bound to arise. Our tastes are sometimes so different that we are apt to declare that all opinions are equal, and no one has a just claim to authority. But when we see that some works of art are widely acknowledged to have greater value than others, we may also understand that some standard indeed functions. He points out certain qualities that one must possess in order to reach such a standard in one's own judgments. For instance, one must have had a wide experience of art works, comparing them to one another, to develop a good sense of what is beautiful and to develop what he calls "delicate taste." One must be as free from prejudice as possible so that one may evaluate works of art fairly. Though the kind of person who can establish a standard of taste rarely comes along, such critics are invaluable to society because they can point out subtleties that would otherwise be lost to the rest of us. It is easier to determine quality over time, because judgments of what art is truly great converge, and the great works of the past continue to give pleasure.

Pierre Bourdieu, a contemporary sociologist, disputes the very idea of a universal standard of taste and argues that our social class and background influence our preferences, our judgments, and our enjoyment of art. What kinds of art we find ourselves encountering will largely be a function of our education and our class. Those who have a taste for what is praised as fine or high art have been conditioned for such activities by their privileged social position and so have been given a kind of cognitive "code" to understand so-called high culture. On the other side of the tracks, working-class people who are daily made aware of the basic demands of life have an inclination towards works that seem to mirror life or that display more practical values. If Bourdieu's analysis is correct, then there is little sense to the suggestion that there may be a standard of taste valid for all.

The issue of what approach we optimally should take when experiencing a work of art is taken up by Peggy Zeglin Brand. This question becomes especially complex when we are confronted with works of art that are intentionally controversial and difficult, as is much political art, including the feminist work she discusses. It has been suggested for some time that the ideal way to appreciate art is with an attitude of disinterest, as Jerome Stolnitz suggests in an earlier entry in Part Two. Many feminist critics have claimed that this is a typically masculine approach associated with misguided notions of objectivity. Art, especially feminist art, is supposed to arouse one's interest; the values of art are both social and individual, and therefore it is appropriate that art be taken personally. Brand gives each side of the debate a hearing and, with the help of some studies in the psychology of perception, attempts to mediate a solution. Each approach is only partial, she argues. By being disinterested, we understand features of a work of art that an interested approach could not offer, though this does not prevent us from returning to an interested mode of appreciation to regain our sense of the social and political significance of the artist's efforts.

The distinction between high art and low art already mentioned before may seem perfectly natural to us, but actually this distinction was fairly recently introduced in the early modern period. (For an account of this also see Parker and Pollock's entry in Part One.) Ted Cohen, while acknowledging some usefulness to the distinction, questions its validity to distinguish that which is most valuable to us from that which merely entertains. He attempts to discover what motive lies behind the separation in the first place. A clue to why we value art may be provided by attending to the personal dimensions of our preferences in art. Each of us is personally touched by our experiences of art. Different kinds of art affect us in different ways and so will have different levels of significance for us. In our relations to other people we have a desire to share what is important to us. So in considering what is important enough to us that we feel others ought to share our tastes, we touch upon what is, in our eyes, the most important art. Some art binds us to large communities of people who share similar tastes, while other art is appreciated by only a very few. This distinction, however, cuts across both "high" and "low" art and rarely gives us grounds for maintaining that distinction.

There is a sense in which, in matters of aesthetic evaluation, the question "who decides?" may be ultimately unanswerable. Yet in attempting to supply answers we may come to see that we did not have as firm a grasp of what is involved in these issues as we first thought. From this perspective, the articles in this section may be seen as taking some steps toward clarification.

David Kaspar

14   Of the Standard of Taste

David Hume

The great variety of Taste, as well as of opinion, which prevails in the world, is too obvious not to have fallen under every one's observation. Men of the most confined knowledge are able to remark a difference of taste in the narrow circle of their acquaintance, even where the persons have been educated under the same government, and have early imbibed the same prejudices. But those, who can enlarge their view to contemplate distant nations and remote ages, are still more surprized at the great inconsistency and contrariety. We are apt to call *barbarous* whatever departs widely from our own taste and apprehension: But soon find the epithet of reproach retorted on us. And the highest arrogance and self-conceit is at last startled, on observing an equal assurance on all sides, and scruples, amidst such a contest of sentiment, to pronounce positively in its own favour.

As this variety of taste is obvious to the most careless enquirer; so will it be found, on examination, to be still greater in reality than in appearance. The sentiments of men often differ with regard to beauty and deformity of all kinds, even while their general discourse is the same. There are certain terms in every language, which import blame, and others praise; and all men, who use the same tongue, must agree in their application of them. Every voice is united in applauding elegance, propriety, simplicity, spirit in writing; and in blaming fustian, affectation, coldness, and a false brilliancy: But when critics come to particulars, this seeming unanimity vanishes; and it is found, that they had affixed a very different meaning to their expressions. In all matters of opinion and science, the case is opposite: The difference among men is there oftener found to lie in generals than in particulars; and to be less in reality than in appearance. An explanation of the terms commonly ends the controversy; and the disputants are surprised to find, that they had been quarrelling, while at bottom they agreed in their judgment.

Those who found morality on sentiment, more than on reason, are inclined to comprehend ethics under the former observation, and to maintain, that, in all questions, which regard conduct and manners, the difference among men is really greater than at first sight it appears. It is indeed obvious, that writers of all nations and all ages concur in applauding justice, humanity, magnanimity, prudence, veracity; and in blaming the opposite qualities. Even poets and other authors, whose compositions are chiefly calculated to please the imagination, are yet found from Homer down to Fenelon, to inculcate the same moral precepts, and to bestow their applause and blame on the same virtues and vices. This great unanimity is usually ascribed to the influence of plain reason; which, in all these cases, maintains similar sentiments in all men, and prevents those controversies, to which the abstract sciences are so much exposed. So far as the unanimity is real, this account may be admitted as satisfactory: But we must also allow that some part of the seeming harmony in morals may be accounted for from the very nature of language. The word *virtue*, with its equivalent in every tongue, implies praise; as that of *vice* does blame: And no one, without the most obvious and grossest impropriety, could affix reproach to a term, which in general acceptation is understood in a good sense; or bestow applause, where the idiom requires disapprobation. Homer's general precepts, where he delivers any such, will never be controverted; but it is obvious, that, when he draws particular pictures of manners, and represents heroism in Achilles and prudence in Ulysses, he intermixes a much greater degree of ferocity in the former, and of cunning and fraud in the latter, than Fenelon would admit of. The sage Ulysses in the Greek poet seems to delight in lies and fictions, and often employs them without any necessity or even advantage: But his more scrupulous son, in the French epic writer, exposes himself to the most imminent perils, rather than depart from the most exact line of truth and veracity.

The admirers and followers of the Alcoran insist on the excellent moral precepts interspersed throughout that wild and absurd performance. But it is to be supposed, that the Arabic words, which correspond to the English, equity, justice, temperance, meekness, charity, were such as, from the constant use of that tongue, must always be taken in a good sense; and it would have argued the ignorance, not of morals, but of language, to have mentioned them with any epithets, besides those of applause and approbation. But would we know, whether the pretended prophet had really attained a just sentiment of morals? Let us attend to his narration; and we shall soon find, that he bestows praise on such instances of treachery, inhumanity, cruelty, revenge, bigotry, as are utterly incompatible with civilized society. No steady rule of right seems there to be attended to; and every action is blamed or praised, so far only as it is beneficial or hurtful to the true believers.

The merit of delivering true general precepts in ethics is indeed very small. Whoever recommends any moral virtues, really does no more than is implied in the terms themselves. That people, who invented the word *charity*, and used it in a good sense, inculcated more clearly and much more efficaciously, the precept, *be charitable*, than any pretended legislator or prophet, who should insert such a *maxim* in his writings. Of all expressions, those, which, together with their other meaning, imply a degree either of blame or approbation, are the least liable to be perverted or mistaken.

It is natural for us to seek a *Standard of Taste*; a rule, by which the various sentiments of men may be reconciled; at least, a decision, afforded, confirming one sentiment, and condemning another.

There is a species of philosophy, which cuts off all hopes of success in such an attempt, and represents the impossibility of ever attaining any standard of taste. The difference, it is said, is very wide between judgment and sentiment. All sentiment is right; because sentiment has a reference to nothing beyond itself, and is always real, wherever a man is conscious of it. But all determinations of the understanding are not right; because they have a reference to something beyond themselves, to wit, real matter of fact; and are not always conformable to that standard. Among a thousand different opinions which different men may entertain of the same subject, there is one, and but one, that is just and true; and the only difficulty is to fix and ascertain it. On the contrary, a thousand different sentiments, excited by the same object, are all right: Because no sentiment represents what is really in the object. It only marks a certain conformity or relation between the object and the organs or faculties of the mind; and if that conformity did not really exist, the sentiment could never possibly have being. Beauty is no quality in things themselves: It exists merely in the mind which contemplates them; and each mind perceives a different beauty. One person may even perceive deformity, where another is sensible of beauty; and every individual ought to acquiesce in his own sentiment, without pretending to regulate those of others. To seek the real beauty, or real deformity, is as fruitless an enquiry, as to pretend to ascertain the real sweet or real bitter. According to the disposition of the organs, the same object may be both sweet and bitter, and the proverb has justly determined it to be fruitless to dispute concerning tastes. It is very natural, and even quite necessary, to extend this axiom to mental, as well as bodily taste; and thus common sense, which is so often at variance with philosophy, especially with the sceptical kind, is found, in one instance at least, to agree in pronouncing the same decision.

But though this axiom, by passing into a proverb, seems to have attained the sanction of common sense; there is certainly a species of common sense which opposes it, at least serves to modify and restrain it. Whoever would assert an equality of genius and elegance between Ogilby and Milton, or Bunyan and Addison, would be thought to defend no less an extravagance, than if he had maintained a mole-hill to be as high as Teneriffe, or a pond as extensive as the ocean. Though there may be found persons, who give the preference to the former authors; no one pays attention to such a taste; and we pronounce without scruple the sentiment of these pretended critics to be absurd and ridiculous. The principle of the natural equality of tastes is then totally forgot, and while we admit it on some occasions, where the objects seem near an equality, it appears an extravagant paradox, or rather a palpable absurdity, where objects so disproportioned are compared together.

It is evident that none of the rules of composition are fixed by reasonings a priori, or can be esteemed abstract conclusions of the understanding, from comparing these habitudes and relations of ideas, which are eternal and immutable. Their foundation is the same with that of all the practical sciences, experience; nor are they any thing but general observations, concerning what has been universally found to please in all countries and in all ages. Many of the beauties of poetry and even of eloquence are founded on falsehood and fiction, on hyperboles, metaphors, and an abuse or perversion of terms from their natural meaning. To check the sallies of the imagination, and to reduce every expression to geometrical truth and exactness, would be the most contrary to the laws of criticism; because it would produce a work, which, by universal experience, has been found the most insipid and disagreeable. But though poetry can never submit to exact truth, it must be confined by rules of art, discovered to the author either by genius or observation. If some negligent or irregular writers have pleased, they have not pleased by their transgressions of rule or order, but in spite of these transgressions: They have possessed other beauties, which were conformable to just criticism; and the force of these beauties has been able to overpower censure, and give the mind a satisfaction superior to the disgust arising from the blemishes. Ariosto pleases; but not by his monstrous and improbable fictions, by his bizarre mixture of the serious and comic style, by the want of coherence in his stories, or by the continual interruptions of his narration. He charms by the force and clearness of his expression, by the readiness and variety of his inventions, and by his natural pictures of the passions, especially those of the gay and amorous kind: And however his faults may diminish our satisfaction, they are not able entirely to destroy it. Did our pleasure really arise from those parts of his poem, which we denominate faults, this would be no objection to criticism in general: It would only be an objection to those particular rules of criticism, which would establish such circumstances to be faults, and would represent them as universally blameable. If they are found to please, they cannot be faults; let the pleasure, which they produce, be ever so unexpected and unaccountable.

But though all the general rules of art are founded only on experience and on the observation of the common sentiments of human nature, we must not imagine, that, on every occasion, the feelings of men will be conformable to these rules. Those finer emotions of the mind are of a very tender and delicate nature, and require the concurrence of many favourable circumstances to make them play with facility and exactness, according to their general and established principles. The least exterior hindrance to such small springs, or the least internal disorder, disturbs their motion, and confounds the operation of the whole machine. When we would make an experiment of this nature, and would try the force of any beauty or deformity, we must choose with care a proper time and place, and bring the fancy to a suitable situation and disposition. A perfect serenity of mind, a recollection of thought, a due attention to the object; if any of these circumstances be wanting, our experiment will be fallacious, and we shall be unable to judge of the catholic and universal beauty. The relation, which nature has placed between the form and the sentiment, will at least be more obscure; and it will require greater accuracy to trace and discern it. We shall be able to ascertain its influence not so much from the operation of each particular beauty, as from the durable admiration, which attends those works, that have survived all the caprices of mode and fashion, all the mistakes of ignorance and envy.

The same Homer, who pleased at Athens and Rome two thousand years ago, is still admired at Paris and at London. All the changes of climate, government, religion, and language, have not been able to obscure his glory. Authority or prejudice may give a temporary vogue to a bad poet or orator, but his reputation will never be durable or general. When his compositions are examined by posterity or by foreigners, the enchantment is dissipated, and his faults appear in their true colours. On the contrary, a real genius, the longer his works endure, and the more wide they are spread, the more sincere is the admiration which he meets with. Envy and jealousy have too much place in a narrow circle; and even familiar acquaintance with his person may diminish the applause due to his performances: But when these obstructions are removed, the beauties, which are naturally fitted to excite agreeable sentiments, immediately display their energy, and while the world endures, they maintain their authority over the minds of men.

It appears then, that, amidst all the variety and caprice of taste, there are certain general principles of approbation or blame, whose influence a careful eye may trace in all operations of the mind. Some particular forms or qualities, from the original structure of the internal fabric, are calculated to please, and others to displease; and if they fail of their effect in any particular instance, it is from some apparent defect or imperfection in the organ. A man in a fever would not insist on his palate as able to decide concerning flavours; nor would one, affected with the jaundice, pretend to give a verdict with regard to colours. In each creature, there is a sound and a defective state; the former alone can be supposed to afford us a true standard of taste and sentiment. If, in the sound state of the organ, there be an entire or a considerable uniformity of sentiment among men, we may thence derive an idea of the perfect beauty; in like manner as the appearance of objects in daylight, to the eye of a man in health, is denominated their true and real colour, even while colour is allowed to be merely a phantasm of the senses.

Many and frequent are the defects in the internal organs, which prevent or weaken the influence of those general principles, on which depends our sentiment of beauty or deformity. Though some objects, by the structure of the mind, be naturally calculated to give pleasure, it is not to be expected, that in every individual the pleasure will be equally felt. Particular incidents and situations occur, which either throw a false light on the objects, or hinder the true from conveying to the imagination the proper sentiment and perception.

One obvious cause, why many feel not the proper sentiment of beauty, is the want of that *delicacy* of imagination, which is requisite to convey a sensibility of those finer emotions. This delicacy every one pretends to: Every one talks of it; and would reduce every kind of taste or sentiment to its standard. But as our intention in this essay is to mingle some light of the understanding with the feelings of sentiment, it will be proper to give a more accurate definition of delicacy, than has hitherto been attempted. And not to draw our philosophy from too profound a source, we shall have recourse to a noted story in Don Quixote.

It is with good reason, says Sancho to the squire with the great nose, that I pretend to have a judgment in wine: This is a quality hereditary in our family. Two of my kinsmen were once called to give their opinion of a hogshead, which was supposed to be excellent, being old and of a good vintage. One of them tastes it; considers it; and after mature reflection pronounces the wine to be good, were it not for a small taste of leather, which he perceived in it. The other, after using the same precautions, gives also his verdict in favour of the wine; but with the reserve of a taste of iron, which he could easily distinguish. You cannot imagine how much they were both ridiculed for their judgment.

But who laughed in the end? On emptying the hogshead, there was found at the bottom, an old key with a leathern thong tied to it.

The great resemblance between mental and bodily taste will easily teach us to apply this story. Though it be certain, that beauty and deformity, more than sweet and bitter, are not qualities in objects, but belong entirely to the sentiment, internal or external; it must be allowed, that there are certain qualities in objects, which are fitted by nature to produce those particular feelings. Now as these qualities may be found in a small degree, or may be mixed and confounded with each other, it often happens, that the taste is not affected with such minute qualities, or is not able to distinguish all the particular flavours, amidst the disorder, in which they are presented. Where the organs are so fine, as to allow nothing to escape them; and at the same time so exact as to perceive every ingredient in the composition: This we call delicacy of taste, whether we employ these terms in the literal or metaphorical sense. Here then the general rules of beauty are of use; being drawn from established models, and from the observation of what pleases or displeases, when presented singly and in a high degree: And if the same qualities, in a continued composition and in a smaller degree, affect not the organs with a sensible delight or uneasiness, we exclude the person from all pretensions to this delicacy. To produce these general rules or avowed patterns of composition is like finding the key with the leathern thong, which justified the verdict of Sancho's kinsmen, and confounded those pretended judges who had condemned them. Though the hogshead had never been emptied, the taste of the one was still equally delicate, and that of the other equally dull and languid: But it would have been more difficult to have proved the superiority of the former, to the conviction of every bystander. In like manner, though the beauties of writing had never been methodized, reduced to general principles; though no excellent models had ever been acknowledged; the different degrees of taste would still have subsisted, and the judgment of one man been preferable to that of another, but it would not have been so easy to silence the bad critic, who might always insist upon his particular sentiment, and refuse to submit to his antagonist. But when we show him an avowed principle of art; when we illustrate this principle by examples, whose operation, from his own particular taste, he acknowledges to be conformable to the principle; when we prove, that the same principle may be applied to the present ease, where he did not perceive or feel its influence: He must conclude, upon the whole, that the fault lies in himself, and that he wants the delicacy, which is requisite to make him sensible of every beauty and every blemish, in any composition or discourse.

It is acknowledged to be the perfection of every sense or faculty, to perceive with exactness its most minute objects, and allow nothing to escape its notice and observation. The smaller the objects are, which become sensible to the eye, the finer is that organ, and the more elaborate its make and composition. A good palate is not tried by strong flavours; but by a mixture of small ingredients, where we are still sensible of each part, notwithstanding its minuteness and its confusion with the rest. In like manner, a quick and acute perception of beauty and deformity must be the perfection of our mental taste; nor can a man be satisfied with himself while he suspects, that any excellence or blemish in a discourse has passed him unobserved. In this case, the perfection of the man, and the perfection of the sense or feeling, are found to be united. A very delicate palate, on many occasions, may be a great inconvenience both to a man himself and to his friends: But a delicate taste of wit or beauty must always be a desirable quality; because it is the source of all the finest and most innocent enjoyments, of which human nature is susceptible. In this decision the sentiments of all mankind are agreed. Wherever you can ascertain a delicacy of taste, it is sure to meet with approbation; and the best way of ascertaining it is to appeal to those models and principles, which have been established by the uniform consent and experience of nations and ages.

But though there be naturally a wide difference in point of delicacy between one person and another, nothing tends further to encrease and improve this talent, than *practice* in a particular art, and the frequent survey or contemplation of a particular species of beauty. When objects of any kind are first presented to the eye or imagination, the sentiment, which attends them, is obscure and confused; and the mind is, in a great measure, incapable of pronouncing concerning their merits or defects. The taste cannot perceive the several excellencies of the performance; much less distinguish the particular character of each excellency, and ascertain its quality and degree. If it pronounce the whole in general to be beautiful or deformed, it is the utmost that can be expected; and even this judgment, a person, so unpractised, will be apt to deliver with great hesitation and reserve. But allow him to acquire experience in those objects, his feeling becomes more exact and nice: He not only perceives the beauties and defects of each part, but marks the distinguishing species of each quality, and assigns it suitable praise or blame. A clear and distinct sentiment ascends him through the whole survey of the objects; and he discerns that very degree and kind of approbation or displeasure, which each part is naturally fitted to produce. The mist dissipates, which seemed formerly to hang over the object: The organ acquires greater perfection in its operations; and can pronounce, without danger of mistake, concerning the merits of every performance. In a word, the same address and dexterity, which practice gives to the execution of any work, is also acquired by the same means, in the judging of it.

So advantageous is practice to the discernment of beauty, that, before we can give judgment on any work of importance, it will even be requisite, that that very individual performance be more than once perused by us, and be surveyed in different lights with attention and deliberation. There a flutter or hurry of thought which attends the first perusal of any piece, and which confounds the genuine sentiment of beauty. The relation of the parts is not discerned: The true characters of style are little distinguished: The several perfections and defects seem wrapped up in a species of confusion, and present themselves indistinctly to the imagination. Not to mention, that there is a species of beauty, which, as it is florid and superficial, pleases at first; but being found incompatible with a just expression either of reason or passion, soon palls upon the taste, and is then rejected with disdain, at least rated at a much lower value.

It is impossible to continue in the practice of contemplating any order of beauty, without being frequently obliged to form *comparisons* between the several species and degrees of excellence, and estimating their proportion to each other. A man, who has had no opportunity of comparing the different kinds of beauty, is indeed foully unqualified to pronounce an opinion with regard to any object presented to him. By comparison alone we fix the epithets of praise or blame, and learn how to assign the due degree of each. The coarsest daubing contains a certain lustre of colours and exactness of imitation, which are so far beauties, and would affect the mind of a peasant or Indian with the highest admiration. The most vulgar ballads are not entirely destitute of harmony or nature; and none but a person, familiarized to superior beauties, would pronounce their numbers harsh, or narration uninteresting. A great inferiority of beauty gives pain to a person conversant in the highest excellence of the kind, and is for that reason pronounced a deformity: As the most finished object, with which we are acquainted, is naturally supposed to have reached the pinnacle of perfection, and to be entitled to the highest applause. One accustomed to see, and examine, and weigh the several performances, admired in different ages and nations, can alone rate the merits of a work exhibited to his view, and assign its proper rank among the productions of genius.

But to enable a critic the more fully to execute this undertaking, he must preserve his mind free from all *prejudice*, and allow nothing to enter into his consideration, but the very object which is submitted to his examination. We may observe, that every work of art, in order to produce its due effect on the mind, must be surveyed in a certain point of view, and cannot be fully relished by persons, whose situation, real or imaginary, is not conformable to that which is required by the performance. An orator addresses himself to a particular audience, and must have a regard to their particular genius, interests, opinions, passions, and prejudices; otherwise he hopes in vain to govern their resolutions, and inflame their affections. Should they even have entertained some prepossessions against him, however unreasonable, he must not overlook this disadvantage; but, before he enters upon the subject, must endeavour to conciliate their affection, and acquire their good graces. A critic of a different age or nation, who should peruse this discourse, must have all these circumstances in his eye, and must place himself in the same situation as the audience, in order to form a true judgment of the oration. In like manner, when any work is addressed to the public, though I should have a friendship or enmity with the author, I must depart from this situation; and considering myself as a man in general, forget, if possible, my individual being and my peculiar circumstances. A person influenced by prejudice, complies not with this condition; but obstinately maintains his natural position, without placing himself in that point of view, which the performance supposes. If the work be addressed to persons of a different age or nation, he makes no allowance for their peculiar views and prejudices; but, full of the manners of his own age and country, rashly condemns what seemed admirable in the eyes of those for whom alone the discourse was calculated. If the work be executed for the public, he never sufficiently enlarges his comprehension, or forgets his interest as a friend or enemy, as a rival or commentator. By this means, his sentiments are perverted; nor have the same beauties and blemishes the same influence upon him, as if he had imposed a proper violence on his imagination, and had forgotten himself for a moment. So far his taste evidently departs from the true standard; and of consequence loses all credit and authority.

It is well known, that in all questions, submitted to the understanding, prejudice is destructive of sound judgment, and perverts all operations of the intellectual faculties: It is no less contrary to good taste; nor has it less influence to corrupt our sentiment of beauty. It belongs to *good sense* to check its influence in both cases; and in this respect, as well as in many others, reason, if not an essential part of taste, is at least requisite to the operations of this latter faculty. In all the nobler productions of genius, there is a mutual relation and correspondence of parts; nor can either the beauties or blemishes be perceived by him, whose thought is not capacious enough to comprehend all those parts, and compare them with each other, in order to perceive the consistence and uniformity of the whole. Every work of art has also a certain end or purpose, for which it is calculated; and is to be deemed more or less perfect, as it is more or less fitted to attain this end. The object of eloquence is to persuade, of history to instruct, of poetry to please by means of the passions and the imagination. These ends we must carry constantly in our view, when we peruse any performance; and we must be able to judge how far the means employed are adapted to their respective purposes. Besides, every kind of composition, even the most poetical, is nothing but a chain of propositions and reasonings; not always, indeed, the justest and most exact, but still plausible and specious, however disguised by the colouring of the imagination. The persons introduced in tragedy and epic poetry, must be represented as reasoning, and thinking, and concluding, and acting, suitably to their character and circumstances; and without judgment, as well as taste and invention, a poet can never hope to succeed in so delicate an undertaking. Not to mention, that the same excellence of faculties which contributes to the improvement of reason, the same clearness of conception, the same exactness of distinction, the same vivacity of apprehension, are essential to the operations of true taste, and are its infallible concomitants. It seldom, or never happens, that a man of sense, who has experience in any art, cannot judge of its beauty; and it is no less rare to meet with a man who has a just taste without a sound understanding.

Thus, though the principles of taste be universal, and nearly, if not entirely the same in all men; yet few are qualified to give judgment on any work of art, or establish their own sentiment as the standard of beauty. The organs of internal sensation are seldom so perfect as to allow the general principles their full play, and produce a feeling correspondent to those principles. They either labour under some defect, or are vitiated by some disorder; and by that means, excite a sentiment, which may be pronounced erroneous. When the critic has no delicacy, he judges without any distinction, and is only affected by the grosser and more palpable qualities of the object: The finer touches pass unnoticed and disregarded. Where he is not aided by practice, his verdict is attended with confusion and hesitation. Where no comparison has been employed, the most frivolous beauties, such as rather merit the name of defects, are the object of his

admiration. Where he lies under the influence of prejudice, all his natural sentiments are perverted. Where good sense is wanting, he is not qualified to discern
the beauties of design and reasoning, which are the highest and most excellent.
Under some or other of these imperfections, the generality of men labour; and
hence a true judge in the finer arts is observed, even during the most polished
ages, to be so rare a character: Strong sense, united to delicate sentiment, improved by practice, perfected by comparison, and cleared of all prejudice, can
alone entitle critics to this valuable character, and the joint verdict of such,
wherever they are to be found, is the true standard of taste and beauty.

But where are such critics to be found? By what marks are they to be known?
How distinguish them from pretenders? These questions are embarrassing; and
seem to throw us back into the same uncertainty, from which, during the course
of this essay, we have endeavoured to extricate ourselves.

But if we consider the matter aright, these are questions of fact, not of sentiment. Whether any particular person be endowed with good sense and a delicate imagination, free from prejudice, may often be the subject of dispute and
be liable to great discussion and enquiry: But that such a character is valuable
and estimable will be agreed in by all mankind. Where these doubts occur, men
can do no more than in other disputable questions, which are submitted to the
understanding: They must produce the best arguments, that their invention
suggests to them; they must acknowledge a true and decisive standard to exist
somewhere, to wit, real existence and matter of fact; and they must have indulgence to such as differ from them in their appeals to this standard. It is sufficient
for our present purpose, if we have proved, that the taste of all individuals is not
upon an equal footing, and that some men in general, however difficult to be
particularly pitched upon, will be acknowledged by universal sentiment to have
a preference above others.

But in reality the difficulty of finding, even in particulars, the standard of
taste, is not so great as it is represented. Though in speculation, we may readily
avow a certain criterion in science and deny it in sentiment, the matter is found
in practice to be much more hard to ascertain in the former case than in the
latter. Theories of abstract philosophy, systems of profound theology, have prevailed during one age: In a successive period, these have been universally ex-
ploded: Their absurdity has been detected: Other theories and systems have
supplied their place, which again gave place to their successors: And nothing
has been experienced more liable to the revolutions of chance and fashion than
these pretended decisions of science. The case is not the same with the beauties
of eloquence and poetry. Just expressions of passion and nature are sure, after a
little time, to gain public applause, which they maintain for ever. Aristotle, and
Plato, and Epicurus, and Descartes, may successively yield to each other: But
Terence and Virgil maintain an universal, undisputed empire over the minds of
men. The abstract philosophy of Cicero has lost its credit: The vehemence of
his oratory is still the object of our admiration.

Though men of delicate taste be rare, they are easily to be distinguished in
society, by the soundness of their understanding and the superiority of their
faculties above the rest of mankind. The ascendant, which they acquire, gives a

prevalence to that lively approbation, with which they receive any productions of genius, and renders it generally predominant. Many men, when left to themselves, have but a faint and dubious perception of beauty, who yet are capable of relishing any fine stroke, which is pointed out to them. Every convert to the admiration of the real poet or orator is the cause of some new conversion. And though prejudices may prevail for a time, they never unite in celebrating any rival to the true genius, but yield at last to the force of nature and just sentiment. Thus, though a civilised nation may easily be mistaken in the choice of their admired philosopher, they never have been found long to err, in their affection for a favourite epic or tragic author.

But notwithstanding all our endeavours to fix a standard of taste, and reconcile the discordant apprehensions of men, there still remain two sources of variation, which are not sufficient indeed to confound all the boundaries of beauty and deformity, but will often serve to produce a difference in the degrees of our approbation or blame. The one is the different humours of particular men; the other, the particular manners and opinions of our age and country. The general principles of taste are uniform in human nature: Where men vary in their judgments, some defect or perversion in the faculties may commonly be remarked; proceeding either from prejudice, from want of practice, or want of delicacy; and there is just reason for approving one taste, and condemning another. But where there is such a diversity in the internal frame or external situation as is entirely blameless on both sides, and leaves no room to give one the preference above the other, in that case a certain degree of diversity in judgment is unavoidable, and we seek in vain for a standard, by which we can reconcile the contrary sentiments.

A young man, whose passions are warm, will be more sensibly touched with amorous and tender images, than a man more advanced in years, who takes pleasure in wise, philosophical reflections concerning the conduct of life and moderation of the passions. At twenty, Ovid may be the favourite author; Horace at forty; and perhaps Tacitus at fifty. Vainly would we, in such cases, endeavour to enter into the sentiments of others, and divest ourselves of those propensities, which are natural to us. We choose our favourite author as we do our friend, from a conformity of humour and disposition. Mirth or passion, sentiment or reflection; whichever of these most predominates in our temper, it gives us a peculiar sympathy with the writer who resembles us.

One person is more pleased with the sublime; another with the tender; a third with raillery. One has a strong sensibility to blemishes, and is extremely studious of correctness: Another has a more lively feeling of beauties, and pardons twenty absurdities and defects for one elevated or pathetic stroke. The ear of this man is entirely turned towards conciseness and energy; that man is delighted with a copious, rich, and harmonious expression. Simplicity is affected by one; ornament by another. Comedy, tragedy, satire, odes, have each its partizans, who prefer that particular species of writing to all others. It is plainly an error in a critic, to confine his approbation to one species or style of writing, and condemn all the rest. But it is almost impossible not to feel a predilection for that which suits our particular turn and disposition. Such preferences are innocent and unavoidable, and can never reasonably be the object of dispute, because there is no standard, by which they can be decided.

For a like reason, we are more pleased, in the course of our reading, with pictures and characters, that resemble objects which are found in our own age or country, than with those which describe a different set of customs. It is not without some effort, that we reconcile ourselves to the simplicity of ancient manners, and behold princesses carrying water from the spring, and kings and heroes dressing their own victuals. We may allow in general, that the representation of such manners is no fault in the author, nor deformity in the piece; but we are not so sensibly touched with them. For this reason, comedy is not easily transferred from one age or nation to another. A Frenchman or Englishman is not pleased with the Andria of Terence, or Clitia of Machiavel; where the fine lady, upon whom all the play turns, never once appears to the spectators, but is always kept behind the scenes, suitably to the reserved humour of the ancient Greeks and modern Italians. A man of learning and reflection can make allowance for these peculiarities of manners; but a common audience can never divest themselves so far of their usual ideas and sentiments, as to relish pictures which no wise resemble them.

But here there occurs a reflection, which may, perhaps, be useful in examining the celebrated controversy concerning ancient and modern learning; where we often find the one side excusing any seeming absurdity in the ancients from the manners of the age, and the other refusing to admit this excuse, or at least, admitting it only as an apology for the author, not for the performance. In my opinion, the proper boundaries in this subject have seldom been fixed between the contending parties. Where any innocent peculiarities of manners are represented, such as those above mentioned, they ought certainly to be admitted; and a man, who is shocked with them, gives an evident proof of false delicacy and refinement. The poet's *monument more durable than brass,* must fall to the ground like common brick or clay, were men to make no allowance for the continual revolutions of manners and customs, and would admit of nothing but what was suitable to the prevailing fashion. Must we throw aside the pictures of our ancestors, because of their ruffs and fardingales? But where the ideas of morality and decency alter from one age to another, and where vicious manners are described, without being marked with the proper characters of blame and disapprobation; this must be allowed to disfigure the poem, and to be a real deformity. I cannot, nor is it proper I should, enter into such sentiments; and however I may excuse the poet, on account of the manners of his age, I never can relish the composition. The want of humanity and of decency, so conspicuous in the characters drawn by several of the ancient poets, even sometimes by Homer and the Greek tragedians, diminishes considerably the merit of their noble performances, and gives modern authors an advantage over them. We are not interested in the fortunes and sentiments of such rough heroes: We are displeased to find the limits of vice and virtue so much confounded: And whatever indulgence we may give to the writer on account of his prejudices, we cannot prevail on ourselves to enter into his sentiments, or bear an affection to characters, which we plainly discover to be blameable.

The case is not the same with moral principles, as with speculative opinions of any kind. These are in continual flux and revolution. The son embraces a different system from the father. Nay, there scarcely is any man, who can boast of great constancy and uniformity in this particular. Whatever speculative errors may be found in the polite writing of any age or country, they detract but little from the value of those compositions. There needs but a certain turn of thought or imagination to make us enter into all the opinions, which then prevailed, and relish the sentiments or conclusions derived from them. But a very violent effort is requisite to change our judgment of manners, and excite sentiments of approbation or blame, love or hatred, different from those to which the mind from long custom has been familiarized. And where a man is confident of the rectitude of that moral standard, by which he judges, he is justly jealous of it, and will not pervert the sentiments of his heart for a moment, in complaisance to any writer whatsoever.

Of all speculative errors, those, which regard religion, are the most excusable in compositions of genius; nor is it ever permitted to judge of the civility or wisdom of any people, or even of single persons, by the grossness or refinement of their theological principles. The same good sense, that directs men in the ordinary occurrences of life, is not hearkened to in religious matters, which are supposed to be placed altogether above the cognizance of human reason. On this account, all the absurdities of the pagan system of theology must be overlooked by every critic, who would pretend to form a just notion of ancient poetry; and our posterity, in their turn, must have the same indulgence to their forefathers. No religious principles can ever be imputed as a fault to any poet, while they remain merely principles, and take not such strong possession of his heart, as to lay him under the imputation of *bigotry* or *superstition*. Where that happens, they confound the sentiments of morality, and alter the natural boundaries of vice and virtue. They are therefore eternal blemishes, according to the principle abovementioned; nor are the prejudices and false opinions of the age sufficient to justify them.

It is essential to the Roman catholic religion to inspire a violent hatred of every other worship, and to represent all pagans, mahometans, and heretics as the objects of divine wrath and vengeance. Such sentiments, though they are in reality very blameable, are considered as virtues by the zealots of that communion, and are represented in their tragedies and epic poems as a kind of divine heroism. This bigotry has disfigured two very fine tragedies of the French theatre, Polieucte and Athalia; where an intemperate zeal for particular modes of worship is set off with all the pomp imaginable, and forms the predominant character of the heroes. 'What is this,' says the sublime Joad to Josabet, finding her in discourse with Mathan, the priest of Baal, 'Does the daughter of David speak to this traitor? Are you not afraid, lest the earth should open and pour forth flames to devour you both? Or lest these holy walls should fall and crush you together? What is his purpose? Why comes that enemy of God hither to poison the air, which we breathe, with his horrid presence?' Such sentiments are received with great applause on the theatre of Paris; but at London the spectators would be full as much pleased to hear Achilles tell Agamemnon, that he was a dog in his forehead, and a deer in his heart, or Jupiter threaten Juno with a sound drubbing, if she will not be quiet.

Religious principles are also a blemish in any polite composition, when they rise up to superstition, and intrude themselves into every sentiment, however remote from any connection with religion. It is no excuse for the poet, that the customs of his country had burthened life with so many religious ceremonies and observances, that no part of it was exempt from that yoke. It must for ever be ridiculous in Petrarch to compare his mistress, Laura, to Jesus Christ. Nor is it less ridiculous in that agreeable libertine, Boccace, very seriously to give thanks to God Almighty and the ladies, for their assistance in defending him against his enemies.

---

15   From *Distinction*

Pierre Bourdieu

There is an economy of cultural goods, but it has a specific logic. Sociology endeavours to establish the conditions in which the consumers of cultural goods, and their taste for them, are produced, and at the same time to describe the different ways of appropriating such of these objects as are regarded at a particular moment as works of art, and the social conditions of the constitution of the mode of appropriation that is considered legitimate. But one cannot fully understand cultural practices unless 'culture', in the restricted, normative sense of ordinary usage, is brought back into 'culture' in the anthropological sense, and the elaborated taste for the most refined objects is reconnected with the elementary taste for the flavours of food.

Whereas the ideology of charisma regards taste in legitimate culture as a gift of nature, scientific observation shows that cultural needs are the product of upbringing and education: surveys establish that all cultural practices (museum visits, concert-going, reading etc.), and preferences in literature, painting or music, are closely linked to educational level (measured by qualifications or length of schooling) and secondarily to social origin. The relative weight of home background and of formal education (the effectiveness and duration of which are closely dependent on social origin) varies according to the extent to which the different cultural practices are recognized and taught by the educational system, and the influence of social origin is strongest – other things being equal – in 'extra-curricular' and avant-garde culture. To the socially recognized hierarchy of the arts, and within each of them, of genres, schools or periods, corresponds a social hierarchy of the consumers. This predisposes tastes to function as markers of 'class'. The manner in which culture has been acquired lives on in the manner of using it: the importance attached to manners can be understood once it is seen that it is these imponderables of practice which distinguish the different – and ranked – modes of culture acquisition, early or late, domestic or scholastic, and the classes of individuals which they characterize (such as 'pedants' and *mondains*). Culture also has its title of nobility – awarded by the educational system – and its pedigrees, measured by seniority in admission to the nobility.

The definition of cultural nobility is the stake in a struggle which has gone on unceasingly, from the seventeenth century to the present day, between groups differing in their ideas of culture and of the legitimate relation to culture and to works of art, and therefore differing in the conditions of acquisition of which these dispositions are the product. Even in the classroom, the dominant definition of the legitimate way of appropriating culture and works of art favours those who have had early access to legitimate culture, in a cultured household, outside of scholastic disciplines, since even within the educational system it devalues scholarly knowledge and interpretation as 'scholastic' or even 'pedantic' in favour of direct experience and simple delight.

The logic of what is sometimes called, in typically 'pedantic' language, the 'reading' of a work of art, offers an objective basis for this opposition. Consumption is, in this case, a stage in a process of communication, that is, an act of deciphering, decoding, which presupposes practical or explicit mastery of a cipher or code. In a sense, one can say that the capacity to see (*voir*) is a function of the knowledge (*savoir*), or concepts, that is, the words, that are available to name visible things, and which are, as it were, programmes for perception. A work of art has meaning and interest only for someone who possesses the cultural competence, that is, the code, into which it is encoded. The conscious or unconscious implementation of explicit or implicit schemes of perception and appreciation which constitutes pictorial or musical culture is the hidden condition for recognizing the style characteristic of a period, a school or an author, and, more generally, for the familiarity with the internal logic of works that aesthetic enjoyment presupposes. A beholder who lacks the specific code feels lost in a chaos of sounds and rhythms, colours and lines, without rhyme or reason. Not having learnt to adopt the adequate disposition, he stops short at what Erwin Panofsky calls the 'sensible properties,' perceiving a skin as downy or lace-work as delicate, or at the emotional resonances aroused by these properties, referring to 'austere' colours or a 'joyful' melody. He cannot move from the 'primary stratum of the meaning we can grasp on the basis of our ordinary experience' to the 'stratum of secondary meanings', i.e., the 'level of the meaning of what is signified', unless he possesses the concepts which go beyond the sensible properties and which identify the specifically stylistic properties of the work.[1] Thus the encounter with a work of art is not 'love at first sight' as is generally supposed, and the act of empathy, *Einfühlung*, which is the art-lover's pleasure, presupposes an act of cognition, a decoding operation, which implies the implementation of a cognitive acquirement, a cultural code.

This typically intellectualist theory of artistic perception directly contradicts the experience of the art-lovers closest to the legitimate definition; acquisition of legitimate culture by insensible familiarization within the family circle tends to favour an enchanted experience of culture which implies forgetting the acquisition. The 'eye' is a product of history reproduced by education. This is true of the mode of artistic perception now accepted as legitimate, that is, the aesthetic disposition, the capacity to consider in and for themselves, as form rather than function, not only the works designated for such apprehension, i.e., legitimate works of art but everything in the world, including cultural objects which are not yet consecrated – such as, at one time, primitive arts, or, nowadays, popular photography or kitsch – and natural objects. The 'pure' gaze is a historical invention linked to the emergence of an autonomous field of artistic production, that is, a field capable of imposing its own norms on both the production and the consumption of its products. An art which, like all Post-Impressionist painting, is the product of an artistic intention which asserts the primacy of the mode of representation over the object of representation demands categorically an attention to form which previous art only demanded conditionally.

The pure intention of the artist is that of a producer who aims to be autonomous, that is, entirely the master of his product, who tends to reject not only the 'programmes' imposed a priori by scholars and scribes, but also – following the old hierarchy of doing and saying – the interpretations superimposed a posteriori on his work. The production of an 'open work', intrinsically and deliberately polysemic, can thus be understood as the final stage in the conquest of artistic autonomy by poets and, following in their footsteps, by painters, who had long been reliant on writers and their work of 'showing' and 'illustrating'. To assert the autonomy of production is to give primacy to that of which the artist is master, i.e., form, manner, style, rather than the 'subject', the external referent, which involves subordination to functions – even if only the most elementary one, that of representing, signifying, saying something. It also means a refusal to recognize any necessity other than that inscribed in the specific tradition of the artistic discipline in question: the shift from an art which imitates nature to an art which imitates art, deriving from its own history the exclusive source of its experiments and even of its breaks with tradition. An art which ever increasingly contains reference to its own history demands to be perceived historically; it asks to be referred not to an external referent, the represented or designated 'reality', but to the universe of past and present works of art. Like artistic production, in that it is generated in a field, aesthetic perception is necessarily historical, inasmuch as it is differential, relational, attentive to the deviations (*écarts*) which make styles. Like the so-called naive painter who, operating outside the field and its specific traditions, remains external to the history of the art, the 'naive' spectator cannot attain a specific grasp of works of art which only have meaning – or value – in relation to the specific history of an artistic tradition. The aesthetic disposition demanded by the products of a highly autonomous field of production is inseparable from a specific cultural competence. This historical culture functions as a principle of pertinence which enables one to identify, among the elements offered to the gaze, all the distinctive features and only these, by referring them, consciously or unconsciously, to the universe of possible alternatives. This mastery is, for the most part, acquired simply by contact with works of art – that is, through an implicit learning analogous to that which makes it possible to recognize familiar faces without explicit rules or criteria – and it generally remains at a practical level; it is what makes it possible to identify styles, i.e., modes of expression characteristic of a period, a civilisation or a school, without having to distinguish clearly, or state explicitly, the features which constitute their originality. Everything seems to suggest that even among professional valuers, the criteria which define the stylistic properties of the 'typical works' on which all their judgements are based usually remain implicit.

The pure gaze implies a break with the ordinary attitude towards the world, which, given the conditions in which it is performed, is also a social separation. Ortega y Gasset can be believed when he attributes to modern art a systematic refusal of all that is 'human', i.e., generic, common – as opposed to distinctive, or distinguished – namely, the passions, emotions and feelings which 'ordinary' people invest in their 'ordinary' lives. It is as if the 'popular aesthetic' (the quotation marks are there to indicate that this is an aesthetic 'in itself' not 'for itself') were based on the affirmation of the continuity between art and life, which implies the subordination of form to function. This is seen clearly in the case of the novel and especially the theatre, where the working-class audience refuses any sort of formal experimentation and all the effects which, by introducing a distance from the accepted conventions (as regards scenery, plot etc.), tend to distance the spectator, preventing him from getting involved and fully identifying with the characters (I am thinking of Brechtian 'alienation' or the disruption of plot in the *nouveau roman*). In contrast to the detachment and disinterestedness which aesthetic theory regards as the only way of recognizing the work of art for what it is, i.e, autonomous, *selbständig*, the 'popular aesthetic' ignores or refuses the refusal of 'facile' involvement and 'vulgar' enjoyment, a refusal which is the basis of the taste for formal experiment. And popular judgements of paintings or photographs spring from an 'aesthetic' (in fact it is an ethos) which is the exact opposite of the Kantian aesthetic. Whereas, in order to grasp the specificity of the aesthetic judgement, Kant strove to distinguish that which pleases from that which gratifies and, more generally, to distinguish disinterestedness, the sole guarantor of the specifically aesthetic quality of contemplation, from the interest of reason which defines the Good, working-class people expect every image to explicitly perform a function, if only that of a sign, and their judgements make reference, often explicitly, to the norms of morality or agreeableness. Whether rejecting or praising, their appreciation always has an ethical basis.

Popular taste applies the schemes of the ethos, which pertain in the ordinary circumstances of life, to legitimate works of art, and so performs a systematic reduction of the things of art to the things of life. The very seriousness (or naivety) which this taste invests in fictions and representations demonstrates a contrario that pure taste performs a suspension of 'naive' involvement which is one dimension of a 'quasi-ludic' relationship with the necessities of the world. Intellectuals could be said to believe in the representation – literature, theatre, painting – more than in the things represented, whereas the people chiefly expect representations and the conventions which govern them to allow them to believe 'naively' in the things represented. The pure aesthetic is rooted in an ethic, or rather, an ethos of elective distance from the necessities of the natural and social world, which may take the form of moral agnosticism (visible when ethical transgression become an artistic *parti pris*) or of an aestheticism which presents the aesthetic disposition as a universally valid principle and takes the bourgeois denial of the social world to its limit. The detachment of the pure gaze cannot be dissociated from a general disposition towards the world which is the paradoxical product of conditioning by negative economic necessities – a life of ease – that tends to induce an active distance from necessity.

Although art obviously offers the greatest scope to the aesthetic disposition, there is no area of practice in which the aim of purifying, refining and sublimating primary needs and impulses cannot assert itself, no area in which the stylization of life, that is, the primacy of forms over function, of manner over matter, does not produce the same effects. And nothing is more distinctive, more distinguished, than the capacity to confer aesthetic status on objects that are banal or even 'common' (because the 'common' people make them their own, especially for aesthetic purposes), or the ability to apply the principles of a 'pure' aesthetic to the most everyday choices of everyday life, e.g., in cooking, clothing or decoration, completely reversing the popular disposition which annexes aesthetics to ethics.

In fact, through the economic and social conditions which they presuppose, the different ways of relating to realities and fictions, of believing in fictions and the realities they simulate, with more or less distance and detachment, are very closely linked to the different possible positions in social space and, consequently, bound up with the systems of dispositions (habitus) characteristic of the different classes and class fractions. Taste classifies, and it classifies the classifier. Social subjects, classified by their classifications, distinguish themselves by the distinctions they make between the beautiful and the ugly, the distinguished and the vulgar, in which their position in the objective classifications is expressed or betrayed. And statistical analysis does indeed show that oppositions similar in structure to those found in cultural practices also appear in eating habits. The antithesis between quantity and quality, substance and form, corresponds to the opposition – linked to different distances from necessity – between the taste of necessity, which favours the most 'filling' and most economical foods, and the taste of liberty – or luxury – which shifts the emphasis to the manner (of presenting, serving, eating etc.) and tends to use stylized forms to deny function.

The science of taste and of cultural consumption begins with a transgression that is in no way aesthetic: it has to abolish the sacred frontier which makes legitimate culture a separate universe, in order to discover the intelligible relations which unite apparently incommensurable 'choices', such as preferences in music and food, painting and sport, literature and hairstyle. This barbarous reintegration of aesthetic consumption into the world of ordinary consumption abolishes the opposition, which has been the basis of high aesthetics since Kant, between the 'taste of sense' and the 'taste of reflection', and between facile pleasure, pleasure reduced to a pleasure of the senses, and pure pleasure, pleasure purified of pleasure, which is predisposed to become a symbol of moral excellence and a measure of the capacity for sublimation which defines the truly human man. The culture which results from this magical division is sacred. Cultural consecration does indeed confer on the objects, persons and situations it touches, a sort of ontological promotion akin to a transubstantiation. [. . .]

The denial of lower, coarse, vulgar, venal, servile – in a word, natural – enjoyment, which constitutes the sacred sphere of culture, implies an affirmation of the superiority of those who can be satisfied with the sublimated, refined, disinterested, gratuitous, distinguished pleasure forever closed to the profane. That is why art and cultural consumption are predisposed, consciously and deliberately or not, to fulfil a social function of legitimating social differences.

Note

1   E. Panofsky, 'Iconography and Iconology: An Introduction to the Study of Renaissance Art', *Meaning in the Visual Arts* (New York: Doubleday, 1955), p. 28.

16   Disinterestedness and Political Art

Peggy Zeglin Brand

Can an ordinary viewer ever experience art – particularly politically charged, socially relevant art – in a neutral, detached, and objective way? The familiar philosophical notion of disinterestedness has its roots in eighteenth-century theories of taste and was refined throughout the twentieth century. In contrast, many contemporary theorists have argued for what I call an "interested approach" in order to expand beyond the traditional emphasis on neutrality and universality. Each group, in effect, has argued for the value of a work of art by excluding the other's approach. This essay will consider the legacy of the concept of disinterestedness for contemporary aesthetic theory in light of challenges posed by postmodern skepticism regarding the possibility of disinterestedness, and by the difficulties involved in appreciating political art with a disinterested attitude. My principal examples of political art will be drawn from feminist art.[1]

Unlike traditional philosophers, I will advocate that an interested stance toward art is, at times, inevitable and appropriate. I will also argue not only that feminist art – and by extension political art of all kinds – *can* be experienced disinterestedly, but that it should be. As a position inconsistent with both traditionalists and feminist critics of tradition, my recommendation of both disinterestedness and interestedness affords what I take to be the fullest and fairest experience of a work of art.

In the early eighteenth century Anthony, Earl of Shaftesbury, proposed disinterestedness as both a moral and an aesthetic ideal in opposition to the notion of private interest (derived from Hobbes) in order to isolate the aspects of a mental state that precluded serving one's own ends. Disinterestedness was contrasted with the desire to possess or use an object. Francis Hutcheson concurred and recommended the exclusion of "feeling to what farther advantage or detriment the use of such objects might tend."[2] Edmund Burke placed disinterestedness at the center of his theory of beauty, frequently citing the female body as a beautiful object which can be perceived as beautiful only if the sole interest of the perceiver is in perceiving for its own sake and not in the desire for possession. In speaking of the quality of beauty exemplified in "gradual vari-ation," he states:

> Observe that part of a beautiful woman where she is perhaps the most beautiful, about the neck and breasts; the smoothness; the softness; the easy and insensible swell; the variety of the surface, which is never for the smallest space the same; the deceitful maze, through which the unsteady eye slides giddily, without knowing where to fix, or whither it is carried.[3]

Archibald Alison maintained that it was not enough to lack self-seeking motives; rather, we must attain a state of mind in which

> the attention is so little occupied by any private or particular object of thought, as to leave us open to all the impressions, which the objects that are before us can produce.[4]

David Hume contrasted private and public interest; public interest was communal and free of individual bonds. Hume adumbrated Kant's sense of disinterestedness in his recommendation that a true judge is one who is free from personal prejudice:

> considering myself as a man in general, [I must] forget, if possible, my individual being and my peculiar circumstances.[5]

Kant expanded the notion of aesthetic disinterestedness, separating it from the practical and conceptual realms: to be disinterested was to be without interest in the object's existence. Making the notion of disinterestedness central transferred the focus of the aesthetic experience to the perceiver and away from the work of art. It was only a short step to the aesthetic attitude theorists' insistence that attitude was the primary determinant of one's aesthetic judgments. Jerome Stolnitz, a twentieth-century aesthetic attitude theorist, extended the previous ideas of Alison:

> To perceive disinterestedly is to make oneself a pure, unflawed mirror, prepared to receive without distortion "all the impressions, which the objects that are before us can produce."[6]

On this view, no object could be excluded from the realm of the aesthetic; by properly adopting a particular mode of perception, any object could be perceived with an aesthetic attitude, i.e., disinterestedly. Thus, far from acknowledging what some would consider a thoroughly human and "natural" reaction we have to images of the body – especially to the many depictions we find in the history of art of the female nude – these philosophers promulgated a self-conscious, deliberate and controlled transformation of interest into the more acceptable form of dispassionate *dis*-interest.

Consider what this means in practical terms for viewing art and the ways in which we have been taught to look at art. Let us review a typical explanation of an artwork by the noted psychologist of art, Rudolf Arnheim, in his landmark publication, *Art and Visual Perception*: an 1856 painting by Jean Auguste Ingres entitled *La Source* (Plate 9). Arnheim concurs with the generally accepted view

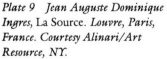

Plate 9 Jean Auguste Dominique Ingres, La Source. *Louvre, Paris, France. Courtesy Alinari/Art Resource, NY.*

that visual perception "is not a passive recording of stimulus material but an active concern of the mind."[7] Note the process by which he analyzes the ways in which an image can be perceived and subsequently interpreted. First, he refers to the painted nude girl standing upright in a frontal position and holding a water jug as follows:

> At first sight it shows such qualities as lifelikeness, sensuousness, simplicity ... Ingres' nudes make the observer almost forget that he is looking at works of art.[8]

Gazing as a male (which he unavoidably is), this initial reaction is not based so much on confusion over disambiguating what he sees as on an automatic response to the sexuality depicted, a reaction perhaps not unlike the one the painter may have felt who found himself painting the actual nude model before him. The implication is that it is difficult for a male viewer to maintain a disengagement of interest given the lifelikeness of the painted girl posed and displayed before him. Arnheim's initial reaction is unabashedly interested as he points out how the jug and the girl are both vessels with "uterine connotations," i.e.,

> the vessel openly releases the stream whereas the lap is locked. In short, the picture plays on the theme of withheld but promised femininity.[9]

He goes on, however, to provide a lengthy description of the formal properties of the scene: the unnatural posture of the girl as she tilts the jug she's holding, the tilt to the left of both head and jug, the analogous flows of water and hair, the vertical axis and the oblique central axes and their contrasting curves and contours. He concludes:

> The remarkable fact about a masterpiece like "La Source" is that in looking at it we sense the effect of the formal devices whose meaning makes it such a complete representation of life and yet we may not be conscious of these devices at all.[10]

How does he isolate and interpret these formal devices that so deceptively convince us that there is a lifelike girl before us?

His answer, found in another of his works entitled *Visual Thinking*, provides a useful lesson as to how the mind is able to abstract an object under observation from its context. He calls this process "subtracting the context."

> The observer may wish to peel off the context in order to obtain the object as it is and as it behaves by itself, as though it existed in complete isolation. This may seem to be the only possible way of performing an abstraction.[11]

By this route, he attains a disinterested approach, by stripping away as much interest as he can. In attempting to treat the depicted object "as though it existed in complete isolation" from its context, he abstracts the compositional elements by blocking their associations and similarity to actual nude girls (and thereby subtracting the context). Arnheim sees this as a clear indication of the "intelligence of visual perception" (this is the chapter title in which the visual exercise is embedded); such intelligence exemplifies the cognitive, i.e., rational activity – the "active concern of the mind" – that plays so crucial a role in perception and interpretation.

Denying one's identification and involvement with the work on a personal level is what many feminists see as a masculinist stance, that is, one that seeks mastery even over one's own bodily responses. Inhibiting one's natural and instinctive *gendered* reactions in a self-conscious, controlling way is seen as psychological censure. According to feminist thinking, disinterestedness is a prime example of a masculinist mode of thought in which it is assumed that the best (and only?) way to experience a work of art is as a neutral, unbiased, selfless observer. Feminists doubt one can ever really be neutral and they discourage its use as a tool in the evaluation of art.

What is notable for our purposes here is that a feminist stance toward art recommends the antithesis of the suggestions listed by the eighteenth-century philosophers. In stark contrast, a feminist stance – often considered subjective or emotional – encourages interest in, identification with, and nurturing of awareness. Thus, it promotes interest with regard to how the image of woman is used or possessed; an inclusion of feeling for advantage or detriment; a nurturing of one's personal, individual interests; and the open admission that no viewer is a "pure, unflawed mirror" ready to receive with openness all the impressions which the objects that are before us can produce. In effect, to adopt a feminist stance is to refuse to "dis" one's interest and to acknowledge and even encourage an interested approach. For feminists, there can be no such thing as a disinterested approach to a work of art; the very attempt participates in an endeavor to posit a particular type of viewer as an ideal, neutral spectator. The only recommended way to properly and fully experience a work of art is with an avowedly gendered, identificatory, interested stance.

According to feminist art critic Katy Deepwell,

> Feminism's critique of the disinterested observer exposed the partisan nature of all readings (when that "neutral" figure was identified as white, male and middle-class), and began to explore how reading is inevitably informed by political positions.[12]

On this view, disinterestedness is a masculinist stance toward art that involves what feminists have recently come to identify as the male gaze.

The most familiar and influential articulation of a theory of the gaze comes from the 1975 film criticism of Laura Mulvey. In an essay entitled "Visual Pleasure and Narrative Cinema," Mulvey initiated an analysis of women characters in the films of Hitchcock and Sternberg based on psychoanalytic readings that identified women as objects of the male gaze.[13] In uncovering and explicating a notion of the male gaze Mulvey sought to challenge the conventional notions of pleasure derived from mainstream film by highlighting the role of gender in the spectator's viewing of the female body on the screen. When a male viewer looks at the image of a woman, he typically looks with a possessing, desiring, objectifying look. His gaze succumbs to his scopophilic tendency to look at her as *erotic* object, to derive masculine pleasure from the power of his gaze over her body — a body on view for his delectation. This gaze is similar to two other types of male gazing that goes on within film: the gaze of the film-maker and camera men who manipulate the technology that defines the medium, and the gaze of the male actors who look at and interact with the woman being filmed. For Mulvey, cinema is uniquely positioned as the artistic medium that provides the paradigm of the male gaze:

> The place of the look defines cinema, the possibility of shifting it, varying it and exposing it. This is what makes cinema quite different in its voyeuristic potential from, say, striptease, theatre, shows and so on. Going far beyond high-lighting a woman's to-be-looked-at-ness, cinema builds the way she is to be looked at into the spectacle itself.[14]

Thus, the person looked at is the woman. Her spectator is male: Hitchcock as film-maker, his camera men, the male "heroes" within the films, and the male audience.[15]

In a later essay, Mulvey addresses the challenge from many readers that film-goers are presumed to be exclusively male. Rather than attempt to isolate and explain a particularly female look or gaze which might give rise to a particularly feminine sort of pleasure, she instead extended her earlier analysis to female viewers, claiming that women who watch the same films come to view them *as men* – with a male gaze – learned through habituation and training. The female spectator's masculine point of view is a "trans-sex identification," i.e., "a *habit* that very easily becomes *second nature*."[16] In other words, women gaze at women in films as men do: by viewing them as erotic objects on view for the pleasure of heterosexual males (both inside and outside the filmic structure), as potential possessions of males, as subjects of male fantasies and desires.[17]

Clearly, Mulvey's thesis is not without problems. It has spawned an enormous amount of commentary and debate. It is undeniably the source, however, of two important consequences: (1) an ongoing investigation into the question of how women artists and film-makers can utilize a woman's body in visual representations without becoming complicit voyeurs, and (2) spin-off notions of the male gaze such as bell hooks' "oppositional gaze." What these varied analyses share is a deep and unyielding skepticism of anything like a neutral, distanced, disinterested mode of perception. The general consensus is that there is no disinterested gazer of visual images, only one whose gaze is saturated *with interest*. With this recognition, it comes as no surprise that most feminists advocate a pro-active, self-conscious, *interested* form of looking: one that blocks our learned tendency to view any subject according to conventional values of critical reception.

For instance, along the lines of Mulvey's concept of trans-sex identification, bell hooks proposes a similar notion: what might aptly be called trans-race identification. In the early days of television and film, black spectators became habituated to look at blacks on the screen the same way as whites, that is, to fail to notice the absence of blacks in television and Hollywood film, to accept without challenge stereotypically degrading and dehumanizing representations of blacks, and to laugh condescendingly at black characters in early shows like *Our Gang* and *Amos and Andy*. Only within the last few years has a body of film theory and criticism begun to emerge that recommends a self-consciousness about the embeddedness of color within one's gaze, especially an awareness of the way in which race and racism determines the visual construction of gender. In an essay entitled, "The Oppositional Gaze: Black Female Spectators," hooks writes:

> Looking at films with an oppositional gaze, black women were able to critically assess the cinema's construction of white womanhood as object of phallocentric gaze and choose not to identify with either the victim or the perpetrator. Black female spectators, who refused to identify with white womanhood, who would not take on the phallocentric gaze of desire and possession, created a critical space where the binary opposition Mulvey posits of "woman as image, man as bearer of the look" was continually deconstructed.[18]

On hooks' analysis, another layer is added to the construction of a feminist interested stance. Besides gender, one is also encouraged to gaze with interest in the racial dynamics of the representations of women. Many other layers of interest can be added as well: class, sexual orientation, ethnicity, disability, and so on.[19] This returns us to the topic of political art and my initial question, can one experience a work of art, particularly a feminist work of art, in a neutral, detached, objective, disinterested way?

Consider one example of particularly provocative feminist art: the performances of Orlan, a French artist who began her career as a painter and has systematically undergone a series of reconstructive surgeries by which she will totally transform her face. Entitled *The Reincarnation of St Orlan*, each "performance" since 1990 is an actual surgical operation designed to alter a specific facial feature and bring it into conformity with some art historically defined criteria of beauty. According to art critic Barbara Rose:

> Supplying surgeons with computer-generated images of the nose of a famous, unattributed School of Fontainebleau sculpture of Diana, the mouth of Boucher's Europa, the forehead of Leonardo's Mona Lisa, the chin of Botticelli's Venus and the eyes of Gerome's Psyche as guides to her transformation, Orlan also decorates the operating rooms with enlarged reproductions of the relevant details from these same works.[20]

Orlan's goal is not to be beautiful, but rather "to represent an ideal formulated by male desire" as she "uses her body as a medium of transformation . . . to deconstruct mythological images of women."[21] Orlan's guides are paintings by past male artists; she creates the ultimate *self*-portrait: not with paint, but with a scalpel.[22] In true 1990s style, she calls her work "techno-art."[23] She claims her

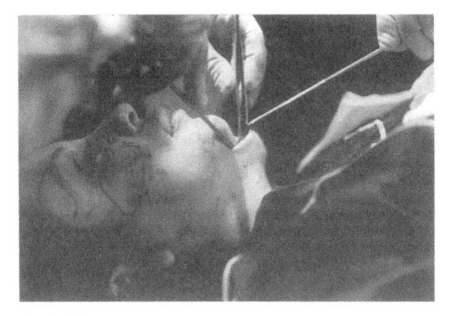

Plate 10 Orlan, Omnipresence, *scene from Seventh Plastic Surgical Operation, November 21, 1993. Courtesy Sichov/Sipa.*

goal is to show that no woman can ever attain a male-defined ideal of beauty and therefore, all attempts are futile. Her art is meant to discourage women from reconstructive surgery.

The still photographs that serve as documents of videotaped performances such as *Omnipresence* (Orlan's seventh operation: November 21, 1993) form fascinating compositions of lights and darks, body parts and surgical instruments, that are at first glance somewhat indecipherable (Plates 10 and 11). They are like ambiguous images: difficult to read. Once deciphered, most viewers are incredulous as to their grisly realism.[24] Initially repelled by the blood and gore depicted in these photos, viewers tend to identify with Orlan to some degree or other, explainable in a variety of ways. Some may empathize with the pain she is apparently enduring (until learning she has undergone epidural anaesthesia) while some may assume a physically-charged male gaze that implies domination and possession. Women viewers in particular may identify with her as the *object* of the masculine gaze, sympathizing with her goal "to represent an ideal formulated by male desire" since they care greatly about whether they conform to prevailing standards of beauty. Insofar as any of these viewers identify with the work, they take an interest in it. To the degree that their interest is self-conscious and self-directed, it becomes an *interested* stance. According to feminist theories advocating an interested stance, such viewers are correctly and fully experiencing the work. But according to the legacy of philosophical notions of disinterestedness, these viewers should block any empathy felt for the artist and attempt to experience the art *dis*interestedly. Is this possible and if so, how might this be accomplished?

I believe it is not only possible but also advisable. I would like to explore a

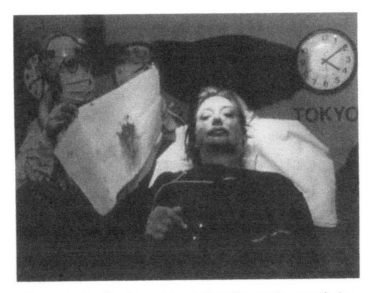

Plate 11 Orlan, Omnipresence, *scene from the operating room during Seventh Plastic Surgical Operation, November 21, 1993. Courtesy Sandra Gering Gallery, New York.*

position that lies somewhere between the two extremes: the traditional endorsement of masculinist disinterestedness on the one hand and its feminist antithesis on the other. What I suggest here is a bit of "gender treason" defined as "the simultaneous endorsement of both authority and freedom, order and flexibility, objectivity and subjectivity, and reason and feeling."[25] I will argue that although the adoption of a stance of traditional disinterestedness is a masculinist approach to the experiencing of a work of art, it is still a possible and appropriate, useful mode of experiencing art, including feminist art, when reconfigured along revisionist lines. What I call Interested Attention (IA) may persist only for the duration of one's initial encounter. It may last for the first few seconds, or it may come later. It may be interspersed with brief moments or long intervals of what I will call Disinterested Attention (DA). The "toggle" between the two types of attention might be deliberate or not. In any case, one cannot "see" with both types of attention at once. One either experiences the work with IA or DA. This is analogous to a person switching between seeing the duck and seeing the rabbit in the well-known duck-rabbit drawing (Figure 2). Sometimes one intends to switch from reading it one way to the other and is successful. At other times, no matter how strongly one attempts to switch, one is not successful. Finally, there are times when one finds the switch occurring involuntarily, in spite of an attempt to focus on the duck or the rabbit exclusively.

Although he was not commenting on such a picture in particular, Hume's observations on one's initial encounter with a work of art are worth noting:

> There is a flutter or hurry of thought which attends the first perusal of any piece, and which confounds the genuine sentiment of beauty. The relation of the parts is

Figure 2   Duck-rabbit drawing

not discerned; The true characters of style are little distinguished: The several perfections and defects seem wrapped up in a species of confusion, and present themselves indistinctly to the imagination.[27]

Clearly a duck-rabbit picture does not present us with as much "confusion" as a more complicated work of art like a photograph of an incision of Orlan's face, since there are only two choices: the duck and the rabbit. But the analogy is worth pursuing. Current theories of the psychology of perception utilize ambiguous images to demonstrate the same point: that there is what Hume called a "flutter or hurry of thought" that confuses and confounds one's cognitive processing of the image in a work of art. Moreover, what one expects to see can often affect what one does see.

Take another recognizable ambiguous figure: the well-known old woman/ young woman illustration (Figure 3A).[28] According to the perceptual construction hypothesis, a viewer's choice of seeing an image one way or another depends upon the perceptual organization she chooses, i.e., the context. This context may be within the stimulus pattern itself or it may be provided by the subject's expectations. If a viewer has been shown a less ambiguous image of the young woman (Figure 3B) before viewing the ambiguous one, she is more likely to see the latter as the young woman rather than the old. Similarly, if she has been shown a less ambiguous image of the old woman (Figure 3C) before viewing the original ambiguous one, she is more likely to see the latter as the old woman rather than the young. Far from being passive receptors of external stimuli, our sensory systems "actively transform their stimulus inputs."[29] Visual patterns are constructions created by the perceiver, and the perception of patterns is heavily affected by experience and expectations.

It is said that we are typically unaware of our mental sets; we can be predisposed toward one particular perceptual organization without knowing that we are. But surely it is possible to also deliberately manipulate the awareness we

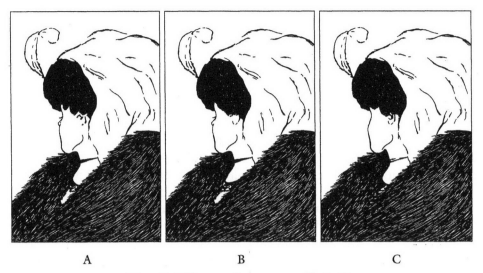

A   B   C

Figure 3   Old woman/young woman illustration

have of our mental sets. One's initial confusion upon encountering a work of art is a preliminary configuring of our mental set to construct both a pattern and an interpretation from what is perceived. Some parts of this process are under our control. Seeing a still photograph out of its original context – a videotape of the surgical process – a viewer of a single image documenting Orlan's "Omnipresence" scrambles to clarify the ambiguities of what is seen. She may be confused at first since freeze-framing the action is not usually the way performances are viewed. But as documents of a performance, they are often studied as individual still shots, and upon encountering such an image, she may attend disinterestedly to the image and ask, "What am I seeing?" Recognizing what the forms and colors depict, the more pressing question becomes whether one can actually believe what one is seeing (thinking that perhaps it's only a computer-generated image). Once verified as a photographic document of real surgery, a viewer (as noted earlier) might empathize with the artist: either by imagining the pain and discomfort of the procedure or, in the case of female viewers, by sympathizing with the need to aspire toward some socially prescribed ideal of beauty. A quick reminder that the image is a work of art and not just a picture of someone's cosmetic surgery might cause another reversal, this time a disengagement with the rapport one has established – a reversal of personal interest – to an intellectual engagement with the content of the work of art. In keeping with the legacy of conceptual art of the 1960s, this engagement with the work of art as art would involve the recognition of Orlan's goal to deconstruct mythological images of women plus the contemplation of herself as the representation of an ideal "formulated by male desire." This final phase (although the possibility of toggling between IA and DA still remains) embodies the revisionist notion of DA sketched earlier: one that attempts to capture what it means to engage intellectually and disengage emotionally with the work of art. Similar though not wholly adoptive of eighteenth-century con-

Figure 4   Pronged figures. © American Psychological Association.
By permission of APA, D. Medin, and R. Goldstone

ceptions of disinterestedness, it encourages attending with a dismissal of as many interests or prejudices as possible, with the full realization that – try as one might – we cannot be pure, unflawed mirrors that reflect the work.

The important point is that the experience and concomitant effect of the work of art rely upon input from both modes of attention, each with its own conceptual framework. After all, one can look at an image of a nude female body with DA by attending – as best as possible – to its color, texture, and overall balance as well as viewing it with a possessing or objectifying male gaze (IA). A viewer's contextual structuring is analogous to wearing different glasses or lenses that affect one's vision; switching and adding mental sets is like changing one's lenses or wearing multiple lenses. One can view representations with a gendered lens, a raced lens, or any other designated lens, but one cannot view and interpret an image with no lens at all. Thus, there is no pure disinterested stance; there is only something *approximating* it. Donning a lens of formal appreciation and intellectual analysis – voluntarily or not – strips away as many of the lenses as one is capable of discarding.[30]

There is recent evidence that shows that *similarity* plays an important role in deciding between incompatible readings. In an experiment in which subjects were given incompatible visual contextual clues before interpreting an ambiguous picture, properties were attributed to the picture based on whether it was being compared with one or the other *even if* the interpretations yielded were mutually exclusive. It was the context of comparison (or the comparison class) that determined the mental set for the processing of the picture based on similarity. For instance, an ambiguous pronged figure could be interpreted as possessing three or four prongs, depending on whether the right-most protrusion is considered to be part of the base or a prong (Figure 4A). When a subject viewed an unambiguous three-pronged version (Figure 4B), it influenced the reading of the ambiguous figure as three-pronged. When s/he viewed an unambiguous four-pronged figure (Figure 4C), it influenced the reading of the ambiguous figure as four-pronged. Similarity played a key role in influencing the predispositional mental set that affected the resultant interpretation.[31]

Reconsider the ambiguous figures of the old woman/young woman and the duck/rabbit. As already noted, when provided with a disambiguated visual clue, viewers tended to interpret the ambiguous figure of the woman based on its similarity to the given clue. In the case of the duck/rabbit, a discussion of one animal or the other affected the interpretation of the ambiguous image, again based on similarity. The sensory contexts enabled viewers to choose between two incompatible interpretations. Incompatible interpretations were considered viable and there was clearly no problem vacillating between them as long as the two were not considered simultaneously. I would like to suggest that the same possibility holds with vacillating between the mutually incompatible approaches of DA and IA.

Extrapolating from the results of these experiments, I would suggest that the reason Arnheim and others viewing with a male gaze find themselves initially responding with interest in a physical, eroticized way to the nude body in *La Source* and perhaps even to the bruised and bloody face of Orlan is that their initial response is *similar to* their unambiguous sexualized predispositions. In confronting the images of nude body and bloody face, they scramble to sort through the confusion of interpretations in much the same way as do viewers of more trivial ambiguous images. In these cases, like the more trivial cases of duck/rabbit and old woman/young woman, the resulting interpretations are mutually exclusive yet viable provided they are not held at one and the same time. What is taking place is a deliberate dis-ing of the gazer's tendency to use, take advantage of, desire, or possess the girl that is pictured; it is an attempt to be open to receiving all the impressions that the work can provide. It is a shift toward the eighteenth-century concept of disinterestedness, which is clearly a denial of Arnheim's initial and intrusive interests: an attraction to the work's sensuality singularly "locked" within (the forbidden femininity). To say that images and works of art "yield" impressions is to misconstrue the process and to philosophically rely on precedent and the weight of tradition; both Alison in the eighteenth century and Stolnitz in the twentieth were incorrect to empha- size the art object and its potential to yield impressions (as if the possibilities were simply there for the taking by passive percipients). However Arnheim, for example, self-consciously reconfigures his mental set to perform "an abstrac- tion/subtraction" on the nude body under his gaze in order to attain some form of DA, thus adding to his experiences of the painting. In striving to be- come an impure, flawed mirror (remember there is no pure, unflawed mirror and hence, no pure DA), he is more open to all the impressions that the work might provide. From this exercise we learn how to attend disinterestedly to art.

But – in switching to a disinterested stance – can one be said to be *fully* experiencing the work of art? Certainly not. Large components of the signifi- cance and the meaning of art are blocked by the assumption of DA. But they may be retrieved through the imaginative exercise of IA. Can a viewer — male or female — who is conditioned to view the image of a woman with a male gaze reconfigure his/her mental set yet again to allow for an interpretation that is similar to a feminist interpretation, *viz.*, that the girl on display is embarrassed by her nakedness, is outraged by being reduced to body parts on display for (clothed) male viewers, is feeling exploited and abused at the expense of male pleasure? Succeeding at this reading of the image may count as "adding" a context instead of subtracting. In any case, it constitutes a deliberate *building* (not dis-ing) of interest in the nude body on display: a clear case of IA with a feminist lens. Changing lenses would enable one to be open to more impressions than ever before, although a viewer might admittedly prefer some to others.

Finally, this extensive detour through IA, DA, and then lA(s) again, provides a model for the feminist who is committed to the goal of expanding viewers' reactions to art. The feminist viewer of Ingres' nude or Orlan's surgeries – whose tendency is to adopt a more physically and bodily based interested stance (IA) like Arnheim's – may also benefit from the lesson of undergoing an intellectualizing and abstracting process. Like the viewer with the male gaze, who undergoes a radical shift by learning to view with a feminist lens, the feminist who looks upon Ingres' nude formalistically is self-consciously and deliberately shedding her feminist lens to view the work as disinterestedly as possible. Viewing *La Source* in terms of geometry and color adds to the variety of experiences she gains from the piece. Again, such shedding of lenses might arise involuntarily or it may become a habitual, learned practice.[32]

One final question still needs to be answered. Granted, a feminist can jump between IA and DA when viewing women in Hitchcock films and Ingres paintings, but can she do so when the image in question is intentionally feminist? Leaving aside the complications philosophers are prone to raise when dealing with artists' intentions, suffice it to say for the purpose of this investigation that Orlan has been up front about the feminist intent of her art and more than one feminist art critic has sanctioned *The Reincarnation* as feminist. (In this case, the well-known art critic Barbara Rose.) I do not foresee the mental exercise required of a viewer (any viewer, but more particularly, a feminist viewer) to be any different in kind from the types of reconfigurations mentioned above on the part of a critic like Arnheim or the feminist viewer of Ingres' nude girl. The adoption of a Revised Disinterested mode of Attention might be more challenging with difficult political art, but only in the level of exertion required and not in the type. Switching from feminist IA to DA with regard to feminist art is still an exercise in subtracting the context. In the case of Orlan, it is a deliberate shift toward viewing bloody facial features as combinations of reds and purples, darks and lights, and a shift to reflection on the concept of women and of art exploited by the performance series. The former switch is in fact, at the heart of every feminist analysis of the formal properties of women's quilts, the composition of the vaginal iconography of Judy Chicago's *Dinner Party*, and Cindy Sherman's recent photographs of maimed mannequins and bloody body parts.

Works of art can yield multiple, even conflicting, sorts of experiences. But we must give them the chance to do so by encouraging ourselves to be open to all the impressions such a representation might yield. We may not be pure, unflawed mirrors, but we are mirrors whose cognitive mechanisms function, at least in part, on perceived similarities between our mental sets and what we disambiguate. One of the most laudatory aspects of art is its ability to make us look within: at our inner selves, our predispositions, our mental sets. We can attempt to be neutral and objective, in the spirit of the traditional notion of disinterestedness, while recognizing that a Revised notion of DA is not co-extensive with that notion.

Notes

1   Some political art is also activist art especially when the art intends to convey an ideological message or motivation. For a defense of the work of Jenny Holzer, Barbara Kruger, and Adrian Piper against charges by art critic Donald Kuspit, see my essay, "Revising the Aesthetic–Nonaesthetic Distinction: The Aesthetic Value of Activist Art," in *Feminism and Tradition in Aesthetics*, eds Peggy Zeglin Brand and Carolyn Korsmeyer (Philadelphia: Penn State Press, 1995), 245–72.

2   Francis Hutcheson, *An Inquiry into the Original of our Ideas of Beauty and Virtue* [1725], in George Dickie and Richard J. Sclafani, eds, *Aesthetics: A Critical Anthology* (New York: St Martin's Press, 1977), 573.

3   Edmund Burke, *A Philosophical Enquiry into the Origin of our Ideas of the Sublime and Beautiful*, ed. J. T. Boulton (London: Routledge and Kegan Paul, 1958), 115.

4   Archibald Alison, *Essays on the Nature and Principles of Taste*, 5th ed. (London: Ward, Lock, and Co., 1817), 71.

5   David Hume, "Of the Standard of Taste" [1757] in *Aesthetics: A Critical Anthology*, 600.

6   Jerome Stolnitz, "On the Origins of 'Aesthetic Disinterestedness'," originally published in *The Journal of Aesthetics and Art Criticism* (Winter, 1961), 131–43, reprinted in *Aesthetics: A Critical Anthology*, 618. [See the selection by Stolnitz in Section II of this volume.]

7   Rudolf Arnheim, *Visual Thinking* (Berkeley: University of California Press, 1969), 37.

8   Rudolf Arnheim, *Art and Visual Perception: A Psychology of the Creative Eye* (Berkeley: University of California Press, 1964), 117.

9   Ibid.

10   Ibid., 120.

11   Arnheim, *Visual Thinking*, 38.

12   Katy Deepwell, ed., *New Feminist Art Criticism* (Manchester: Manchester University Press, 1995), 8. Deepwell refers to Christine Battersby's critique of Kantian aesthetics in "Situating the Aesthetic: A Feminist Defence," in A. Benjamin and P. Osborne, eds, *Thinking Art: Beyond Traditional Aesthetics* (London: ICA (Philosophical Forum), 1991), 31–44.

13   Laura Mulvey, "Visual Pleasure and Narrative Cinema," in *Visual and Other Pleasures* (Indianapolis: Indiana University Press, 1989), 14–26; originally published in *Screen* (Autumn, 1975).

14   Ibid., 25.

15   The heroes include the policeman in *Vertigo*, the dominant male possessing money and power in *Marnie*, and the photo-journalist whose sole enterprise is the viewing of others through a camera lens, in particular a woman in another apartment in *Rear Window*.

16   Laura Mulvey, "Afterthoughts on 'Visual Pleasure and Narrative Cinema' inspired by *Duel in the Sun*," in *Visual and Other Pleasures*, 33. Reprinted from *Framework* (Summer, 1981).

17   Art historians such as Griselda Pollock have extended this analysis to painting. See her *Vision and Difference: Femininity, Feminism and the Histories of Art* (New York: Routledge, 1988).

18   bell hooks, "The Oppositional Gaze: Black Female Spectators," *Feminism and*

Tradition in Aesthetics, 149–50; originally published in *Black Looks: Race and Representation* (Boston: South End Press, 1992), 115–31. hooks laments the slow increase in the number of black critics writing about art in *Art On My Mind: Visual Politics* (New York: New Press, 1995).

19 For an account of the dynamics of whites assuming black face and vice versa, see Susan Gubar's *Racechanges: White Skin, Black Face in American Culture* (New York: Oxford University Press, 1997)

20 Barbara Rose, "Is It Art? Orlan and the Transgressive Act," *Art in America* 81 (2) (February, 1993), 82–7, 125. See also Kathy Davis, "'My Body is My Art' Cosmetic Surgery as Feminist Utopia?" *The European Journal of Women's Studies* 4 (1) February, 1997), 23–37.

21 Ibid., 84.

22 She remains awake to orchestrate her performances. During one surgery, which was broadcast live to several galleries around the world, she answered faxes from viewers. One can purchase videos of her performances as well as ceremonial containers containing a "relic" of her flesh. She is currently represented by the Sandra Gering Gallery in New York.

23 Orlan interviewed in "The Doyenne of Divasection," by Miryam Sas, *Mondo 2000*, 13 (January, 1995), 106–11.

24 A particularly shocking image is one that shows the skin of her face being lifted away from her cheek structure below, pictured on the cover of Parveen Adams' collection of essays, *The Emptiness of the Image: Psychoanalysis and Sexual Differences* (London and New York: Routledge, 1996). This, and related images, form the content of Adams' essay, "Operation Orlan," 140–59.

25 Sara Munson Deats and Langretta Tallen Lenker, eds, *Gender and Academe: Feminist Pedagogy and Politics* (Maryland: Rowman and Littlefield Publishers, Inc., 1994), xxiv.

26 The duck-rabbit figure was first used in 1900 by Joseph Jastrow. See Henry Gleitman, *Psychology* (New York: W. W. Norton and Co., 1981), 231.

27 Hume, "Of the Standard of Taste," 599.

28 Formerly referred to as the "Wife/Mistress" figure, it dates from 1930, the work of E. G. Boring. See Gleitman, *Psychology*, 252. Gleitman labels Figures 2B and 2C "unambiguous" but I have called them "less ambiguous" since they are sometimes difficult to interpret as either an unambiguously young or old woman in spite of the visual clues: the prominent eyelash of the young woman (in profile on the left side of the face) in Figure 2B and the more prominent ear-as-eye on the right side of the face of the old woman in Figure 2C.

29 See, for instance, the theories of Julian Hochberg and Ulric Neisser in Gleitman, *Psychology*, 246.

30 This is similar to E. H. Gombrich's claim "the innocent eye is a myth," except for the fact that Gombrich never suggested gender or race as part of a viewer's mental makeup, opting instead for more general categories of "fears, guesses, expectations which sort and model the incoming messages, testing and transforming and testing again." See *Art and Illusion: A Study in the Psychology of Pictorial Representation* (Princeton: Princeton University Press, 1960), 298.

31 D. Medin, R. Goldstone, and D. Gentner, "Respects for Similarity," *Psychological Review* 100 (2) (1993), 254–78. (I have changed the letters of the figures from the original article in order to have them conform with the previous convention from Gleitman's *Psychology*, of Figure A designating the ambiguous image.) It might be noteworthy to add that the authors of this essay were inspired by Nelson Goodman's

claims about similarity; "he called similarity 'invidious, insidious, a pretender, an imposter, a quack' " (254).

32 I hasten to add that some feminist critics and theorists would reject this suggestion. Andrea Dworkin and Susanne Kappeler, for example, claim that it is impossible for them to look at images of nude women in any way other than through a feminist lens. See Andrea Dworkin, *Pornography: Men Possessing Women* (Perigree Book, G. P. Putnam's Sons, 1979) and Susanne Kappeler, *The Pornography of Representation* (Minneapolis: University of Minnesota Press, 1986). Kappeler specifically denounces feminists who are "busy rescuing a female artist," for example, Judy Chicago and her immense project, *The Dinner Party*. Her complaint is that "The overriding stumbling block here is art – to be rescued at all costs, and to be filled up, moreover, by a quota of women" (39).

33 In fact, Laura Mulvey speaks of a similar process with regard to Cindy Sherman's photographs which she calls an "oscillation effect . . . between reverence and revulsion." See "Cosmetics and Abjection: Cindy Sherman 1977–87," in *Fetishism and Curiosity* (Indianapolis: Indiana University Press, 1996), 75–6. The essay was originally published as "A Phantasmagoria of the Female Body: The Work of Cindy Sherman," in *New Left Review* (July/August 1991).

---

17 High and Low Thinking about High and Low Art

Ted Cohen

[. . .] A year ago I was listening to a movie review on a television news program. I do not remember the movie. I think it was a *Police Academy* movie, or some movie such as *Dead Shot*, but I am not sure. The reviewer was Gene Siskel (I do remember who is Siskel and who is Ebert), and he said that he would not give a serious review because this was not a serious movie. I remember thinking that as far as I could remember, Siskel has never given what I think of as a *serious* review of any movie at all. But Siskel himself has, nevertheless, some sense of a difference between serious movies and other movies. I wonder how he would articulate this difference.

A distinction between high art and low art (or perhaps between fine art and popular art) is like the distinction between art and non-art. The distinctions are alike in at least these two respects: (1) Each distinction is, probably, as a serious philosophical distinction – as a distinction, say, that would satisfy Carnap – indefensible; (2) each distinction is indispensable. Such distinctions, indefensible and indispensable, are an abiding and startling feature of my thought, and not only of mine. I would like to understand the place of such distinctions, but this is not the place to go into them: all I will do here is illustrate some of them. Let me begin with this question: If the distinction between high art and low art is like the distinction between art and non-art, then why do we need *both* distinctions? Suppose I am already lumbered with an art/non-art device, shouldering it because I cannot seem to go along without it. Why do I also drag along a wedge for separating high art from low art? What extra work does it do? What can I do with it that I cannot do with my art/non-art distinction? Or, on the other hand, if I am already tolerably comfortable with some high/low gauge, why do I also need a separation between art and what isn't art? (If paintings are high and pots are low, what difference does it make whether both are art?) Let me try asking it this way – If you think that Shakespeare is better or deeper or nicer or something than *The Simpsons*, why do you feel a need to say anything more than that? And if you do, why do you feel a need to distinguish the *kind* of thing Shakespeare is from the *kind* of thing *The Simpsons* is?

In recent years, increasingly, I have found that when I need to find a way to think about some topic in the philosophy of art, I do best when I begin with some other topic and then try to make a connection. Let me begin, then, with some ruminations on my moral landscape, and see if this helps get a fix on my aesthetics.

A few years ago I spent some days in Krakow. When the meetings I was attending were nearly over, the conference participants were invited to make a trip to the nearby town of Oswiecim and take a tour. About twenty of my colleagues made the trip, I think: another American, two or three Britons, two Germans, a man from Holland, and the rest from Eastern Europe (Romania, Bulgaria, Yugoslavia, the Soviet Union, and, of course, Poland).

I had to decide whether to go. Oswiecim, as you may know, is more often known under its German name, Auschwitz. I did not expect to enjoy this trip. And I did not think that I could *learn* anything. Once before, I had made a tour of a German death camp, Maydanek, the one near Lublin in Eastern Poland; I made that tour with my wife and two children and I had an idea what the experience would be like.

This time my wife and son, who had been with me in Warsaw, Gdansk, and Krakow, had departed for the United States some days before the Auschwitz tour was to be held, and so I was making a decision by myself, for myself. I decided to go: I decided I would go: I thought I *ought* to go (and I still think that I ought to have gone). The morally obtuse, the spiritually crude may ask: "Is that a *moral* obligation?" And I refuse to answer. "Is it the moral sense of the word 'ought'?" they ask, and I say, "You are the one with the categories, the boxes, the petrifying distinctions, and the dead sensibility: put my 'ought' wherever you like, and leave me alone."

Why am I so recalcitrant, so uncooperative, so mean-spirited? Well, I know that anyone who asks questions about moral senses of 'ought' and different kinds of obligations, has lurking in his professor's briefcase, some theory. A *theory*, God help us, of morality. And this theory, whatever it is, will distort my sense of why I ought to have gone to Auschwitz. It will appropriate an acutely painful decision of mine, one which I felt and made with special intensity and a sense of unique need, and put it in one of those God-damned boxes. Not on your life. At least not on my life.

Well, what is so peculiar about this 'ought' for me? It is not simple to say, but I can make this beginning: do I think everyone ought to visit Auschwitz? No. Do I think anyone should make a long trip, say across the Atlantic, in order to visit Auschwitz? No, probably not. Do I think every German ought to visit Auschwitz? No, not necessarily. Do I think every Jew ought to visit Auschwitz? No. Do I think my family and friends ought to visit Auschwitz? No. Do I think every Jew who finds it not terribly inconvenient or unbearably painful to do so, should visit Auschwitz? Maybe; but I am not sure. Do I think that I, on that occasion, six years or so ago, when I was in Krakow for other reasons, when I had been speaking German during the conference, and elsewhere with some non-English-speaking Poles, ought to have gone to Auschwitz? Yes.

Well, then, how much like me would someone have to be in order for me to think that this hypothetical person ought to visit Auschwitz? This is not a bad question. My interest in the question, however, seems to be an interest in my own, autobiographical morality, and not an interest in what I have been taught to think of as conceptual morality. How does it strike you?

I have done a number of other things, gone to many other places, when I have visited Poland. I have gone to the boardwalk in Sopot. I have lectured in Gdansk. I have gone to a site in the Tatra Mountains where a Polish resistance fighter leaped from a mountain-traversing gondola in order to escape the Gestapo. I have stayed up all night helping Polish friends put essays of theirs into idiomatic English. I have gone to see an American sailing ship in the harbor at Gdynia, and in Krakow I have gone to a piano recital by a young Italian woman, and to a meeting with the mayor. I did not think I *ought* to do any of those things, not in the way I think I ought to have gone to Auschwitz.

But there certainly are a number of things I think I ought to do. I ought to refrain from telling children that I know how they feel and will feel. I ought to share my money with others. I ought to teach, to teach the young, and to teach the old. And I ought to remember the Sabbath day, to keep it holy. And I believe just about everyone ought to do almost all of those things.

This is a messy catalogue, isn't it? Well, it is a messy business which I do not understand very well. My moral sensibility encompasses a range of things I decide to do, and I can mark them off from one another, trying desperately to keep them from being collapsed into crude, general categories, but also believing that they must somehow be related to one another, some closely, some not closely at all. Do you have, or could you make, your own catalogue?

My moral landscape requires a number of landmarks. It is my idea that so does my aesthetic landscape. The categories of the forbidden, the permitted, the obligatory, and the supererogatory will not do justice to the sensibility of my moral landscape (nor, I daresay, to that of anyone besides the caricatured example figures of moral theories); and neither will the categories of art and non-art, nor those of high and low art illuminate what I see in my aesthetic life: they just blur and blotch.

Here are a few things I care about and pay attention to: the television programs *The Simpsons* and *Northern Exposure*; *King Lear*; some pieces by Mose Allison and some by the Neville Brothers; Pasternak's *Dr Zhivago*; some short stories by A. B. Yehoshua; Hitchcock's *North by Northwest*; some pieces by Paul Desmond; some poems by Paul Celan; Mozart's *Marriage of Figaro*; some guitar work by Doc Watson; some raspy singing by Leon Redbone; a lot of Hoagy Carmichael; Ravel's setting of some Hebrew melodies, and also those of Prokofiev and Shostakovich; a couple of novels by Russell Hoban; the Hebrew *Bible*; some paintings by Rembrandt and some by Manet; photographs by Edward Weston; and – why not? – a couple of stories by me. It would be a small, quick matter for me to increase this list tenfold, but this partial inventory is enough for purposes at hand.

Are all these *art*? I suppose so, but I'm not sure that I care, and I will not advance the assertion that they are. If you would like to say that some aren't, go ahead, give your reasons, and we will see how long you can hold your ground. But let us be cordial and cooperative for at least a moment, and I will speak freely, even confessionally.

I think I feel a need to think of all these things as art because it somehow matters to me how they stand with other people. That is, it is somehow important to me that others respond to Aaron Neville's amazing version of "Will the Circle be Unbroken?" And I need others to gasp at the Bach-like character of Paul Desmond's saxophone. And I need others to shudder when Paul Celan says that Death is *ein Meister aus Deutschland.* . . .

What others? Everyone? This is, for me, the subtle and endlessly interesting question. In some cases I hold out the vain but necessary, beautiful hope that the work will – or at least *could* – reach everyone, that it could be our entrée into what we desperately wish to be our universal humanity, that it could be what Kant, in all the profound, obtuse, crystalline opacity of the optimism of the Enlightenment thought beauty is, the mark of the "universal substrate of humanity." But in most cases the net of my hopes is cast less widely. This is not a bad or limiting thing: it is essential to my location of myself.

Some of these objects link me to some of my fellows, some of the objects link me to other people. Some lead me into rather small groups, some lead me into large and varied groups. And it is my membership in these groups that locates me aesthetically, as I think of it, that reflects the dimensions of my sensibility.

No doubt you have your own list of things you care about, and of things you care that others also care about. Some of your things will not be on my list, even on my complete list, and that is just as it should be. My absence from these groups you inhabit is just as important in defining me as your membership is in defining you.

And it is also important that there are things I care for which I do not, in my caring, suppose link me to others in any way that matters to me. Chocolate ice cream (at least some brands), Bob Marley's song "Buffalo Soldiers," the movie *The Blues Brothers*, and a photograph I once made of my son with his bicycle are a few examples. I do not think of any of these things as art, and I believe the reason I do not think of them in this way is that I do not suppose them to link me to any others who might care for them.

I hope this rings the bell sounded in the brief discussion of moral sensibility in terms of my visiting-Auschwitz example. When I try to understand the character and quality of my attachment to a prospective action, or to an object I may cultivate an appreciation of, I tend to think of how, through this action or object, I am related to others who may contemplate undertaking this action or appreciating this object.

Although I have participated in discussions of what art is, I have always been in a negative position, arguing that someone's attempt to say what art is fails, and until recently it did not seem to me that I had anything to say about what art is. And that was because, although I could think of reasons for denying what someone says art is, I could think of no way to begin thinking about what art seems (at least to me) to be. Now I have begun to find a way, and I am finding it by trying to understand why I (or anyone, for that matter) would ever *seriously* care to assert or deny that something is art. I have gotten this far: When I feel like insisting or denying that something is art it is because I wish to insist on or resist the idea that the thing is to be taken seriously, that there is a kind of obligation to recognize the thing as a significant item in my life.

And I have gotten this much farther: to explain the significance of the thing in my life I must suppose that it also has a place, or deserves to have a place, in the lives of others. That's as far as I've gotten. In this paper, a work in progress if ever there was one, I will not go much farther nor will I attempt to justify going as far as I have. I am just seeing out this fledgling conviction in order to see, given this proto-conception of art, what place in it, or beside it, there is for a distinction between high and low art, or between popular and not-so-popular art. Before I do that, let me say just a little more about art as a focus for a mutuality that locates a community. I will try another example.

A year ago I participated in a memorial service for a friend who had died during the summer. The program for the service was a number of remembrances and two musical selections. The musical selections, performed by a string quartet, were chosen by someone who had known my friend and knew that both were favorites of his. Why is this music appropriate? There are a number of answers, good answers, to this question. I draw your attention to one. My friend has died and is not present. I listen to music I know he cared for. It is a fact about my friend that he cared for this music, perhaps even a constitutive fact about his sensibility: it partially defines who and what he was. It is, thus, an entrance into that sensibility. I sit listening, not merely thinking that this music meant something to my friend, but bending my imagination to the task of *reaching* and *comprehending* an aspect of my friend which responded to this music, that is, feeling what it was to be my friend.

It is the significance of occasions like this one that has prompted me to think and write about *intimacy* for the past few years, and has led me to try to understand this characteristic of the interpersonal status of certain objects, particularly works of art. On the occasion in question, all of us present who were bent on this imaginative act of joining our lost friend in a response to that music were ourselves also joined to one another: we were finding one another and our friend in that music of Mozart and Haydn. Does it matter that Mozart and Haydn are high art (very high art indeed)?

When I had given this example last October, Professor Robert Yanal replied that it did not seem significant that the Mozart and Haydn are art. It would have done as well, he said, for some favorite object of my friend's, say a saddle, to have been displayed. I was unconvinced because there does not seem to me to be any presumption that an arbitrary favorite of my friend's could reach us, those of us remembering him; but I am not sure of this. A few days ago I was privileged to deliver the Frances Rooz Memorial Lecture at Temple Sholom in Chicago. When I had finished, Mrs Claire Rooz, Frances Rooz's sister, an exceptionally gracious and cordial person, told me that her sister would have enjoyed the lecture. Of course I was pleased. And I wondered whether I had supplied for Frances Rooz's friends and relatives what Mozart and Haydn had supplied for me when I attended my friend's memorial. I don't think so. I think I was more like the saddle in Professor Yanal's example. But just what is the difference?

It is a commonplace, I suppose, that works of art have trans-personal significance. It is not commonly noted that the breadth of their reach is understood in two mutually incongruous ways. On the one hand, very popular works are typically thought to be slight, to be "easy," to be superficial, as if these characteristics explained why so many people are able to appreciate them. On the other hand, it is a very old, well-established, favorite idea about the greatest art that precisely because of its enormous, penetrating depth, it *must* be able to reach all who are genuinely human. Thus the great appeal of *Hamlet* (one of Shakespeare's two most often performed plays) is attributed to its greatness; and the virtually complete international appeal of American popular culture is attributed to its allegedly glib superficiality: on this account, *Hamlet* is transcendental, *Dallas* is subterranean. (And what, then, about *The Merchant of Venice*, the other of Shakespeare's two most popular plays?)

This striking incongruity has been present for some time. Hume, for instance, tells us that the truly beautiful has pleased at all times, in all places, and he also tells us that there are ages in which no one can apprehend the truly beautiful. He seems to say both that the truest beauty is for everyone, and that it is reserved for a very special very few. (What do you suppose Hume really thinks?)

Let us go a little more deeply into the idea that the highest art is for only a few. If you were one of those critics, say, like Barbara Rose or John Simon, who pride themselves on their exquisite, refined taste, and revel in how rare that makes them, you must be supposing a link between you and those unfortunates who do not share your appreciation of the precious. You must think they are missing something they would be better not to miss: you must think, at least with regard to these artistic items, the crude fellows *should* be like you. If you do not think this, your contempt for them barely makes sense, and it is certainly not justified. Unless they *should* be like you, you cannot blame them for any objective failure: all you can do is blame them for not being like you – period. Now even God does not blame us for not being like God, and we are certainly not going to feel a shortcoming just because we are not like you unless you supply a reason why we should be like that. The converse situation is similar. Your contempt for my devotion to television is unfounded, except, again, as your contempt for any who deviate from you, unless you supply a reason why it would be better to join you in sneering at television. I know of no empirical proposition that will do as a reason.

John Simon may think that his fine appreciation of the theatre and movies goes hand-in-hand with his disdain for television; but I stand ready to show that my interest in television has left me able to more than match Simon in refined responses to movies (in fact Simon has virtually no taste in movies because, I imagine, his sneer is so wide it has distorted his ability to see what is before him).

That is enough sneering, even by me. Let me try a brief, inconclusive conclusion:

My conception of art as the focus of a *community* needs explanation and defense – but not here. I ask you only to entertain the idea of an affective community, a group whose intimacy is underwritten by their conviction that they feel the same about something, and that that thing – the art – is their bond. They feel that one another respond in the same way, and for the same reasons. If I understand art in terms of this communitarian character, how do distinctions between high and low, and rare and popular, figure in the reckoning? Like this, perhaps: they cut across the main differentiating dimension, the distinction between wide and narrow ranges of human connection. Some works connect me with many people, including, sometimes, considerable varieties of kinds of people. Thus *The Simpsons* and some Marx brothers movies connect me with both very young people and some widely varying kinds of people my own age and older. And some works connect me with very few people. Thus some stories by I. B. Singer and some by Richard Stern seem to connect me with only a few people, people who are much like me.

It seems that a wide connection, a link between me and many others can be made through a work either because the work has great depth or because it is all pretty much on the surface. At least that is how it seems. And sometimes a work of depth connects many of us partly because we do not relate ourselves to it in the same way. At least parts of the Hebrew *Bible* are very great works of art, and they hold the attention of an enormously wide and numerous audience; and yet the members of the audience find quite different ways into these books, leaving it an extremely interesting question just how these different readers are linked to one another.

However we choose to explain and understand wide and narrow connections, I think we should assume, at least at the start, that width is neither better or worse than narrowness. I need both. Urgently. *Hamlet* and *The Marriage of Figaro* connect me with most of you, I would guess, perhaps all of you. Elaine May's movie *Ishtar*, which I am very fond of, leaves me virtually alone. That's all fine: I need to be with you, and I need to be alone. I need to be like you, and I need to be unlike you. A world in which you and I never connected would be a horror. And so would a world in which we were exactly the same, and therefore connected unfailingly, with every object on every occasion. *The Marriage of Figaro* helps us be us. *Ishtar* helps me be me. Thank God for them both.

Suggestions for Further Reading

Barnes, Annette. *On Interpretation*. Oxford: Blackwell, 1988.

Beardsley, Monroe. *Aesthetics: Problems in the Philosophy of Criticism*. Second edition. Indianapolis: Hackett Publishing Co., 1981.

Dickie, George. *The Century of Taste: The Philosophical Odyssey of Taste in the Eighteenth Century*. New York: Oxford University Press, 1996.

—— *Evaluating Art*. Philadelphia: Temple University Press, 1988.

Eagleton, Terry. *The Ideology of the Aesthetic*. Oxford: Blackwell, 1990.

Felski, Rita. *Beyond Feminist Aesthetics*. Cambridge, Mass.: Harvard University Press, 1989.

Foster, Hal, ed. *The Anti-Aesthetic: Essays on Postmodern Culture*. Port Townsend, Wash.: Bay Press, 1983.

Isenberg, Arnold. "Critical Communication," *Philosophical Review* 58 (1949).

Kaplan, E. Ann. "Is the Gaze Male?" in *Women and Values*, ed. Marilyn Pearsall. Second edition. Belmont, Calif.: Wadsworth, 1993.

Kupfer, Joseph. *Experience as Art*. Albany: State University of New York Press, 1983.

Margolis, Joseph. "Robust Relativism," *Journal of Aesthetics and Art Criticism* 35 (1976).

Novitz, David. "Towards a Robust Realism," *Journal of Aesthetics and Art Criticism* 41 (1982).

Shusterman, Richard. *Pragmatist Aesthetics*. Oxford: Blackwell, 1992.

Sibley, Frank. "Aesthetic Concepts," *Philosophical Review* 48 (1959).

Walton, Kendall. "Categories of Art," *Philosophical Review* 89 (1970).

PART FOUR

CAN WE LEARN FROM ART?

Preface

The question of whether we can learn from art has been debated since the dawn of philosophical inquiry. No one can deny that art can affect us powerfully, but the question has been whether it can affect us in a way that benefits our understanding of the world or of ourselves. Typically, those who say we can learn from art argue that our engagement with works of art engenders certain emotions or activities that either result in or facilitate the development of knowledge. That is, some aspect of the work of art can produce in us greater clarity with respect to our understanding of the world. Those who deny we can learn from art generally claim that the way art affects us inhibits both our capacity to understand the real world and our ability to think critically. This section presents five responses to the question of whether we can learn from art that range from thinkers of ancient Greece to philosophers of the twentieth century.

Plato, perhaps the first philosopher who dealt with the question of whether we can learn from art, focused primarily on the negative effects art can produce in us. He was highly suspicious of the ability of art to inform our understanding of reality. For Plato, knowledge entails acquiring an understanding of the Forms, which are the ultimate reality of the world. The Forms serve as the transcendent patterns or "universals" of the physical world which we inhabit. His suspicion of art was grounded in the fact that it offers images which are merely imitations or representations of the physical world. As such, art objects are incapable of emulating the Forms and in fact lead us away from true knowledge. According to Plato, artistic representations arouse emotions which undermine a clear path to knowledge of the Forms. Since genuine knowledge can be only found by intuiting the Forms, art objects actually deter the process of acquiring knowledge by confusing the perceiver. By looking at mere images of the physical world, one becomes confused as to where knowledge of the real lies. This view of the dangers of art raises obvious questions about the degree to which art ought to be controlled. Although it is not clear that Plato advocates wide-ranging censorship, he believes that the artistic images of reality are potentially dangerous for those who do not recognize the images as such. Therefore his theory does suggest that certain individuals' access to images should be restricted.

Continuing in the platonic tradition, Iris Murdoch seizes upon the one positive aspect that Plato saw in art, namely, beauty. According to Murdoch, appreciating both natural and artistic beauty can benefit us morally. Beauty has this positive effect because when we appreciate it, we shift out of our typically self-interested mode of attention, becoming more sensitive and aesthetically aware. While Murdoch maintains that various activities can result in our moral improvement, a number of those activities would be difficult and unenjoyable. Beauty is especially useful because it not only has the potential to benefit us, but it is something we enjoy instinctively. In encouraging us to move from our self-absorbed orientation, Murdoch argues, the appreciation of art makes us forget our selfish concerns about the material world – concerns which can distort our understanding. Thus by seeking beauty in our lives we can have a clearer understanding of the world because we are not limited by self-interest.

Shifting attention from the arts in general to literature, Martha Nussbaum argues that narratives can enhance our moral understanding in a way that is complementary to philosophies of ethics. This is possible because the style of literary writings is more attentive to particulars and to the significance of emotion than the typically abstract style employed by much philosophical writing. According to Nussbaum in order to have a sufficiently comprehensive appreciation of ethics, one must acknowledge both the uniqueness of particulars as well as the role that emotion plays in moral judgment. Nussbaum argues that literature can enhance our moral understanding not only because it presents us with an attentive depiction of moral situations but also because it encourages a certain sensitivity on the part of the reader. Literature engenders sympathetic identification with characters that contributes to the reader's development. Moreover, Nussbaum contends, because literature allows us to identify with individuals and events that would be unavailable under normal circumstances, it gives us epistemic access to a wider range of situations than our own empirical existence permits.

Michael Norman focuses on the instructive capacity of film – in particular war movies. While he maintains that film has a heuristic function, he asserts that learning from movies is problematic because they necessarily distort reality, especially when that reality is unbearably painful. War stories in particular tend to romanticize or over-dramatize the events that they portray. Where films typically have a neat beginning, middle, and end (and are judged partly on how well those are created), real life rarely has such a convenient structure. Despite their degree of distortion, Norman argues, narratives of war inevitably affect our perception of the real thing. He suggests that we need these "lies" or illusions because the truth of war is too horrible to apprehend unmitigated. War movies, however, simply cannot capture the truth of their subject. The question of what we can learn through this art form raises a disturbing prospect: do the tempered representations of war allow us to stomach a reality and persist in a practice, which, if represented differently, we might try harder to avoid?

Unlike the previous accounts, Susan Feagin subjects the question of how we can learn from art to a different kind of scrutiny. She argues that the question of whether we can learn from art presupposes a distinction between art and reality and assumes that art teaches us in some distinctive way. Feagin suggests that this distinction is problematic to the extent that if art stands apart from reality, how could we learn anything that would be applicable to our own realities? For Feagin, art and reality are not distinct but are closely intertwined. She argues that art objects such as paintings which make up alterpieces are real things with which we sometimes engage in a very practical fashion. Such artworks serve as substitutes for absent objects, and in so doing, they create spaces that invite activity. We relate to the artistic substitute almost as we would engage with the original subject. For example, in the presence of a religious icon one might offer the reverence appropriate to the actual deity. For Feagin, the significance of art lies less in what it can teach us than in the activities or spaces of engagement that it encourages.

Perhaps the guiding theme in all of these readings is art's capacity to affect us in ways that influence our cognitive ability. (In this way the concept of the aesthetic they presume has much in common with Gadamer's in Part Two.) Art does not necessarily have a so-called propositional content that can be learned, but it can be seen to generate effects that either encourage or undermine the development of understanding. In short, for the authors included here, the importance of art lies as much in what it does as what it says.

Jennifer McMahon Railey and Sarah Worth

18   From the *Republic*, Books II, III, X

Plato

[The main speaker in this dialogue is Socrates, who is discussing with friends the roles that poets and painters should have in a just society.]

II

[...]

You know, don't you, that the beginning of any process is most important especially for anything young and tender? It's at that time that it is most malleable and tales on any pattern one wishes to impress on it.

Exactly.

Then shall we carelessly allow the children to hear any old stories, told by just anyone, and to take beliefs into their souls that are for the most part opposite to the ones we think they should hold when they are grown up?

We certainly won't

Then we must first of all, it seems, supervise the storytellers. We'll select their stories whenever they are fine or local and reject them when they aren't. And we'll persuade nurses and mothers to tell their children the ones we have selected, since they will shape their children's souls with stories much more than they shape their bodies by handling them. Many of the stories they tell now, however, must be thrown out.

Which ones do you mean?

We'll first look at the major stories, and by seeing how to deal with them, we'll see how to deal with the minor ones as well, for they exhibit the same pattern and have the same effects whether they're famous or not. Don't you think so?

I do, but I don't know which ones you're calling major.

Those that Homer, Hesiod, and other poets tell us, for surely they composed false stories, told them to people, and are still telling them.

Which stories do you mean, and what fault do you find in them?

The fault one ought to find first and foremost especially if the falsehood isn't well told.

For example?

When a story gives a bad image of what the gods and heroes are like, the way a painter does whose picture is not at all like the things he's trying to paint.

You're right to object to that. But what sort of thing in particular do you have in mind?

First, telling the greatest falsehood about the most important things doesn't make a fine story – I mean Hesiod telling us about how Ouranos behaved, how

Cronos punished him for it, and how he was in turn punished by his own son.[1] But even if it were true, it should be passed over in silence, not told to foolish young people. And if, for some reason, it has to be told, only a very few people – pledged to secrecy and after sacrificing not just a pig but something great and scarce – should hear it, so that their number is kept as small as possible.

Yes, such stories are hard to deal with.

And they shouldn't be told in our city, Adeimantus. Nor should a young person hear it said that in committing the worst crimes he's doing nothing out of the ordinary, or that if he inflicts every kind of punishment on an unjust father, he's only doing the same as the first and greatest of the gods.

No, by god, I don't think myself that these stories are fit to be told.

Indeed, if we want the guardians of our city to think that it's shameful to be easily provoked into hating one another, we mustn't allow any stories about gods warring, fighting, or plotting against one another, for they aren't true. The battles of gods and giants, and all the various stories of the gods hating their families or friends, should neither be told nor even woven in embroideries. If we're to persuade our people that no citizen has ever hated another and that it's impious to do so, then *that's* what should be told to children from the beginning by old men and women; and as these children grow older, poets should be compelled to tell them the same sort of thing. We won't admit stories into our city – whether allegorical or not – about Hera being chained by her son, nor about Hephaestus being hurled from heaven by his father when he tried to help his mother, who was being beaten, nor about the battle of the gods in Homer. The young can't distinguish what is allegorical from what isn't, and the opinions they absorb at that age are hard to erase and apt to become unalterable. For these reasons, then, we should probably take the utmost care to insure that the first stories they hear about virtue are the best ones for them to hear.

That's reasonable. But if someone asked us what stories these are, what should we say?

You and I, Adeimantus, aren't poets, but we *are* founding a city. And it's appropriate for the founders to know the patterns on which poets must base their stories and from which they mustn't deviate. But we aren't actually going to compose their poems for them.

All right. But what precisely are the patterns for theology or stories about the gods?

Something like this: Whether in epic, lyric, or tragedy, a god must always be represented as he is.

Indeed, he must.

Now, a god is really good, isn't he, and must be described as such?

What else?

And surely nothing good is harmful, is it?

I suppose not.

And can what isn't harmful do harm?

Never.

Or can what does no harm do anything bad?

No.

And can what does nothing bad be the cause of anything bad?

How could it?

Moreover, the good is beneficial?

Yes.

It is the cause of doing well?

Yes.

The good isn't the cause of all things, then, but only of good ones; it isn't the cause of bad ones.

I agree entirely.

Therefore, since a god is good, he is not – as most people claim – the cause of everything that happens to human beings but of only a few things, for good things are fewer than bad ones in our lives. He alone is responsible for the good things, but we must find some other cause for the bad ones, not a god.

That's very true, and I believe it.

Then we won't accept from anyone the foolish mistake Homer makes about the gods when he says:

> There are two urns at the threshold of Zeus,
> One filled with good fates, the other with bad ones. . . .

and the person to whom he gives a mixture of these

> Sometimes meets with a bad fate, sometimes with good,

but the one who receives his fate entirely from the second urn,

> Evil famine drives him over the divine earth.

We won't grant either that Zeus is for us

> The distributor of both good and bad.

And as to the breaking of the promised truce by Pandarus, if anyone tells us that it was brought about by Athena and Zeus or that Themis and Zeus were responsible for strife and contention among the gods, we will not praise him. Nor will we allow the young to hear the words of Aeschylus:

> A god makes mortals guilty
> When he wants utterly to destroy a house.[2]

And if anyone composes a poem about the sufferings of Niobe, such as the one in which these lines occur, or about the house of Pelops, or the tale of Troy, or anything else of that kind, we must require him to say that these things are not the work of a god. Or, if they are, then poets must look for the kind of account of them that we are now seeking, and say that the actions of the gods are good and just, and that those they punish are benefited thereby. We won't allow poets to say that the punished are made wretched and that it was a god who made them so. But we will allow them to say that bad people are wretched because they are in need of punishment and that, in paying the penalty, they are benefited by the gods. And, as for saying that a god, who is himself good, is the cause of bad things we'll fight that in every way, and we won't allow anyone to say it in his own city, if it's to be well governed, or anyone to hear it either – whether young or old, whether in verse or prose. These stories are not pious, not advantageous to us, and not consistent with one another.

I like your law, and I'll vote for it.

This, then, is one of the laws or patterns concerning the gods to which speakers and poets must conform, namely, that a god isn't the cause of all things but only of good ones.

And it's a fully satisfactory law.

What about this second law? Do you think that a god is a sorcerer, able to appear in different forms at different times, sometimes changing himself from his own form into many shapes, sometimes deceiving us by making us think that he has done it? Or do you think he's simple and least of all likely to step out of his own form?

I can't say offhand.

[. . .]

What? Would a god be willing to be false, either in word or deed, by presenting an illusion?

I don't know.

Don't you know that a *true* falsehood, if one may call it that, is hated by all gods and humans?

What do you mean?

I mean that no one is willing to tell falsehoods to the most important part of himself about the most important things, but of all places he most afraid to have falsehood there.

I still don't understand.

That's because you think I'm saying something deep. I simply mean that to be false to one's soul about the things that are, to be ignorant and to have and hold falsehood there, is what everyone would least of all accept, for everyone hates a falsehood in that place most of all.

That's right.

Surely, as I said just now, this would be most correctly called true falsehood – ignorance in the soul of someone who has been told a falsehood. Falsehood in words is a kind of imitation of this affection in the soul, an image of it that comes into being after it and is not a pure falsehood. Isn't that so?

Certainly.

And the thing that is really a falsehood is hated not only by the gods but by human beings as well.

It seems so to me.

[. . .]

A god, then, is simple and true in word and deed. He doesn't change himself or deceive others by images, words, or signs, whether in visions or in dreams.

That's what I thought as soon as I heard you say it.

You agree, then, that this is our second pattern for speaking or composing poems about the gods: They are not sorcerers who change themselves, nor do they mislead us by falsehoods in words or deeds.

I agree.

So, even though we praise many things in Homer, we won't approve of the dream Zeus sent to Agamemnon, nor of Aeschylus when he makes Thetis say that Apollo sang in prophecy at her wedding:

> About the good fortune my children would have,
> Free of disease throughout their long lives,
> And of all the blessings that the friendship of the gods would bring me.
> I hoped that Phoebus' divine mouth would be free of falsehood,
> Endowed as it is with the craft of prophecy.
> But the very god who sang, the one at the feast,
> The one who said all this, he himself it is
> Who killed my son.[3]

Whenever anyone says such things about a god, we'll be angry with him, refuse him a chorus,[4] and not allow his poetry to be used in the education of the young, so that our guardians will be as god-fearing and godlike as human beings can be.

I completely endorse these patterns, he said, and I would enact them as laws.

III

Such, then, I said, are the kinds of stories that I think future guardians should and should not hear about the gods from childhood on, if they are to honor the gods and their parents and not take their friendship with one another lightly.

I'm sure we're right about that, at any rate.

What if they are to be courageous as well? Shouldn't they be told stories that will make them least afraid of death? Or do you think that anyone ever becomes courageous if he's possessed by this fear?

No, I certainly don't.

And can someone be unafraid of death, preferring it to defeat in battle or slavery, if he believes in a Hades full of terrors?

Not at all.

Then we must supervise such stories and those who tell them, and ask them not to disparage the life in Hades in this unconditional way, but rather to praise it, since what they now say is neither true nor beneficial to future warriors.

We must.

Then we'll expunge all that sort of disparagement, beginning with the following lines:

I would rather labour on earth in service to another,
To a man who is landless, with little to live on,
Than be king over all the dead.[5]

and also these:

He feared that his home should appear to gods and men
Dreadful, dank and hated even by the gods.[6]

and

Alas, there survives in the Halls of Hades
A soul, a mere phantasm, with its wits completely gone.[7]

and this:

And he alone could think; the others are flitting shadows.[8]

and

The soul, leaving his limbs, made its way to Hades,
Lamenting its fate, leaving manhood and youth behind.[9]

[. . .]

We'll ask Homer and the other poets not to be angry if we delete these passages and all similar ones. It isn't that they aren't poetic and pleasing to the majority of hearers but that, the more poetic they are, the less they should be heard by children or by men who are supposed to be free and to fear slavery more than death. Most certainly.

[. . .] We need to come to an agreement about whether we'll allow poets to narrate through imitation, and, if so, whether they are to imitate some things but not others – and what things these are, or whether they are not to imitate at all.

I divine that you're looking into the question of whether or not we'll allow tragedy and comedy into our city.

Perhaps, and perhaps even more than that, for I myself really don't know yet, but whatever direction the argument blows us, that's where we must go.

Fine.

Then, consider, Adeimantus, whether our guardians should be imitators or not. Or does this also follow from our earlier statement that each individual would do a fine job of one occupation, not of many, and that if he tried the latter and dabbled in many things, he'd surely fail to achieve distinction in any of them?

He would indeed.

Then, doesn't the same argument also hold for imitation – a single individual can't imitate many things as well as he can imitate one?

No, he can't.

Then, he'll hardly be able to pursue any worthwhile way of life while at the same time imitating many things and being an imitator. Even in the case of two kinds of imitation that are thought to be closely akin, such as tragedy and comedy, the same people aren't able to do both of them well. Did you not just say that these were both imitations?

I did, and you're quite right that the same people can't do both.

Nor can they be both rhapsodes and actors.

True.

Indeed, not even the same actors are used for tragedy and comedy. Yet all these are imitations, aren't they?

They are.

And human nature, Adeimantus, seems to me to be minted in even smaller coins than these, so that it can neither imitate many things well nor do the actions themselves, of which those imitations are likenesses.

That's absolutely true.

Then, if we're to preserve our first argument, that our guardians must be kept away from all other crafts so as to be the craftsmen of the city's freedom and be exclusively that, and do nothing at all except what contributes to it, they must neither do nor imitate anything else. If they do imitate, they must imitate from childhood what is appropriate for them, namely, people who are courageous, self controlled, pious, and free, and their actions. They mustn't be clever at doing or imitating slavish or shameful actions, lest from enjoying the imitation, they come to enjoy the reality. Or haven't you noticed that imitations practiced from youth become part of nature and settle into habits of gesture, voice, and thought?

I have indeed.

Then we won't allow those for whom we profess to care, and who must grow into good men, to imitate either a young woman or an older one, or one abusing her husband, quarreling with the gods, or bragging because she thinks herself happy, or one suffering misfortune and possessed by sorrows and lamentations, and even less one who is ill, in love, or in labor.

That's absolutely right.

Nor must they imitate either male or female slaves doing slavish things.

No, they mustn't.

Nor bad men, it seems, who are cowards and are doing the opposite of what we described earlier, namely, libeling and ridiculing each other, using shameful language while drunk or sober, or wronging themselves and others, whether in word or deed, in the various other ways that are typical of such people. They mustn't become accustomed to making themselves like madmen in either word or deed, for, though they must know about mad and vicious men and women, they must neither do nor imitate anything they do.

That's absolutely true.

Should they imitate metal workers or other craftsmen, or those who row in triremes, or their time-keepers, or anything else connected with ships?

How could they, since they aren't to concern themselves with any of those occupations?

And what about this? Will they imitate neighing horses, bellowing bulls, roaring rivers, the crashing sea, thunder, or anything of that sort?

They are forbidden to be mad or to imitate mad people.

If I understand what you mean, there is one kind of style and narrative that someone who is really a gentleman would use whenever he wanted to narrate something, and another kind, unlike this one, which his opposite by nature and education would favor, and in which he would narrate.

Which styles are those?

Well, I think that when a moderate man comes upon the words or actions of a good man in his narrative, he'll be willing to report them as if he were that man himself, and he won't be ashamed of that kind of imitation. He'll imitate this good man most when he's acting in a faultless and intelligent manner, but he'll do so less, and with more reluctance, when the good man is upset by disease, sexual passion, drunkenness, or some other misfortune. When he comes upon a character unworthy of himself, however, he'll be unwilling to make himself seriously resemble that inferior character – except perhaps for a brief period in which he's doing something good. Rather he'll be ashamed to do something like that, both because he's unpracticed in the imitation of such people and because he can't stand to shape and mould himself according to a worse pattern. He despises this in his mind, unless it's just done in play.

That seems likely.

[. . .]

X

Indeed, I said, our city has many features that assure me that we were entirely right in founding it as we did, and, when I say this, I'm especially thinking of poetry.

What about it in particular? Glaucon said.

That we didn't admit any that is imitative. Now that we have distinguished the separate parts of the soul, it is even clearer, I think, that such poetry should be altogether excluded.

What do you mean?

Between ourselves – for *you* won't denounce me to the tragic poets or any of the other imitative ones – all such poetry is likely to distort the thought of anyone who hears it, unless he has the knowledge of what it is really like, as a drug to counteract it.

What exactly do you have in mind in saying this?

I'll tell you, even though the love and respect I've had for Homer since I was a child make me hesitate to speak, for he seems to have been the first teacher and leader of all these fine tragedians. All the same, no one is to be honored or valued more than the truth. So, as I say, it must be told.

That's right.

Listen then, or, rather, answer.

Ask and I will.

Could you tell me what imitation in general is? I don't entirely understand what sort of thing imitations are trying to be.

Is it likely, then, that *I'll* understand?

That wouldn't be so strange, for people with bad eyesight often see things before those whose eyesight is keener.

That's so, but even if something occurred to me, I wouldn't be eager to talk about it in front of you. So I'd rather that you did the looking.

Do you want us to begin our examination, then, by adopting our usual procedure? As you know, we customarily hypothesise a single form in connection with each of the many things to which we apply the same name. Or don't you understand?

I do.

Then let's now take any of the manys you like. For example, there are many beds and tables.

Of course.

But there are only two forms of such furniture, one of the bed and one of the table.

Yes.

And don't we also customarily say that their makers look towards the appropriate form in making the beds or tables we use, and similarly in the other cases? Surely no craftsman makes the form itself. How could he?

There's no way he could.

Well, then, see what you'd call *this* craftsman?

Which one?

The one who makes all the things that all the other kinds of craftsmen severally make.

That's a clever and wonderful fellow you're talking about.

Wait a minute, and you'll have even more reason to say that, for this same craftsman is able to make, not only all kinds of furniture, but all plants that grow from the earth, all animals (including himself), the earth itself, the heavens, the gods, all the things in the heavens and in Hades beneath the earth.

He'd be amazingly clever!

You don't believe me? Tell me, do you think that there's no way any craftsman could make all these things, or that in one way he could and in another he couldn't? Don't you see that there is a way in which you yourself could make all of them?

What way is that?

It isn't hard: You could do it quickly and in lots of places, especially if you were willing to carry a mirror with you, for that's the quickest way of all. With it you can quickly make the sun, the things in the heavens, the earth, yourself, the other animals, manufactured items, plants, and everything else mentioned just now.

Yes, I could make them appear, but I couldn't make the things themselves as they truly are.

Well put! You've extracted the point that's crucial to the argument. I suppose that the painter too belongs to this class of makers,[10] doesn't he?

Of course.

But I suppose you'll say that he doesn't truly make the things he makes. Yet, in a certain way, the painter does make a bed, doesn't he?

Yes, he makes the appearance of one.

What about the carpenter? Didn't you just say that he doesn't make the form – which is our term for the being of a bed – but only *a* bed?

Yes, I did say that.

Now, if he doesn't make the being of a bed, he isn't making that which is, but something which is like that which is, but is not it. So, if someone were to say that the work of a carpenter or any other craftsman is completely that which is, wouldn't he risk saying what isn't true?[11]

That, at least, would be the opinion of those who busy themselves with arguments of this sort.

Then let's not be surprised if the carpenter's bed, too, turns out to be a somewhat dark affair in comparison to the true one.

All right.

Then, do you want us to try to discover what an imitator is by reference to these same examples?

I do, if you do.

We get, then, these three kinds of beds. The first is in nature a bed, and I suppose we'd say that a god makes it, or does someone else make it?

No one else, I suppose.

The second is the work of a carpenter.

Yes.

And the third is the one the painter makes. Isn't that so?

It is.

Then the painter, carpenter, and god correspond to three kinds of bed?

Yes, three.

Now, the god, either because he didn't want to or because it was necessary for him not to do so, didn't make more than one bed in nature, but only one, the very one that is the being of a bed. Two or more of these have not been made by the god and never will be.

Why is that?

Because, if he made only two, then again one would come to light whose form they in turn would both possess, and *that* would be the one that is the being of a bed and not the other two.

That's right.

The god knew this, I think and wishing to be the real maker of the truly real bed and not just *a* maker of *a* bed, he made it to be one in nature.

Probably so.

Do you want us to call him its natural maker or something like that?

It would be right to do so, at any rate, since he is by nature the maker of this and everything else.

What about a carpenter? Isn't he the maker of a bed?

Yes.

And is a painter also a craftsman and maker of such things?

Not at all.

Then what do you think he does do to a bed?

He imitates it. He is an imitator of what the others make. That, in my view, is the most reasonable thing to call him.

All right. Then wouldn't you call someone whose product is third from the natural one an imitator?

I most certainly would.

Then this will also be true of a tragedian, if indeed he is an imitator. He is by nature third from the king and the truth, as are all other imitators.

It looks that way.

We're agreed about imitators, then. Now, tell me this about a painter. Do you think he tries in each case to imitate the thing itself in nature or the works of craftsmen?

The works of craftsmen.

As they are or as they appear? You must be clear about that.

How do you mean?

Like this. If you look at a bed from the side or the front or from anywhere else is it a different bed each time? Or does it only appear different, without being at all different? And is that also the case with other things?

That's the way it is – it appears different without being so.

Then consider this very point: What does painting do in each case? Does it imitate that which is as it is, or does it imitate that which appears as it appears? Is it an imitation of appearances or of truth?

Of appearances.

Then imitation is far removed from the truth, for it touches only a small part of each thing and a part that is itself only an image. And that, it seems, is why it can produce everything. For example, we say that a painter can paint a cobbler, a carpenter, or any other craftsman, even though he knows nothing about these crafts. Nevertheless, if he is a good painter and displays his painting of a carpenter at a distance, he can deceive children and foolish people into thinking that it is truly a carpenter.

Of course.

Then this, I suppose, is what we must bear in mind in all these cases. Hence, whenever someone tells us that he has met a person who knows all the crafts as well as all the other things that anyone else knows and that his knowledge of any subject is more exact than any of theirs is, we must assume that we're talking to a simple-minded fellow who has apparently encountered some sort of magician or imitator and been deceived into thinking him omniscient and that the reason he has been deceived is that he himself can't distinguish between knowledge, ignorance, and imitation.

That's absolutely true.

[. . .]

Then let this be our defense – now that we've returned to the topic of poetry – that, in view of its nature, we had reason to banish it from the city earlier, for our argument compelled us to do so. But in case we are charged with a certain harshness and lack of sophistication, let's also tell poetry that there is an ancient quarrel between it and philosophy, which is evidenced by such expressions as "the dog yelping and shrieking at its master," "great in the empty eloquence of fools," "the mob of wise men that has mastered Zeus," and "the subtle thinkers, beggars all."[12] Nonetheless, if the poetry that aims at pleasure and imitation has any argument to bring forward that proves it ought to have a place in a well-governed city, we at least would be glad to admit it, for we are well aware of the charm it exercises. But, be that as it may, to betray what one believes to be the truth is impious. What about you, Glaucon, don't you feel the charm of the pleasure-giving Muse, especially when you study her through the eyes of Homer?

Very much so.

Therefore, isn't it just that such poetry should return from exile when it has successfully defended itself, whether in lyric or any other meter?

Certainly.

Then we'll allow its defenders, who aren't poets themselves but lovers of poetry, to speak in prose on its behalf and to show that it not only gives pleasure but is beneficial both to constitutions and to human life. Indeed, we'll listen to them graciously, for we'd certainly profit if poetry were shown to be not only pleasant but also beneficial.

How could we fail to profit?

However, if such a defense isn't made, we'll behave like people who have fallen in love with someone but who force themselves to stay away from him, because they realize that their passion isn't beneficial. In the same way, because the love of this sort of poetry has been implanted in us by the upbringing we have received under our fine constitutions, we are well disposed to any proof that it is the best and truest thing. But if it isn't able to produce such a defence, then, whenever we listen to it, we'll repeat the argument we have just now put forward like an incantation so as to preserve ourselves from slipping back into that childish passion for poetry which the majority of people have. And we'll go on chanting that such poetry is not to be taken seriously or treated as a serious undertaking with some kind of hold on the truth, but that anyone who is anxious about the constitution within him must be careful when he hears it and must continue to believe what we have said about it.

I completely agree.

Notes

1 Ourenos prevented his wife Gaia from giving birth to his children, by blocking them up inside her. Gaia gave a sickle to one of these children, Cronos, with which he castrated his father when the latter next had intercourse with her. Cronos ate the children he had by his wife Rheia, until, by deceiving him with a stone, she was able to save Zeus from suffering this fate. Zeus then overthrew his father. See Hesiod, *Theogony* 154–210, 453–506.

2 The first three quotations are from *Iliad* 24.527–32. The sources for the fourth and for the quotation from Aeschylus are unknown. The story of Athena urging Pandarus to break the truce is told in *Iliad* 4.73–126.

3 In the *Iliad* 2.1–34, Zeus sends a dream to Agamemnon to promise success if he attacks Troy immediately. The promise is false. The source for the quotation from Aeschylus is unknown.

4 i.e. deny him the funding necessary to hire a chorus of actors and produce his play.

5 *Odyssey* 11.489–91. Odysseus is being addressed by the dead Achilles in Hades.

6 *Iliad* 20.64–5. The speaker is Hades – god of Hades or the underworld – who is afraid that the earth will split open and reveal that his home is dreadful, etc.

7 *Iliad* 23.103–4. Achilles speaks these lines as the soul of the dead Patroclus leaves for Hades.

8 *Odyssey* 10.493–5. Circe is speaking to Odysseus about the prophet Tiresias.

9 *Iliad* 16.856–7. The words refer to Patroclus, who has just been mortally wounded by Hector.

10 Throughout the following passage, Plato takes advantage of the fact that the Greek word *poiein* means both "to make" generally and also "to compose poetry." Indeed, the word *poiētēs* means both "poet" and "maker" so that to class the poet (and the painter) as "makers" is much more natural in Greek than it is in English.

11 This sentence is best understood as follows: "If the carpenter doesn't make the being of e.g. a bed, he isn't making that which a bed is, but something which, though it is like what a bed is, isn't the same as what a bed is. So if someone were to say that the work of a carpenter or other craftsman is completely that which it is (e.g. a bed), wouldn't he risk saying what isn't true?"

12 Philosophers, such as Xenophanes and Heraclitus, attacked Homer and Hesiod for their immoral tales about the gods. Poets, such as Aristophanes in his *Clouds*, attacked philosophers for subverting traditional ethical and religious values. But the sources of these particular quotations are unknown.

19 The Sovereignty of Good Over Other Concepts

Iris Murdoch

The development of consciousness in human beings is inseparably connected with the use of metaphor. Metaphors are not merely peripheral decorations or even useful models, they are fundamental forms of our awareness of our condition: metaphors of space, metaphors of movement, metaphors of vision. Philosophy in general, and moral philosophy in particular, has in the past often concerned itself with what it took to be our most important images, clarifying existing ones and developing new ones. Philosophical argument which consists of such image-play, I mean the great metaphysical systems, is usually inconclusive, and is regarded by many contemporary thinkers as valueless. The status and merit of this type of argument raises, of course, many problems. However, it seems to me impossible to discuss certain kinds of concepts without resort to metaphor, since the concepts are themselves deeply metaphorical and cannot be analysed into non-metaphorical components without a loss of substance. Modern behaviouristic philosophy attempts such an analysis in the case of certain moral concepts, it seems to me without success. One of the motives of the attempt is a wish to 'neutralize' moral philosophy, to produce a philosophical discussion of morality which does not take sides. Metaphors often carry a moral charge, which analysis in simpler and plainer terms is designed to remove. This too seems to me to be misguided. Moral philosophy cannot avoid taking sides, and would-be neutral philosophers merely take sides surreptitiously. Moral philosophy is the examination of the most important of all human activities, and I think that two things are required of it. The examination should be realistic. Human nature, as opposed to the natures of other hypothetical spiritual beings, has certain discoverable attributes, and these should be suitably considered in any discussion of morality. Secondly, since an ethical system cannot but commend an ideal, it should commend a worthy ideal. Ethics should not be merely an analysis of ordinary mediocre conduct, it should be a hypothesis about good conduct and about how this can be achieved. How can we make ourselves better? is a question moral philosophers should attempt to answer. And if I am right the answer will come partly at least in the form of explanatory and persuasive metaphors. The metaphors which I myself favour and the philosopher under whose banner I am fighting I will make clear shortly.

First, however, I wish to mention very briefly two fundamental assumptions of my argument. If either of these is denied what follows will be less convincing. I assume that human beings are naturally selfish and that human life has no external point or τέλος. That human beings are naturally selfish seems true on the evidence, whenever and wherever we look at them, in spite of a very small number of apparent exceptions. About the quality of this selfishness modern psychology has had something to tell us. The psyche is a historically determined individual relentlessly looking after itself. In some ways it resembles a machine; in order to operate it needs sources of energy, and it is predisposed to certain patterns of activity. The area of its vaunted freedom of choice is not usually very great. One of its main pastimes is day-dreaming. It is reluctant to face unpleasant realities. Its consciousness is not normally a transparent glass through which it views the world, but a cloud of more or less fantastic reverie designed to protect the psyche from pain. It constantly seeks consolation, either through imagined inflation of self or through fictions of a theological nature. Even its loving is more often than not an assertion of self. I think we can probably recognize ourselves in this rather depressing description.

That human life has no external point or τέλος is a view as difficult to argue as its opposite, and I shall simply assert it. I can see no evidence to suggest that human life is not something self-contained. There are properly many patterns and purposes within life, but there is no general and as it were externally guaranteed pattern or purpose of the kind for which philosophers and theologians used to search. We are what we seem to be, transient mortal creatures subject to necessity and chance. This is to say that there is, in my view, no God in the traditional sense of that term; and the traditional sense is perhaps the only sense. When Bonhoeffer says that God wants us to live as if there were no God I suspect he is misusing words. Equally the various metaphysical substitutes for God – Reason, Science, History – are false deities. Our destiny can be examined but it cannot be justified or totally explained. We are simply here. And if there is any kind of sense or unity in human life, and the dream of this does not cease to haunt us, it is of some other kind and must be sought within a human experience which has nothing outside it. [. . .]

By opening our eyes we do not necessarily see what confronts us. We are anxiety-ridden animals. Our minds are continually active, fabricating an anxious, usually self-preoccupied, often falsifying *veil* which partially conceals the world. Our states of consciousness differ in quality, our fantasies and reveries are not trivial and unimportant, they are profoundly connected with our energies and our ability to choose and act. And if quality of consciousness matters, then anything which alters consciousness in the direction of unselfishness, objectivity and realism is to be connected with virtue.

Following a hint in Plato (*Phaedrus* 250) I shall start by speaking of what is perhaps the most obvious thing in our surroundings which is an occasion for 'unselfing', and that is what is popularly called beauty. Recent philosophers tend to avoid this term because they prefer to talk of reasons rather than of experiences. But the implication of experience with beauty seems to me to be something of great importance which should not be bypassed in favour of analysis of critical vocabularies. Beauty is the convenient and traditional name of something which art and nature share, and which gives a fairly clear sense to the idea of quality of experience and change of consciousness. I am looking out of my window in an anxious and resentful state of mind, oblivious of my surroundings, brooding perhaps on some damage done to my prestige. Then suddenly I observe a hovering kestrel. In a moment everything is altered. The brooding self with its hurt vanity has disappeared. There is nothing now but kestrel. And when I return to thinking of the other matter it seems less important. And of course this is something which we may also do deliberately: give attention to nature in order to clear our minds of selfish care. It may seem odd to start the argument against what I have roughly labelled as 'romanticism' by using the case of attention to nature. In fact I do not think that any of the great romantics really believed that we receive but what we give and in our life alone does nature live, although the lesser ones tended to follow Kant's lead and use nature as an occasion for exalted self-feeling. The great romantics, including the one I have just quoted, transcended 'romanticism'. A self-directed enjoyment of nature seems to me to be something forced. More naturally, as well as more properly, we take a self-forgetful pleasure in the sheer alien pointless independent existence of animals, birds, stones and trees. 'Not how the world is, but that it is, is the mystical.'

I take this starting-point, not because I think it is the most important place of moral change, but because I think it is the most accessible one. It is so patently a good thing to take delight in flowers and animals that people who bring home potted plants and watch kestrels might even be surprised at the notion that these things have anything to do with virtue. The surprise is a product of the fact that, as Plato pointed out, beauty is the only spiritual thing which we love by instinct. When we move from beauty in nature to beauty in art we are already in a more difficult region. The experience of art is more easily degraded than the experience of nature. A great deal of art, perhaps most art, actually is self-consoling fantasy, and even great art cannot guarantee the quality of its consumer's consciousness. However, great art exists and is sometimes properly experienced and even a shallow experience of what is great can have its effect. Art, and by 'art' from now on I mean good art, not fantasy art, affords us a pure delight in the independent existence of what is excellent. Both in its genesis and its enjoyment it is a thing totally opposed to selfish obsession. It invigorates our best faculties and, to use Platonic language, inspires love in the highest part of the soul. It is able to do this partly by virtue of something which it shares with nature: a perfection of form which invites unpossessive contemplation and resists absorption into the selfish dream life of the consciousness.

Art however, considered as a sacrament or a source of good energy, possesses an extra dimension. Art is less accessible than nature but also more edifying since it is actually a human product, and certain arts are actually 'about' human affairs in a direct sense. Art is a human product and virtues as well as talents are required of the artist. The good artist, in relation to his art, is brave, truthful, patient, humble; and even in nonrepresentational art we may receive intuitions of these qualities. One may also suggest, more cautiously, that non-representational art does seem to express more positively something which is to do with virtue. The spiritual role of music has often been acknowledged, though theorists have been chary of analysing it. However that may be, the representational arts, which more evidently hold the mirror up to nature, seem to be concerned with morality in a way which is not simply an effect of our intuition of the artist's discipline.

These arts, especially literature and painting, show us the peculiar sense in which the concept of virtue is tied on to the human condition. They show us the absolute pointlessness of virtue while exhibiting its supreme importance; the enjoyment of art is a training in the love of virtue. The pointlessness of art is not the pointlessness of a game; it is the pointlessness of human life itself, and form in art is properly the simulation of the self-contained aimlessness of the universe. Good art reveals what we are usually too selfish and too timid to recognise, the minute and absolutely random detail of the world, and reveals it together with a sense of unity and form. This form often seems to us mysterious because it resists the easy patterns of the fantasy, whereas there is nothing mysterious about the forms of bad art since they are the recognizable and familiar rat-runs of selfish day-dream. Good art shows us how difficult it is to be objective by showing us how differently the world looks to an objective vision. We are presented with a truthful image of the human condition in a form which can be steadily contemplated; and indeed this is the only context in which many of us are capable of contemplating it at all. Art transcends selfish and obsessive limitations of personality and can enlarge the sensibility of its consumer. It is a kind of goodness by proxy. Most of all it exhibits to us the connection, in *human* beings, of clear realistic vision with compassion. The realism of a great artist is not a photographic realism, it is essentially both pity and justice. [. . .]

Art then is not a diversion or a side-issue, it is the most educational of all human activities and a place in which the nature of morality can be *seen*. Art gives a clear sense to many ideas which seem more puzzling when we meet with them elsewhere, and it is a clue to what happens elsewhere. An understanding of any art involves a recognition of hierarchy and authority. There are very evident degrees of merit, there are heights and distances; even Shakespeare is not perfect. Good art, unlike bad art, unlike 'happenings', is something pre-eminently outside us and resistant to our consciousness. We surrender ourselves to its *authority* with a love which is unpossessive and unselfish. Art shows us the only sense in which the permanent and incorruptible is compatible with the transient; and whether representational or not it reveals to us aspects of our world which our ordinary dull dream-consciousness is unable to see. Art pierces the veil and gives sense to the notion of a reality which lies beyond appearance; it exhibits virtue in its true guise in the context of death and chance.

Plato held that beauty could be a starting-point of the good life, but he came to mistrust art and we can see played out in that great spirit the peculiarly distressing struggle between the artist and the saint. Plato allowed to the beauty of the lovely boy an awakening power which he denied to the beauty of nature or of art. He seems to have come to believe that all art is bad art, a mere fiction and consolation which distorts reality. About nature he seems, in the context of the theory of forms, to have been at least once in doubt. Are there forms of mud, hair and dirt? If there are then nature is redeemed into the area of truthful vision. (My previous argument assumes of course, in Platonic terms, that there are.) Another starting-point, or road, which Plato speaks of more often however is the way of the τέχναι, the sciences, crafts, and intellectual disciplines excluding the arts. I think there is a way of the intellect, a sense in which intellectual disciplines arc moral disciplines, and this is not too difficult to discern. There are important bridge ideas between morality and other at first sight different human activities, and these ideas are perhaps most clearly seen in the context of the τέχναι. And as when we use the nature of art as a clue, we may be able to learn more about the central area of morality if we examine what are essentially the same concepts more simply on display elsewhere. I mean such concepts as justice, accuracy, truthfulness, realism, humility, courage as the ability to sustain clear vision, love as attachment or even passion without sentiment or self.

The τέχνη which Plato thought was most important was mathematics, because it was most rigorous and abstract. I shall take an example of a τέχνη more congenial to myself: learning a language. If I am learning, for instance, Russian, I am confronted by an authoritative structure which commands my respect. The task is difficult and the goal is distant and perhaps never entirely attainable. My work is a progressive revelation of something which exists independently of me. Attention is rewarded by a knowledge of reality. Love of Russian leads me away from myself towards something alien to me, something which my consciousness cannot take over, swallow up, deny or make unreal. The honesty and humility required of the student – not to pretend to know what one does not know – is the preparation for the honesty and humility of the scholar who does not even feel tempted to suppress the fact which damns his theory. Of course a τέχνη can be misused; a scientist might feel he ought to give up a certain branch of study if he knew that his discoveries would be used wickedly. But apart from special contexts, studying is normally an exercise of virtue as well as of talent, and shows us a fundamental way in which virtue is related to the real world.

20   Form and Content, Philosophy and Literature

Martha C. Nussbaum

How should one write, what words should one select, what forms and structures and organization, if one is pursuing understanding? (Which is to say, if one is, in that sense, a philosopher?) Sometimes this is taken to be a trivial and uninteresting question. I shall claim that it is not. Style itself makes its claims, expresses its own sense of what matters. Literary form is not separable from philosophical content, but is, itself, a part of content – an integral part, then, of the search for and the statement of truth.

But this suggests, too, that there may be some views of the world and how one should live in it – views, especially, that emphasize the world's surprising variety, its complexity and mysteriousness, its flawed and imperfect beauty – that cannot be fully and adequately stated in the language of conventional philosophical prose, a style remarkably flat and lacking in wonder – but only in a language and in forms themselves more complex, more allusive, more attentive to particulars. Not perhaps, either, in the expositional structure conventional to philosophy, which sets out to establish something and then does so, without surprise, without incident – but only in a form that itself implies that life contains significant surprises, that our task, as agents, is to live as good characters in a good story do, caring about what happens, resourcefully confronting each new thing. If these views are serious candidates for truth, views that the search for truth ought to consider along its way, then it seems that this language and these forms ought to be included within philosophy. [. . .]

In his preface to *The Golden Bowl*, Henry James describes the author's selection of appropriate terms and sentences, using two metaphors. One is a metaphor of plant growth. Focusing on his theme or idea, the author causes it "to flower before me as into the only terms that honorably expressed it."[1] And elsewhere in the prefaces, James frequently compares the author's sense of life to soil, the literary text to a plant that grows out of that soil and expresses, in its form, the soil's character and composition.

James's second metaphor is more mysterious. The fully imagined text is next compared (in its relation, apparently, to whatever simpler, more inert, less adequate language may have been, before its invention, on the scene to cover the subject) to some creatures of the air, perhaps birds, perhaps angels. The novelist's imagined words are called "the immense array of terms, perceptional and expressional, that, after the fashion I have indicated, in sentence, passage and page, simply looked over the heads of the standing terms – or perhaps rather, like alert winged creatures, perched on those diminished summits and aspired to a clearer air."[2]

These two metaphors point to two claims about the writer's art that seem worth investigating. To investigate and defend them is a central purpose of [this essay]. The first is the claim that there is, with respect to any text carefully written and fully imagined, an organic connection between its form and its content. Certain thoughts and ideas, a certain sense of life, reach toward expression in writing that has a certain shape and form, that uses certain structures, certain terms. Just as the plant emerges from the seeded soil, taking its form from the combined character of seed and soil, so the novel and its terms flower from and express the conceptions of the author, his or her sense of what matters. Conception and form are bound together; finding and shaping the words is a matter of finding the appropriate and, so to speak, the honorable, fit between conception and expression. If the writing is well done, a paraphrase in a very different form and style will not, in general, express the same conception.

The second claim is that certain truths about human life can only be fittingly and accurately stated in the language and forms characteristic of the narrative artist. With respect to certain elements of human life, the terms of the novelist's art are alert winged creatures, perceiving where the blunt terms of ordinary speech, or of abstract theoretical discourse, are blind, acute where they are obtuse, winged where they are dull and heavy. [. . .]

In Plato's attack upon the poets we find a profound insight: that all of the ways of writing that were characteristic of tragic (and much of epic) poetry are committed to a certain, albeit very general, view of human life, a view from which one might dissent. Tragedies state this view in the very way they construct their plots, engage the attention of their audience, use rhythm and music and language. The elements of this view include at least the following: that happenings beyond the agent's control are of real importance not only for his or her feelings of happiness or contentment, but also for whether he or she manages to live a fully good life, a life inclusive of various forms of laudable action. That, therefore, what happens to people by chance can be of enormous importance to the ethical quality of their lives; that, therefore, good people are right to care deeply about such chance events. That, for these same reasons, an audience's pity and fear at tragic events are valuable responses, responses for which there is an important place in the ethical life, since they embody a recognition of ethical truths. That other emotions as well are appropriate, and based upon correct beliefs about what matters. That, for example, it is right to love certain things and people that lie beyond one's own control, and to grieve when these people die, when these things are removed. The tragic genre depends on such beliefs for its very structure and literary shape: for its habit is to tell stories of reversals happening to good but not invulnerable people, and to tell these stories as if they matter for all human beings. And the form sets up in its audience responses, particularly those of pity for the characters and fear for oneself, that presuppose a similar set of beliefs. It feeds the tendency of the spectator to identify with a hero who weeps uncontrollably over the body of a loved one, or goes mad with rage, or is terrified by the force of an insoluble dilemma.

But one may or may not accept these beliefs, this view of life. If one believes, with Socrates, that the good person cannot be harmed, that the only thing of real importance is one's own virtue, then one will not think that stories of reversal have deep ethical significance, and one will not want to write as if they did, or to show as worthy heroes people who believe that they do. Like Plato's *Republic*, we will omit the tears of Achilles at Patroclus' death, if we wish to teach that the good person is self-sufficient. Nor will we want works around that make their connection with the audience through the emotions – since all of them seem to rest on the belief (a false belief, from this point of view) that such external happenings do have significance. In short, one's beliefs about the ethical truth shape one's view of literary forms, seen as ethical statements. [. . .]

The "ancient quarrel" had an exemplary clarity, since the participants shared a view of what the quarrel was about. However much Plato and the poets disagreed, they agreed that the aim of their work was to provide illumination concerning how one should live. Of course they were at odds concerning what the ethical truth was, and also concerning the nature of understanding. But still, there was some roughly single goal, however much in need of further specification, that they did share, some question to which they could be seen as offering competing answers.

One obstacle to any contemporary version of the ancient project is the difficulty of arriving at any account of what we are looking for that will be shared by the various parties. My aim is to establish that certain literary texts (or texts similar these in certain relevant ways) are indispensable to a philosophical inquiry in the ethical sphere: not by any means sufficient but sources of insight without which the inquiry cannot be complete. But then it is important to have some conception, however general and flexible, of the inquiry inside which I wish to place the novels, the project in which I see them as helping to state a distinctive alternative to Kantian and Utilitarian conceptions. A difficulty here is that some influential accounts of what moral philosophy includes are cast in the terms of one or another of the competing ethical conceptions; thus they will prove unsuitable, if we want to organize a fair comparison among them. For example, if we begin with the Utilitarian's organizing question, "How can one maximize utility?," we accept, already, a certain characterization of what is salient in the subject matter of ethics, of the right or relevant descriptions for practical situations – one that would rule out from the start, as irrelevant, much of what the novels present as highly relevant. Similarly, reliance on a Kantian characterization of the domain of the moral, and of its relation to what happens in the empirical realm, together with reliance on the Kantian's organizing question "What is my moral duty?," would have the effect of artificially cutting off from the inquiry some elements of life that the novels show as important and link to others – all in advance of a sensitive study of the sense of life that the novels themselves have to offer. So we would, it seems, be ill advised to adopt either of these methods and questions as architectonic guides to the pursuit of a comparison among different conceptions, different senses of life – among these the views of life expressed in the novels. It seems that we should see whether we can find an account of the methods, subject maker, and questions of moral philosophy (ethical inquiry) that is more inclusive.

And here, it must be stressed, what we really want is an account of ethical inquiry that will capture what we actually do when we ask ourselves the most pressing ethical questions. For the activity of comparison I describe is a real practical activity, one that we undertake in countless ways when we ask ourselves how to live, what to be; one that we perform together with others, in search of ways of living together in a community, country, or planet. To bring novels into moral philosophy is not – as I understand this proposal – to bring them to some academic discipline which happens to ask ethical questions. It is to bring them into connection with our deepest practical searching, for ourselves and others, the searching in connection with which the influential philosophical conceptions of the ethical were originally developed, the searching we pursue as we compare these conceptions, both with one another and with our active sense of life. Or rather, it is to recognize that the novels are in this search already: to insist on and describe, the connections the novels have already for readers who love them and who read, like David Copperfield, for life. [. . .]

Nothing could be further from my intentions than to suggest that we *substitute* the study of novels for the study of the recognized great works of the various philosophical traditions in ethics. Although this may disappoint some who find moderate positions boring, I have no interest in dismissive assaults on systematic ethical theory, or on "Western rationality," or even on Kantianism or Utilitarianism, to which the novels, to be sure, display their own oppositions. I make a proposal that should be acceptable even to Kantians or Utilitarians, if, like Rawls and Sidgwick, they accept the Aristotelian question and the Aristotelian dialectical procedure as good overall guides in ethics, and are thereby methodologically committed to the sympathetic study of alternative conceptions. The proposal is that we should *add* the study of certain novels to the study of these works, on the grounds that without them we will not have a fully adequate statement of a powerful ethical conception, one that we ought to investigate. It will be clear that I sympathize with this ethical conception and that I present, in alliance with the novels, the beginning of a defense of it. But that's just it, it is the beginning, not the completion. And in the full working out of the inquiry the investigation of alternative views, in their own styles and structures, would play a central role. [. . .]

"But novels both represent and activate the emotions: so our dealings with them are marred by irrationality. They are not likely, therefore, to contribute to rational resection." No other objection has been so frequently made against the literary style, and no other has been so damaging to its claims. Emotions, it is said, are unreliable, animal, seductive. They lead away from the cool reflection that alone is capable of delivering a considered judgment. Certainly the novel as form is profoundly committed to the emotions; its interaction with its readers takes place centrally through them. So this challenge must be confronted.

A central purpose of [this essay] is to call this view of rationality into question and to suggest, with Aristotle, that practical reasoning unaccompanied by emotion is not sufficient for practical wisdom; that emotions are not only not more unreliable than intellectual calculations, but frequently are more reliable, and less deceptively seductive. But before we can go very far with this issue, it is very important to notice that the traditional objection is actually two very different objections, which have been confused in some contemporary versions of the debate. According to one version of the objection, emotions are unreliable and distracting because they have nothing to do with cognition at all. According to the second objection, they have a great deal to do with cognition, but they embody a view of the world that is in fact false.

According to the first view, then, emotions are blind animal reactions, like or identical with bodily feelings, that are in their nature unmixed with thought, undiscriminating, and impervious to reasoning. This version of the objection relies on a very impoverished conception of emotion that cannot survive scrutiny. It has had a certain influence; but by now it has been decisively rejected by cognitive psychology, by anthropology, by psychoanalysis, and even by philosophy – not to speak of our sense of life itself. However much these disciplines differ about the further analysis of emotions such as fear, grief, love, and pity, they agree that these emotions are very closely linked to beliefs in such a way that a modification of beliefs brings about a modification of emotion. In drawing this conclusion, they are in fact returning to the conception of emotion that Aristotle shared with most of the other Greek philosophers. For they all held that emotions are not simply blind surges of affect, recognized, and discriminated from one another, by their felt quality alone; rather they are discriminating responses closely connected with beliefs about how things are and what is important. Being angry, for example, is not like experiencing a bodily appetite. Hunger and thirst do seem to be relatively impervious to changes in belief, but anger seems to require and to rest upon a belief that one has been wronged or damaged in some significant way by the person toward whom the anger is directed. The discovery that this belief is false (either that the event in question did not take place, or that the damage is after all trivial, or that it was not caused by that person) can be expected to remove the anger toward that person. Feeling grief presupposes, in a similar way, a family of beliefs about one's circumstances: that a loss has taken place; that the loss is of something that has value. Once again, a change in the relevant beliefs, either about what has happened or about its importance, will be likely to alter or remove the emotion. Love, pity, fear, and their relatives—all are belief-based in a similar way: all involve the acceptance of certain views of how the world is and what has importance.

There are various subtly different positions available (in both the ancient discussion and the contemporary literature) about the precise relationship between emotions and beliefs. But the major views all make the acceptance of a certain belief or beliefs at least a necessary condition for emotion, and, in most cases, also constituent part of what an emotion is. And the most powerful accounts, furthermore, go on to argue that if one *really* accepts or takes in a certain belief, one will experience the emotion: belief is sufficient for emotion, emotion necessary for full belief. For example, if a person believes that X is the most important person in her life and that X has just died, she will feel grief. If she does not, this is because in some sense she doesn't fully comprehend or has not taken in or is repressing these facts. Again, if Y *says* that racial justice is very important to her and also that a racially motivated attack has just taken place before her eyes, and yet she is in no way angry – this, again, will lead us to question the sincerity, either of Y's belief-claims, or of her denial of emotion.

Because the emotions have this cognitive dimension in their very structure, it is very natural to view them as intelligent parts of our ethical agency, responsive to the workings of deliberation and essential to its completion. (Dante's *intelligenza d'amore* is not an intellectual grasp of emotion; it is an understanding that is not available to the non-lover, and the loving itself is part of it.) On this view, there will be certain contexts in which the pursuit of intellectual reasoning apart from emotion will actually prevent a full rational judgment – for example by preventing an access to one's grief, or one's love, that is necessary for the full understanding of what has taken place when a loved one dies Emotions can, of course, be unreliable – in much the same ways that beliefs can. People get angry because of false beliefs about the facts, or their importance; the relevant beliefs might also be true but unjustified, or both false and unjustified. [. . .]

But the fact that some beliefs are irrational has rarely led philosophers to dismiss all beliefs from practical reasoning. So it is not easy to see why parallel failings in the emotions should have led to their dismissal. And the Aristotelian view holds, in fact, that frequently they are more reliable in deliberation than detached intellectual judgments, since emotions embody some of our most deeply rooted views about what has importance, views that could easily be lost from sight during sophisticated intellectual reasoning. [. . .]

But why not life itself? Why can't we investigate whatever we want to investigate by living and reflecting on our lives? Why, if it is the Aristotelian ethical conception we wish to scrutinize, can't we do that without literary texts, without texts at all – or, rather, with the texts of our own lives set before us? Here, we must first say that of course we do this as well, both apart from our reading of the novels and (as Proust insists) in the process of reading. In a sense Proust is right to see the literary text as an "optical instrument" through which the reader becomes a reader of his or her own heart. But, why do we need, in that case, such optical instruments?

One obvious answer was suggested already by Aristotle: we have never lived enough. Our experience is, without fiction, too confined and too parochial. Literature extends it, making us reflect and feel about what might otherwise be too distant for feeling.[3] The importance of this for both morals and politics cannot be underestimated. [. . .]

We can clarify and extend this point by emphasizing that novels do not function, inside this account, as pieces of "raw" life: they are a close and careful interpretative description. All living is interpreting; all action requires seeing the world *as* something. So in this sense no life is "raw," and (as James and Proust insist) throughout our living we are, in a sense, makers of fictions. The point is that in the activity of literary imagining we are led to imagine and describe with greater precision, focusing our attention on each word, feeling each event more keenly – whereas much of actual life goes by without that heightened awareness, and is thus, in a certain sense, not fully or thoroughly lived. Neither James nor Proust thinks of ordinary life as normative, and the Aristotelian conception concurs: too much of it is obtuse, routinized, incompletely sentient. So literature is an extension of life not only horizontally, bringing the reader into contact with events or locations or persons or problems he or she has not otherwise met, but also, so to speak, vertically, giving the reader experience that is deeper, sharper, and more precise than much of what takes place in life.

To this point we can add three others that have to do with our relation, as readers, to the literary text, and the differences between that relation and other relations in which life involves us. As James frequently stresses, novel reading places us in a position that is both like and unlike the position we occupy in life: like, in that we are emotionally involved with the characters, active with them, and aware of our incompleteness; unlike, in that we are free of certain sources of distortion that frequently impede our real-life deliberations. Since the story is not ours, we do not find ourselves caught up in the "vulgar heat" of our personal jealousies or angers or in the sometimes blinding violence of our loves. Thus the (ethically concerned) aesthetic attitude shows us the way. Proust's Marcel concurs, making a far stronger (and, perhaps, to that extent less compelling) claim: that it is only in relation to the literary text, and never in life, that we can have a relation characterized by genuine altruism, and by genuine acknowledgment of the otherness of the other. [. . .] There is something about the act of reading that is exemplary for conduct.

Furthermore, another way in which the enterprise of reading is exemplary is that it brings readers together. And, as Lionel Trilling emphasized, it brings them together in a particular way, a way that is constitutive of a particular sort of community: one in which each person's imagining and thinking and feeling are respected as morally valuable. The Aristotelian dialectical enterprise was characterized as a social or communal endeavor in which people who will share a form of life try to agree on the conception by which they can live together. Each person's solitary scrutiny of his or her own experience may, then, be too private and non-shared an activity to facilitate such a shared conversation – especially if we take seriously, as the novels all do, the moral value of privacy regarding one's own personal thoughts and feelings. We need, then, texts we can read together and talk about as friends, texts that are available to all of us. [. . .]

A community is formed by author and readers. In this community separateness and qualitative difference are not neglected; the privacy and the imagining of each is nourished and encouraged. But at the same time it is stressed that living together is the object of our ethical interest. [. . .]

Philosophy has often seen itself as a way of transcending the merely human, of giving the human being a new and more godlike set of activities and attachments. The alternative I explore sees it as a way of being human and speaking humanly. That suggestion will appeal only to those who actually want to be human, who see in human life as it is, with its surprises and connections, its pains and sudden joys, a story worth embracing. This in no way means not wishing to make life better than it is. But [. . .] there are ways of transcending that are human and "internal," and other ways that involve flight and repudiation. It seems plausible that in pursuit of the first way – in pursuit of human self-understanding and of a society in which humanity can realize itself more fully – the imagination and the terms of the literary artist are indispensable guides: as James suggests, angels of and in the fallen world, alert in perception and sympathy, lucidly bewildered, surprised by the intelligence of love.

Notes

1 Henry James, Preface to *The Golden Bowl*, in *The Art of the Novel* (New York, 1907), 339. In the volumes of the New York Edition (Scribners, 1907–9) containing *The Golden Bowl*, this passage occurs on I.xvi. James is actually talking here of the activity of "revision," the author/reader's re-imagining of the language and form of his text.
2 James, *Art of the Novel*, 339.
3 I am thinking of Aristotle's claims, in both *Rhetoric* and *Poetics*, about the connection between our interest in literature and our love of learning.

---

21 Carnage and Glory, Legends and Lies

Michael Norman

For the record, I know the drill. I've saluted my superiors and spit shined my shoes and marched till my arches were aching. I've aimed a rifle and reeled at the awful result. In short, I'm a typical American paradox, a veteran who still boils at the Beltway blockheads who bloodied his generation and a former marine who will always step forward for his beloved corps.

One fine Tuesday many movie seasons ago I carried this baggage into the Sherry Netherland Hotel in Manhattan to interview a film maker, then relatively unknown, named Oliver Stone. Someone thought it might make interesting reading if a combat-hardened reporter was dispatched to encounter a combat-hardened director, especially when that director was peddling his war record as the bona fides for his new movie, *Platoon*.

"So – what did you think?" he said as I settled into a chair opposite him. The marketing campaign, as I remember, was to position *Platoon* as the real thing, the first Vietnam movie to present the war as it really was. "You were there too," he kept saying. "What do you think?"

I was a little naive in those days; I'd been covering politicians and murderers and had no experience with the more dangerous characters from Hollywood. I took the director's question literally; I thought he was talking about psychological sense, existential verity, the real war, the one that rages in a warrior's head and heart and soul. I thought – God forgive me my innocence – I thought he was talking about the *truth*.

I went on to write some polite and, I now know, some very wrongheaded things about *Platoon*. In truth I hated the movie almost as much as I hated the war. But the legacy of that day is not the feckless story I delivered. It is in the last words of the director as I thanked him for his time and turned to leave. He asked if I'd seen his movie *Salvador*, and as it happened I had.

"Wasn't the makeup on the corpses great?" he said, beaming. "I'm proud of those corpses."

I thought about that bizarre remark for a long time. I was sure that Mr Stone was talking about verisimilitude, how he'd tried to make the dead seem so lifelike, so real. Then two years later I found myself in Chicago in the middle of winter with Gene Hackman.

The actor had just finished shooting a scene for Andrew Davis's film *The Package*, and we were sitting on the set, a small neighborhood restaurant, drinking cups of tepid coffee to ward off the bitter cold. Mr Hackman is a former marine, and the conversation soon turned to the corps and war movies – he'd made a few – and finally *Platoon*. I mentioned Mr Stone's bizarre remark about the makeup on corpses, then told Mr Hackman how I had never been able to figure out exactly what the director was trying to say.

"My friend," said the actor, smiling a big, knowing smile, "maybe he was trying to tell you that *Platoon* was only a movie, get it?"

I'm not sure – on both counts – so we'll just let the question of truth and art hang for a moment. Let's flash forward to a few weeks ago. Edward Zwick, the director, was sitting in a tiny, cramped office not far from a scoring stage in Studio City, California, talking on the telephone about his new movie *Courage under Fire*, a combat film set in the Persian Gulf war, that very brief demonstration of the latest in lethal technology.

Courage Under Fire, which stars Denzel Washington, Meg Ryan and Lou Diamond Phillips [. . .] is about the investigation into the last hours of a helicopter pilot, a woman nominated for a Congressional Medal of Honor. It is one of a spate of films [. . .] that turn on war or invoke a military motif or milieu.

Sergeant Bilko, for example, is a revival of the ingenious con-man capers that Phil Silvers made famous in his television barracks and motor pool decades ago; *Down Periscope* evokes the close-quarters laughs of 1959's *Operation Petticoat*; *Executive Decision* employs the now familiar device of the military antiterrorist squad, this time on board a nuclear-rigged jetliner; *The Rock* has a renegade band of Marines and mercenaries on Alcatraz Island armed with bitter memories and poison gas rockets. But in *Independence Day*, [. . .] there's no doubting who the good guys are when the Marine fighter pilots take on alien invaders.

No other genre offers a film maker as much background or as many cultural reference points. Set the scene on a battlefield and the director instantly has a clearly defined conflict, a catalyst for violence and all the elements to create the one quality that will draw people to the big screen – spectacle. Put the characters in uniform and the scriptwriter instantly inherits story lines and narrative conventions that are at least 4,000 years old.

If the war film, or military movie, is not the oldest genre in Hollywood, surely it is the most enduring. A century ago the earliest film makers were restaging scenes from the Spanish-American War to show in the old nickelodeons. D. W. Griffith's *Birth of a Nation*, the 1915 12-reeler that heralded the era of modern movie making, turned on the Civil War and its aftermath. Two years later, America entered World War I, and with that fight and every subsequent slaughter, Hollywood has had plenty of raw material to produce battle epics, war dramas, military comedies and musicals, propaganda films, action movies with military motifs, love stories in uniform, Pentagon intrigues and, lately, high technology hardware parades and shoot-em-ups. (*Wings*, the 1927 silent film about air combat in World War I was the techno-thriller of its day and so amazed audiences that it won the first Oscar for best picture.)

The martial genre has produced some of the most remarkable movies ever made, films that approach art. *All Quiet on the Western Front*, Lewis Milestone's 1930 version of Erich Maria Remarque's novel, set the standard for war-movie realism, mise en scène and message. (Sixteen years later, Milestone reprised the "platoon on patrol" plot with *A Walk in the Sun*, and, in 1959, he came back with the Korean War drama *Pork Chop Hill* – based on a book by Brig. Gen. S. L. A. Marshall – a stark film as gimlet-eyed as *All Quiet* and as powerful.)

Preston Sturges's 1944 *Hail the Conquering Hero* exposes heroism and home-front hero worship in one satirical swipe and presages Robert Altman's 1970 bloody burlesque, *M*A*S*H*. In 1946, William Wyler built indirectly on the sociologist Dixon Wecter's work and gave us the Oscar-winning home-coming drama *The Best Years of our Lives*, a clean, frank look at how the warrior stirs society and how war lingers in the psyche. Stanley Kubrick's *Paths of Glory* in 1957 was relentlessly haunting, with a last scene so honest – the work on the killing fields never ends – that it can serve as a coda for the whole genre.

Art aside, military movies can also be fine entertainment: Victor Fleming's *Gone With the Wind*, John Ford's *Horse Soldiers*, David Lean's *Lawrence of Arabia*, Ken Annikan's *Longest Day*, Franklin Schaffner's *Patton*, John Frankenheimer's *Manchurian Candidate*, Michael Cimino's *Deer Hunter* and two by Francis Ford Coppola, his Conradian bolus *Apocalypse Now* and his attempt to embrace the same subject, this time without pretension and pyrotechnics, in *Gardens of Stone*, one of my favorites.

But most of this year's war or military movies borrow from the genre rather than trade in it. Ed Harris tries to walk and talk and even die like a Marine Corps general, but *The Rock* is really Indiana Jones meets James Bond on Alcatraz Island. And in *Broken Arrow*, when John Travolta and Christian Slater as Air

Force officers have a boxing match in the cockpit of a stealth fighter carrying nuclear weapons, the audience knows that it has walked in on Rocky Rocks the Bomb.

Mr Zwick's first sortie into the subject was his 1989 Civil War Epic *Glory*, the story of the 54th Massachusetts, a black infantry outfit. As a war movie, *Glory* suggested both the desolate beauty of battle and the ecstasy of comradeship. It also illustrated the idea of genre.

"In genre you make the old, the familiar, current," said the film historian Jeanine Basinger, the director of the Cinema Archives at Wesleyan University in Connecticut. "What a genre must do is repeat elements the audience knows and understands and also update itself so it deals with current issues and values. With *Glory*, Mr Zwick used the Civil War to talk to us about race. It's not that it doesn't reflect historical truth. It's an example of using history in an atmosphere the audience understands to make a story about a modern contemporary issue."

But with *Courage Under Fire* the director is trying to do more, much more, maybe too much. The story by the screenwriter Patrick Sheane Duncan, is told indirectly through the character of a veteran officer (Mr Washington) who is assigned to investigate the case of the dead pilot to make sure her deeds warranted the Medal of Honor. The officer brings to the task his own ghost from the battlefield: he accidentally killed one of his own men. Taking the twin storylines, the director shifts between the issues – the accountability of command and the debate about women in combat. And his main theme, alas, is truth.

"The gulf war was a war whose truth was carefully presented and indeed controlled," Mr Zwick said. "The images we have of the war are only those images that were very slickly and artfully presented to us in sound bites and photo ops. I did have the agenda of trying to present an additional set of images. There is a wonderful quote from Hiram Johnson that in war the first victim is always the truth."

What Hiram Johnson actually told his colleagues in the United States Senate during a 1917 speech was, "The first casualty when war comes is the truth," suggesting, of course, that the desire to go to war turns politicians into liars. But Mr Zwick uses Johnson's remark as an epigraph for his film and in so doing expands its meaning to include everything from literal truth – What really happened out there in the crucible of battle? – to a postmodern inquiry about the nature of truth itself. The problem is that film may be the worst medium to talk about truth because every film is a lie, even a documentary.

The lie begins as soon as the first cut is made and time and reality are altered. The lie continues when drama is added, a neat beginning, middle and end. (Resolution? Catharsis? In players, perhaps, not in people.) Everything on the screen is bigger, brighter, louder, more beautiful, more desolate, more dangerous and sensual than anything in life. In other words film romanticizes whatever it portrays, including the worst of war.

But film makers want it both ways. They need the freedom of fiction to create their dramas, yet want to advertise their products as representations of reality so they can touch – "manipulate" – their audience. And in no genre is verisimili-tude more advertised, or more essential, than in war or military movies. Every director wants to bring his audience onto the battlefield for 113 minutes, then send them safely home. The best way to do this is to make the movie war seem as real, as truthful, as possible. Oliver Stone brags about the makeup on his corpses; Edward Zwick brags about the makeup on his tanks. ("We found 11 Centurions in Australia that a brilliant set and production designer clad into Abrams.")

None of this is to suggest that any film should be held to some standard of authenticity. "We don't want to say our movies are accurate or inaccurate or that the world of movies is a false vision of society," said Robert Sklar, a profes-sor of cinema studies at New York University. "The question is, How do they relate?"

Truth? No war film has ever, or will ever, capture the fierce savagery, the ineffable suffering and the galling waste of combat. Samuel Fuller, a combat veteran of World War II and the director of *The Steel Helmet*, *The Big Red One* and other war films, once told an interviewer that the only way to recapture the reality of war on film was to put a machine gun behind the screen and gun down the audience. I'd amend that with: then prop up the wounded and cut their hearts out.

So what is the truth? "For the average person war is the war movie," says Ms Basinger, who has studied and written about the films of World War II. "When a combat veteran asks me, 'How do you know what you're talking about?' I say, 'I'm a veteran of war movies, and I put my service up against anybody.' The audience comes into a war film with the knowledge of other war movies, so war films become a faithful recreation of other war movies."

In this vein no one can say to what degree our fictions reflect our feelings. The debate about the flow of attitudes and ideas between art and society is an endless one. For example, many films this year that employ a military motif treat the military with ambivalence. On the one hand there is the ambitious, often immoral officer engaged in a conspiracy to either blow something up or cover something up (*The Rock*, *Broken Arrow*), a convention that may reflect society's abiding suspicion of the coterie of command and the military's real-life pen-chant for secrecy and prevarication.

On the other hand, in the post-modern era the military may represent the only institution whose story line has not changed. It still stands for duty, honor, sacrifice. And in a culture in which the concept of accountability has been deconstructed into abject self-interest, the notion of old-fashioned standards and values has enormous appeal. "Even when you make the military into a villain, you still have the idea of a mission, an obligation to be fulfilled, and a set of rules," Ms Basinger said.

I think that's one reason I like war movies, particularly those made during and immediately after World War II. The characters are often allegorical: Gary Cooper in the 1941 biographical epic *Sergeant York* as the embodiment of the conflict between faith and duty; William Bendix and Brian Donlevy in 1942's *Wake Island*, as stalwart as the Spartans at Thermopylae; John Wayne, particularly in his signature war film, *Sands of Iwo Jima*, from 1949, dauntless comrade and surrogate father rolled into one; finally Kirk Douglas in *Paths of Glory* as the *sine qua non* of conscience.

The best war movies have certain stylistic similarities. They often begin *in medias res*: Fade in. Ext.: A hill in the jungle, a squad of 10 men on patrol. The best war movies also have more tension than gore. Submarine movies like Dick Powell's powerful 1957 film *The Enemy Below* or the taut *Das Boot* (1981), by Wolfgang Peterson, are tales of suspense that turn on the cunning of the hunter or the endurance of the hunted. The best war movies have dialogue that is epigrammatic, thus memorable, rather than expository. In *Pork Chop Hill*, someone asks Gregory Peck, "This hill worth it?" He answers, "Worth it? This hill hasn't much military value. I doubt if any American would give you a dollar for it, any Chinese two bits, but the value changed somehow, some time, maybe when the first man was killed."

The truth about war movies is that they are not really about war; they are about our fantasies of war, our notions of what happens when we arm our children and send them off to fight. They are the images we can't summon on our own or are too afraid to imagine. They are the stories we need to hear, the explanations we require to deal with mysteries of living. Without war movies we would be left only with the truth and the truth of war is simply too terrible to tell.

---

22   Paintings and Their Places

Susan L. Feagin

> *These conditions of presentation [of a sign] necessarily occupy the space we share with them, and it is in this space that images . . . uniquely articulate and create meaning.*
> David Summers, 'Real Metaphor'

Many suggestions as to how art can provide knowledge have been offered through the years, some of which are even plausible and interesting. Writers too numerous to mention have argued that art gives us knowledge of what it is like to be a certain sort of person, or to be in certain sorts of situations, and what it is like to have certain kinds of emotions or experiences. Art 'educates the emotions'; Martha Nussbaum, in particular, argues that our affective responses to fiction give us moral knowledge.[1] We can learn from poetry and novels to see the 'shape and significance' of life differently.[2] R. G. Collingwood touted art as giving us knowledge of ourselves. Art is alleged also to give us knowledge of social scientific facts: Rom Harré claims that 'one can study the conventions of women's speech quite successfully by analysing certain properties of the speech of women that is displayed in novels and plays'.[3] If art at least partially 'constructs' culture, we can learn about that aspect of culture through its art. And art has even been seen as a source of propositional knowledge of a variety of kinds.[4]

These views on how art can give us knowledge are commonly advanced in relation to poetry, prose or music that has words, such as opera. Paintings and sculptures, on the other hand, are generally touted as giving us visual insights, through changing the way we see things, or as giving us insights into character or personality, in the case of portraits. Paintings and sculptures can reveal attitudes and social structures prevalent at the time when they were produced; we can reflect on cultural differences and similarities and come to a better understanding of ourselves and how we are embedded within the styles, institutions and attitudes of our own culture.

These moves are familiar. Instead of adding to or expanding on one or more of them, I will examine how certain presuppositions have standardly been made when asking the question, 'Can art give us knowledge?'. The points I make are addressed only to the visual arts of painting and sculpture. Whether analogous moves can be made in relation to literature is an intricate and difficult issue, though after having made my points, I will return briefly to why there is this difference between painting and sculpture on the one hand, and poetry and music on the other. I first point out how the inquiry into whether we can obtain knowledge from the visual arts of painting and sculpture is different from other kinds of epistemic inquiries about the possibility of obtaining knowledge through visual perception. It presupposes a special kind of separation between art and 'reality', 'life', or whatever it is about which we are to obtain knowledge. This separation, that is taken for granted in the question, is a major constituent in many traditional theories of art and the aesthetic. In the remainder of the paper I discuss some recent work in art history that challenges the assumption of this distance between art and life so fundamental to much aesthetic theory. Once this distance is collapsed, the presuppositions of the inquiry are no longer satisfied. Art becomes a part of life, rather than something through which we learn about life. This is not to deny that one may learn from art; intelligent people can learn from virtually anything. But the presuppositions of the inquiry place special emphasis on the fact that it is art whose epistemic potential we are questioning in a way that is different from the way we question how knowledge comes from other forms of experience. When the presuppositions of our questioning are not satisfied, the inquiry itself comes to look peculiar and inappropriate, revealing the narrowness of the ways we have been thinking about the visual arts.

I. Presuppositions of the Question

'Can we obtain knowledge from perception?' This question is a staple of the epistemologist's repertoire. To motivate the question, one must understand how perceptual experience might fail to give knowledge, i.e., how it can mis-represent or mislead us with respect to the way things are. Perception clearly fails to give us knowledge when we are victims of various kinds of illusions or hallucination. But does perception give us knowledge under 'normal' circum-stances? Visual perception is a process during which we obtain 'input' from the environment in the form of retinal stimulation, and, biologically speaking, its functional role is to provide us with information about that environment. Per-ception will fail to give knowledge if we could have the visual experiences we have, given our background knowledge and beliefs, and what we claim to know could still be untrue.[5] That is, visual experience, along with a certain number of background beliefs, must ensure the truth of what we claim to know, and it may well be that things are not as we perceive them to be.

But the question 'Can art give us knowledge?' has different presuppositions from the question, 'Can perceptual experience give us knowledge?' It is not only *not* a staple of the epistemologist's repertoire, but the inquiry is not moti-vated by doubts about the reliability of perception. Artworks are perceived, and there are questions about whether we perceive them correctly in given cases, and even whether it makes sense to talk about perceiving them 'correctly'. But the inquiry into whether artworks are a source of knowledge is not initiated by doubts about the reliability of our perception of those artworks. It is motivated by the realization that, even if we correctly perceive them, the artworks them-selves may not accurately reflect the way real things are.

Thus, our initial question presumes a distinction between art objects and real objects or reality – what we allegedly want to have knowledge about. This dis-tinction is clearly and firmly embedded within theories of art that identify an art object, or its aesthetically or artistically relevant aspects, with a phenomenal object, or an aesthetic object, rather than a material object. Aesthetic attitudes, disinterestedness and distance are all theoretical constructs that supposedly de-scribe the ways in which we acquaint ourselves with the ontologically special objects, aesthetic objects, that are relevant to appreciating and understanding works of art. Vincent Tomas succinctly sums up the view, clearly borrowing from a Kantian notion of disinterestedness defined in terms of a lack of interest in the real existence of the object: 'When we see things aesthetically, our atten-tion is directed toward appearances . . . the question of reality does not arise.'[6] Even without making the ontological move to a different type of object, J. Urmson distinguishes aesthetic appreciation from other kinds (moral, economic, religious, etc.) by concentration on how a thing looks rather than how it is. What is aesthetically important about a sculpture (or a building), for example is whether it looks top heavy, not whether it is top heavy. We don't even need to perceive the real qualities the art object has to view it aesthetically, but only what some have called its 'phenomenal' qualities. 'What makes the appreciation aesthetic is that it is concerned with a thing's looking somehow without con-cern for whether it really is like that; beauty we may say, to emphasize the point, is not even skin-deep.'[7]

If theories of the aesthetic have traditionally traded on the distinction be-tween appearance and reality, so have some theories of art. '[I]n the case of art an argument may be mounted to show that its possibility and value is logically tied up with putting reality at a distance.'[8] Arthur Danto then proceeds to make such a case, arguing that art is distinguished from real things by being embedded in the history and theory of art. '[C]onsciousness of the difference between reality and art is part of what makes the difference between art and reality.'[9] On the other hand, a tree is not a tree because it is embedded within the history and theory of trees;[10] the same is true with non-art artefacts – a chair, for instance, is not a chair because it is embedded within the history and theory of chairs.

According to Danto real things may become incorporated into art by being transfigured by theory. The challenge to viewers is to be able to see real things as art, by utilizing a knowledge of the history and theory of art. Julian Schnabel's cracked crockery, John Chamberlain's auto parts, Tony Cragg's beakers and test tubes tell us more about art than they do about crockery, automobiles and scientific glassware, just as the snippets of newspaper and wine labels in Picasso's paintings/collages tell us more about art than about newspapers or wine labels, or the news or wine they apparently describe.

Once artworks are accessed – either as artworks or aesthetic objects – by special modes of perception or understanding, the question is how we can return to the world of real things with knowledge about it gained from our experience with the artworld. If we are attending to how things appear, rather than the way they are, or if our attention and experience is informed by knowledge of the history and theory of the artworld, the relevance of our perceptions and experiences of paintings to understanding anything about the real world is certainly suspect. Even more puzzling is how engaging in these special modes of attention and understanding would give us any distinctive insights into the operations of the 'real world'.

II. Art as Physical Object

The fact that real things can be artworks has occupied Arthur Danto's theoretical attentions for some time.[11] According to Danto, artworks are real things in a special sense of the verb 'to be': the 'is' of artistic identification. Artworks, as Danto claims, are subject to interpretation. To say of Rauschenberg's work, 'This is a bed', is to interpret it, and the 'is' functions differently from the 'is' in the following: 'the object under the north window in my bedroom is a bed'. It is not an interpretation of my bed that it is a bed. To say of the first component of Joseph Kosuth's work which consists of a chair, a picture of a chair, and a description of a chair, 'This is a chair', is to interpret it. But to say of John Chamberlain's work, 'These are auto parts', is to misinterpret it. Just because real things are used in artworks does not mean that one interprets the artworks correctly in saying the work 'is' the real thing that is transfigured within it. In Chamberlain's work the auto parts are used as materials out of which a sculpture is made, losing their identity as those materials as they are metamorphosed into art.[12]

If we back up just one more step, and describe artworks not in kind terms (e.g., 'it is a bed') but in terms of ontological status, there is more hope. Artworks, at least some artworks, such as paintings and sculptures, are physical objects. At least, there is nothing in the fact that they are objects of interpretation that prevents them from being physical objects.[13] If they are indeed physical objects, they have at least this in common with the ordinary objects of our everyday existence. This may seem a singularly unremarkable fact, but I think not, and I shall spend the remainder of this paper drawing out some of its implications.

The first implication of the fact that paintings and sculptures are physical objects is that they move out of the realm of 'pure' perception and into the realm of action. Indeed, the notion of 'pure' perception is misguided; human perception cannot be understood without understanding the effect of the object's literal distance from us. The muscles of the eyes move as the focal point shifts from nearer to farther, and side to side. Alterations in this input from the eye muscles change what 'computations' are made in the process of understanding what one sees. The ways the eyes have to adjust to the physical objects in front of them make a difference to our identifications of what we see. This is one reason why, at fairly close range, a two dimensional depiction of a scene in relatively deep space cannot 'look like' what it depicts.

More important than this, however, is the fact that a painting or sculpture as an object relates physically to our whole body, not just to our eyes. Ernst Gombrich reflected on the significance of this fact in his well-known 'Meditations on a Hobby Horse'.[14] He uses the term 'icons' for images whose content is identified in terms of what they visually resemble, and 'representations' for images whose content is identified by how they are used. Whether something can function as a representation of x depends on how one wants to use the representation. If one merely wants to denote x, i.e., refer to it, literally anything that can serve as a symbol will do, though for most symbolic purposes, huge immobile objects will not function well as symbols of anything.[15] But if one wants parts of the representation to function differently, it must have a fairly well-articulated number of parts that can be brought into the appropriate relations with one another. The only issue of resemblance here is whether the parts can be made to function in appropriate ways, whether one would or would not otherwise say that there was a visual resemblance between the symbol and what it symbolizes.

Ken Walton builds on Gombrich's notion of representation in his analysis of pictorial representation.[16] According to Walton, a picture (pictorial representation, depiction) is something that has the function of serving as a prop in a visual game of make-believe. If the picture is a picture of x, one is to imagine of one's seeing that it is a seeing of x. This analysis places constraints on what counts as a picture, and on what is a picture of x, since it will not be psychologically possible to imagine of just anything that one's seeing of it is a seeing of x.

Notice that in Walton's analysis of depiction that the games we play with paintings are visual games of make-believe so we are back to thinking of paintings in the perceptual mode, in terms of what they depict, rather than as something with which we interact in some bodily way. However, art historically, we may want to understand not merely what a painting pictures or depicts, its status as a work of art, or its character as an aesthetic object. We may want to understand it as a painting, which is a physical object that stands in certain spatial relationships to us and our bodies, not just our eyes, and which represents – in Gombrich's sense – what it does partly because of the nature of those relationships.

Some of these relationships are explored by David Summers in 'Real Metaphor'.[17] A 'real metaphor' is a substitute for a real thing, as opposed to what Summers calls 'images', for which, like Gombrich's 'icons', resemblance is the key to their pictorial content. Substitutes, or real metaphors, create 'subjunctive spaces', in which desires are fulfilled, created and sustained through their capacity to serve as substitutes. Real metaphors – such as paintings – are themselves real objects, and subjunctive spaces are real spaces. They are the spaces where the paintings become substitutes for the real thing. Paintings become substitutes partly by their ability to transform the spaces in which they exist, by making them into spaces where it is appropriate to do things, and not merely to look and contemplate visual forms.

If Walton is right about depiction, in seeing what a painting represents one plays a visual game of make-believe with the painting. But to describe a particular painting, such as an altar-piece, as an object that has the function of serving as a prop in a visual game of make-believe, and leave it at that, would be to misrepresent the character of that painting as an altar-piece, i.e., as that physical object. An altar-piece creates a space wherein certain devotions and rituals are appropriate, whether it be in a private or public devotional space. Atheists may want to call these games of make-believe, of course, but that description from the perspective of someone not actually engaged in the activity is clearly not what either Gombrich or Walton had in mind. These are not games, but rituals. And there is nothing make-believe about this activity in the psychology of the supplicant. Rather, the paintings transform the space, and place, where they are, into one where certain ritual observances are appropriate.

Altar-pieces don't transform spaces the same way when they are hung on walls in museums. Neither do paintings originally produced for chapels in churches and cathedrals when they are also hung in museums. Neither do miniature portraits for lockets, nor segments cut from ceiling paintings (now, of course, hanging approximately eye-level on the wall), nor seventeenth-century Dutch vanitas paintings that created an occasion within a domestic space for viewers to reflect on the impermanence of worldly possessions, nor ancestral or royal portraits. Neither do African masks, nor Japanese cups for the tea ceremony, nor Chinese tomb figures of guardians, nor Greek funerary monuments nor sarcophagi. And certainly neither do pieces of furniture nor architectural fragments.

My point is not merely that, given the different conditions of presentation in museums and original contexts, these objects look different to us. They function differently. Once in museums, they have been stripped of their power to transform the spaces in which they reside into spaces where a viewer is to use them as props in something other than visual games of make-believe.

Summers relates these matters to what he calls 'the defect of distance'. An aesthetician reading this phrase might interpret it as another critique of aesthetic attitude theories, thinking of Edward Bullough's famous article on 'psychical distance' from early in the twentieth century.[18] That is, until it is realized that Summers' use of the phrase 'the defect of distance' derives from one Gabriele Paleotti, who wrote of it in 1582. The defect of distance to which Summers and Paleotti refer is the distance between us and the things we desire. Paintings fulfil desires for absent objects by making them present through a substitute. But the substitute is no mirage or mere mirror image. It is something that can function, in material respects, as what it represents does or did. This functioning is not merely as an object of our visual attention; the things we desire are not merely objects to look at. They are God, Jesus or the Virgin Mary; one's beloved whose portrait one wears around one's neck; the ascent into the heavens, or eternal life; communion with spirit forces, with the order and harmony of the universe, with our loved ones who are now deceased.

Various kinds of actions are sanctioned in the absence of things we desire, such as prayer, reverence, reflection, and meditation. Paintings are vehicles that transform the spaces into those wherein such actions are sanctioned. At least, they are such vehicles when in their original spaces. In museums, they are vehicles for the purpose of visual pleasure, and sometimes, as with objects in the British Museum, vehicles for producing awe at the extent and efficacy of British imperialism, or with various private collections donated en masse to museums, vehicles for producing awe and admiration for the taste and acquisitive talents of their collectors.[19] Paintings in museums transform spaces differently. British imperialism is past and most of the collectors who donated their collections to museums have passed, but the objects have acquired the power to transform their spaces in a new way. Put negatively, they have been kidnapped and enslaved to a new master, the ideology of the aesthetic; put positively, they have been rescued from deterioration and obsolescence to contribute to aesthetic culture.

As objects with altered powers to transform spaces, they function as props to visual games of make-believe, and they transform the museum spaces in which they appear into spaces where one is to play those games. But notice that no longer is there a defect of distance, in Paleotti's sense. The painting no longer functions as a substitute for the absent, since its own physical presence is the object of attention. Rapt attention to the object itself is so often described as a condition of aesthetic appreciation, even to the extent of ignoring a work's representational content as urged by Clive Bell. The only distance now is psychical distance, a distance that protects us from the power of images to transform the spaces in which we move into sites of action. For, as we know, 'psychical distance' puts us 'out of gear' with our ordinary, practical self.

Modernism incorporated this relatively civilized manoeuvre into its ideological apparatus, enabling us to preserve and savour paintings and sculptures of the past by transforming the powers of alien objects, rather than having to destroy the objects to strip them of their powers. The same principle was followed by early Christianity, which appropriated pagan rites and deities to its own religious purposes, for example, in grafting the celebration of Jesus' birth onto the celebrations of the winter solstice. The Renaissance, in turn, was depicted by Walter Benjamin as neutralizing the powers of the ancient gods by aestheticization. As summed up by Michael Camille, 'Rather than a rebirth, the Renaissance was for Benjamin a pompous funeral parade of dead divinities that had been rendered innocuous in their aesthetic embalming'.[20]

Sometimes the attack on paintings and sculptures has been destructive rather than appropriative, as during the waves of iconoclasm that have washed over Western civilization, e.g., in the form of Pope Gregory's demolition of Roman idols, and the destruction of images and condemnation of image-making during the Reformation.[21] Whereas the problem of pictorial representation is often described as the problem of rendering three-dimensional reality on a two-dimensional surface, Camille describes a problem of representation that emerged in the late Middle Ages out of an opposite worry. The problem was not how to make something realistic or life-like, but rather how to avoid introducing the power of the originals into the image: the problem in depicting pagan idols, even in the 'fall of idols,' was to represent them without making the representations themselves idolatrous objects.[22]

Our attitude since Plato has been that images that function as substitutes for real things have a kind of 'second-class' status. They are not as real, true or powerful as the original, and so they are condemned as being weak imitations of the real thing, with a correlative tendency to confuse us about the nature of truth and reality. But what this tradition has ignored is that substitutes extend the power of the original: a bust of the emperor in every province, a painting of the Virgin Mary on every altar-piece, portraits of the ancestors in every vestibule, a picture of the president in every post office. What travels under the self-effacing guise of a second-class citizen is actually an arm of the law; images are a device for making something present by functioning as a substitute for that thing. No one can be in two places at the same time, but through substitutes one can transform multiple spaces at the same time as sites for human actions.

So how can paintings give us knowledge? The question itself would have struck many people, through much of the history of what we now call the visual arts, as bizarre. Paintings as 'real metaphors' creating 'subjunctive spaces' weren't creating opportunities to learn, but provocations to act in various ways. They function to reinforce certain habitual modes of acting and thinking, rather than to impart knowledge. The distance between substitute and object or person is not the distance between appearance and reality, or between truth and a piece of possible evidence. The distance is between the viewer and objects that relate to our desires, and the desires are sustained and satisfied by substitutes for those objects, substitutes that take the form of representations of them. The presuppositions of the question, 'Can we get knowledge from painting?' are confounded when paintings serve to transform the spaces in which we act, rather than to give us clues or ideas about the nature of reality.

One reason for separating a discussion of paintings and sculptures from other arts such as poetry and music should now be clearer. Interestingly, it doesn't really have to do with the fact that a painting is a physical object, but a poem or a musical composition is not. For poems have instances or tokens that are physical objects, and musical compositions have instances or tokens that are particular sonic arrays that might, *qua* physical object or auditory array, function the way paintings do, as described above. It has rather to do with the fact that poetry and music were traditionally associated with the 'liberal arts,' and included within the studies of educated people.[23] It wouldn't be surprising to find poetry, literary prose and music to be conceived of and used as vehicles for teaching important lessons about the nature of living and the value of life. And it has been traditional to see them as playing this type of instructive role. On the other hand, profound and significant insights about what it is like to be a certain sort of person, or to live in certain sorts of circumstances, or about ourselves or our emotions would simply not have been in the 'brief' of the visual arts.

None of this is to deny that one can learn from the visual arts, that many have been designed to convey certain sorts of knowledge, and that such important benefits can be derived from them. What I have tried to do is rather to explain how asking that question of paintings makes presuppositions which in many respects are simply not fulfilled. The question focuses our attention on our visual interactions with paintings, excluding how they have served to transform the spaces in which people live. The question presupposes a certain distance between art and life that is contrary to the historical mode of functioning of many of the visual arts. Moreover, a great number of the philosophical issues receiving attention today concern paintings simply as objects of visual attention, rather than as physical objects that have their own social and cultural roles as creators of environments where certain actions and behaviours are sanctioned.

Notes

1 Martha Nussbaum, ' "Finely Aware and Richly Responsible". Moral Attention and the Moral Task of Literature', *The Journal of Philosophy* 82 (1985) pp. 516–29.
2 R. W. Beardsmore, 'Learning From a Novel' in *Philosophy and the Arts, Lectures of the Royal Institute of Philosophy*, 1971–72 (New York: St Martin's, 1973) pp. 23–46, esp. p. 32.
3 Rom Harré, *Personal Being: A Theory for Individual Psychology* (Oxford: Blackwell, 1983) p. 121.
4 John W. Bender, 'Art as a Source of Knowledge: Linking Analytic Aesthetics and Epistemology' in *Contemporary Philosophy of Art: Readings in Analytic Aesthetics* (eds) John W. Bender and H. Gene Blocker (Englewood Cliffs, NJ: Prentice-Hall, 1993) pp. 593–607.
5 I have borrowed here from Fred Dretske's views about knowledge and perception. See *Knowledge and the Flow of Information* (Cambridge Mass.: MIT Press, 1981). Not everyone will agree with this general approach to an analysis of knowledge and perception. I use it to set up the issue: the particular analysis of knowledge is not crucial to the point.
6 Vincent Tomas, 'Aesthetic Vision', *The Philosophical Review* 68 (1959) pp. 52–67, esp. p. 53.
7 J. O. Urmson, 'What Makes a Situation Aesthetic?' in Francis J. Coleman (ed.), *Contemporary Studies in Aesthetics* (New York: McGraw-Hill, 1968) pp. 355–369, esp. p. 367.

8   Arthur C. Danto, 'Artworks and Real Things', *Theoria* 39 (1973) pp. 1–17; re-printed in William E. Kennick (ed.), *Art and Philosophy: Readings in Aesthetics*, 2nd edn (New York: St Martin's Press, 1979) pp. 98–110, esp. p. 99.

9   Ibid., p. 105.

10 Ethnobotanists, on the other hand, study the ways in which various groups have classified and categorized trees and plants.

11 Most notably, in addition to 'Artworks and Real Things', see 'The Artistic Enfran-chisement of Real Objects: The Artworld', *The Journal of Philosophy* 61 (1964) pp. 571–584 and *The Transfiguration of the Commonplace: A Philosophy of Art* (Cam-bridge, MA: Harvard University Press, 1981) ch. 1. [See entry in Part One of this volume.]

12 I thank Mary Wessel for help with the examples in this paragraph.

13 Richard Wollheim, *Art and Its Objects*, 2nd edn (New York: Cambridge University Press, 1980) §§9–19, pp. 10–34.

14 Ernst Gombrich, 'Meditations on a Hobby Horse or the Roots of Artistic Form' in *Meditations on a Hobby Horse and Other Essays on the Theory of Art* (New York: Phaidon, 1963).

15 Then again, if one wants to characterize the whole earth as endowed with symbolic significance by some deity, the more grandiose the symbols – mountains stand for one thing, oceans for another – the better.

16 Kendall L. Walton, *Mimesis as Make-Believe: On the Foundations of the Representa-tional Arts* (Cambridge, Mass.: Harvard University Press, 1990) pp. 293–6.

17 David Summers, 'Real Metaphor' in *Visual Theory: Painting and Interpretation* (eds) Norman Bryson, Michael Ann Holly, and Keith Moxey (New York: HarperCollins, 1991) pp. 231–59. I have used Summers' ideas of real metaphor and subjunctive spaces to address the question of whether we obtain knowledge from art. I thank Frances Connelly for extremely helpful discussion in connection with this material, which provided the stimulus for this paper. For some related work, see David Freedberg, *The Power of Images: Studies in the History and Theory of Response* (Chicago: University of Chicago Press, 1989).

18 Edward Bullough, ' "Psychical Distance" as a Factor in Art and an Aesthetic Prin-ciple', *British Journal of Psychology* 5 (1912) pp. 87–98; reprinted in Morris Weitz, *Problems in Aesthetics: An Introductory Book of Readings*, 2nd edn (London: Macmillan, 1970) pp. 782–92.

19 And paintings need not even be in museums to play this role. Michael Baxandall quotes Rucellai, a prominent patron of the arts in Renaissance Florence, to the effect that the paintings he commissioned 'serve[d] the glory of God, the honour of the city, and the commemoration of myself'. *Painting and Experience in Fif-teenth Century Italy: A Primer in the Social History of Pictorial Style* (Oxford: Clarendon Press, 1972) p. 2.

20 Michael Camille, *The Gothic Idol: Ideology and Image-making in Medieval Art* (New York: Cambridge University Press, 1989) p. 338.

21 Ibid., p. 346. Camille suggests there is a universal fear of the power of images as substitutes, and a need to strip them of that power. See his comments on p. 350.

22 Ibid., ch. 1, 'Fallen Idols'.

23 P. O. Kristeller, 'The Modern System of the Arts', *Journal of the History of Ideas* 12 (1951) pp. 496–527 and 13 (1952) pp. 17–46.

Suggestions for Further Reading

Bender, John W. "Art as a Source of Knowledge," in *Contemporary Philosophy of Art*, ed. John W. Bender and H. Gene Blocker. Englewood Cliffs, NJ: Prentice-Hall, 1993.

Booth, Wayne. *The Company We Keep*. Berkeley and Los Angeles: University of California Press, 1988.

Davies, Steven. *Art and Its Messages*. University Park Penn.: Pennsylvania State University Press, 1997.

Eldridge, Richard. *On Moral Personhood*. Chicago: University of Chicago Press, 1989.

Feagin, Susan. *Reading with Feeling*. Ithaca: Cornell University Press, 1996.

Gadamer, Hans-Georg. *Truth and Method* [1960]. Trans. Joel Weinsheimer and Donald G. Marshall. New York: Continuum Press,1975.

Goodman, Nelson. *Ways of Worldmaking*. Indianapolis: Hackett Publishing Co., 1978.

Lamarque, Peter. *Fictional Points of View*. Ithaca: Cornell University Press, 1996.

Lamarque, Peter and Stein Olson. *Truth, Fiction, and Literature*. Oxford: Clarendon Press, 1994.

Novitz, David. *Knowledge, Fiction, and Imagination*. Philadelphia: Temple University Press, 1987.

Nussbaum, Martha. *Poetic Justice: The Literary Imagination and Public Life*. Boston: Beacon Press, 1995.

Putnam, Hilary. *Meaning, and the Moral Sciences*. Boston: Routledge and Kegan Paul, 1978.

Walton, Kendall. *Mimesis and Make-Believe*. Cambridge, Mass.: Harvard University Press, 1990.

PART FIVE

TRAGEDY, SUBLIMITY, HORROR:
WHY DO WE ENJOY PAINFUL EXPERIENCE IN ART?

Preface

The development of theories of the aesthetic in Part Two concentrates on aesthetic pleasure, a general way of considering the experience of beauty. A little reflection, however, reveals the fact that a good deal of what we appreciate in art and in nature is not really beautiful or aesthetically delightful at all. Sometimes it is tragic or terrible or even horrific, qualities that would seem to induce pain rather than pleasure, an experience that we normally avoid when conducting our own lives. Painful subjects and the arousal of strong emotions constitute a large portion of works of art that are held in high esteem, however, either for the profundity of the ideas expressed, the moral and emotional insight they convey, or the sheer entertainment they afford. Three categories of difficult or painful aesthetic experiences may be identified as tragedy, sublimity, and horror.

One of the earliest questions about art treated by philosophers concerns tragedy. In the *Poetics* Aristotle posed what has come to be known as the "paradox of tragedy" when he asked, how can it be that human beings have an aversion to pain in reality but enjoy it in art? His answer is that it is human nature to enjoy learning, to be curious about one's surroundings no matter how painful or difficult they may be. We are by nature imitative creatures, and we learn by imitating in our actions and by experiencing the imitations of art. (Aristotle adopts the mimetic theory of art mentioned in Part One.) The genre of art he treats in the *Poetics*, or at least the part of it that has survived the centuries (for only a fragment of this treatise is extant), is tragic poetry – the theatrical dramas that were a part of religious and civic festivals in ancient Athens. (A choral ode from Sophocles' *Oedipus at Colonus* precedes Aristotle's discussion. It expresses an essential idea of tragic vision – that human life is destined for sorrow.) Aristotle offers a conception of tragedy that emphasizes a plot that details the downfall of a person of sufficiently noble character to earn our admiration, and yet enough like ordinary people to engage our sympathies. Tragedy arouses in the audience the emotions of pity and terror, he observes, and these emotions are discharged or resolved in the experience of *catharsis* that a well-structured tragedy brings about. While the exact nature of catharsis has been debated ever since Aristotle posed this view, it is clear that he departs from Plato, who as we saw in the previous section considered the arousal of such emotions by art to be dangerous both personally and politically. Aristotle holds that the recognition of the vulnerability of human existence that tragedy induces, and the catharsis of the emotions thereby aroused, tends to cleanse the soul and invite moral understanding.

More than two millennia after Aristotle, Friedrich Nietzsche (1844–1900) pondered the nature of Greek tragedy and the kind of artistic experience that it induces. Nietzsche recognizes two categories of art and by extension two types of aesthetic experience. One, which he designates "Apollinian" (after the god Apollo), is an art of order or reason that creates beauty of form. Static arts such as painting and sculpture are likely to be of this sort; they distill the messiness of life into a graspable, bounded aesthetic form which we may contemplate and enjoy with deliberation and calm. A counterpart category is the "Dionysian" (named after the god Dionysus who was the cult figure for an ecstatic mystery religion of antiquity), which is an art of participation and excess in which one loses a sense of one's individual identity in an experience of cosmic chaos and disorder. Dionysian art glimpses the forces of life that relentlessly power the world, but they may be brutal and destructive, and they are the antithesis of the order and harmony of Apollinian creations. Greek tragedy, argues Nietzsche, is an art form that partakes of both Dionysian and Apollinian elements, as it presents the savagery and pain of life in a poetic form that makes it capable of being understood. The concept of Dionysian art may be extended to a variety of artistic experiences other than tragedy, including participatory dance and music in which one loses a sense of the distance between oneself and the object of appreciation, and in extreme forms (if we employ Nietzsche's terms) may lose one's sense of self entirely.

While Nietzsche is not directly invoking the concept of the sublime, in certain respects Dionysian experience is related to what other philosophers label an encounter with sublimity. There are several different types of experience that have been theorized as "sublime," and this term pertains to encounters with both art and nature that present a vastness and infinity of dimension or power that defies human rationality and our ability to contain or manipulate or even to understand what we confront. The concept of sublimity also has ancient roots, though the entries in this section are all from the eighteenth and nineteenth centuries. The first is a short story by the American writer Edgar Allen Poe (1809–49), and as such is not a "theory" of the sublime at all. "The Descent into the Maelström" narrates a fictional encounter with the mystery and might of nature, a terrible whirlpool off the coast of Norway in which a hapless fisherman is caught. Poe describes the maelstrom as overwhelming, terrifying, vast – and in its power both awesome and glorious. The experience detailed in his story may be analyzed according to the categories offered by two philosophers of the sublime, Edmund Burke (1729–97) and Immanuel Kant (1724–1804). Burke, like Aristotle, is intrigued with the enjoyment of painful experience, and part of his essay is a study of the phenomena of pleasure and pain. The sublime derives from pain, but it has been transformed into delight because of the awe and interest it inspires. Kant, one of the most influential philosophers of the western tradition, divides the sublime into two sub-categories, the "dynamic" sublime of nature, whose power and vastness exceed the capacity of the human mind to comprehend, and the "mathematical" sublime, which similarly leads the mind to the concept of infinity and dimensions so vast that they cannot be clearly grasped with the use of what he calls "determinate" concepts. The experience of the sublime has an important moral dimension for Kant. Because we recognize in encounters with the sublime the limitations of human imagination, Kant speculates, we also recognize the distinction between human minds and nature. This leads us to realize our freedom from the laws of nature, which lends the sublime a moral dimension as we recognize that despite our physical incapacity to control nature, we can legislate our own moral law.

The concept of the sublime is very close to the concept of the terrible, and this lends to sublimity an extreme and painful edge. With the artistic genre of horror, this edge is crossed. While the sublime may be afforded by both nature and art, the enjoyment of horror is exclusively an enjoyment of art (for those who enjoy in reality what occurs in horror stories are considered too perverse to deserve the dignity of an aesthetic category). Indeed, horror is often considered a popular, "low" genre of entertainment, not really "art" at all. But philosopher Noël Carroll analyzes horror as a distinctive genre of art that presents many of the same philosophical puzzles as tragedy. Indeed, he poses a "paradox of horror" to match the paradox of tragedy: how is it that we can enjoy the horrific subjects treated by this genre of art? Like Aristotle, he appeals to the satisfaction of curiosity in his response.

Carroll restricts his analysis to what he calls "art horror," classic horror stories that aim at arousing in the viewer or reader – for the genres of horror are largely film and literature – the same kind of emotion that is aroused by the protagonist in the story or on the screen. This type of experience is paradigmatic for the category of horror. Cynthia Freeland questions the adequacy of this understanding to do justice to all types of horror film or literature. In particular, she argues, an increasingly popular type of film she calls "Realist Horror" bridges the gap between fiction and reality and must be accounted for in different terms. Freeland's study situates contemporary horror films and television shows in a social context and offers a political analysis for their meaning and importance. This approach reminds us that art has origins in social interests and expectations. The entries in this section, which range from classical antiquity to the present, invite the reader to consider the cultural contexts for tragedy and sublimity as well as for horror, and to speculate about contemporary versions of experiences in all of these categories.

Tragedy

23 Choral Ode from *Oedipus at Colonus*

Sophocles

CHORUS
Show me a man who longs to live a day beyond his time
who turns his back on a decent length of life,
I'll show the world a man who clings to folly.
For the long, looming days lay up a thousand things
closer to pain than pleasure, and the pleasures disappear,
you look and know not where
when a man's outlived his limit, plunged in age
and the good comrade comes who comes at last to all,
not with a wedding-song, no lyre, no singers dancing –
the doom of the Deathgod comes like lightning
always death at the last.

Not to be born is best
when all is reckoned in, but once a man has seen the light
the next best thing, by far, is to go back
back where he came from, quickly as he can.
For once his youth slips by, light on the wing
lightheaded . . . what mortal blows can he escape
what griefs won't stalk his days?
Envy and enemies, rage and battles, bloodshed
and last of all despised old age overtakes him,
stripped of power, companions, stripped of love –
the worst this life of pain can offer,
old age our mate at last.

This is the grief he faces – I am not alone –
like some great headland fronting the north
hit by the winter breakers beating down
from every quarter – so he suffers,
terrible blows crashing over him
head to foot, over and over
down from every quarter –
now from the west, the dying sun

now from the first light rising
now from the blazing beams of noon
now from the north engulfed in endless night.

trans. Robert Fagles

---

24   From the *Poetics*

Aristotle

Poetry in general can be seen to owe its existence to two causes, and these are rooted in nature. First, there is man's natural propensity, from childhood onwards, to engage in mimetic activity (and this distinguishes man from other creatures, that he is thoroughly mimetic and through mimesis takes his first steps in understanding). Second, there is the pleasure which all men take in mimetic objects.

An indication of the latter can be observed in practice: for we take pleasure in contemplating the most precise images of things whose sight in itself causes us pain – such as the appearance of the basest animals, or of corpses. Here too the explanation lies in the fact that great pleasure is derived from exercising the understanding, not just for philosophers but in the same way for all men, though their capacity for it may be limited. It is for this reason that men enjoy looking at images, because what happens is that, as they contemplate them, they apply their understanding and reasoning to each element (identifying this as an image of such-and-such a man, for instance). Since, if it happens that one has no previous familiarity with the sight, then the object will not give pleasure *qua* mimetic object but because of its craftsmanship, or colour, or for some other such reason.

Given, then, that mimetic activity comes naturally to us – together with melody and rhythm (for it is evident that metres are species of rhythm) – it was originally those with a special natural capacity who, through a slow and gradual process, brought poetry into being by their improvisations. And poetry was split into two types according to the poets' own characters: the more dignified made noble actions and noble agents the object of their mimesis; while lighter poets took the actions of base men and began by composing invectives, just as the other group produced hymns and encomia. Now, we cannot cite an invective by any individual poet before Homer's time, though it is likely there were many such poets; their known history starts with Homer, with his *Margites* and other such works. It was appropriate that in these works the iambic metre came to find its place – and this is why it is called 'iambic' now, because it was in this metre that they abused one another (in the manner called *iambizein*).

Of the old poets, some composed in epic hexameters, others in iambics. Just as Homer was the supreme poet of serious subjects (for he was unique both in the quality and in the *dramatic* nature of his poetry), similarly he was the first to reveal the form of comedy, by producing dramatic poetry which dealt not with invective but with the ridiculous. For the *Margites* stands in the same relation to later comedies as do the *Iliad* and *Odyssey* to tragedies. And when the possibility of tragedy and comedy had been glimpsed, men aspired to either type of poetry according to their personal capacities; so some became poets of comedy instead of iambic verses, while others abandoned epic for tragedy, because the latter's forms were greater than, and superior to, epic's.

To consider whether tragedy is by now sufficiently developed in its types – judging it both in itself and in relation to audiences – is a separate matter. At any rate, having come into being from an improvisational origin (which is true of both tragedy and comedy, the first starting from the leaders of the dithyramb, the second from the leaders of the phallic songs which are still customary in many cities), tragedy was gradually enhanced as poets made progress with the potential which they could see in the genre. And when it had gone through many changes, tragedy ceased to evolve, since it had attained its natural fulfilment.

It was Aeschylus who first increased the number of actors from one to two, reduced the choral parts, and gave speech the leading role; the third actor and scene-painting came with Sophocles. A further aspect of change concerns scale: after a period of slight plots and humorous diction, it was only at a late stage that tragedy attained dignity by departing from the style of satyr-plays, and that the iambic metre replaced the trochaic tetrameter. To begin with, poets used the tetrameter because the poetry had more of the tone of a satyr-play and of dance; and it was only when speech was brought in that the nature of the genre found its appropriate metre (the iambic is the most colloquial of metres, as we see from the fact that we frequently produce the rhythm of iambic lines in our conversation, while we rarely produce hexameters and only by departing from the register of ordinary speech).

There were further developments concerning the number of episodes, and we shall take as read the other particular elaborations which are said to have been effected, since it would be a large task to give a thorough account of every detail.

Comedy, as I earlier said, is a mimesis of men who are inferior, but not in a way which involves complete evil: the comic is one species of the shameful. For the comic is constituted by a fault and a mark of shame, but lacking in pain or destruction: to take an obvious example, the comic mask is ugly and misshapen, but does not express pain. Now, while the stages of tragedy's development, and those responsible for them, have been preserved, comedy's have not been, because it was not originally given serious attention: the archon first granted a comic chorus at quite a late date; before that, the performers were volunteers. The first recorded comic poets belong to the era when the genre already possessed some established forms. We are simply ignorant about such matters as who invented masks, or introduced prologues, or increased the number of actors, and other such details. But as for the use of poetic plot-structures, that originally came from Sicily; and of Athenian poets Crates was the first to abandon the iambic concept and to compose generalised stories and plots.

Epic conforms with tragedy in so far as it is a mimesis, in spoken metre, of ethically serious subjects; but it differs by virtue of using *only* spoken verse and of being in the narrative mode. There is also a difference of scale: whereas tragedy strives as far as possible to limit itself to a single day, epic is distinctive by its lack of a temporal limit, although in the early days poets of tragedy were as free in this respect as those of epic. The parts of epic are all common to tragedy, but the latter has some peculiar to itself. Consequently, whoever knows the difference between a good and a bad tragedy knows the same for epic too; for epic's attributes all belong to tragedy as well, though not all of tragedy's are shared by epic.

I shall discuss epic mimesis and comedy later. But let us deal with tragedy by taking up the definition of its essential nature which arises out of what has so far been said.

Tragedy, then, is a representation of an action which is serious, complete and of a certain magnitude – in language which is garnished in various forms in its different parts in the mode of dramatic enactment, not narrative – and through the arousal of pity and fear effecting the *katharsis* of such emotions.

By 'garnished' language I mean with rhythm and melody; and by the 'various forms' I mean that some parts use spoken metre, and others use lyric song. Since the mimesis is enacted by agents, we can deduce that one element of tragedy must be the adornment of visual spectacle, while others are lyric poetry and verbal style, for it is in these that the mimesis is presented. By 'style' I mean the composition of the spoken metres; the meaning of 'lyric poetry' is entirely evident.

Since tragedy is a representation of an action, and is enacted by agents, who must be characterized in both their character and their thought (for it is through these that we can also judge the qualities of their actions, and it is in their actions that all men either succeed or fail), we have the plot-structure as the mimesis of the action (for by this term 'plot-structure' I mean the organization of the events) while characterization is what allows us to judge the nature of the agents, and 'thought' represents the parts in which by their speech they put forward arguments or make statements.

So then, tragedy as a whole must have six elements which make it what it is: they are plot-structure, character, style, thought, spectacle, lyric poetry. Two of these are the media, one the mode and three the objects, of the mimesis – and that embraces everything. [. . .]

Given these definitions, my next topic is to prescribe the form which the structure of events ought to take, since this is the first and foremost component of tragedy. We have already laid down that tragedy is a representation of an action which is complete, whole and of a certain magnitude (for something can be whole but of no magnitude).

By 'whole' I mean possessing a beginning, middle and end. By 'beginning' I mean that which does not have a necessary connection with a preceding event, but which can itself give rise naturally to some further fact or occurrence. An 'end', by contrast, is something which naturally occurs after a preceding event, whether by necessity or as a general rule, but need not be followed by anything else. The 'middle' involves causal connections with both what precedes and what ensues. Consequently, well designed plot-structures ought not to begin or finish at arbitrary points, but to follow the principles indicated.

Moreover, any beautiful object, whether a living creature or any other structure of parts, must possess not only ordered arrangement but also an appropriate scale (for beauty is grounded in both size and order). A creature could not be beautiful if it is either too small – for perception of it is practically instantaneous and so cannot be experienced – or too great, for contemplation of it cannot be a single experience, and it is not possible to derive a sense of unity and wholeness from our perception of it (imagine an animal a thousand miles long). Just, therefore, as a beautiful body or creature must have some size, but one which allows it to be perceived all together, so plot-structures should be of a length which can be easily held in the memory. [. . .]

It is a further clear implication of what has been said that the poet's task is to speak not of events which have occurred, but of the kind of events which *could* occur, and are possible by the standards of probability or necessity. For it is not the use or absence of metre which distinguishes poet and historian (one could put Herodotus' work into verse, but it would be no less a sort of history with it than without it): the difference lies in the fact that the one speaks of events which have occurred, the other of the sort of events which could occur.

It is for this reason that poetry is both more philosophical and more serious than history, since poetry speaks more of universals, history of particulars. A 'universal' comprises the *kind* of speech or action which belongs by probability or necessity to a certain *kind* of character – something which poetry aims at *despite* its addition of particular names. A 'particular', by contrast, is (for example) what Alcibiades did or experienced.

This point has become clear in the case of comedy, where it is only after constructing a plot in terms of probable event that they give the characters ordinary names, so diverging from the iambic poets' practice of writing about individuals. In tragedy, on the other hand, the poets hold to the actual names. (The reason for this is that people are ready to believe in what is possible; and while we may not yet believe in the possibility of things that have not already happened, actual events are evidently possible, otherwise they would not have occurred.) Even so, there are some tragedies in which one or two of the familiar names are kept, while others are due to the poet; and some plays in which all are new, as in Agathon's *Antheus*: for in this play both the events and the names are equally the poet's work, yet the pleasure it gives is just as great. So, fidelity to the traditional plots which are the subject of tragedies is not to be sought at all costs. Indeed, to do this is absurd, since even familiar material is familiar only to a minority, but it can still afford pleasure to all. [. . .]

Reversal, as indicated, is a complete swing in the direction of the action; but this, as we insist, must conform to probability or necessity. Take, for example, Sophocles' *Oedipus Tyrannus*, where the person comes to bring Oedipus happiness, and intends to free him from his fear about his mother; but he produces the opposite effect, by revealing Oedipus' identity. And in *Lynceus*, the one person is led off to die, while Danaus follows to kill him; yet it comes about that the latter's death and the former's rescue result from the chain of events.

Recognition, as the very name shows, is from ignorance to knowledge, bringing the characters into either a close bond, or enmity, with one another, and concerning matters which bear on their prosperity or affliction. The finest recognition occurs in direct conjunction with reversal – as with the one in the *Oedipus*. There are, of course, other kinds of recognition, for recognition can relate to inanimate or fortuitous objects, or reveal that someone has, or has not, committed a deed. But the type I have mentioned is the one which is most integral to the plot-structure and its action: for such a combination of recognition and reversal will produce pity or fear (and it is events of this kind that tragedy, on our definition, is a mimesis of), since both affliction and prosperity will hinge on such circumstances. And since recognition involves people, there are cases where one person's recognition by another takes place (when this other's own identity is clear), and cases where the recognition must be reciprocal: for instance, Iphigeneia was recognized by Orestes through the sending of the letter, but another means of recognition was needed for Iphigeneia's identification of *him*.

Well then, reversal and recognition form two components of the plot-structure; the third is suffering. To the definitions of reversal and recognition already given we can add that of suffering: a destructive or painful action, such as visible deaths, torments, woundings and other things of the same kind. [. . .]

It follows on from my earlier argument that I should define what ought to be aimed at and avoided in plot-construction, as well as the source of tragedy's effect. Since, then, the structure of the finest tragedy should be complex, not simple, and, moreover, should portray fearful and pitiful events (for this is the distinctive feature of this type of mimesis), it is to begin with clear that:

(a) good men should not be shown passing from prosperity to affliction, for this is neither fearful nor pitiful but repulsive;

(b) wicked men should not be shown passing from affliction to prosperity, for this is the most untragic of all possible cases and is entirely defective (it is neither moving nor pitiful nor fearful);

(c) the extremely evil man should not fall from prosperity to affliction, for such a plot-structure might move us, but would not arouse pity or fear, since pity is felt towards one whose affliction is undeserved, fear towards one who is like ourselves (so what happens in such a case will be neither pitiful nor fearful).

We are left, then, with the figure who falls between these types. Such a man is one who is not preeminent in virtue and justice, and one who falls into affliction not because of evil and wickedness, but because of a certain fallibility (*hamartia*). He will belong to the class of those who enjoy great esteem and prosperity, such as Oedipus, Thyestes and outstanding men from such families. [. . .]

Events which are impossible but plausible should be preferred to those which are possible but implausible. Plots should not consist of parts which are irrational. So far as possible, there should be no irrational component; otherwise, it should lie outside the plot-structure, as with Oedipus' ignorance of how Laius died,[1] rather than inside the drama, as with the report of the Pythian games in *Electra*,[2] or with the silent character's arrival at Mysia from Tegea in the *Mysians*. To say that otherwise the plot-structure would be ruined is a ridiculous defence: such plot-construction should be avoided *from the start*. But even absurdity can sometimes be handled more or less reasonably. It would be obvious, if they were handled by an inferior poet, just how intolerable the absurdities regarding the disembarkation in the *Odyssey* could be: as it is, Homer uses his other virtues to disguise the absurdity and to make it enjoyable.[3]

Notes

1 Cf. Sophocles, *Oedipus Tyrannus* 112–13.
2 Sophocles, *Electra* 680ff.
3 *Odyssey* 13.116ff.

25 From *The Birth of Tragedy*

Friedrich Nietzsche

We shall have gained much for the science of aesthetics, once we perceive not merely by logical inference, but with the immediate certainty of vision, that the continuous development of art is bound up with the *Apollinian* and *Dionysian* duality – just as procreation depends on the duality of the sexes, involving perpetual strife with only periodically intervening reconciliations. The terms Dionysian and Apollinian we borrow from the Greeks, who disclose to the discerning mind the profound mysteries of their view of art, not to be sure, in concepts, but in the intensely clear figures of their gods. Through Apollo and Dionysus, the two art deities of the Greeks, we come to recognize that in the Greek world there existed a tremendous opposition, in origin and aims, between the Apollinian art of sculpture and the nonimagistic, Dionysian art of music. These two different tendencies run parallel to each other, for the most part openly at variance; and they continually incite each other to new and more powerful births, which perpetuate an antagonism, only superficially reconciled by the common term "art"; till eventually, by a metaphysical miracle of the

Hellenic "will," they appear coupled with each other, and through this coupling ultimately generate an equally Dionysian and Apollinian form of art – Attic tragedy.

In order to grasp these two tendencies, let us first conceive of them as the separate art worlds of *dreams* and *intoxication*. These physiological phenomena present a contrast analogous to that existing between the Apollinian and the Dionysian. [...]

The beautiful illusion of the dream worlds, in the creation of which every man is truly an artist, is the prerequisite of all plastic art, and, as we shall see, of an important part of poetry also. In our dreams we delight in the immediate understanding of figures; all forms speak to us; there is nothing unimportant or superfluous. But even when this dream reality is most intense, we still have, glimmering through it, the sensation that it is *mere appearance*: at least this is my experience, and for its frequency – indeed, normality – I could adduce many proofs, including the sayings of the poets. [...]

This joyous necessity of the dream experience has been embodied by the Greeks in their Apollo: Apollo, the god of all plastic energies, is at the same time the soothsaying god. He, who (as the etymology of the name indicates) is the "shining one," the deity of light, is also ruler over the beautiful illusion of the inner world of fantasy. The higher truth, the perfection of these states in contrast to the incompletely intelligible everyday world, this deep consciousness of nature, healing and helping in sleep and dreams, is at the same time the symbolic analogue of the soothsaying faculty and of the arts generally, which make life possible and worth living. But we must also include in our image of Apollo that delicate boundary which the dream image must not overstep lest it have a pathological effect (in which case mere appearance would deceive us as if it were crude reality). We must keep in mind that measured restraint, that freedom from the wilder emotions, that calm of the sculptor god. His eye must be "sunlike," as befits his origin; even when it is angry and distempered it is still hallowed by beautiful illusion. And so, in one sense, we might apply to Apollo the worlds of Schopenhauer when he speaks of the man wrapped in the veil of *maya*[1] (*Welt als Wille und Vorstellung* [*The World as Will and Idea*], I, p;. 416[2]): "Just as in a stormy sea that, unbounded in all directions, raises and drops mountainous waves, howling, a sailor sits in a boat and trusts in his frail bark: so in the midst of a world of torments the individual human being sits quietly, supported by and trusting in the *principium individuationis*."[3] In fact, we might say of Apollo that in him the unshaken faith in this *principium* and the calm repose of the man wrapped up in it received their most sublime expression; and we might call Apollo himself the glorious divine image of the *principium individuationis*, through whose gestures and eyes all the joy and wisdom of "illusion," together with its beauty, speak to us.

In the same work Schopenhauer has depicted for us the tremendous *terror* which seizes man when he is suddenly dumbfounded by the cognitive form of phenomena because the principle of sufficient reason, in some one of its manifestations, seems to suffer an exception. If we add to this terror the blissful ecstasy that wells from the innermost depths of man, indeed of nature, at this collapse of the *principium individuationis*, we steal a glimpse into the nature of the *Dionysian*, which is brought home to us most intimately by the analogy of intoxication.

Either under the influence of the narcotic draught, of which the songs of all primitive men and peoples speak, or with the potent coming of spring that penetrates all nature with joy, these Dionysian emotions awake, and as they grow in intensity everything subjective vanishes into complete self-forgetfulness. In the German Middle Ages, too, singing and dancing crowds, ever increasing in number, whirled themselves from place to place under this same Dionysian impulse. In these dancers of St John and St Vitus, we rediscover the Bacchic choruses of the Greeks, with their prehistory in Asia Minor, as far back as Babylon and the orgiastic Sacaea.[4] There are some who, from obtuseness or lack of experience, turn away from such phenomena as from "folk-diseases," with contempt or pity born of the consciousness of their own "healthy-mindedness." But of course such poor wretches have no idea how corpselike and ghostly their so-called "healthy-mindedness" looks when the glowing life of the Dionysian revelers roars past them.

Under the charm of the Dionysian not only is the union between man and man reaffirmed, but nature which has become alienated, hostile, or subjugated, celebrates once more her reconciliation with her lost son, man. Freely, earth proffers her gifts, and peacefully the beasts of prey of the rocks and desert approach. The chariot of Dionysus is covered with flowers and garlands; panthers and tigers walk under its yoke. Transform Beethoven's "Hymn to Joy" into a painting; let your imagination conceive the multitudes bowing to the dust, awestruck – then you will approach the Dionysian. Now the slave is a free man; now all the rigid, hostile barriers that necessity, caprice, or "impudent convention"[5] have fixed between man and man are broken. Now, with the gospel of universal harmony, each one feels himself not only united, reconciled, and fused with his neighbor, but as one with him, as if the veil of *maya* had been torn aside and were now merely fluttering in tatters before the mysterious primordial unity.

In song and in dance man expresses himself as a member of a higher community; he has forgotten how to walk and speak and is on the way toward flying into the air, dancing. His very gestures express enchantment. Just as the animals now talk, and the earth yields milk and honey, supernatural sounds emanate from him, too: he feels himself a god, he himself now walks about enchanted, in ecstasy, like the gods he saw walking in his dreams. He is no longer an artist, he has become a work of art: in these paroxysms of intoxication the artistic power of all nature reveals itself to the highest gratification of the primordial unity. The noblest clay, the most costly marble, man, is here kneaded and cut, and to the sound of the chisel strokes of the Dionysian world-artist rings out the cry of the Eleusinian mysteries: "Do you prostrate yourselves, millions? Do you sense your Maker, world?[6]

Thus far we have considered the Apollinian and its opposite, the Dionysian, as artistic energies which burst forth from nature herself, *without the mediation of the human artist* –energies in which nature's art impulses are satisfied in the most immediate and direct way – first in the image world of dreams, whose completeness is not dependent upon the intellectual attitude or the artistic culture of any single being; and then as intoxicated reality, which likewise does not heed the single unit, but even seeks to destroy the individual and redeem him by a mystic feeling of oneness. With reference to these immediate art-states of nature, every artist is an "imitator," that is to say, either an Apollinian artist in dreams, or a Dionysian artist in ecstasies, or finally – as for example in Greek tragedy – at once artist in both dreams and ecstasies: so we may perhaps picture him sinking down in his Dionysian intoxication and mystical self-abnegation, alone and apart from the singing revelers, and we may imagine how, through Apollinian dream-inspiration, his own state, i.e., his oneness with the inmost ground of the world, is revealed to him in a *symbolical dream image*. [. . .]

[O]nly the curious blending and duality in the emotions of the Dionysian revelers remind us – as medicines remind us of deadly poisons – of the phenomenon that pain begets joy, that ecstasy may wring sounds of agony from us. At the very climax of joy there sounds a cry of horror or a learning lamentation for an irretrievable loss. In these Greek festivals, nature seems to reveal a sentimental[7] trait; it is as if she were heaving a sigh at her dismemberment into individuals. The song and pantomime of such dually-minded revelers was something new and unheard-of in the Homeric-Greek world; and the Dionysian *music* in particular excited awe and terror. If music, as it would seem, had been known previously as an Apollinian art, it was so, strictly speaking, only as the wave beat of rhythm, whose formative power was developed for the representation of Apollinian states. The music of Apollo was Doric architectonics in tones, but in tones that were merely suggestive, such as those of the cithara. The very element which forms the essence of Dionysian music (and hence of music in general) is carefully excluded as un-Apollinian – namely, the emotional power of the tone, the uniform flow of the melody, and the utterly incomparable world of harmony. In the Dionysian dithyramb man is incited to the greatest exaltation of all his symbolic faculties; something never before experienced struggles for utterance – the annihilation of the veil of *maya*, oneness as the soul of the race and of nature itself. The essence of nature is now to be expressed symbolically; we need a new world of symbols; and the entire symbolism of the body is called into play, not the mere symbolism of the lips, face, and speech but the whole pantomime of dancing, forcing every member into rhythmic movement. Then the other symbolic powers suddenly press forward, particularly those of music, in rhythmics, dynamics, and harmony. To grasp this collective release of all the symbolic powers, man must have already attained that height of self-abnegation which seeks to express itself symbolically through all these powers – and so the dithyrambic votary of Dionysus is understood only by his peers. With what astonishment must the Apollinian Greek have beheld him! With an astonishment that was all the greater the more it was mingled with the shuddering suspicion that all this was actually not so very alien to him after all, in fact, that it was only his Apollinian consciousness which, like a veil, hid this Dionysian world from his vision.

To understand this, it becomes necessary to level the artistic structure of the *Apollinian culture*, as it were, stone by stone, till the foundations on which it rests become visible. First of all we see the glorious *Olyhmpian* figures of the gods, standing on the gables of this structure. Their deeds, pictured in brilliant reliefs, adorn its friezes. We must not be misled by the fact that Apollo stands side by side with the others as an individual deity, without any claim to priority of rank. For the same impulse that embodied itself in Apollo gave birth to this entire Olympian world, and in this sense Apollo is its father. What terrific need was it that could produce such an illustrious company of Olympian beings?

Whoever approaches these Olympians with another religion in his heart, searching among them for moral elevation, even for sanctity, for disincarnate spirituality, for charity and benevolence, will soon be forced to turn his back on them, discouraged and disappointed. For there is nothing here that suggests asceticism, spirituality, or duty. We hear nothing but the accents of an exuberant, triumphant life in which all things, whether good or evil are deified. And so the spectator may stand quite bewildered before this fantastic excess of life, asking himself by virtue of what magic potion these high-spirited men could have found life so enjoyable that, wherever they turned, their eyes beheld the smile of Helen, the ideal picture of their own existence, "floating in sweet sensuality." But to this spectator, who has already turned his back, we must say: "Do not go away, but stay and hear what Greek folk wisdom has to say of this very life, which with such inexplicable gaiety unfolds itself before your eyes.

"There is an ancient story that King Midas hunted in the forest a long time for the wise Silenus, the companion of Dionysus, without capturing him. When Silenus at last fell into his hands, the king asked what was the best and most desirable of all things for man. Fixed and immovable, the demigod said not a word, till at last, urged by the king, he gave a shrill laugh and broke out into these words: 'Oh, wretched ephemeral race, children of chance and misery, why do you compel me to tell you what it would be most expedient for you not to hear? What is best of all is utterly beyond your reach: not to be born, to *be*, to be *nothing*. But the second best for you is – to die soon.' "[8]

How is the world of the Olympian gods related to this folk wisdom? Even as the rapturous vision of the tortured martyr to his suffering.

Now it is as if the Olympian magic mountain[9] had opened before us and revealed its roots to us. The Greek knew and felt the terror and horror of existence. That he might endure this terror at all, he had to interpose between himself and life the radiant dream-birth of the Olympians. That overwhelming dismay in the face of the titanic powers of nature, the Moira[10] enthroned inexorably over all knowledge, the vulture of the great lover of mankind, Prometheus, the terrible fate of the wise Oedipus, the family curse of the Atridae which drove Orestes to matricide: in short, that entire philosophy of the sylvan god, with its mythical exemplars, which caused the downfall of the melancholy Etruscans – all this was again and again overcome by the Greeks with the aid of the Olympian *middle world* of art; or at any rate it was veiled and withdrawn from sight. It was in order to be able to live that the Greeks had to create these gods from a most profound need. Perhaps we may picture the process to ourselves somewhat as follows: out of the original Titanic divine order of terror, the Olympian divine order of joy gradually evolved through the Apollinian impulse toward beauty, just as roses burst from thorny bushes. How else could this people, so sensitive, so vehement in its desires, so singularly capable of *suffering*, have endured existence, if it had not been revealed to them in their gods, surrounded with a higher glory?

The same impulse which calls art into being, as the complement and consummation of existence, seducing one to a continuation of life, was also the cause of the Olympian world which the Hellenic "will" made use of as a transfiguring mirror. Thus do the gods justify the life of man: they themselves live it – the only satisfactory theodicy! Existence under the bright sunshine of such gods is regarded as desirable in itself, and the real pain of Homeric men is caused by parting from it, especially by early parting: so that now, reversing the wisdom of Silenus, we might say of the Greeks that "to die soon is worst of all for them, the next worst – to die at all." Once heard, it will ring out again; do not forget the lament of the short-lived Achilles, mourning the leaflike change and vicissitudes of the race of men and the decline of the heroic age. It is not unworthy of the greatest hero to long for a continuation of life, even though he live as a day laborer. At the Apollinian stage of development, the "will" longs so vehemently for this existence, the Homeric man feels himself so completely at one with it, that lamentation itself becomes a song of praise. [. . .]

For the rapture of the Dionysian stage with its annihilation of the ordinary bounds and limits of existence contains, while it lasts, a *lethargic* element in which all personal experiences of the past become immersed. This chasm of oblivion separates the worlds of everyday reality and of Dionysian reality. But as soon as this everyday reality re-enters consciousness, it is experienced as such with nausea: an ascetic, will-negating mood is the fruit of these states.

In this sense the Dionysian man resembles Hamlet: both have once looked truly into the essence of things, they have *gained knowledge*, and nausea inhibits action; for their action could not change anything in the eternal nature of things; they feel it to be ridiculous or humiliating that they should be asked to set right a world that is out of joint. Knowledge kills action; action requires the veils of illusion: that is the doctrine of Hamlet, not that cheap wisdom of Jack the Dreamer who reflects too much and, as it were, from an excess of possibilities does not get around to action. Not reflection, no – true knowledge, an insight into the horrible truth, outweighs any motive for action, both in Hamlet and in the Dionysian man.

Now no comfort avails any more; longing transcends a world after death, even the gods; existence is negated along with its glittering reflection in the gods or in an immortal beyond. Conscious of the truth he has once seen, man now sees everywhere only the horror or absurdity of existence; now he understands what is symbolic in Ophelia's fate; now he understands the wisdom of the sylvan god, Silenus: he is nauseated.

Here, when the danger to his will is greatest, *art* approaches as a saving sorceress, expert at healing. She alone knows how to turn these nauseous thoughts about the horror or absurdity of existence into notions with which one can live:

these are the *sublime* as the artistic taming of the horrible, and the *comic* as the artistic discharge of the nausea of absurdity. The satyr chorus of the dithyramb is the saving deed of Greek art; faced with the intermediary world of these Dionysian companions, the feelings described here exhausted themselves.[11]

Music and tragic myth are equally expressions of the Dionysian capacity of a people, and they are inseparable. Both derive from a sphere of art that lies beyond the Apollinian; both transfigure a region in whose joyous chords dissonance as well as the terrible image of the world fade away charmingly; both play with the sting of displeasure, trusting in their exceedingly powerful magic arts; and by means of this play both justify the existence of even the "worst world." Thus the Dionysian is seen to be, compared to the Apollinian, the eternal and original artistic power that first calls the whole world of phenomena into existence – and it is only in the midst of this world that a new transfiguring illusion becomes necessary in order to keep the animated world of individuation alive.

If we could imagine dissonance become man – and what else is man? – this dissonance, to be able to live, would need a splendid illusion that would cover dissonance with a veil of beauty. This is the true artistic aim of Apollo in whose name we comprehend all those countless illusions of the beauty of mere appearance that at every moment make life worth living at all and prompt the desire to live on in order to experience the next moment.

Of this foundation of all existence – the Dionysian basic ground the world – not one whit more may enter the consciousness of the human individual than can be overcome again by this Apollinian power of transfiguration. Thus these two art drives must unfold their powers in a strict proportion, according to the law of eternal justice. Where the Dionysian powers rise up as impetuously as we experience them now, Apollo, too, must already have descended among us, wrapped in a cloud; and the next generation will probably behold his most ample beautiful effects.

That this effect should be necessary, everybody should be able to feel most assuredly by means of intuition, provided he has ever felt, if only in a dream, that he was carried back into an ancient Greek existence. Walking under lofty Ionic colonnades, looking up toward a horizon that was cut off by pure and noble lines, finding reflections of his transfigured shape in the shining marble at his side, and all around him solemnly striding or delicately moving human beings, speaking with harmonious voices and in a rhythmic language of gestures – in view of this continual influx of beauty, would he not have to exclaim, raising his hand to Apollo: "Blessed people of Hellas! How great must Dionysus be among you if the god of Delos considers such magic necessary to heal your dithyrambic madness!"

To a man in such a mood, however, an old Athenian, looking up at him with the sublime eyes of Aeschylus, might reply: "But say this, too, curious stranger: how much did this people have to suffer to be able to become so beautiful! But now follow me to witness a tragedy, and sacrifice with me in the temple of both deities!"

Notes

1   A Sanskrit word usually translated as illusion.
2   This reference, like subsequent references to the same work, is Nietzsche's own and refers to the edition of 1873 edited by Julius Frauenstädt – still one of the standard editions of Schopenhauer's works.
3   Principle of individuation.
4   A Babylonian festival that lasted five days and was marked by general license. During this time slaves are said to have ruled their masters, and a criminal was given all royal rights before he was put to death at the end of the festival. For references, see, e.g., *The Oxford Classical Dictionary*.
5   An allusion to Friedrich Schiller's hymn *An die Freude* (to joy), used by Beethoven in the final movement of his Ninth Symphony.
6   Quotation from Schiller's hymn.
7   *Sentimentalisch* (not *sentimental*): an allusion to Schiller's influential contrast of *naïve* (Goethean) poetry with his own *sentimentalische Dichtung*.
8   Cf. Sophocles, *Oedipus at Colonus*, reprinted above.
9   *Zauberberg*, as in the title of Thomas Mann's novel.
10   Fate.
11   Having finally broken loose from Schopenhauer, Nietzsche for the first time shows the brilliancy of his own genius. It is doubtful whether anyone before him had illuminated *Hamlet* so extensively in so few words: the passage invites comparison with Freud's great footnote on *Hamlet* in the first edition of *Die Traumdeutung* (interpretation of dreams), 1900. Even more obviously, the last three paragraphs invite comparison with existentialist literature, notably, but by no means only, Sartre's *La Nausée* (1938).

Sublimity

26　A Descent into the Maelström

Edgar Allan Poe

The ways of God in Nature, as in Providence, are not as our ways; nor are the models that we frame in any way commensurate to the vastness, profundity, and unsearchableness of His works, which have a depth in them greater than the well of Democritus.

Joseph Glanville

We had now reached the summit of the loftiest crag. For some minutes the old man seemed too much exhausted to speak.

"Not long ago," said he at length, "and I could have guided you on this route as well as the youngest of my sons; but, about three years past, there happened to me an event such as never happened before to mortal man – or at least such as no man ever survived to tell of – and the six hours of deadly terror which I then endured have broken me up body and soul. You suppose me a *very* old man – but I am not. It took less than a single day to change these hairs from a jetty black to white, to weaken my limbs, and to unstring my nerves, so that I tremble at the least exertion, and am frightened at a shadow. Do you know I can scarcely look over this little cliff without getting giddy?"

The "little cliff," upon whose edge he had so carelessly thrown himself down to rest that the weightier portion of his body hung over it, while he was only kept from falling by the tenure of his elbow on its extreme and slippery edge – this "little cliff" arose, a sheer unobstructed precipice of black shining rock, some fifteen or sixteen hundred feet from the world of crags beneath us. Nothing would have tempted me to be within half a dozen yards of its brink. In truth so deeply was I excited by the perilous position of my companion, that I fell at full length upon the ground, clung to the shrubs around me, and dared not even glance upward at the sky – while I struggled in vain to divest myself of the idea that the very foundations of the mountain were in danger from the fury of the winds. It was long before I could reason myself into sufficient courage to sit up and look out into the distance.

"You must get over these fancies," said the guide, "for I have brought you here that you might have the best possible view of the scene of that event I mentioned – and to tell you the whole story with the spot just under your eye."

"We are now," he continued, in that particularising manner which distinguished him – "we are now close upon the Norwegian coast – in the sixty-eighth degree of latitude – in the great province of Nordland – and in the dreary district of Lofoden. The mountain upon whose top we sit is Helseggen, the Cloudy. Now raise yourself up a little higher – hold on to the grass if you feel giddy – so – and look out, beyond the belt of vapor beneath us, into the sea."

I looked dizzily, and beheld a wide expanse of ocean, whose waters wore so inky a hue as to bring at once to my mind the Nubian geographer's account of the *Mare Tenebrarum*. A panorama more deplorably desolate no human imagination can conceive. To the right and left, as far as the eye could reach, there lay outstretched, like ramparts of the world, lines of horridly black and beetling cliff, whose character of gloom was but the more forcibly illustrated by the surf which reared high up against it its white and ghastly crest, howling and shrieking for ever. Just opposite the promontory upon whose apex we were placed, and at a distance of some five or six miles out at sea, there was visible a small, bleak-looking island; or, more properly, its position was discernible through the wilderness of surge in which it was enveloped. About two miles nearer the land, arose another of smaller size, hideously craggy and barren, and encompassed at various intervals by a cluster of dark rocks.

The appearance of the ocean, in the space between the more distant island and the shore, had something very unusual about it. Although, at the time, so strong a gale was blowing landward that a brig in the remote offing lay to under a double-reefed trysail, and constantly plunged her whole hull out of sight, still there was here nothing like a regular swell, but only a short, quick, angry cross dashing of water in every direction – as well in the teeth of the wind as otherwise. Of foam there was little except in the immediate vicinity of the rocks.

"The island in the distance," resumed the old man, "is called by the Norwegians Vurrgh. The one midway is Moskoe. That a mile to the northward is Ambaaren. Yonder are Islesen, Hotholm, Keildhelm, Suarven, and Buckholm. Further off – between Moskoe and Vurrgh – are Otterholm, Flimen, Sandflesen, and Stockholm. These are the true names of the places – but why it has been thought necessary to name them at all, is more than either you or I can understand. Do you hear any thing? Do you see any change in the water?"

We had now been about ten minutes upon the top of Helseggen, to which we had ascended from the interior of Lofoden, so that we had caught no glimpse of the sea until it had burst upon us from the summit. As the old man spoke, I became aware of a loud and gradually increasing sound, like the moaning of a vast herd of buffaloes upon an American prairie; and at the same moment I perceived that what seamen term the *chopping* character of the ocean beneath us, was rapidly changing into a current which set to the eastward. Even while I gazed, this current acquired a monstrous velocity. Each moment added to its speed – to its headlong impetuosity. In five minutes the whole sea, as far as Vurrgh, was lashed into ungovernable fury; but it was between Moskoe and the coast that the main uproar held its sway. Here the vast bed of the waters, seamed and scarred into a thousand conflicting channels, burst suddenly into phrensied convulsion – heaving, boiling, hissing – gyrating in gigantic and innumerable vortices, and all whirling and plunging on to the eastward with a rapidity which water never elsewhere assumes, except in precipitous descents.

In a few minutes more, there came over the scene another radical alteration. The general surface grew somewhat more smooth, and the whirlpools, one by one, disappeared, while prodigious streaks of foam became apparent where none had been seen before. These streaks, at length, spreading out to a great distance, and entering into combination, took unto themselves the gyratory motion of the subsided vortices, and seemed to form the germ of another more vast. Suddenly – very suddenly – this assumed a distinct and definite existence, in a circle of more than a mile in diameter. The edge of the whirl was represented by a broad belt of gleaming spray; but no particle of this slipped into the mouth of the terrific funnel, whose interior, as far as the eye could fathom it, was a smooth, shining, and jet-black wall of water, inclined to the horizon at an angle of some forty-five degrees, speeding dizzily round and round with a swaying and sweltering motion, and sending forth to the winds an appalling voice, half shriek, half roar, such as not even the mighty cataract of Niagara ever lifts up in its agony to Heaven.

The mountain trembled to its very base, and the rock rocked. I threw myself upon my face, and clung to the scant herbage in an excess of nervous agitation.

"This," said I at length, to the old man – "this can be nothing else than the great whirlpool of the Maelström."

"So it is sometimes termed," said he. "We Norwegians call it the Moskoeström, from the island of Moskoe in the midway."

The ordinary account of this vortex had by no means prepared me for what I saw. That of Jonas Ramus, which is perhaps the most circumstantial of any, cannot impart the faintest conception either of the magnificence, or of the horror of the scene – or of the wild bewildering sense of *the novel* which confounds the beholder. I am not sure from what point of view the writer in question surveyed it, nor at what time; but it could neither have been from the summit of Helseggen, nor during a storm. There are some passages of his description, nevertheless, which may be quoted for their details, although their effect is exceedingly feeble in conveying an impression of the spectacle.

"Between Lofoden and Moskoe," he says, "the depth of the water is between thirty-six and forty fathoms; but on the other side, toward Ver (Vurrgh) this depth decreases so as not to afford a convenient passage for a vessel, without the risk of splitting on the rocks, which happens even in the calmest weather. When it is flood, the stream runs up the country between Lofoden and Moskoe with a boisterous rapidity; but the roar of its impetuous ebb to the sea is scarce equalled by the loudest and most dreadful cataracts; the noise being heard several leagues off, and the vortices or pits are of such an extent and depth, that if a ship comes within its attraction, it is inevitably absorbed and carried down to the bottom, and there beat to pieces against the rocks; and when the water relaxes, the fragments thereof are thrown up again. But these intervals of tranquility are only at the turn of the ebb and flood, and in calm weather, and last but a quarter of an hour, its violence gradually returning. When the stream is most boisterous, and its fury heightened by a storm, it is dangerous to come within a Norway mile of it. Boats, yachts, and ships have been carried away by not guarding against it before they were carried within its reach. It likewise happens frequently, that whales come too near the stream, and are overpowered by its violence; and then

it is impossible to describe their howlings and bellowings in their fruitless struggles to disengage themselves. A bear once, attempting to swim from Lofoden to
Moskoe, was caught by the stream and borne down, while he roared terribly, so
as to be heard on shore. Large stocks of firs and pine trees, after being absorbed
by the current, rise again broken and torn to such a degree as if bristles grew
upon them. This plainly shows the bottom to consist of craggy rocks, among
which they are whirled to and fro. This stream is regulated by the flux and reflux
of the sea – it being constantly high and low water every six hours. In the year
1645, early in the morning of Sexagesima Sunday, it raged with such noise and
impetuosity that the very stones of the houses on the coast fell to the ground."

In regard to the depth of the water, I could not see how this could have been
ascertained at all in the immediate vicinity of the vortex. The "forty fathoms"
must have reference only to portions of the channel close upon the shore either
of Moskoe or Lofoden. The depth in the centre of the Moskoe-ström must be
unmeasurably greater; and no better proof of this fact is necessary than can be
obtained from even the sidelong glance into the abyss of the whirl which may
be had from the highest crag of Helseggen. Looking down from this pinnacle
upon the howling Phlegethon below, I could not help smiling at the simplicity
with which the honest Jonas Ramus records, as a matter difficult of belief, the
anecdotes of the whales and the bears, for it appeared to me, in fact, a self-
evident thing, that the largest ships of the line in existence, coming within the
influence of that deadly attraction, could resist it as little as a feather the hurricane, and must disappear bodily and at once.

The attempts to account for the phenomenon – some of which I remember,
seemed to me sufficiently plausible in perusal – now wore a very different and
unsatisfactory aspect. The idea generally received is that this, as well as three
smaller vortices among the Ferroe Islands, "have no other cause than the colli-
sion of waves rising and falling, at flux and reflux, against a ridge of rows and
shelves; which confines the water so that it precipitates itself like a cataract; and
thus the higher the flood rises, the deeper must the fall be, and the natural
result of all is a whirlpool or vortex, the prodigious suction of which is sufficiently known by lesser experiments." – These are the words of the Encyclopae-
dia Britannica. Kircher and others imagine that in the centre of the channel of
the maelström is an abyss penetrating the globe, and issuing in some very remote part – the Gulf of Bothnia being somewhat decidedly named in one instance. This opinion, idle in itself, was the one to which, as I gazed, my
imagination most readily assented; and, mentioning it to the guide, I was rather
surprised to hear him say that, although it was the view almost universally entertained of the subject by the Norwegians, it nevertheless was not his own. As to
the former notion he confessed his inability to comprehend it; and here I agreed
with him – for, however conclusive on paper, it becomes altogether unintelligi-
ble, and even absurd, amid the thunder of the abyss.

"You have had a good look at the whirl now," said the old man, "and if you
will creep round this crag, so as to get in its lee, and deaden the roar of the
water, I will tell you a story that will convince you I ought to know something
of the Moskoe-ström."

I placed myself as desired, and he proceeded.

"Myself and my two brothers once owned a schooner-rigged smack of about seventy tons burthen, with which we were in the habit of fishing among the islands beyond Moskoe, nearly to Vurrgh. In all violent eddies at sea there is good fishing, at proper opportunities, if one has only the courage to attempt it; but among the whole of the Lofoden coastmen, we three were the only ones who made a regular business of going out to the islands, as I tell you. The usual grounds are a great way lower down to the southward. There fish can be got at all hours, without much risk, and therefore these places are preferred. The choice spots over here among the rocks, however, not only yield the finest variety, but in far greater abundance; so that we often got in a single day, what the more timid of the craft could not scrape together in a week. In fact, we made it a matter of desperate speculation – the risk of life standing instead of labor, and courage answering for capital.

"We kept the smack in a cove about five miles higher up the coast than this; and it was our practice, in fine weather, to take advantage of the fifteen minutes' slack to push across the main channel of the Moskoe-ström, far above the pool, and then drop down upon anchorage somewhere near Otterholm, or Sandflesen, where the eddies are not so violent as elsewhere. Here we used to remain until nearly time for slack-water again, when we weighed and made for home. We never set out upon this expedition without a steady side wind for going and coming – one that we felt sure would not fail us before our return – and we seldom made a miscalculation upon this point. Twice, during six years, we were forced to stay all night at anchor on account of a dead calm, which is a rare thing indeed just about here; and once we had to remain on the grounds nearly a week, starving to death, owing to a gale which blew up shortly after our arrival, and made the channel too boisterous to be thought of. Upon this occasion we should have been driven out to sea in spite of every thing (for the whirlpools threw us round and round so violently, that, at length, we fouled our anchor and dragged it), if it had not been that we drifted into one of the innumerable cross currents – here to-day and gone tomorrow – which drove us under the lee of Flimen, where, by good luck, we brought up.

"I could not tell you the twentieth part of the difficulties we encountered 'on the ground' – it is a bad spot to be in, even in good weather – but we make shift always to run the gauntlet of the Moskoe-ström itself without accident; although at times my heart has been in my mouth when we happened to be a minute or so behind or before the slack. The wind sometimes was not as strong as we thought it at starting, and then we made rather less way than we could wish, while the current rendered the smack unmanageable. My eldest brother had a son eighteen years old, and I had two stout boys of my own. These would have been of great assistance at such times, in using the sweeps as well as afterward in fishing – but, somehow, although we ran the risk ourselves, we had not the heart to let the young ones get into the danger – for, after all said and done, it *was* a horrible danger, and that is the truth.

"It is now within a few days of three years since what I am going to tell you occurred. It was on the tenth of July, 18—, a day which the people of this part of the world will never forget – for it was one in which blew the most terrible hurricane that ever came out of the heavens. And yet all the morning, and indeed until late in the afternoon, there was a gentle and steady breeze from the southwest, while the sun shone brightly, so that the oldest seaman among us could not have foreseen what was to follow.

"The three of us – my two brothers and myself – had crossed over to the islands about two o'clock P.M., and soon nearly loaded the smack with fine fish, which, we all remarked, were more plenty that day than we had ever known them. It was just seven, *by my watch*, when we weighed and started for home, so as to make the worst of the Ström at slack water, which we knew would be at eight.

"We set out with a fresh wind on our starboard quarter, and for some time spanked along at a great rate, never dreaming of danger, for indeed we saw not the slightest reason to apprehend it. All at once we were taken aback by a breeze from over Helseggen. This was most unusual – something that had never happened to us before – and I began to feel a little uneasy, without exactly knowing why. We put the boat on the wind, but could make no headway at all for the eddies, and I was upon the point of proposing to return to the anchorage, when, looking astern, we saw the whole horizon covered with a singular copper-colored cloud that rose with the most amazing velocity.

"In the meantime the breeze that had headed us off fell away and we were dead becalmed, drifting about in every direction. This state of things, however, did not last long enough to give us time to think about it. In less than a minute the storm was upon us – in less than two the sky was entirely overcast – and what with this and the driving spray, it became suddenly so dark that we could not see each other in the smack.

"Such a hurricane as then blew it is folly to attempt describing. The oldest seaman in Norway never experienced any thing like it. We had let our sails go by the run before it cleverly took us; but, at the first puff, both our masts went by the board as if they had been sawed off – the mainmast taking with it my youngest brother, who had lashed himself to it for safety.

"Our boat was the lightest feather of a thing that ever sat upon water. It had a complete flush deck, with only a small hatch near the bow, and this hatch it had always been our custom to batten down when about to cross the Ström, by way of precaution against the chopping seas. But for this circumstance we should have foundered at once – for we lay entirely buried for some moments. How my elder brother escaped destruction I cannot say, for I never had an opportunity of ascertaining. For my part, as soon as I had let the foresail run, I threw myself flat on deck, with my feet against the narrow gunwale of the bow, and with my hands grasping a ring-bolt near the foot of the foremast. It was mere instinct that prompted me to do this – which was undoubtedly the very best thing I could have done – for I was too much flurried to think.

"For some moments we were completely deluged, as I say, and all this time I held my breath, and clung to the bolt. When I could stand it no longer I raised myself upon my knees, still keeping hold with my hands, and thus got my head clear. Presently our little boat gave herself a shake, just as a dog does in coming out of the water, and thus rid herself, in some measure, of the seas. I was now trying to get the better of the stupor that had come over me, and to collect my senses so as to see what was to be done, when I felt somebody grasp my arm. It was my elder brother, and my heart leaped for joy, for I had made sure that he was overboard – but the next moment all the joy was turned into horror – for he put his mouth close to my ear, and screamed out the word *'Moskoe-ström!'*

"No one ever will know what my feelings were at that moment. I shook from head to foot as if I had had the most violent fit of the ague. I knew what he meant by that one word well enough – I knew what he wished to make me understand. With the wind that now drove us on, we were bound for the whirl of the Ström, and nothing could save us!

"You perceive that in crossing the Ström *channel*, we always went a long way up above the whirl, even in the calmest weather, and then had to wait and watch carefully for the slack – but now we were driving right upon the pool itself, and in such a hurricane as this! 'To be sure,' I thought, 'we shall get there just about the slack – there is some little hope in that' – but in the next moment I cursed myself for being so great a fool as to dream of hope at all. I knew very well that we were doomed, had we been ten times a ninety-gun ship.

"By this time the first fury of the tempest had spent itself, or perhaps we did not feel it so much, as we scudded before it, but at all events the seas, which at first had been kept down by the wind, and lay flat and frothing, now got up into absolute mountains. A singular change, too, had come over the heavens. Around in every direction it was still as black as pitch, but nearly overhead there burst out, all at once, a circular rift of clear sky – as clear as I ever saw – and of a deep bright blue – and through it there blazed forth the full moon with a lustre that I never before knew her to wear. She lit up every thing about us with the greatest distinctness – but, oh God, what a scene it was to light up!

"I now made one or two attempts to speak to my brother – but in some manner which I could not understand, the din had so increased that I could not make him hear a single word, although I screamed at the top of my voice in his ear. Presently he shook his head, looking as pale as death, and held up one of his fingers, as if to say *'listen!'*

"At first I could not make out what he meant – but soon a hideous thought flashed upon me. I dragged my watch from its fob. It was not going. I glanced at its face by the moonlight, and then burst into tears as I flung it far away into the ocean. *It had run down at seven o'clock! We were behind the time of the slack, and the whirl of the Ström was in full fury!*

"When a boat is well built, properly trimmed, and not deep laden, the waves in a strong gale, when she is going large, seem always to slip from beneath her – which appears strange to a landsman – and this is what is called *riding*, in sea phrase.

"Well, so far we had ridden the swells very cleverly; but presently a gigantic sea happened to take us right under the counter, and bore us with it as it rose – up – up – as if into the sky. I would not have believed that any wave could rise so high. And then down we came with a sweep, a slide, and a plunge that made me feel sick and dizzy, as if I was falling from some lofty mountain-top in a dream. But while we were up I had thrown a quick glance around – and that one glance was all-sufficient. I saw our exact position in an instant. The Moskoe-ström whirlpool was about a quarter of a mile dead ahead – but no more like the everyday Moskoe-ström than the whirl, as you now see it, is like a mill-race. If I had not known where we were, and what we had to expect, I should not have recognized the place at all. As it was, I involuntarily closed my eyes in horror. The lids clenched themselves together as if in a spasm.

"It could not have been more than two minutes afterwards until we suddenly felt the wave subside, and were enveloped in foam. The boat made a sharp half turn to larboard, and then shot off in its new direction like a thunderbolt. At the same moment the roaring noise of the water was completely drowned in a kind of shrill shriek – such a sound as you might imagine given out by the water-pipes of many thousand steam-vessels letting off their steam all together. We were now in the belt of surf that always surrounds the whirl; and I thought, of course, that another moment would plunge us into the abyss, down which we could only see indistinctly on account of the amazing velocity with which we were borne along. The boat did not seem to sink into the water at all, but to skim like an air-bubble upon the surface of the surge. Her starboard side was next the whirl, and on the larboard arose the world of ocean we had left. It stood like a huge writhing wall between us and the horizon.

"It may appear strange, but now, when we were in the very jaws of the gulf, I felt more composed than when we were only approaching it. Having made up my mind to hope no more, I got rid of a great deal of that terror which unmanned me at first. I supposed it was despair that strung my nerves.

"It may look like boasting – but what I tell you is truth – I began to reflect how magnificent a thing it was to die in such a manner, and how foolish it was in me to think of so paltry a consideration as my own individual life, in view of so wonderful a manifestation of God's power. I do believe that I blushed with shame when this idea crossed my mind. After a little while I became possessed with the keenest curiosity about the whirl itself. I positively felt a *wish* to explore its depths, even at the sacrifice I was going to make; and my principal grief was that I should never be able to tell my old companions on shore about the mysteries I should see. These, no doubt, were singular fancies to occupy a man's mind in such extremity – and I have often thought since, that the revolutions of the boat around the pool might have rendered me a little light-headed.

"There was another circumstance which tended to restore my self-possession; and this was the cessation of the wind, which could not reach us in our present situation – for, as you saw for yourself, the belt of the surf is considerably lower than the general bed of the ocean, and this latter now towered above us, a high, black, mountainous ridge. If you have never been at sea in a heavy gale, you can form no idea of the confusion of mind occasioned by the wind and spray together. They blind, deafen, and strangle you, and take away all power of action or reflection. But we were now, in a great measure, rid of these annoyances – just as death-condemned felons in prison are allowed petty indulgences, forbidden them while their doom is yet uncertain.

"How often we made the circuit of the belt it is impossible to say. We careered round and round for perhaps an hour, flying rather than floating, getting gradually more and more into the middle of the surge, and then nearer and nearer to its horrible inner edge. All this time I had never let go of the ring-bolt. My brother was at the stern, holding on to a small empty water-cask which had been securely lashed under the coop of the counter, and was the only thing on deck that had not been swept overboard when the gale first took us. As we approached the brink of the pit he let go his hold upon this, and made for the ring, from which, in the agony of his terror, he endeavored to force my hands, as it was not large enough to afford us both a secure grasp. I never felt deeper grief than when I saw him attempt this act – although I knew he was a madman when he did it – a raving maniac through sheer fright. I did not care, however, to contest the point with him. I knew it could make no difference whether either of us held on at all; so I let him have the bolt, and went astern to the cask. This there was no great difficulty in doing; for the smack flew round steadily enough, and upon an even keel – only swaying to and fro with the immense sweeps and swelters of the whirl. Scarcely had I secured myself in my new position, when we gave a wild lurch to starboard, and rushed headlong into the abyss. I muttered a hurried prayer to God, and thought all was over.

"As I felt the sickening sweep of the descent, I had instinctively tightened my hold upon the barrel, and closed my eyes. For some seconds I dared not open them – while I expected instant destruction, and wondered that I was not already in my death-struggles with the water. But moment after moment elapsed. I still lived. The sense of falling had ceased; and the motion of the vessel seemed much as it had been before, while in the belt of foam, with the exception that she now lay more along. I took courage and looked once again upon the scene.

"Never shall I forget the sensation of awe, horror, and admiration with which I gazed about me. The boat appeared to be hanging, as if by magic, midway down, upon the interior surface of a funnel vast in circumference, prodigious in depth, and whose perfectly smooth sides might have been mistaken for ebony, but for the bewildering rapidity with which they spun around, and for the gleaming and ghastly radiance they shot forth, as the rays of the full moon, from that circular rift amid the clouds which I have already described, streamed in a flood of golden glory along the black walls, and far away down into the inmost recesses of the abyss.

"At first I was too much confused to observe any thing accurately. The general burst of terrific grandeur was all that I beheld. When I recovered myself a little, however, my gaze fell instinctively downward. In this direction I was able to obtain an unobstructed view, from the manner in which the smack hung on the inclined surface of the pool. She was quite upon an even keel – that is to say, her deck lay in a plane parallel with that of the water – but this latter sloped at an angle of more than forty-five degrees, so that we seemed to be lying upon our beam-ends. I could not help observing, nevertheless, that I had scarcely more difficulty in maintaining my hold and footing in this situation, than if we had been upon a dead level; and this, I suppose, was owing to the speed at which we revolved.

"The rays of the moon seemed to search the very bottom of the profound gulf; but still I could make out nothing distinctly on account of a thick mist in which every thing there was enveloped, and over which there hung a magnificent rainbow, like that narrow and tottering bridge which Mussulmen say is the only pathway between Time and Eternity. This mist, or spray, was no doubt occasioned by the clashing of the great walls of the funnel, as they all met together at the bottom – but the yell that went up to the Heavens from out of that mist I dare not attempt to describe.

"Our first slide into the abyss itself, from the belt of foam above, had carried us to a great distance down the slope; but our farther descent was by no means proportionate. Round and round we swept – not with any uniform movement – but in dizzying swings and jerks, that sent us sometimes only a few hundred yards – sometimes nearly the complete circuit of the whirl. Our progress downward, at each revolution, was slow, but very perceptible.

"Looking about me upon the wide waste of liquid ebony on which we were thus borne, I perceived that our boat was not the only object in the embrace of the whirl. Both above and below us were visible fragments of vessels, large masses of building-timber and trunks of trees, with many smaller articles, such as pieces of house furniture, broken boxes, barrels and staves. I have already described the unnatural curiosity which had taken the place of my original terrors. It appeared to grow upon me as I drew nearer and nearer to my dreadful doom. I now began to watch, with a strange interest, the numerous things that floated in our company. I *must* have been delirious, for I even sought *amusement* in speculating upon the relative velocities of their several descents toward the foam below. 'This fir-tree,' I found myself at one time saying, 'will certainly be the next thing that takes the awful plunge and disappears,' – and then I was disappointed to find that the wreck of a Dutch merchant ship overtook it and went down before. At length, after making several guesses of this nature, and being deceived in all – this fact – the fact of my invariable miscalculation, set me upon a train of reflection that made my limbs again tremble, and my heart beat heavily once more.

"It was not a new terror that thus affected me, but the dawn of a more exciting *hope*. This hope arose partly from memory, and partly from present observation. I called to mind the great variety of buoyant matter that strewed the coast of Lofoden, having been absorbed and then thrown forth by the Moskoe-ström. By far the greater number of the articles were shattered in the most extraordinary way – so chafed and roughened as to have the appearance of being stuck full of splinters – but then I distinctly recollected that there were *some* of them which were not disfigured at all. Now I could not account for this difference except by supposing that the roughened fragments were the only ones which had been *completely absorbed* – that the others had entered the whirl at so late a period of the tide, or, from some reason, had descended so slowly after entering, that they did not reach the bottom before the turn of the flood came, or of the ebb, as the case might be. I conceived it possible, in either instance, that they might thus be whirled up again to the level of the ocean, without undergoing the fate of those which had been drawn in more early or absorbed more rapidly. I made, also, three important observations. The first was, that as a general rule, the larger the bodies were, the more rapid their descent – the second, that, between two masses of equal extent, the one spherical, and the other *of any other shape*, the superiority in speed of descent was with the sphere – the third, that, between two masses of equal size, the one cylindrical, and the other of any other shape, the cylinder was absorbed the more slowly. Since my escape, I have had several conversations on this subject with an old school-master of the district; and it was from him that I learned the use of the words 'cylinder' and 'sphere.' He explained to me – although I have forgotten the explanation – how what I observed was, in fact, the natural consequence of the forms of the floating fragments – and showed me how it happened that a cylinder, swimming in a vortex, offered more resistance to its suction, and was drawn in with greater difficulty than an equally bulky body, of any form whatever.[1]

"There was one startling circumstance which went a great way in enforcing these observations, and rendering me anxious to turn them to account, and this was that, at every revolution, we passed something like a barrel, or else the yard or the mast of a vessel, while many of these things, which had been on our level when I first opened my eyes upon the wonders of the whirlpool, were now high up above us, and seemed to have moved but little from their original station.

"I no longer hesitated what to do. I resolved to lash myself securely to the water cask upon which I now held, to cut it loose from the counter, and to throw myself with it into the water. I attracted my brother's attention by signs, pointed to the floating barrels that came near us, and did every thing in my power to make him understand what I was about to do. I thought at length that he comprehended my design – but, whether this was the case or not, he shook his head despairingly, and refused to move from his station by the ringbolt. It was impossible to reach him; the emergency admitted of no delay; and so, with a bitter struggle, I resigned him to his fate, fastened myself to the cask by means of the lashings which secured it to the counter, and precipitated myself with it into the sea, without another moment's hesitation.

"The result was precisely what I had hoped it might be. As it is myself who now tell you this tale – as you see that I *did* escape – and as you are already in possession of the mode in which this escape was effected, and must therefore anticipate all that I have farther to say – I will bring my story quickly to conclusion. It might have been an hour, or thereabout, after my quitting the smack, when, having descended to a vast distance beneath me, it made three or four wild gyrations in rapid succession, and, bearing my loved brother with it, plunged headlong, at once and forever, into the chaos of foam below. The barrel to which I was attached sunk very little farther than half the distance between the bottom of the gulf and the spot at which I leaped overboard, before a great change took place in the character of the whirlpool. The slope of the sides of the vast funnel became momently less and less steep The gyrations of the whirl grew, gradually, less and less violent. By degrees, the froth and the rainbow disappeared, and the bottom of the gulf seemed slowly to uprise. The sky was clear, the winds had gone down, and the full moon was setting radiantly in the west, when I found myself on the surface of the ocean, in full view of the shores of Lofoden, and above the spot where the pool of the Moskoe-ström *had been*. It was the hour of the slack – but the sea still heaved in mountainous waves from the effects of the hurricane. I was borne violently into the channel of the Ström, and in a few minutes, was hurried down the coast into the 'grounds' of the fishermen. A boat picked me up – exhausted from fatigue – and (now that the danger was removed) speechless from the memory of its horror. Those who drew me on board were my old mates and daily companions – but they knew me no more than they would have known a traveller from the spirit-land. My hair, which had been raven black the day before, was as white as you see it now. They say too that the whole expression of my countenance had changed. I told them my story – they did not believe it. I now tell it to *you* – and I can scarcely expect you to put more faith in it than did the merry fishermen of Lofoden."

Notes

1   See Archimedes, "*De Incidentibus in Fluido.*" – lib. 2.

---

27   From *A Philosophical Enquiry into the Origin of Our Ideas of the Sublime and Beautiful*

Edmund Burke

It seems then necessary towards moving the passions of people advanced in life to any considerable degree, that the objects designed for that purpose, besides their being in some measure new, should be capable of exciting pain or pleasure from other causes. Pain and pleasure are simple ideas, incapable of definition. People are not liable to be mistaken in their feelings, but they are very frequently wrong in the names they give them, and in their reasonings about them. Many are of opinion, that pain arises necessarily from the removal of some pleasure; as they think pleasure does from the ceasing or diminution of some pain. For my part I am rather inclined to imagine, that pain and pleasure in their most simple and natural manner of affecting, are each of a positive nature, and by no means necessarily dependent on each other for their existence. The human mind is often, and I think it is for the most part, in a state neither of pain nor pleasure, which I call a state of indifference. When I am carried from this state into a state of actual pleasure, it does not appear necessary that I should pass through the medium of any sort of pain. If in such a state of indifference, or ease, or tranquillity, or call it what you please, you were to be suddenly entertained with a concert of music; or suppose some object of a fine shape, and bright lively colours to be presented before you; or imagine your smell is gratified with the fragrance of a rose; or if without any previous thirst you were to drink of some pleasant kind of wine; or to taste of some sweetmeat without being hungry; in all the several senses, of hearing, smelling, and tasting, you undoubtedly find a pleasure; yet if I enquire into the state of your mind previous to these gratifications, you will hardly tell me that they found you in any kind of pain; or having satisfied these several senses with their several pleasures, will you say that any pain has succeeded, though the pleasure is absolutely over? Suppose on the other hand, a man in the same state of indifference, to receive a violent blow, or to drink of some bitter potion, or to have his ears wounded with some harsh and grating sound; here is no removal of pleasure; and yet here is felt, in every sense which is affected, a pain very distinguishable. It may be said perhaps, that the pain in these cases had its rise from the removal of the pleasure which the man enjoyed before, though that pleasure was of so low a degree as to be perceived only by the removal. But this seems to me a subtilty, that is not discoverable in nature. For if, previous to the pain, I do not feel any actual pleasure, I have no reason to judge that any such thing exists; since pleasure is only pleasure as it is felt. The same may be said of pain, and with equal reason. I can never persuade myself that pleasure and pain are mere relations, which can only exist as they are contrasted: but I think I can discern clearly that there are positive pains and pleasures, which do not at all depend upon each other. Nothing is more certain to my own feelings than this. There is nothing which I can distinguish in my mind with more clearness than the three states, of indifference, of pleasure, and of pain. [. . .]

Most of the ideas which are capable of making a powerful impression on the mind, whether simply of Pain or Pleasure, or of the modifications of those, may be reduced very nearly to these two heads, *self-preservation* and *society*; to the ends of one or the other of which all our passions are calculated to answer. The passions which concern self-preservation, turn mostly on *pain* or *danger*. The ideas of *pain, sickness*, and *death*, fill the mind with strong emotions of horror; but *life* and *health*, though they put us in a capacity of being affected with pleasure, they make no such impression by the simple enjoyment. The passions therefore which are conversant about the preservation of the individual, turn chiefly on *pain* and *danger*, and they are the most powerful of all the passions.

Whatever is fitted in any sort to excite the ideas of pain, and danger, that is to say, whatever is in any sort terrible, or is conversant about terrible objects, or operates in a manner analogous to terror, is a source of the *sublime*; that is, it is productive of the strongest emotion which the mind is capable of feeling. I say the strongest emotion, because I am satisfied the ideas of pain are much more powerful than those which enter on the part of pleasure. Without all doubt, the torments which we may be made to suffer, are much greater in their effect on the body and mind, than any pleasures which the most learned voluptuary could suggest, or than the liveliest imagination, and the most sound and exquisitely sensible body could enjoy. Nay I am in great doubt, whether any man could be found who would earn a life of the most perfect satisfaction, at the price of ending it in the torments, which justice inflicted in a few hours on the late unfortunate regicide in France. But as pain is stronger in its operation than pleasure, so death is in general a much more affecting idea than pain; because there are very few pains, however exquisite, which are not preferred to death; nay, what generally makes pain itself, if I may say so, more painful, is, that it is considered as an emissary of this king of terrors. When danger or pain press too nearly, they are incapable of giving any delight, and are simply terrible; but at certain distances, and with certain modifications, they may be, and they are delightful, as we every day experience. The cause of this I shall endeavour to investigate hereafter. [. . .]

Under this denomination of society, the passions are of a complicated kind, and branch out into a variety of forms agreeable to that variety of ends they are to serve in the great chain of society. The three principal links in this chain are *sympathy, imitation, and ambition.*

It is by the first of these passions that we enter into the concerns of others; that we are moved as they are moved, and are never suffered to be indifferent spectators of almost any thing which men can do or suffer. For sympathy must be considered as a sort of substitution, by which we are put into the place of another man, and affected in many respects as he is affected; so that this passion may either partake of the nature of those which regard self-preservation, and turning upon pain may be a source of the sublime; or it may turn upon ideas of pleasure; and then, whatever has been said of the social affections, whether they regard society in general, or only some particular modes of it, may be applicable here. It is by this principle chiefly that poetry, painting, and other affecting arts, transfuse their passions from one breast to another, and are often capable of grafting a delight on wretchedness, misery, and death itself. It is a common observation, that objects which in the reality would shock, are in tragical, and such like representations, the source of a very high species of pleasure. This taken as a fact, has been the cause of much reasoning. The satisfaction has been commonly attributed, first, to the comfort we receive in considering that so melancholy a story is no more than a fiction; and next, to the contemplation of our own freedom from the evils which we see represented. I am afraid it is a practice much too common in inquiries of this nature, to attribute the cause of feelings which merely arise from the mechanical structure of our bodies, or from the natural frame and constitution of our minds, to certain conclusions of the reasoning faculty on the objects presented to us; for I should imagine, that the influence of reason in producing our passions is nothing near so extensive as it is commonly believed.

To examine this point concerning the effect of tragedy in a proper manner, we must previously consider, how we are affected by the feelings of our fellow creatures in circumstances of real distress. I am convinced we have a degree of delight, and that no small one, in the real misfortunes and pains of others; for let the affection be what it will in appearance, if it does not make us shun such objects, if on the contrary it induces us to approach them, if it makes us dwell upon them, in this case I conceive we must have a delight or pleasure of some species or other in contemplating objects of this kind. Do we not read the authentic histories of scenes of this nature with as much pleasure as romances or poems, where the incidents are fictitious? The prosperity of no empire, nor the grandeur of no king, can so agreeably affect in the reading, as the ruin of the state of Macedon, and the distress of its unhappy prince. Such a catastrophe touches us in history as much as the destruction of Troy does in fable. Our delight in cases of this kind, is very greatly heightened, if the sufferer be some excellent person who sinks under an unworthy fortune. Scipio and Cato are both virtuous characters; but we are more deeply affected by the violent death of the one, and the ruin of the great cause he adhered to, than with the deserved triumphs and uninterrupted prosperity of the other; for terror is a passion which always produces delight when it does not press too close, and pity is a passion accompanied with pleasure, because it arises from love and social affection. Whenever we are formed by nature to any active purpose, the passion which animates us to it, is attended with delight, or a pleasure of some kind, let the subject matter be what it will; and as our Creator has designed we should be united by the bond of sympathy, he has strengthened that bond by a proportionable delight; and there most where our sympathy is most wanted, in the distresses of others. If this passion was simply painful, we would shun with the greatest care all persons and places that could excite such a passion; as, some who are so far gone in indolence as not to endure any strong impression actually do. But the case is widely different with the greater part of mankind; there is no spectacle we so eagerly pursue, as that of some uncommon and grievous calamity; so that whether the misfortune is before our eyes, or whether they are turned back to it in history, it always touches with delight. This is not an unmixed delight, but blended with no small uneasiness. The delight we have in such things, hinders us from shunning scenes of misery; and the pain we feel prompts us to relieve ourselves in relieving those who suffer; and all this antecedent to any reasoning, by an instinct that works us to its own purposes, without our concurrence.

It is thus in real calamities. In imitated distresses the only difference is the pleasure resulting from the effects of imitation; for it is never so perfect, but we can perceive it is an imitation, and on that principle are somewhat pleased with it. And indeed in some cases we derive as much or more pleasure from that source than from the thing itself. But then I imagine we shall be much mistaken if we attribute any considerable part of our satisfaction in tragedy to a consideration that tragedy is a deceit, and its representations no realities. The nearer it approaches the reality, and the further it removes us from all idea of fiction, the more perfect is its power. But be its power of what kind it will, it never approaches to what it represents. Chuse a day on which to represent the most sublime and affecting tragedy we have; appoint the most favourite actors; spare no cost upon the scenes and decorations; unite the greatest efforts of poetry, painting and music; and when you have collected your audience, just at the moment when their minds are erect with expectation, let it be reported that a state criminal of high rank is on the point of being executed in the adjoining square;[1] in a moment the emptiness of the theatre would demonstrate the comparative weakness of the imitative arts, and proclaim the triumph of the real sympathy. I believe that this notion of our having a simple pain in the reality, yet a delight in the representation, arises from hence, that we do not sufficiently distinguish what we would by no means chuse to do, from what we should be eager enough to see if it was once done. We delight in seeing things, which so far from doing, our heartiest wishes would be to see redressed. This noble capital, the pride of England and of Europe, I believe no man is so strangely wicked as to desire to see destroyed by a conflagration or an earthquake, though he should be removed himself to the greatest distance from the danger. But suppose such a fatal accident have happened, what numbers from all parts would croud to behold the ruins, and amongst them many who would have been content never to have seen London in its glory? Nor is it either in real or fictitious distresses, our immunity from them which produces our delight; in my own mind I can discover nothing like it. I apprehend that this mistake is owing to a sort of sophism, by which we are frequently imposed upon; it arises from our not distinguishing between what is indeed a necessary condition to our doing or suffering any thing in general, and what is the *cause* of some particular act. If a man kills me with a sword, it is a necessary condition to this that we should have been both of us alive before the fact; and yet it would be absurd to say, that our being both living creatures was the cause of his crime and of my death. So it is certain, that it is absolutely necessary my life should be out of any imminent hazard before I can take a delight in the sufferings of others, real or imaginary, or indeed in any thing else from any cause whatsoever. But then it is a sophism to argue from thence, that this immunity is the cause of my delight either on these or on any occasions. No one can distinguish such a cause of satisfaction in his own mind I believe; nay when we do not suffer any very acute pain, nor are exposed to any imminent danger of our lives, we can feel for others, whilst we suffer ourselves; and often then most when we are softened by affliction; we see with pity even distresses which we would accept in the place of our own. [. . .]

Besides these things which *directly* suggest the idea of danger, and those which produce a similar effect from a mechanical cause, I know of nothing sublime which is not some modification of power. And this branch rises as naturally as the other two branches, from terror, the common stock of every thing that is sublime. The idea of power at first view, seems of the class of these indifferent ones, which may equally belong to pain or to pleasure. But in reality, the affection arising from the idea of vast power, is extremely remote from that neutral character. For first, we must remember, that the idea of pain, in its highest degree, is much stronger than the highest degree of pleasure; and that it preserves the same superiority through all the subordinate gradations. From hence it is, that where the chances for equal degrees of suffering or enjoyment are in any sort equal, the idea of the suffering must always be prevalent. And indeed the ideas of pain, and above all of death, are so very affecting, that whilst we remain in the presence of whatever is supposed to have the power of inflicting either, it is impossible to be perfectly free from terror. Again, we know by experience, that for the enjoyment of pleasure, no great efforts of power are at all necessary; nay we know, that such efforts would go a great way towards destroying our satisfaction: for pleasure must be stolen, and not forced upon us; pleasure follows the will; and therefore we are generally affected with it by many things of a force greatly inferior to our own. But pain is always inflicted by a power in some way superior, because we never submit to pain willingly. So that strength, violence, pain and terror, are ideas that rush in upon the mind together. Look at a man, or any other animal of prodigious strength, and what is your idea before reflection? Is it that this strength will be subservient to you, to your ease, to your pleasure, to your interest in any sense? No; the emotion you feel is, lest this enormous strength should be employed to the purposes of rapine and destruction. That power derives all its sublimity from the terror with which it is generally accompanied, will appear evidently from its effect in the very few cases, in which it may be possible to strip a considerable degree of strength of its ability to hurt. When you do this, you spoil it of every thing sublime, and it immediately becomes contemptible. An ox is a creature of vast strength; but he is an innocent creature, extremely serviceable, and not at all dangerous; for which reason the idea of an ox is by no means grand. A bull is strong too; but his strength is of another kind; often very destructive, seldom (at least amongst us) of any use in our business; the idea of a bull is therefore great, and it has frequently a place in sublime descriptions, and elevating comparison. Let us look at another strong animal in the two distinct lights in which we may consider him. The horse in the light of an useful beast, fit for the plough, the road, the draft, in every social useful light the horse has nothing of the sublime; but is it thus that we are affected with him, *whose neck is cloathed with thunder, the glory of whose nostrils is terrible, who swalloweth the ground with fierceness and rage, neither believeth that it is the sound of the trumpet?*[2] In this description the useful character of the horse entirely disappears, and the terrible and sublime blaze out together. We have continually about us animals of a strength that is considerable, but not pernicious. Amongst these we never look for the sublime: it comes upon us in the gloomy forest, and in the howling wilderness, in the form of the lion, the tiger, the panther, or rhinoceros. Whenever strength is only useful, and employed for our benefit or our pleasure, then it is never sublime; for nothing can act agreeably to us, that does not act in conformity to our will; but to act agreeably to our will, it must be subject to us; and therefore can never be the cause of a grand and commanding conception. The description of the wild ass, in Job, is worked up into no small sublimity, merely by insisting on his freedom, and his setting mankind at defiance; otherwise the description of such an animal could have had nothing noble in it. *Who hath loosed* (says he) *the bands of the wild ass? whose house I have made the wilderness, and the barren land his dwellings. He scorneth the multitude of the city, neither regardeth he the voice of the driver. The range of the mountains is his pasture.*[3] The magnificent description of the unicorn and of leviathan in the same book, is full of the same heightening circumstances. *Will the unicorn be willing to serve thee? canst thou bind the unicorn with his band in the furrow? wilt thou trust him because his strength is great? – Canst thou draw out leviathan with an hook? will he make a covenant with thee? wilt thou take him for a servant for ever? shall not one be cast down even at the sight of him?*[4] In short, wheresoever we find strength, and in what light soever we look upon power, we shall all along observe the sublime the concomitant of terror, and contempt the attendant on a strength that is subservient and innoxious. [. . .]

In the scripture, wherever God is represented as appearing or speaking, every thing terrible in nature is called up to heighten the awe and solemnity of the divine presence. The psalms, and the prophetical books, are crouded with instances of this kind. *The earth shook* (says the psalmist) *the heavens also dropped at the presence of the Lord.*[5] And what is remarkable, the painting preserves the same character, not only when he is supposed descending to take vengeance upon the wicked, but even when he exerts the like plenitude of power in acts of beneficence to mankind. *Tremble, thou earth at the presence of the Lord, at the presence of the God of Jacob; which turned the rock into standing water, the flint into a fountain of waters.*[6] It were endless to enumerate all the passages both in the sacred and profane writers, which establish the general sentiment of mankind, concerning the inseparable union of a sacred and reverential awe, with our ideas of the divinity. [. . .]

Thus we have traced power through its several gradations unto the highest of all, where our imagination is finally lost; and we find terror quite throughout the progress, its inseparable companion, and growing along with it, as far as we can possibly trace them. Now as power is undoubtedly a capital source of the sublime, this will point out evidently from whence its energy is derived, and to what class of ideas we ought to unite it. [. . .]

Greatness of dimension, is a powerful cause of the sublime. [. . .]

Another source of the sublime, is *infinity*, if it does not rather belong to the last. Infinity has a tendency to fill the mind with that sort of delightful horror, which is the most genuine effect, and truest test of the sublime. There are scarce any things which can become the objects of our senses that are really, and in their own nature infinite. But the eye not being able to perceive the bounds of many things, they seem to be infinite, and they produce the same effects as if they were really so. We are deceived in the like manner, if the parts of some large object are so continued to any indefinite number, that the imagination meets no check which may hinder its extending them at pleasure. [. . .]

Another source of greatness is *Difficulty*. When any work seems to have required immense force and labour to effect it, the idea is grand. Stonehenge, neither for disposition nor ornament, has any thing admirable; but those huge rude masses of stone, set on end, and piled each on other, turn the mind on the immense force necessary for such a work. Nay the rudeness of the work increases this cause of grandeur, as it excludes the idea of art, and contrivance; for dexterity produces another sort of effect which is different enough from this.

Magnificence is likewise a source of the sublime. A great profusion of things which are splendid or valuable in themselves, is *magnificent*. The starry heaven, though it occurs so very frequently to our view, never fails to excite an idea of grandeur. This cannot be owing to any thing in the stars themselves, separately considered. The number is certainly the cause. The apparent disorder augments the grandeur, for the appearance of care is highly contrary to our ideas of magnificence. Besides, the stars lye in such apparent confusion, as makes it impossible on ordinary occasions to reckon them. This gives them the advantage of a sort of infinity. In works of art, this kind of grandeur, which consists in multitude, is to be very cautiously admitted; because, a profusion of excellent things is not to be attained, or with too much difficulty; and, because in many cases this splendid confusion would destroy all use, which should be attended to in most of the works of art with the greatest care; besides it is to be considered, that unless you can produce an appearance of infinity by your disorder, you will have disorder only without magnificence. There are, however, a sort of fireworks, and some other things, that in this way succeed well, and are truly grand. There are also many descriptions in the poets and orators which owe their sublimity to a richness and profusion of images, in which the mind is so dazzled as to make it impossible to attend to that exact coherence and agreement of the allusions, which we should require on every other occasion. [. . .]

The Sublime and Beautiful Compared

On closing this general view of beauty, it naturally occurs, that we should compare it with the sublime; and in this comparison there appears a remarkable contrast. For sublime objects are vast in their dimensions, beautiful ones comparatively small; beauty should be smooth, and polished; the great, rugged and negligent; beauty should shun the right line, yet deviate from it insensibly; the great in many cases loves the right line, and when it deviates, it often makes a strong deviation; beauty should not be obscure; the great ought to be dark and gloomy; beauty should be light and delicate; the great ought to be solid, and even massive. They are indeed ideas of a very different nature, one being founded on pain, the other on pleasure; and however they may vary afterwards from the direct nature of their causes, yet these causes keep up an eternal distinction between them, a distinction never to be forgotten by any whose business it is to affect the passions. In the infinite variety of natural combinations we must expect to find the qualities of things the most remote imaginable from each other united in the same object. We must expect also to find combinations of the same kind in the works of art. But when we consider the power of an object upon our passions, we must know that when any thing is intended to affect the mind by the force of some predominant property, the affection produced is like to be the more uniform and perfect, if all the other properties or qualities of the object be of the same nature, and tending to the same design as the principal;

> If black, and white blend, soften, and unite,
> A thousand ways, are there no black and white?[7]

If the qualities of the sublime and beautiful are sometimes found united, does this prove, that they are the same, does it prove, that they are any way allied, does it prove even that they are not opposite and contradictory? Black and white may soften, may blend, but they are not therefore the same. Nor when they are so softened and blended with each other, or with different colours, is the power of black as black, or of white as white, so strong as when each stands uniform and distinguished. [. . .]

Having considered terror as producing an unnatural tension and certain violent emotions of the nerves; it easily follows, from what we have just said, that whatever is fitted to produce such a tension, must be productive of a passion similar to terror, and consequently must be a source of the sublime, though it should have no idea of danger connected with it. So that little remains towards shewing the cause of the sublime, but to shew that the instances we have given of it in the second part, relate to such things, as are fitted by nature to produce this sort of tension, either by the primary operation of the mind or the body. With regard to such things as affect by the associated idea of danger, there can be no doubt but that they produce terror, and act by some modification of that passion; and that terror, when sufficiently violent, raises the emotions of the body just mentioned, can as little be doubted. But if the sublime is built on terror, or some passion like it, which has pain for its object; it is previously proper to enquire how any species of delight can be derived from a cause so apparently contrary to it. I say, delight, because, as I have often remarked, it is very evidently different in its cause, and in its own nature, from actual and positive pleasure.

How pain can be a cause of delight

Providence has so ordered it, that a state of rest and inaction, however it may flatter our indolence, should be productive of many inconveniences; that it should generate such disorders, as may force us to have recourse to some labour, as a thing absolutely requisite to make us pass our lives with tolerable satisfaction; for the nature of rest is to suffer all the parts of our bodies to fall into a relaxation, that not only disables the members from performing their functions, but takes away the vigorous tone of fibre which is requisite for carrying on the natural and necessary secretions. At the same time, that in this languid inactive state, the nerves are more liable to the most horrid convulsions, than when they are sufficiently braced and strengthened. Melancholy, dejection, despair, and often self-murder, is the consequence of the gloomy view we take of things in this relaxed state of body. The best remedy for all these evils is exercise or labour; and labour is a surmounting of difficulties, an exertion of the contracting power of the muscles; and as such resembles pain, which consists in tension or contraction, in every thing but degree. Labour is not only requisite to preserve the coarser organs in a state fit for their functions, but it is equally necessary to these finer and more delicate organs, on which, and by which, the imagination, and perhaps the other mental powers act. Since it is probable, that not only the inferior parts of the soul, as the passions are called, but the understanding itself makes use of some fine corporeal instruments in its operation;

though what they are, and where they are, may be somewhat hard to settle: but that it does make use of such, appears from hence; that a long exercise of the mental powers induce a remarkable lassitude of the whole body; and on the other hand, that great bodily labour, or pain, weakens, and sometimes actually destroys the mental faculties. Now, as a due exercise is essential to the coarse muscular parts of the constitution, and that without this rousing they would become languid, and diseased, the very same rule holds with regard to those finer parts we have mentioned; to have them in proper order, they must be shaken and worked to a proper degree. [. . .]

Notes

1 Burke's illustration was most likely prompted by the extraordinary popular interest shown in the execution of Lord Lovat (9 April 1747). Burke himself was fully acquainted with the details of the trial and execution: on 28 April 1747 the Trinity College 'Club' heard and debated an 'Oration' from its President (William Dennis) on the subject. (See Samuels, *Early Life*, p. 231.)
2 Job, XXXIX, 19b, 20b, 24 (misquoted). Lowth quotes this passage to prove his contention that Job "is adapted in every respect to the incitement of terror; and . . . is universally animated with the true spirit of sublimity" (*Lectures on the Sacred Poetry of the Hebrews*, trans. G. Gregory, 1787, II, 428, 424).
3 Job, XXXIX, 5b–8a (misquoted).
4 Ibid., XXXIX, 9a, 10a, 11a; XLI, 1a, 4, 9b.
5 Psalms, LXVIII, 8 (misquoted).
6 Ibid., CXIV, 7–8 (misquoted).
7 Pope, *Essay on Man*, II, 213–14 (misquoted).

28 Analytic of the Sublime from the *Critique of Judgment*

Immanuel Kant

The beautiful and the sublime are similar in some respects. We like both for their own sake, and both presuppose that we make a judgment of reflection rather than either a judgment of sense or a logically determinative one. Hence in neither of them does our liking depend on a sensation, such as that of the agreeable, nor on a determinate concept, as does our liking for the good; yet we do refer the liking to concepts, though it is indeterminate which concepts these are. Hence the liking is connected with the mere exhibition or power of exhibition, i.e., the imagination, with the result that we regard this power, when an intuition is given us, as harmonizing with the *power of concepts*, i.e., the understanding or reason, this harmony furthering [the aims of] these. That is also why both kinds of judgment are *singular* ones that nonetheless proclaim themselves universally valid for all subjects, though what they lay claim to is merely the feeling of pleasure, and not any cognition of the object.

But some significant differences between the beautiful and the sublime are also readily apparent. The beautiful in nature concerns the form of the object, which consists in [the object's] being bounded. But the sublime can also be found in a formless object, insofar as we present *unboundedness*, either [as] in the object or because the object prompts us to present it, while yet we add to this unboundedness the thought of its totality. So it seems that we regard the beautiful as the exhibition of an indeterminate concept of the understanding, and the sublime as the exhibition of an indeterminate concept of reason. Hence in the case of the beautiful our liking is connected with the presentation of *quality*, but in the case of the sublime with the presentation of *quantity*. The two likings are also very different in kind. For the one liking ([that for] the beautiful) carries with it directly a feeling of life's being furthered, and hence is compatible with charms and with an imagination at play. But the other liking (the feeling of the sublime) is a pleasure that arises only indirectly: it is produced by the feeling of a momentary inhibition of the vital forces followed immediately by an outpouring of them that is all the stronger. Hence it is an emotion,[1] and so it seems to be seriousness, rather than play, in the imagination's activity. Hence, too, this liking is incompatible with charms, and, since the mind is not just attracted by the object but is alternately always repelled as well, the liking for the sublime contains not so much a positive pleasure as rather admiration and respect, and so should be called a negative pleasure.[2]

But the intrinsic and most important distinction between the sublime and the beautiful is presumably the following. If, as is permissible, we start here by considering only the sublime in natural objects (since the sublime in art is always confined to the conditions that [art] must meet to be in harmony with nature), then the distinction in question comes to this: (Independent) natural beauty carries with it a purposiveness in its form, by which the object seems as it were predetermined for our power of judgment, so that this beauty constitutes in itself an object of our liking. On the other hand, if something arouses in us, merely in apprehension and without any reasoning on our part, a feeling of the sublime, then it may indeed appear, in its form, contrapurposive for our power of judgment, incommensurate with our power of exhibition, and as it were violent to our imagination and yet we judge it all the more sublime for that. [...]

But we do have to make one division in analyzing the sublime that the analysis of the beautiful did not require: we must divide the sublime into the *mathematically* and the *dynamically* sublime.

For while taste for the beautiful presupposes and sustains the mind in *restful* contemplation, the feeling of the sublime carries with it, as its character, a mental agitation connected with our judging of the object. [...]

Of the Mathematically Sublime

[. . .] Estimation of magnitude by means of numerical concepts (or their signs in algebra) is mathematical; estimation of magnitudes in mere intuition (by the eye) is aesthetic. It is true that to get determinate concepts of how large something is we must use numbers (or, at any rate, approximations [expressed] by numerical series progressing to infinity), whose unity is [the unit we use as] the measure; and to that extent all logical estimation of magnitude is mathematical. Yet the magnitude of the measure must be assumed to be known. Therefore, if we had to estimate this magnitude also mathematically, i.e., only by numbers, whose unity would have to be a different measure, then we could never have a first or basic measure, and hence also could have no determinate concept of a given magnitude. Hence our estimation of the magnitude of the basic measure must consist merely in our being able to take it in [*fassen*] directly in one intuition and to use it, by means of the imagination, for exhibiting numerical concepts. In other words, all estimation of the magnitude of objects of nature is ultimately aesthetic (i.e., determined subjectively rather than objectively).

Now even though there is no maximum [*Größtes*] for the mathematical estimation of magnitude (inasmuch as the power of numbers progresses to infinity), yet for the aesthetic estimation of magnitude there is indeed a maximum. And regarding this latter maximum I say that when it is judged as [the] absolute measure beyond which no larger is subjectively possible (i.e., possible for the judging subject), then it carries with it the idea of the sublime and gives rise to that emotion which no mathematical estimation of magnitude by means of numbers can produce (except to the extent that the basic aesthetic measure is at the same time kept alive in the imagination). For a mathematical estimation of magnitude never exhibits more than relative magnitude, by a comparison with others of the same kind, whereas an aesthetic one exhibits absolute magnitude to the extent that the mind can take it in in one intuition.

In order for the imagination to take in a quantum intuitively, so that we can then use it as a measure or unity in estimating magnitude by numbers, the imagination must perform two acts: *apprehension* (*apprehensio*), and *comprehension*[3] (*comprehensio aesthetica*). Apprehension involves no problem, for it may progress to infinity. But comprehension becomes more and more difficult the farther apprehension progresses, and it soon reaches its maximum, namely, the aesthetically largest basic measure for an estimation of magnitude. For when apprehension has reached the point where the partial presentations of sensible intuition that were first apprehended are already beginning to be extinguished in the imagination, as it proceeds to apprehend further ones, the imagination then loses as much on the one side as it gains on the other: and so there is a maximum in comprehension that it cannot exceed.

This serves to explain a comment made by *Savary* in his report on Egypt:[4] that in order to get the full emotional effect from the magnitude of the pyramids one must neither get too close to them nor stay too far away. For if one stays too far away, then the apprehended parts (the stones on top of one another) are presented only obscurely, and hence their presentation has no effect on the subject's aesthetic judgment; and if one gets too close, then the eye needs some time to complete the apprehension from the base to the peak, but during that time some of the earlier parts are invariably extinguished in the imagination before it has apprehended the later ones, and hence the comprehension is never complete. [. . .]

Since the presentation of anything that our merely reflective power of judgment is to like without an interest must carry with it a purposiveness that is subjective and yet universally valid, but since in the sublime (unlike the beautiful) our judging is not based on a purposiveness of the *form* of the object, the following questions arise: What is this subjective purposiveness, and how does it come to be prescribed as a standard, thereby providing a basis for a universally valid liking accompanying the mere estimation of magnitude – an estimation that has been pushed to the point where the ability of our imagination is inadequate to exhibit the concept of magnitude?

When the imagination performs the combination [*Zusammensetzung*] that is required to present a magnitude, it encounters no obstacles and on its own progresses to infinity, while the understanding guides it by means of numerical concepts, for which the imagination must provide the schema;[5] and in this procedure, which is involved in the logical estimation of magnitude, there is indeed something objectively purposive under the concept of a purpose (since any measuring is a purpose). And yet there is nothing in it that is purposive for, and liked by, the aesthetic power of judgment. Nor is there anything in this intentional purposiveness that necessitates our pushing the magnitude of the measure, and hence of the *comprehension* of the many [elements] in one intuition, to the limit of the imagination's ability, and as far as it may extend in exhibiting. For in estimating magnitudes by the understanding (arithmetic) we get equally far whether we pursue the comprehension of the unities to the number 10 (as in the decadic system) or only to 4 (as in the tetradic system): the further generation of magnitudes – in the [process of] combination or, if the quantum is given in intuition, in apprehension – is done merely progressively (rather than comprehensively), under an assumed principle of progression. This mathematical estimation of magnitude serves and satisfies the understanding equally well, whether the imagination selects as the unity a magnitude that we can take in in one glance. such as a foot or a rod, or whether it selects a German mile,[6] or even an earth diameter, which the imagination can apprehend but cannot comprehend in one intuition (by a *comprehensio aesthetica* though it can comprehend it in a numerical concept by a *comprehensio logica*). In either case the logical estimation of magnitude progresses without hindrance to infinity.[7]

But the mind listens to the voice of reason within itself, which demands totality for all given magnitudes, even for those that we can never apprehend in their entirety but do (in presentation of sense) judge as given in their entirety. Hence reason demands comprehension in *one* intuition, and *exhibition* of all the members of a progressively increasing numerical series, and it exempts from this demand not even the infinite (space and past time). Rather, reason makes us unavoidably think of the infinite (in common reason's judgment) as *given in its entirety* (in its totality).

The infinite, however, is absolutely large (not merely large by comparison). Compared with it everything else (of the same kind of magnitude) is small. But – and this is most important – to be able even to think the infinite as a whole indicates a mental power that surpasses any standard of sense. For [thinking the infinite as a whole while using a standard of sense] would require a comprehension yielding as a unity a standard that would have a determinate relation to the infinite, one that could be stated in numbers; and this is impossible. If the human mind is nonetheless to *be able even to think* the given infinite without contradiction, it must have within itself a power that is supersensible, whose idea of a noumenon cannot be intuited but can yet be regarded as the substrate underlying what is mere appearance, namely, our intuition of the world. For only by means of this power and its idea do we, in a pure intellectual estimation of magnitude, comprehend the infinite in the world of sense *entirely under* a concept, even though in a mathematical estimation of magnitude *by means of numerical concepts* we can never think it in its entirety. Even a power that enables us to think the infinite of supersensible intuition as given (in our intelligible substrate) surpasses any standard of sensibility. It is large beyond any comparison even with the power of mathematical estimation – not, it is true, for [the pursuit of] a theoretical aim on behalf of our cognitive power, but still as an expansion of the mind that feels able to cross the barriers of sensibility with a different (a practical) aim.

Hence nature is sublime in those of its appearances whose intuition carries with it the idea of their infinity. But the only way for this to occur is through the inadequacy of even the greatest effort of our imagination to estimate an object's magnitude. In the mathematical estimation of magnitude, however, the imagination is equal to the task of providing, for any object, a measure that will suffice for this estimation, because the understanding's numerical concepts can be used in a progression and so can make any measure adequate to any given magnitude. Hence it must be the *aesthetic* estimation of magnitude where we feel that effort, our imagination's effort to perform a comprehension that surpasses its ability to encompass [*begreifen*] the progressive apprehension in a whole of intuition, and where at the same time we perceive the inadequacy of the imagination – unbounded though it is as far as progressing is concerned – for taking in and using, for the estimation of magnitude, a basic measure that is suitable for this with minimal expenditure on the part of the understanding. Now the proper unchangeable basic measure of nature is the absolute whole of nature, which, in the case of nature as appearance, is infinity comprehended. This basic measure, however, is a self-contradictory concept (because an absolute totality of an endless progression is impossible). Hence that magnitude of a natural object to which the imagination fruitlessly applies its entire ability to comprehend must lead the concept of nature to a supersensible substrate (which underlies both nature and our ability to think), a substrate that is large beyond any standard of sense and hence makes us judge as *sublime* not so much the object as the mental attunement in which we find ourselves when we estimate the object.

Therefore, just as the aesthetic power of judgment in judging the beautiful refers the imagination in its free play to the *understanding* so that it will harmonize with the understanding's *concepts* in general (which concepts they are is left indeterminate), so in judging a thing sublime it refers the imagination to *reason* so that it will harmonize subjectively with reason's *ideas* (which ideas they are is indeterminate), i.e., so that it will produce a mental attunement that conforms to and is compatible with the one that an influence by determinate (practical) ideas would produce on feeling.

This also shows that true sublimity must be sought only in the mind of the judging person, not in the natural object the judging of which prompts this mental attunement. Indeed, who would want to call sublime such things as shapeless mountain masses piled on one another in wild disarray, with their pyramids of ice, or the gloomy raging sea? But the mind feels elevated in its own judgment of itself when it contemplates these without concern for their form and abandons itself to the imagination and to a reason that has come to be connected with it – though quite without a determinate purpose, and merely expanding it – and finds all the might of the imagination still inadequate to reason's ideas. [. . .]

The feeling that it is beyond our ability to attain to an idea *that is a law for us* is RESPECT. Now the idea of comprehending every appearance that may be given us in the intuition of a whole is an idea enjoined on us by a law of reason, which knows no other determinate measure that is valid for everyone and unchanging than the absolute whole. But our imagination, even in its greatest effort to do what is demanded of it and comprehend a given object in a whole of intuition (and hence to exhibit the idea of reason), proves its own limits and inadequacy, and yet at the same time proves its vocation to [obey] a law, namely, to make itself adequate to that idea. Hence the feeling of the sublime in nature is respect for our own vocation. But by a certain subreption (in which respect for the object is substituted for respect for the idea of humanity within our[selves, as] subject[s]) this respect is accorded an object of nature that, as it were, makes intuitable for us the superiority of the rational vocation of our cognitive powers over the greatest power of sensibility.[8]

Hence the feeling of the sublime is a feeling of displeasure that arises from the imagination's inadequacy, in an aesthetic estimation of magnitude, for an estimation by reason, but is at the same time also a pleasure, aroused by the fact that this very judgment, namely, that even the greatest power of sensibility is inadequate, is [itself] in harmony with rational ideas, insofar as striving toward them is still a law for us. For it is a law (of reason) for us, and part of our vocation, to estimate any sense object in nature that is large for us as being small when compared with ideas of reason; and whatever arouses in us the feeling of this supersensible vocation is in harmony with that law. Now the greatest effort of the imagination in exhibiting the unity [it needs] to estimate magnitude is [itself] a reference to something *large absolutely*, and hence also a reference to reason's law to adopt only this something as the supreme measure of magnitude. Hence our inner perception that every standard of sensibility is inadequate for an estimation of magnitude by reason is [itself] a harmony with laws of reason, as well as a displeasure that arouses in us the feeling of our supersensible vocation, according to which finding that every standard of sensibility is inadequate to the ideas of reason is purposive and hence pleasurable. [. . .]

Of the Dynamically Sublime in Nature

Might is an ability that is superior to great obstacles. It is called *dominance* [*Gewalt*] if it is superior even to the resistance of something that itself possesses might. When in an aesthetic judgment we consider nature as a might that has no dominance over us, then it is *dynamically sublime*.

If we are to judge nature as sublime dynamically, we must present it as arousing fear. (But the reverse does not hold: not every object that arouses fear is found sublime when we judge it aesthetically.) For when we judge [something] aesthetically (without a concept), the only way we can judge a superiority over obstacles is by the magnitude of the resistance. But whatever we strive to resist is an evil, and it is an object of fear if we find that our ability [to resist it] is no match for it. Hence nature can count as a might, and so as dynamically sublime, for aesthetic judgment only insofar as we consider it as an object of fear.

We can, however, consider an object *fearful* without being afraid *of* it, namely, if we judge it in such a way that we merely *think* of the case where we might possibly want to put up resistance against it, and that any resistance would in that case be utterly futile. Thus a virtuous person fears God without being afraid of him. For he does not think of wanting to resist God and his commandments as a possibility that should worry *him*. But for every such case, which he thinks of as not impossible intrinsically, he recognizes God as fearful.

Just as we cannot pass judgment on the beautiful if we are seized by inclination and appetite, so we cannot pass judgment at all on the sublime in nature if we are afraid. For we flee from the sight of an object that scares us, and it is impossible to like terror that we take seriously. That is why the agreeableness that arises from the cessation of a hardship is *gladness*. But since this gladness involves our liberation from a danger, it is accompanied by our resolve never to expose ourselves to that danger again. Indeed, we do not even like to think back on that sensation, let alone actively seek out an opportunity for it.

On the other hand, consider bold, overhanging and, as it were, threatening rocks, thunderclouds piling up in the sky and moving about accompanied by lightning and thunderclaps, volcanoes with all their destructive power, hurricanes with all the devastation they leave behind, the boundless ocean heaved up, the high waterfall of a mighty river, and so on. Compared to the might of any of these, our ability to resist becomes an insignificant trifle. Yet the sight of them becomes all the more attractive the more fearful it is, provided we are in a safe place. And we like to call these objects sublime because they raise the soul's fortitude above its usual middle range and allow us to discover in ourselves an ability to reply which is of a quite different kind, and which gives us the courage [to believe] that we could be a match for nature's seeming omnipotence.

For although we found our own limitation when we considered the immensity of nature and the inadequacy of our ability to adopt a standard proportionate to estimating aesthetically the magnitude of nature's *domain*, yet we also found, in our power of reason, a different and nonsensible standard that has this infinity itself under it as a unit; and since in contrast to this standard everything in nature is small, we found in our mind a superiority over nature itself in its immensity. In the same way, though the irresistibility of nature's might makes us, considered as natural beings, recognize our physical impotence, it reveals in us at the same time an ability to judge ourselves independent of nature, and reveals in us a superiority over nature that is the basis of a self-preservation quite different in kind from the one that can be assailed and endangered by nature outside us. This keeps the humanity in our person from being degraded, even though a human being would have to succumb to that dominance [of nature]. Hence if in judging nature aesthetically we call it sublime, we do so not because nature arouses fear, but because it calls forth our strength (which does not belong to nature [within us]), to regard as small the [objects] of our [natural] concerns: property, health, and life, and because of this we regard nature's might (to which we are indeed subjected in these [natural] concerns) as yet not having such dominance over us, as persons, that we should have to bow to it if our highest principles were at stake and we had to choose between upholding or abandoning them. Hence nature is here called sublime [*erhaben*] merely because it elevates [*erhebt*] our imagination, [making] it exhibit those cases where the mind can come to feel its own sublimity, which lies in its vocation and elevates it even above nature.

This self-estimation loses nothing from the fact that we must find ourselves safe in order to feel this exciting liking, so that (as it might seem), since the danger is not genuine, the sublimity of our intellectual ability might also not be genuine. For here the liking concerns only our ability's *vocation*, revealed in such cases, insofar as the predisposition to this ability is part of our nature, whereas it remains up to us, as our obligation, to develop and exercise this ability. And there is truth in this, no matter how conscious of his actual present impotence man may be when he extends his reflection thus far. [. . .]

This analysis of the concept of the sublime, insofar as [sublimity is] attributed to might, may seem to conflict with the fact that in certain situations – in tempests, storms, earthquakes, and so on – we usually present God as showing himself in his wrath but also in his sublimity, while yet it would be both foolish and sacrilegious to imagine that our mind is superior to the effects produced by such a might, and is superior apparently even to its intentions. It seems that here the mental attunement that befits the manifestation of such an object is not a feeling of the sublimity of our own nature, but rather submission, prostration, and a feeling of our utter impotence; and this mental attunement is in fact usually connected with the idea of this object when natural events of this sort occur. It seems that in religion in general the only fitting behavior in the presence of the deity is prostration, worship with bowed head and accompanied by contrite and timorous gestures and voice; and that is why most peoples have in fact adopted this behavior and still engage in it. But, by the same token, this mental attunement is far from being intrinsically and necessarily connected with the idea of the *sublimity* of a religion and its object. A person who is actually afraid and finds cause for this in himself because he is conscious that with his reprehensible attitude he offends against a might whose will is at once irresistible and just is not at all in the frame of mind [needed] to admire divine greatness, which requires that we be attuned to quiet contemplation and that our judgment be completely free. Only if he is conscious that his attitude is sincere and pleasing to God, will these effects of might serve to arouse in him the idea of God's sublimity, insofar as he recognizes in his own attitude a sublimity that conforms to God's will, and is thereby elevated above any fear of such natural effects, which he does not regard as outbursts of God's wrath. [. . .]

Hence sublimity is contained not in any thing of nature, but only in our mind, insofar as we can become conscious of our superiority to nature within us, and thereby also to nature outside us (as far as it influences us). Whatever arouses this feeling in us, and this includes the *might* of nature that challenges our forces, is then (although improperly) called sublime. And it is only by presupposing this idea within us, and by referring to it, that we can arrive at the idea of the sublimity of that being who arouses deep respect in us, not just by his might as demonstrated in nature, but even more by the ability, with which we have been endowed, to judge nature without fear and to think of our vocation as being sublimely above nature. [. . .]

Notes

1 Cf. the *Observations on the Feeling of the Beautiful and Sublime* (1764), Ak. II. 209: "The sublime MOVES us, the beautiful CHARMS us.

2 On admiration, respect, and positive and negative pleasure, cf. the Critique of Practical Reason, Ak. V, 71–89.

3 *Zusammenfassung.* "Comprehension" and "comprehend" are used in this translation only in this sense of "collecting together and holding together" (cf. "comprehensive"), never in the sense of "understanding."

4 *Lettres sur l'Égypte* (*Letters on Egypt*), 1787, by Anne Jean Marie René Savary, Duke of Rovigo, (1774–1833), French general, diplomat, and later minister of police (notorious for his severity) under Napoleon Bonaparte, but active even after the latter's banishment to St Helena in 1815. Savary took part in Bonaparte's expedition to Egypt.

5 A schema is what mediates, and so makes possible, the subsumption of intuitions under concepts of the understanding (and so the application of these concepts to intuitions). It does so by sharing features of both a concept and an intuition. See the *Critique of Pure Reason*, A 137–47 = B 176–87, and cf. Ak. 351–2.

6 The Prussian rod equaled 3.7662 m. (meters), the Saxon 4.2951 m., whereas the English rod equals 5.5 yds or 5.029 m. The German mile was quite long: 7500 m., the English statute mile equals only 1609.35 m. There was also a "geographic" or "Bavarian" as well as a "*Badische*" mile.

7 "*Das Unendliche.*" What the expression says *literally* is "the infinite." Yet here (and similarly in mathematics, where the same expression is used), the expression does

not mean *something infinite* (to which the estimation of magnitude progresses), even though it does mean this in other contexts (e.g., in the next paragraph). "*Unendlichkeit*," on the other hand, usually means "infinity" only in the most abstract sense: "infiniteness," "being infinite."

8   i.e., the imagination "in its greatest expansion."

Horror

---

29 From *The Philosophy of Horror*

Noël Carroll

[. . .] I plan to analyze horror as a genre. However, it should not be assumed that all genres can be analyzed in the same way. Westerns, for example, are identified primarily by virtue of their setting. Novels, films, plays, paintings, and other works, that are grouped under the label "horror" are identified according to a different sort of criteria. Like suspense novels or mystery novels, novels are denominated horrific in respect of their intended capacity to raise a certain *affect*. Indeed, the genres of suspense, mystery, and horror derive their very names from the affects they are intended to promote – a sense of suspense, a sense of mystery, and a sense of horror. The cross-art, cross-media genre of horror takes its title from the emotion it characteristically or rather ideally promotes; this emotion constitutes the identifying mark of horror.

Again, it must be underlined that not all genres are identified in this way. The musical, either on stage or on film, is not tied to any affect. One might think that musicals are by nature light and charming, in the fashion of *Me and My Girl*. But, of course, this is not the case. Musicals can pretend to tragedy (*West Side Story, Pequod, Camelot*), melodrama (*Les Miserables*), worldliness (*A Chorus Line*), pessimism (*Candide*), political indignation (*Sarafina!*), and even terror (*Sweeney Todd*). A musical is defined by a certain proportion of song and perhaps usually dance and can indulge any sort of emotion, the implicit argument of *The Band Wagon* (that it is always entertaining) notwithstanding. The horror genre, however, is essentially linked with a particular affect – specifically, that from which it takes its name.

The genres that are named by the very affect they are designed to provoke suggest a particularly tantalizing strategy through which to pursue their analysis. Like works of suspense, works of horror are designed to elicit a certain kind of affect. I shall presume that this is an emotional state, which emotion I call art-horror. Thus, one can expect to locate the genre of horror, in part, by a specification of art-horror, that is, the emotion works of this type are designed to engender. Members of the horror genre will be identified as narratives and/ or images (in the case of fine art, film, etc.) predicated on raising the affect of horror in audiences. Such an analysis, of course, is not a priori. It is an attempt, in the tradition of Aristotle's *Poetics*, to provide clarificatory generalizations about a body of work that, in everyday discourse, we antecedently accept as constituting a family. [. . .]

[O]ne indicator of that which differentiates works of horror proper from monster stories in general is the affective responses of the positive human characters in the stories to the monsters that beleaguer them. Moreover, though we have only spoken about the emotions of characters in horror stories, nevertheless, the preceding hypothesis is useful for getting at the emotional responses that works of horror are designed to elicit from audiences. For horror appears to be one of those genres in which the emotive responses of the audience, ideally, run parallel to the emotions of characters. Indeed, in works of horror the responses of characters often seem to cue the emotional responses of the audiences.

In "Jonathan Harker's Journal," in *Dracula*, we read:

> As the Count leaned over me and his hands touched me, I could not repress a shudder. It may have been that his breath was rank, but a horrible feeling of nausea came over me, which do what I would, I could not conceal.

This shudder, this recoil at the vampire's touch, this feeling of nausea all structure our emotional reception of the ensuing descriptions of Dracula; for example, when his protruding teeth are mentioned we regard them as shudder-inducing, nauseating, rank – not something one would want either to touch or be touched by. Similarly, in films we model our emotional response upon ones like that of the young, blonde woman in *Night of the Living Dead*, who, when surrounded by zombies, screams and clutches herself in such a way as to avoid contact with the contaminated flesh. The characters in works of horror exemplify for us the way in which to react to the monsters in the fiction. In film and onstage, the characters *shrink* from the monsters, contracting themselves in order to avoid the grip of the creature but also to avert an accidental brush against this unclean being. This does not mean that we believe in the existence of fictional monsters, as the characters in horror stories do, but that we regard the description or depiction of them as unsettling [in] virtue of the same kind of qualities that revolt someone like Jonathan Harker in the preceding quotation.

The emotional reactions of characters, then, provide a set of instructions or, rather, examples about the way in which the audience is to respond to the monsters in the fiction – that is, about the way we are meant to react to its monstrous properties. In the classic film *King Kong*, for example, there is a scene on the ship during the journey to Skull Island in which the fictional director, Carl Denham, stages a screen test for Ann Darrow, the heroine of the film within the film. The offscreen motivations that Denham supplies his starlet can be taken as a set of instructions for the way both Ann Darrow and the audience are to react to the first apparition of Kong. Denham says to Darrow:

> Now you look higher. You're amazed. Your eyes open wider. It's horrible Ann, but you can't look away. There's no chance for you, Ann – no escape. You're helpless, Ann, helpless. There's just one chance. If you can scream – but your throat's paralyzed. Scream, Ann, cry. Perhaps if you didn't see it you could scream. Throw your arms across your face and scream, scream for your life.

In horror fictions, the emotions of the audience are supposed to mirror those of the positive human characters in certain, but not all, respects. In the preceding examples the characters' responses counsel us that the appropriate reactions to the monsters in question comprise shuddering, nausea, shrinking, paralysis, screaming, and revulsion. Our responses are meant, ideally, to parallel those of characters. Our responses are supposed to converge (but not exactly duplicate) those of the characters; like the characters we assess the monster as a horrifying sort of being (though unlike the characters, we do not believe in its existence). This mirroring-effect, moreover, is a key feature of the horror genre. For it is not the case for every genre that the audience response is supposed to repeat certain of the elements of the emotional state of characters.

If Aristotle is right about catharsis, for example, the emotional state of the audience does not double that of King Oedipus at the end of the play of the same name. Nor are we jealous, when Othello is. Also, when a comic character takes a pratfall, he hardly feels joyous, though we do. And though we feel suspense when the hero rushes to save the heroine tied to the railroad tracks he cannot afford to indulge such an emotion. Nevertheless, with horror, the situation is different. For in horror the emotions of the characters and those of the audience are synchronized in certain pertinent respects, as one can easily observe at a Saturday matinee in one's local cinema.

That the audience's emotional responses are modeled to a certain extent on those of the characters in horror fictions provides us with a useful methodological advantage in analyzing the emotion of art-horror. It suggests a way in which we can formulate an objective, as opposed to an introspective, picture of the emotion of art-horror. That is, rather than characterizing art-horror solely on the basis of our own subjective responses, we can ground our conjectures on observations of the way in which characters respond to the monsters in works of horror. That is, if we proceed under the assumption that our emotional responses as audience members are supposed to parallel those of characters in important respects, then we can begin to portray art-horror by noting the typical emotional features that authors and directors attribute to characters molested by monsters.

How do characters respond to monsters in horror stories? Well, of course, they're frightened. After all, monsters are dangerous. But there is more to it than this. In Mary Shelley's famous novel, Victor Frankenstein recounts his reaction to the first movements of his creation: "now that I had finished, the beauty of the dream vanished and disgust filled my heart. Unable to endure the aspect of the being I had created, I rushed out of the room, unable to compose my mind to sleep." Shortly after this, the monster, with an outstretched hand, wakens Victor, who flees from its touch.

In "Sea-Raiders," H. G. Wells, using the third person, narrates Mr Frison's reaction to some unsavory, glistening, tentacled creatures: "he was horrified, of course, and intensely excited and indignant at such *revolting* creatures preying on human skin." In Augustus Muir's "The Reptile," MacAndrew's first response to what he takes (wrongly) to be a giant snake is described as the "paralysing grip of *repulsion* and surprise."

When Miles, in Jack Finney's *Invasion of the Body Snatchers* first encounters the pods, he reports "At the feel of them on my skin, I lost my mind completely, and then I was tramping them, smashing and crushing them under my plunging feet and legs, not even knowing that I was uttering a sort of hoarse meaningless cry – 'Unhh! Unhh! Unhh!' – of fright and animal disgust." And in Peter Straub's *Ghost Story*, Don makes love to the monster Alma Mobley and suddenly senses "a shock of concentrated feeling, a shock of revulsion – as though I had touched a slug."

The theme of visceral revulsion is also evident in Bram Stoker's "Dracula's Guest," originally planned to be the first chapter of his seminal vampire tale. The first-person narrator tells how he was awakened by what commentators take to be a werewolf. He says:

> This period of semi-lethargy seemed to remain a long time, and as it faded away I must have slept or swooned. Then came a sort of *loathing, like the first stage of seasickness*, and a wild desire to be free from something, I know not what. A vast stillness enveloped me, as though the world were asleep or dead – only broken by the low panting as of some animal close to me. I felt a warm rasping at my throat, then came a consciousness of the awful truth, which chilled me to the heart and sent the blood surging up through my brain. Some great animal was lying on me and now licking my throat.

[. . .] From this preliminary inventory of examples, it is possible to derive a theory of the nature of the emotion of art-horror. But before setting out that theory in detail, some comments need to be made about the structure of emotions. I am presupposing that art-horror is an emotion. It is the emotion that horror narratives and images are designed to elicit from audiences. That is, "art-horror" names the emotion that the creators of the genre have perennially sought to instill in their audiences, though they, undoubtedly, would be more disposed to call this emotion "horror" rather than "art-horror."

Furthermore, it is an emotion whose contours are reflected in the emotional responses of the positive human characters to the monsters in works of horror. I am also presuming that art-horror is an occurrent emotional state, like a flash of anger, rather than a dispositional emotional state, such as undying envy.

An occurrent emotional state has both physical and cognitive dimensions. Broadly speaking, the physical dimension of an emotion is a matter of felt agitation. Specifically, the physical dimension is a sensation or a feeling. An emotion, that is, involves some kind of stirring, perturbation, or arrest physiologically registered by an increase in heartbeat, respiration, or the like. The word "emotion" comes from the Latin "emovere" which combines the notion of "to move" with the prefix for "out." An *emotion* originally was a *moving* out. To be in an emotional state involves the experience of a transition or migration – a change of state, a moving out of a normal physical state to an agitated one, one marked by inner movings. To be an occurrent emotion, I want to claim, involves a physical state – a sense of a physiological moving of some sort – a felt agitation or feeling sensation.

In respect to art-horror some of the regularly recurring sensations, or felt-physical agitations, or automatic responses, or feelings are muscular contractions, tension, cringing, shrinking, shuddering, recoiling, tingling, frozenness, momentary arrests, chilling (hence, "spine-chilling"), paralysis, trembling, nausea, a reflex of apprehension or physically heightened alertness (a danger response), perhaps involuntary screaming, and so on.

The word "horror" derives from the Latin "horrere" – to stand on end (as hair standing on end) or to bristle – and the old French "orror" – to bristle or to shudder. And though it need not be the case that our hair must literally stand on end when we are art-horrified, it is important to stress that the original conception of the word connected it with an abnormal (from the subject's point of view) physiological state of felt agitation. [. . .]

No specifiable, recurring feeling or package of feelings can be worked into necessary or sufficient conditions for a given emotion. That is, to summarize the above arguments, in order to be an emotional state some physical agitation must obtain, though an emotional state will not be identified by being associated with a unique physical feeling state or even a uniquely recurring pattern of physical feelings.

What then identifies or individuates given emotional states? Their cognitive elements. Emotions involve not only physical perturbations but beliefs and thoughts, beliefs and thoughts about the properties of objects and situations. Moreover, these beliefs (and thoughts) are not just factual – e.g., there is a large truck coming at me – but also evaluative – e.g., that large truck is dangerous to me. Now when I am in a state of fear with regard to this truck, I am in some physical state – perhaps I involuntarily squeeze my eyes shut while my pulse shoots up – and this physical state has been *caused* by my cognitive state, by my beliefs (or thoughts) that the truck is headed at me and that this situation is dangerous. My eyes closing and my pulse racing could be associated with many emotional states, e.g., ecstasy; what makes my emotional state fear in this particular ease are my beliefs. That is, cognitive states differentiate one emotion from another though for a state to be an emotional one there must also be some kind of physical agitation that has been engendered by the presiding cognitive state (comprised of either beliefs or thoughts).

To illustrate the point here, it may be helpful to indulge in a science-fiction-like thought experiment. Imagine that we have advanced to the point where we an stimulate any sort of physical agitation by applying electrodes to the brain. A scientist observing me nearly run over by the truck in the preceding paragraph notes that when fearful my eyes clamp shut by reflex and my pulse quickens. She then arranges her electrodes in my brain so as to raise these physical states in me. Would we wish to say that, under these laboratory conditions, I am afraid. I suspect not. And the theory outlined above explains why not. For in the laboratory, my physical states are caused by electrical stimulation; they are not caused by beliefs (or thoughts) and, specifically, they are not caused by the kinds of beliefs that are appropriate to the emotional state of fear.

We can summarize this view of the emotions – which might be called a cognitive/evaluative theory – by saying that an occurrent emotional state is one in which some physically abnormal state of felt agitation has been caused by the subject's cognitive construal and evaluation of his/her situation. This is the core of an emotional state, though some emotions may involve wants and desires as well as construals and appraisals. If I am afraid of the approaching truck, then I form the desire to avoid its onslaught. Here the connection between the appraisal element of my emotion and my desire is a rational one, since the appraisal provides a good reason for the want or the desire. However, it is not the case that every emotion links up with a desire; I may be saddened by the realization that I will die some day without that leading to any other desire, such as, for instance, that I shall never die. Thus, though wants and desires may figure in the characterization of some emotions, the core structure of emotions involves physical agitations caused by the construals and evaluations that serve constitutively to identify the emotion as the specific emotion it is.

Using this account of the emotions, we are now in a position to organize these observations about the emotion of art-horror. Assuming that "I-as-audience member" am in an analogous emotional state to that which fictional characters beset by monsters are described to be in, then: I am occurrently art-horrified by some monster X, say Dracula, if and only if 1) I am in some state of abnormal, physically felt agitation (shuddering, tingling, screaming, etc.) which 2) has been *caused* by a) the thought: that Dracula is a possible being; and by the evaluative thoughts: that b) said Dracula has the property of being physically (and perhaps morally and socially) threatening in the ways portrayed in the fiction and that c) said Dracula has the property of being impure, where 3) such thoughts are usually accompanied by the desire to avoid the touch of things like Dracula.

Of course, "Dracula," here, is merely a heuristic device. Any old monster X can be plugged into the formula. Moreover, in order to forestall charges of circularity, let me note that, for our purposes, "monster" refers to any being not believed to exist now according to contemporary science. Thus, dinosaurs and nonhuman visitors from another galaxy are monsters under this stipulation though the former once existed and the latter might exist. Whether they are monsters who are also horrifying in the context of a particular fiction depends upon whether they meet the conditions of the analysis above. Some monsters may be only threatening rather than horrifying, while others may be neither threatening nor horrifying.

Another thing to note about the preceding definition is that it is the evaluative components of the theory that primarily serve to individuate art-horror. And, furthermore, it is crucial that two evaluative components come into play: that the monster is regarded as threatening *and* impure. If the monster were only evaluated as potentially threatening, the emotion would be fear; if only potentially impure, the emotion would be disgust. Art-horror requires evaluation both in terms of threat and disgust.

The threat component of the analysis derives from the fact that the monsters we find in horror stories are uniformly dangerous or at least appear to be so; when they cease to be threatening, they cease to be horrifying. The impurity clause in the definition is postulated as a result of noting the regularity with which literary descriptions of the experiences of horror undergone by fictional

characters include reference to disgust, repugnance, nausea, physical loathing, shuddering, revulsion, abhorrence, abomination, and so on. Likewise, the
gestures actors on stage and on screen adopt when confronting horrific
monsters communicate corresponding mental states. And, of course, these
reactions – abomination, nausea, shuddering, revulsion, disgust, etc. – are characteristically the product of perceiving something to be noxious or impure.
(With regard to the impurity clause of this theory, it is persuasive to recall that
horrific beings are often associated with contamination – sicknesses, disease,
and plague – and often accompanied by infectious vermin – rats, insects and the
like.) [. . .]

There is a theoretical question about horror which, although not unique to
horror, nevertheless is not one that readily arises with respect to other popular
genres, such as mystery, romance, comedy, the thriller, adventure stories, and
the western. The question is: why would anyone be interested in the genre to
begin with? Why does the genre persist? I have written a lot about the internal
elements of the genre; but many readers may feel that in doing that their attention has been deflected away from the central issue concerning horror—viz.,
how can we explain its very existence, for why would anyone *want* to be horrified, or even art-horrified?

This question, moreover, becomes especially pressing if my analysis of the
nature of horror is accepted. For we have seen that a key element in the emotion of art-horror is repulsion or disgust. But – and this is the question of "Why
horror?" in its primary form – if horror necessarily has something repulsive
about it, how can audiences be attracted to it? Indeed, even if horror only
caused fear, we might feel justified in demanding an explanation of what could
motivate people to seek out the genre. But where fear is compounded with
repulsion, the ante is, in a manner of speaking, raised.

In the ordinary course of affairs, people shun what disgusts them. Being re-
pulsed by something that one finds to be loathsome and impure is an unpleasant experience. We do not, for example, attempt to add some pleasure to a
boring afternoon by opening the lid of a steamy trash can in order to savor its
unwholesome stew of broken bits of meat, moldering fruits and vegetables, and
noxious, unrecognizable clumps, riven thoroughly by all manner of crawling
things. And, ordinarily, checking out hospital waste bags is not our idea of a
good time. But, on the other hand, many people – so many, in fact, that we
must concede that they are normal, at least in the statistical sense – do seek out
horror fictions for the purpose of deriving pleasure from sights and descriptions
that customarily repulse them.

In short, there appears to be something paradoxical about the horror genre. It
obviously attracts consumers; but it seems to do so by means of the expressly
repulsive. Furthermore, the horror genre gives every evidence of being pleasurable to its audience, but it does so by means of trafficking in the very sorts of
things that cause disquiet, distress, and displeasure. So different ways of clarifying
the question "Why horror?" are to ask: "Why are horror audiences attracted by
what, typically (in everyday life), should (and would) repel them?," or "How can

horror audiences find pleasure in what by nature is distressful and unpleasant?
[. . .]

[T]o a large extent, the horror story is driven explicitly by curiosity. It engages its audience by being involved in processes of disclosure, discovery, proof, explanation, hypothesis, and confirmation. Doubt, skepticism, and the fear that belief in the existence of the monster is a form of insanity are predictable foils to the revelation (to the audience or to the characters or both) of the existence of the monster.

Horror stories, in a significant number of cases, are dramas of proving the existence of the monster and disclosing (most often gradually) the origin, identity, purposes, and powers of the monster. Monsters, as well, are obviously a perfect vehicle for engendering this kind of curiosity and for supporting the drama of proof, because monsters are (physically, though generally not logically) impossible beings. They arouse interest and attention through being putatively inexplicable or highly unusual *vis-à-vis* our standing cultural categories, thereby instilling a desire to learn and to know about them. And since they are also outside of (justifiably) prevailing definitions of what is, they understandably prompt a need for proof (or the fiction of a proof) in the face of skepticism. Monsters are, then, natural subjects for curiosity, and they straightforwardly warrant the ratiocinative energies the plot lavishes upon them.

All narratives might be thought to involve the desire to know – the desire to know at least the outcome of the interaction of the forces made salient in the plot. However, the horror fiction is a special variation on this general narrative motivation, because it has at the center of it something which is given as in principle *unknowable* – something which, *ex hypothesi*, cannot, given the structure of our conceptual scheme, exist and that cannot have the properties it has. This is why, so often, the real drama in a horror story resides in establishing the existence of the monster and in disclosing its horrific properties. Once this is established, the monster, generally, has to be confronted, and the narrative is driven by the question of whether the creature can be destroyed. However, even at this point, the drama of ratiocination can continue as further discoveries – accompanied by arguments, explanations, and hypotheses – reveal features of the monster that will facilitate or impede the destruction of the creature.
[. . .]

Applied to the paradox of horror, these observations suggest that the pleasure derived from the horror fiction and the source of our interest in it resides, first and foremost, in the processes of discovery, proof, and confirmation that horror fictions often employ. The disclosure of the existence of the horrific being and of its properties is the central source of pleasure in the genre; once that process of revelation is consummated, we remain inquisitive about whether such a creature can be successfully confronted, and that narrative question sees us through to the end of the story. Here, the pleasure involved is, broadly speaking, cognitive. Hobbes, interestingly, thought of curiosity as an appetite of the mind; with the horror fiction, that appetite is whetted by the prospect of knowing the putatively unknowable, and then satisfied through a continuous process of revelation, enhanced by imitations of (admittedly simplistic) proofs, hypotheses, counterfeits of causal reasoning, and explanations whose details and movement intrigue the mind in ways analogous to genuine ones.

Moreover, it should be clear that these particular cognitive pleasures, insofar as they are set in motion by the relevant kind of unknowable beings, are especially well served by horrific monsters. Thus, there is a special functional relationship between the beings that mark off the horror genre and the pleasure and interest that many horror fictions sustain. That interest and that pleasure derive from the disclosure of unknown and impossible beings, just the sorts of things that seem to call for proof, discovery, and confirmation. Therefore, the disgust that such beings evince might be seen as part of the price to be paid for the pleasure of their disclosure. That is, the narrative expectations that the horror genre puts in place is that the being whose existence is in question be something that defies standing cultural categories; thus, disgust, so to say, is itself more or less mandated by the kind of curiosity that the horror narrative puts in place. The horror narrative could not deliver a successful, affirmative answer to its presiding question unless the disclosure of the monster indeed elicited disgust, or was of the sort that was a highly probable object of disgust.

That is, there is a strong relation of consilience between the objects of art-horror, on the one hand, and the revelatory plotting on the other. The kind of plots and the subjects of horrific revelation are not merely compatible, but fit together or agree in a way that is highly appropriate. That the audience is naturally inquisitive about that which is unknown meshes with plotting that is concerned to render the unknown known by processes of discovery, explanation, proof, hypothesis, confirmation, and so on.

Of course, what it means to say that the horrific being is "unknown" here is that it is not accommodated by standing conceptual schemes. Moreover, if Mary Douglas's account of impurity is correct, things that violate our conceptual scheme, by (for example) being interstitial, are things that we are prone to find disturbing. Thus, that horrific beings are predictably objects of loathing and revulsion is a function of the ways they violate our classificatory scheme.[1]

If what is of primary importance about horrific creatures is that their very impossibility *vis-à-vis* our conceptual categories is what makes them function so compellingly in dramas of discovery and confirmation, then their disclosure, insofar as they are categorical violations, will be attached to some sense of disturbance, distress, and disgust. Consequently, the role of the horrific creature in such narratives – where their disclosure captures our interest and delivers pleasure – will simultaneously mandate some probable revulsion. That is, in order to reward our interest by the disclosure of the putatively impossible beings of the plot, said beings ought to be disturbing, distressing, and repulsive in the way that theorists like Douglas predict phenomena that ill fit cultural classifications will be.

So, as a first approximation of resolving the paradox of horror, we may conjecture that we are attracted to the majority of horror fictions because of the way that the plots of discovery and the dramas of proof pique our curiosity, and abet our interest, ideally satisfying them in a way that is pleasurable. But if narrative curiosity about impossible beings is to be satisfied through disclosure, that process must require some element of probable disgust since such impossible beings are, *ex hypothesi*, disturbing, distressful, and repulsive.

One way of making the point is to say that the monsters in such tales of disclosure have to be disturbing, distressful, and repulsive, if the process of their discovery is to be rewarding in a pleasurable way. Another way to get at this is to say that the primary pleasure that narratives of disclosure afford – i.e., the interest we take in them, and the source of their attraction – resides in the processes of discovery, the play of proof, and the dramas of ratiocination that comprise them. It is not that we crave disgust, but that disgust is a predictable concomitant of disclosing the unknown, whose disclosure is a desire the narrative instills in the audience and then goes on to gladden. Nor will that desire be satisfied unless the monster defies our conception of nature which demands that it probably engender some measure of repulsion.

In this interpretation of horror narratives, the majority of which would appear to exploit the cognitive attractions of the drama of disclosure, experiencing the emotion of art-horror is not our absolutely primary aim in consuming horror fictions, even though it is a determining feature for identifying membership in the genre. Rather, art-horror is the price we are willing to pay for the revelation of that which is impossible and unknown, of that which violates our conceptual schema. The impossible being does disgust; but that disgust is part of an overall narrative address which is not only pleasurable, but whose potential pleasure depends on the confirmation of the existence of the monster as a being that violates, defies, or problematizes standing cultural classifications. Thus, we are attracted to, and many of us seek out, horror fictions of this sort despite the fact that they provoke disgust, because that disgust is required for the pleasure involved in engaging our curiosity in the unknown and drawing it into the processes of revelation, ratiocination, etc. [. . .]

Note

1   Mary Douglas, *Implicit Meanings* (London: Routledge and Kegan Paul, 1975); *Purity and Danger* (New York: Praeger, 1966). [C.K.]

---

30   Realist Horror

Cynthia A. Freeland

A Chicago man steals corpses and skins them to make himself a suit. A drifter from Texas confesses to 600 murders. A Milwaukee man cannibalizes and has sex with the corpses of numerous boys he has killed.

These sketches illustrate realist horror narratives.[1] They begin in the newspapers but move swiftly to Hollywood contracts and major motion pictures.[2] It is no news that art imitates life: Mary Shelley's monster was born out of Galvani's experiments on the publicly displayed bodies of executed criminals, and nineteenth-century newspapers inspired the more chilling episodes in Dickens, Poe, and Dostoyevsky.[3] But the ties between fact and fiction have become increasingly intricate and ramified. The fiction of *The Silence of the Lambs*, based partly on facts about real corpse-stealer Ed Gein, permeated media coverage of the arrest of cannibalistic serial killer Jeffrey Dahmer, and publicity over Dahmer's arrest in its turn threatened the box-office take and opening date of the horror film *Body Parts*.

What is it to engage in a philosophical examination of realist horror? An important precedent in the western tradition is the ancient Greek debate about tragedy. Plato faulted tragedy because it (like horror) appeals to the audience's baser instincts, obscuring truth and showcasing scenes of overwhelming terror and violence. Aristotle defended tragedies as worthy *representations* with a distinct cognitive status, and he described a positive aspect, *katharsis*, of our emotional reactions of pity and terror to such representations.

I am not the first to observe a parallel between tragedy and horror. Noël Carroll's recent *The Philosophy of Horror* brings horror into the western aesthetic tradition by supplying a framework that recalls Aristotle's defense of tragedy in the *Poetics*.[4] In this paper I want to show that such a classical approach will not work for realist horror. [. . .]

The Classical Approach

Plato attacked tragic poetry for confusing people who took it to be more vivid than reality itself. It was crucial for Aristotle to show that we recognize and evaluate tragedies as imitations (*mimesis*), in which plot *represents* action and characters *represent* people. Carroll's *The Philosophy of Horror*, like Aristotle's *Poetics*, examines a genre that seems to rely upon our direct, problematic interest in fearful violence. Again like Aristotle, Carroll argues that this genre evokes a distinct aesthetic response built upon a somewhat distanced intellectual interest in plot. We enjoy tracking the suspenseful narrative, and so we put up with the revulsion that Carroll calls "art-horror." Art-horror is a distanced emotional response to a representation: though monsters in horror are repellent and scary, they do not threaten us directly, and we are protected by knowing they are in fact impossible. They fascinate us because they violate our conceptual categories, arousing in us a strong desire to know something unknowable.

This theoretical defense of horror fails to work for the entire subgenre of realist horror because it depends crucially upon the fictitious nature of the monsters at the center of horror. Carroll defines a monster as "any being not believed to exist according to contemporary science." This requirement is essential to keeping the emphasis on narrative or plot and to preserving the particular aesthetic response Carroll approves, art-horror. He seems to see in the psychotic killer a sort of falling away from an essence of horrific monstrousness. So he is forced to discount a film like *Psycho* as horror, for example, because the monster in it is naturalized: "He is a schizophrenic, a type of being that science countenances" (38).

Yet realist horror is a prevalent and important subgenre of horror that deserves consideration. *Psycho* and *Peeping Tom*, both released in 1960, initiated a significant shift in the horror genre. They chillingly depicted "ordinary" men who were unable to connect with the reality around them.[5] Due to traumas of childhood and sexual repression, so the story went, they become mad slashers. This scenario has become formulaic in numerous subsequent variations and the subgenre became the dominant form of horror in the 1980s.[6]

To see the limitations of Carroll's Aristotelian or classical approach to horror, I want to look in some detail at one example, *Henry: Portrait of a Serial Killer* (1990, prod. 1986, John McNaughton), a movie loosely based on the story of real serial murderer Henry Lee Lucas.[7] *Henry* is exceptionally interesting – and also disturbing – for its realism of style and amoral viewpoint. It violates the usual rules of both the horror genre in general and the slasher in particular.[8] It offers no audience identification figure, nor does its plot depict any righting of wrongs. As a horror movie, though, this film succeeds by creating terror and unease, both promising and withholding the spectacle of violence.

Henry flouts horror-movie conventions for suspenseful narrative. Its opening scenes show an array of corpses accompanied by an eerie sound track, intercut with scenes of a young man who, by implication, is the multiple murderer Henry, talking to a waitress in a late night diner. The film sets up the viewer to expect him to attack her, but nothing happens. Next Henry follows a woman home from a shopping mall. Tension rises almost unbearably, but at the last moment as she arrives at home a man greets her, and Henry drives away. Even when Henry finally does kill, the film again flouts conventions by withholding the spectacle of the murder. Henry picks up a hitchhiker carrying a guitar, and returns home later carrying her guitar. Or, in a long shot, we see a woman let Henry into her house with his exterminator's equipment. The audience is set up to expect to enter the house and witness a murder. Instead, the film cuts to a shot of a living room. A slow and impersonal pan reveals the woman, naked, dead. A third killing happens so fast and is so obscured that it barely has time to register. Henry snaps the necks of two prostitutes in his car and then goes with his friend Otis to buy a hamburger.

The plot of *Henry* seems flat and random. Certain events occur when Becky, the sister of Henry's roommate Otis, moves into their small Chicago apartment and disrupts their somewhat repressed homosexual partnership. [. . .]

Otis and Henry had met in prison, and when Becky asks Otis what Henry was in for, he at first refuses to say. "What did he do, kill his mama?" she asks. "Yes, he killed his mama with a baseball bat," Otis replies, as if it's a joke. Later Becky pursues the subject with intense fascination. In the only scene in the film that tells us anything about Henry, the facts remain hazy. Henry says that he did kill his mother, he stabbed her to death. He tells Becky, "Daddy used to drive a truck before he got his legs cut off. My mama was a whore. But I don't fault her for that. She made me watch, she beat me, made me wear a dress and watch." Becky responds by confiding that she too was abused, by her father, then says gushingly "I feel like I know you, have known you for a long time." Henry says, summing up, that yeah, he shot his mother on his fourteenth birthday. "Shot her?" Becky asks, "I thought you stabbed her." "Oh yeah," he says.

From this point on the intensity of the killings in the film escalates. After a fight during a drug deal Otis comments, "I'd like to kill somebody." Henry subsequently takes him out for sport to shoot a young man who stops to help with their car. Again, it's all over in a flash. Next Henry murders a pawn shop owner after an argument over the purchase of a television. He turns murder into a science, explaining to Otis how you must vary the method each time, switch guns so as not to be caught, etc. Henry remarks, "It's either you or them. Open your eyes, look at the world, Otis. You or them, you know what I mean."

The stage is now set for two especially gruesome final killing scenes. First there is the killing of a suburban family. In a long shot the killers are shown approaching a house at night. Then the scene switches to a grainy, tilted home video version of the family's murder. It soon emerges that we are watching this footage alongside the killers who are reviewing it afterwards on their living room sofa, as recorded by their stolen camcorder. Point of view and real time are wrenched in a disconcerting way, with contradictory effects. On the one hand, the scene distances viewers and makes the murders seem less awful. The effect is as if we were just watching something on TV. The people in the family are already dead, depersonalized, not individuals. On the other hand, the amateur camera also makes the murders seem more real: things happen unexpectedly, everything seems unplanned and awkward. The viewpoint is not standard, and the murders are not cleanly centered for our observation.

The most graphic and bloody of the murders in *Henry* is Henry's murder of Otis, whom he has caught raping Becky. Henry blinds Otis and then stabs him while lying atop his body in an orgiastic, sexualized attack. Henry chops up Otis's body and loads it into large garbage bags which he packs into suitcases and dumps in the river. He leaves town with Becky, who looks at him and says "I love you Henry." "I guess I love you too," he says. The car radio plays the song, "Loving you was my mistake." They stop for the night at a motel room and get ready for bed. Becky looks up trustingly at Henry who says it's time to turn in. The next morning we see Henry shaving with a straight razor, getting dressed and leaving the motel room – alone. He piles suitcases into the car, and later stops along the road to set a suitcase along the berm. In close-up we see blood seeping through the soft-sided case. That's it, she's dead. Inevitable. Henry drives on in his beat-up old brown Chevy. The movie ends.

Henry is an example of realist horror: based on a real serial murderer, it features a possible, realistic monster. But the classical account of horror modeled on Aristotle's defense of tragedy will not work for this movie. [. . .]

First, in realist horror like *Henry*, the monster is a true-to-life rather than supernatural being. Henry *is* a monster. Like many movie monsters, he seems all-powerful, unpredictable, and a source of hideous violence. His approach to his fellow humans is loathesome. He is nevertheless a possible being; he is based upon a real Death Row killer, Henry Lee Lucas. [. . .]

Realist horror, whether fictive or factual, like *Henry*, typically showcases the spectacular nature of monstrous violence. Realist horror is like other film genres that rely chiefly upon spectacle (for example the musical or hard-core pornography film[9]); in these genres, plot serves to bridge together the "real thing" the film promises to deliver. Although *The Silence of the Lambs* offers many conventional plot elements, it too allows spectacle a major role. The movie highlights the skinned bodies of Buffalo Bill's victims and the bizarreness of his underground den and moth fetish. In the outer story, Lecter is an even greater master of spectacle, operating with a Nietzschean aesthetic all his own. We witness one of his grotesque aesthetic acts (almost a piece of performance art itself) when he orchestrates the murder of his two guards as part of a seamless whole that includes his drawings of Clarice with a lamb, a dinner of rare lamb chops, and Bach's *Goldberg Variations*. The murder is not simply bloody (it is that) but it is artistically arranged, with one body stretched on high as a disemboweled angel and another man's face skinned off to provide Lecter's own disguise. Significantly the director Demme conspires with Lecter by setting the audience up to see and share the expectations of the local police who have been duped by Lecter, just as it offers the audience the killer's view of Starling when he tracks her with his night-vision glasses.

An emphasis on the spectacle of random violence rather than plot in realist horror would lead philosophers from Plato and Aristotle to Noël Carroll to downgrade this genre. Plato categorized our drive toward violent spectacle as lowest among his rank-ordering of human desires,[10] and in the *Poetics* Aristotle argued that spectacle is the "least artistic" of tragedy's six parts.[11] Carroll follows Aristotle in emphasizing plot, which again, like Aristotle, he sees as the focus of our cognitive interests in horror – hence as having greater legitimacy than a "mere" interest in spectacle. In other words, in this tradition, realist horror has little merit aesthetically and would no doubt have to be condemned as morally perverse.

Against this classical approach I have several things to say. First, I think realist horror is a subgenre of horror. But such films rely crucially upon the realism of their horror, the possibility of their monsters, the showcasing of gruesome spectacle, and (at least in the case of *Henry*) the flat randomness of their structure. And second, realist horror films *can* be good movies. That is, they can be well-made constructions or representations that effectively carry out their aims of evoking suspense and horror. I would cite *Henry* or *The Texas Chain Saw Massacre* as examples; *The Silence of the Lambs* won many Oscars, including Best Motion Picture. Realist horror forces us to attend to the very problem of moral perverseness that Carroll wants to avoid: that we are somehow attracted to monsters and to the horrific spectacle itself. The orchestrated representation of violence evokes an ambivalent thrill as we react to realistic depictions of horrific events we know to be possible.[12] I find standard critiques of our direct interest in such monsters and spectacles both simplistic and naive. We need room for a subtler sort of moral assessment. The intricacy of interconnections between the news and film plots necessitates more reflection upon the representational character of violence in realist horror, and it also calls for the use of a different strategy than the classical approach.

An Alternative Strategy

I have described two key features of realist horror, the fascination of the realistic monster and the foregrounding of gruesome spectacle over plot, that prevent this genre from neatly fitting within a classical theory like Carroll's. As I use the term, a classical theory, like Aristotle's in the *Poetics*, has three elements. We first understand there is a clear relation between art and reality: artworks imitate or represent reality. Second, we describe the construction of such imitations, focusing on plot and narrative. Aristotle discerned key patterns that involve a hero, an action, a mistake or *hamartia*, a downfall, and a denouement or un-winding. Carroll similarly describes variations in horror plot patterns. And third, in a classical theory we describe the aesthetic/emotional reactions that such representations aim at producing or evoking. Both Aristotle and Carroll argue that such reactions are unproblematic or unperverse.

Now, I contend that realist horror problematizes the classical approach by thwarting the initial assumption that we can draw a clear distinction between artistic imitations and reality. Realist horror must be understood as a particularly postmodern phenomenon. I mean by this several things. In the immediacy of transmission of the news and in the growing world of infotainment, realistic elements from news stories are easily, commonly, and quickly integrated into new feature film plots. Conversely, fictitious characters (like Hannibal Lecter) are alluded to in presenting or describing real ones (like Jeffrey Dahmer). In addition, realist horror can present violent spectacles with an uncanny immediacy right before our eyes, with the immediacy that the camera also allows on our nightly news. [. . .]

[A]s news and reality interweave, there is a diminishing role for the constructedness of plot. Plots in realist horror, like stories on the nightly news, are dominated by the three r's: random, reductive, repetitious. Both are about gruesome acts, spectacle, and aftermath, more than about action, downfall, motives, mistakes, and justice. And so, third, it is inappropriate to speak here of any specifically aesthetic or distanced reaction of art-horror. Instead, like the news, realist horror evolves real, albeit paradoxical, reactions: at the same time it is both emotionally flattening (familiar, formulaic, and predictable in showcasing violence), and disturbing (immediate, real, gruesome, random).

I want to move away from talk about the aesthetico-emotional responses of *katharsis*, or art-horror, to seek a subtler and more nuanced moral assessment of realist horror films. I propose a method of *ideological critique*. I am interested in asking these sorts of questions: how do realist horror narratives operate as a discourse that creates knowledge and power? Whose interests do they serve? Ideological critique interprets film texts by identifying how they represent existing power relations so as to naturalize them.[13] Such readings can register contradictions between surface and deeper messages, so can offer more complexity than the moral psychological condemnation of realist horror as perverse. I mean that a good ideological reading can enable the critic to question and resist what she sees as problematic moral messages of films. [. . .]

There is no particular map for ideological critique; it is more like a possible guide to use in studying a film genre. As I use it, it reflects my own concern with issues that are especially likely to be raised in realist horror. These typically concern gender, since so much of realist horror involves male violence against women, but there also may be issues about violence in general as it relates to social class, race, urban alienation, etc. Focusing on the examples I have mentioned so far, I can identify two particular sorts of morally problematic messages typically conveyed in realist horror, related to what I have called the key features of this genre, the monster and the spectacle.

Monsters In Realist Horror

Some argue that the only way to deconstruct or undo the damaging myths of fascination of monstrous killers is to argue, persuasively and rationally, that they are not extraordinary or monstrous, and deserve no particular attention.[14] My response here is somewhat Baudrillardian or cynical: it seems simply too late or impossible to undo the kinds of mechanisms that currently exist for making such figures famous, for portraying Bundy for instance by the "sexiest man alive," as *People* magazine once dubbed Mark Harmon, or for instant hysterical recreations of disasters at Waco or Killeen. So if rational resistance has become impossible in the society of spectacle, than the alternative is to understand that we/the masses are enjoying spectacle as hyperbolic charade. We have begun to take the spectacle to extreme forms that make it deconstruct itself when we make the repulsive one-eyed short and dumpy Henry Lucas into the handsome Brandoesque Michael Rooker, or the cannibal Lecter into the fascinating genius-villain played by Anthony Hopkins in an Oscar-winning performance. As I have argued above, *Henry* glamorizes and eroticizes its central figure at the same time that it raises for the audience real and disturbing issues about our fascination with him and with this spectacle. [. . .]

Though feminist critics have attacked horror films for linking violence against the female body with male spectatorial pleasure, a more insidiously troublesome feature of realist horror is to target and victimize viewers by playing on the fascination of the monster so as to eroticize him.[15] This is equally true in the presentation of real cases (Dahmer, the Menendez brothers, Bundy) and fictive ones like Henry or Hannibal Lecter. In particular, a film like *Henry* eroticizes the killer by linking him to traditional Hollywood film heroes like James Dean and Marlon Brando. Of course, from Gary Cooper to Clint Eastwood this hero has been strong, potentially violent, inept at communicating, independent, etc. Significantly, although many real life serial killers (like Dahmer) prey on young men or boys, this sort of killer has not been made the focus of major films, presumably because he violates the clichéd association between potent maleness and heterosexuality. In other words, realist horror creates links between the dark side of male traits (violence, uncontrolled sexuality) and the heroic side (power, independence, etc.).

This means that realist horror legitimizes patriarchal privilege through the stereotyped and naturalized representation of male violence against women. These cultural narratives treat male violence as an inevitable concomitant of normal male sexuality. [. . .]

In realist horror, male sexuality is a ticking time bomb, a natural force that must be released and will seek its outlet in violence if it is frustrated or repressed. Since women, and usually the monster's mother (as in *Henry*, *Psycho*, *Silent Madness*, or real-life accounts of criminals like John Hinckley), are scapegoated as sources of this repression, they are shown somehow to deserve the violence they evoke. The net effect is that we simply accept as a natural and inevitable reality that there will be vast amounts of male violence against women.[16]

Nevertheless, I believe that the formulaic depictions of violent male sexuality in realist horror can come to be seen *as* just that, formulas. Many prominent examples of contemporary horror employ self-parody and bizarre humor, recognizing and poking fun at the audience's participation in the formulas of the genre (including gender stereotypes). Consider changes that occurred in the sequel to *The Texas Chain Saw Massacre*. Both Part I and its successor are framed by a grim announcement that "this film is based on a true story"; but the realism of *Chain Saw I* has vanished by version II to be replaced by hyperbolic violence, violence as excess. Key scenes in this film play with the sex/slash formula in hilarious ways. The unforgettably frightening Leatherface from the first *Chain Saw* has here become a rather pitiful younger sibling who gets a crush on the heroine and is teased about it by his brother. When Leatherface first moves to attack Stretch he becomes mesmerized by her long naked legs in a scene that blatantly parodies the notion of buzzsaw as phallic substitute. The point is driven home (as if it needed to be) when the patriarch of the cannibalistic family tells his son sternly "Sex or the saw, son, you have to choose."

Films like *Henry* or *The Silence of the Lambs* may actually lead audience members to question their own fascination with the monstrousness of the serial killer and to query associated icons of male heroism. This is a tricky point to demonstrate. Realist horror films may undercut the standard *Psycho* explanation that scapegoats women, particularly mothers, for male violence. I have suggested that something like this occurs in *Henry*, a film that relies upon but simultaneously empties out the formula "he did it because of his mother." [. . .]

As I argued above, realist horror highlights spectacle over plot, and this means that one ideological effect of such narratives is to perpetuate a climate of fear and random violence where anyone is a potential victim. Paradoxically these films send out the comforting message that we are safe because the violence is, at the moment, striking someone else. The emphasis on pessimism and powerlessness in realist horror also obscures the truth about factors that produce a climate of violence: racism; inequities in education, health care, social and economic status, and political power; urban blight and flight; drug use; and gun laws. So instead of the horror prompting action and resistance, it works to produce passivity and legitimize current social arrangements. [. . .]

But there is more to be said about this specularization of gruesome violence. Again, what is going on involves a blurring, even inversion, of the classical relation between *mimesis* and reality – simulations of violence can precede and come to define reality (this is Baudrillard's notion of the hyperreal[17]). There does seem to be a sense in which the spectacle is hyperreal – the depiction of violence sets the standard for the reality. For example, it is common for survivors of real disasters to exhibit flattened responses and to describe the reality by comparing it to television or movie disasters, as in this news account of the scene in Killeen, Texas after the Luby's massacre:

> DPS spokesman Mike Cox said after the attack that the cafeteria looked like a slaughterhouse or a scene from a movie.
> "There are bodies scattered throughout the entire cafeteria," Cox said "the floor is covered with broken glass, bullet holes, bullet fragments, blood."
> "It's almost a surrealistic, nightmarish-looking scene. You think you are on a TV set. You have to remind yourself this is the real thing."[18]

The spokesman here can almost be seen as anticipating the inevitable reenactment soon to be shown (as it was indeed shown) on *America's Most Wanted*. Americans watched virtually the entire Persian Gulf War on live television, and we could see the television movie about David Koresh in Waco right in the same week the apocalyptic fire there ended the long cult standoff.

Of course, it is tempting to stop after pronouncing a negative verdict about this increasing dominance of the spectacle, or making the critical points I made just above. This supposes that audiences are seduced and perhaps controlled or victimized by the increasing spectacles of violence offered by the modern entertainment industry, with as the result an obscene sort of flattening that equates all experiences and produces indifference, as even horrific disasters like Chernobyl or the Challenger explosion become, in Baudrillard's terms, "mere holograms or simulacra."[19] Nevertheless, I again want to insist that as members of the masses, we bear some responsibility for our participation in the specularization of violence. I think that realist horror, by its very hyperbolic excess, may actively encourage the audience in its critical awareness of its own interest in spectacle. Recall that *Henry*, for example, is a particularly self-reflexive movie that forces viewers into the viewpoint of the murderers themselves as we become spectators, alongside Henry and Otis, watching their video-recorded home movies of murders. This naturally prompts audience unrest and questions, so I do not think it is sufficient to analyze it as an exercise in ideological control. Much the same is true, I would argue, of *The Silence of the Lambs*, which problematically encourages the audience to sympathize with brilliant serial killer Hannibal Lecter. Other realist horror films allude to the use of surveillance devices in our culture to problematize the spectacle of violence. For example, in *Menace II Society* the character O-Dog is criticized for repeatedly watching and screening a videotape that recorded his murder of a Korean store owner. [. . .]

Conclusion

Realist horror is like ancient tragedy in that it presents horrific events and features an element of problematic spectacle; these are in each case set within a broader context of somewhat regimented representational devices. The similarity is strong enough to have tempted philosophers to build upon it in fashioning a theory of horror that may work as a defense of the genre. But I have argued that a classical approach to realist horror does not work, for various reasons. Realist horror showcases spectacle, downplays plot, and plays upon serious confusions between representations of fiction and of reality. I do not believe that my task as a philosopher of film is to defend the genre of realist horror. Instead I want to describe it and comment upon its appeal. My own strategy of reading this genre involves me, admittedly, in a sort of tension: ideological critique focuses on problematic ways in which realist horror films create discourses of knowledge and power, serving conservative and patriarchal interests, and it is likely to produce a critical view of realist horror. But I have also tried to foreground the horror and mass media audience's ability to produce subversive interpretations, acknowledging that viewers do indeed have a significant power and interpretive role in reading, and resisting, realist horror films.

Notes

1   I am grateful to Noël Carroll, Anne Jaap Jacobson, Doug Kellner, Justin Leiber, and Tom Wartenberg for comments on earlier versions, and to Doug Ischar, Lynn Randolph, and Bill Simon for watching and discussing *Henry* with me.

2   See Lisa W. Foderaro, "Crimes of Passion, Deals of a Lifetime," *New York Times*, February 10, 1991, 6E.

3   See Anne Mellor, *Mary Shelley: Her Life, Her Fiction, Her Monsters* (New York: Methuen, 1988), 98–100, 105–6; and Thomas Boyle, *Black Swine in the Sewers of Hampstead: Beneath the Surface of Victorian Sensationalism* (New York: Viking, 1989).

4   Noël Carroll, *The Philosophy of Horror, or Paradoxes of the Heart* (New York and London: Routledge, 1990). [See entry in this volume.]

5   There are rare female counterparts in 1960s films, for example, Roman Polanski's *Repulsion* (1965).

6   The prevalence of realist horror featuring psycho killers is confirmed and analyzed in several recent studies. See James B. Twitchell, *Dreadful Pictures: An Anatomy of Modern Horror* (New York and Oxford: Oxford University Press, 1985); Andrew Tudor, *Monsters and Mad Scientists: A Cultural History of the Horror Movie* (Oxford: Blackwell, 1989).

7   Michael Graczyk, "Odyssey of Henry Lee Lucas," *Houston Chronicle*, August 15, 1993, 5D.

8   Carol Clover has shown that slashers usually do obey a certain moral code in *Men, Women, and Chain Saws: Gender in the Modern Horror Film* (Princeton: Princeton University Press, 1992).

9   See Linda Williams, *Hard Core: Power, Pleasure, and the "Frenzy of the Visible"* (Berkeley: University of California Press, 1989), 131–4.

10   Plato, *Republic* X, 439e–40a.

11   Aristotle, *Poetics* 6, 50b16–17.

12   For a similar objection see Robert Solomon, Review of Noël Carroll's *The Philosophy of Horror*, in *Philosophy and Literature* 16 (1992): 163–73 (with reply by Carroll).

13   An example of an ideological analysis of horror is offered in Michael Ryan's and

Douglas Kellner's *Camera Politica: The Politics and Ideology of Contemporary Hollywood Film* (Bloomington: Indiana University Press, 1988).

14 Mary Lou Dietz, "Killing Sequentially: Expanding the Parameters of the Conceptualization of Serial and Mass Killers," paper presented at the First International Conference on "Serial and Mass Murder . . . Theory, Research, and Policy," April 3–5, 1992, University of Windsor, Windsor, Canada.

15 See Tania Modleski, "The Terror of Pleasure: The Contemporary Horror Film and Postmodern Theory," in Tania Modleski, ea., *Studies in Entertainment: Critical Approaches to Mass Culture* (Bloomington: Indiana University Press, 1986), 155–66; and Linda Williams, "When the Woman Looks," in Mary Ann Doane, Patricia Mellencamp, and Linda Williams, eds *Re-Vision: Essays in Feminist Film Criticism* (Los Angeles: American Film Institute Monograph Series, University Publications of America, Frederick MD, 1984), 83–99.

16 See for example R. Emerson Dobash and Russell Dobash, *Violence Against Wives: A Case Against the Patriarchy* (New York: The Free Press, 1979).

17 Jean Baudrillard, "The Precession of Simulacra," in Baudrillard, *Simulations*, trans. Paul Foss and Paul Patton (New York: Semiotext(e), 1983).

18 Cindy Rugeley, "22 slain, 20 hurt as gunman opens fire in cafeteria," *Houston Chronicle*, October 17, 1991, 16A.

19 Douglas Kellner, *Jean Baudrillard: From Marxism to Postmodernism and Beyond* (Stanford: Stanford University Press, 1989), 209.

Suggestions for Further Reading

Auerbach, Eric. *Mimesis*. trans. Willard Trask, Princeton: Princeton University Press, 1953.

Clover, Carol C. *Men, Women, and Chain Saws*. Princeton: Princeton University Press, 1992.

Creed, Barbara. *The Monstrous-Feminine: Film, Feminism, Psychoanalysis*. London: Routledge, 1993.

Crowther, Paul. *The Kantian Sublime: From Morality to Art*. Oxford: Clarendon Press, 1989.

Heller, Terry. *The Delights of Terror*. Urbana: University of Illinois Press, 1987.

Hertz, Neil. *The End of the Line: Essays on Psychoanalysis and the Sublime*. New York: Columbia University Press, 1985.

Kant, Immanuel. *Observations on the Beautiful and Sublime* [1763]. Trans. J. T. Goldthwait. Berkeley and Los Angeles: University of California Press, 1960.

Kaufmann, Walter. *Tragedy and Philosophy*. Garden City, NY: Doubleday, 1968.

Kristeva, Julia. *The Powers of Horror*. Trans. Leon S. Roudiez. New York: Columbia University Press, 1982.

Levinson, Jerrold. "Music and Negative Emotions," *Pacific Philosophical Quarterly* 63 (1982).

Longinus. *On the Sublime*. Trans. James A. Arieti and John M. Crossett. New York: Mellen Press, 1985.

Lyotard, Jean-François. *Lessons on the Analytic of the Sublime*. Trans. Elizabeth Rottenberg. Stanford: Stanford University Press, 1994.

Nussbaum, Martha. *The Fragility of Goodness*. Cambridge: Cambridge University Press, 1986.

Nuttall, A. D. *Why Does Tragedy Give Pleasure*. Oxford: Clarendon Press, 1996.

Twitchell, James B. *Dreadful Pleasures*. New York: Oxford University Press, 1985.

PART SIX

WHERE IS THE ARTIST IN THE WORK OF ART?

Preface

Until now, questions about the producers of art have remained at the periphery of our investigation. At this point, we turn our attention to the following issue: Where is the artist in the work of art? In posing this final question, we are forced to confront both the figure of the artist and our own assumptions about how the artist is to be defined, understood, and interpreted.

In the first part of this section, Immanuel Kant, Christine Battersby, and Linda Nochlin investigate the nature of creativity – a subject that centers around such questions as What qualities are essential for artistic eminence? To what degree is creativity a matter of individual vision and talent? To what extent is it a product of the social conditions that foster expectation and opportunity? And finally, should our current standards of artistic achievement be maintained, modified, or abandoned?

In the first two readings, the discussion of creativity is cast in terms of the concept of genius. Immanuel Kant argues that genius is a rare, innate talent, not for science but for art. According to Kant, the genius is a unique wellspring of creativity; rather than follow the rules other artists have laid down before him, the genius is the source of rules which lesser artists may copy. Endowed with the qualities of originality, imagination, and understanding, the genius serves as the conduit through which nature "gives the rule to art." Situating his idea in historical context, Christine Battersby criticizes the influential notion of genius. Rather than capturing the essence of creativity in general, genius focuses on one particular concept of the artist that appropriates feminine qualities of creativity but assigns them exclusively to male artists. Battersby contends that this vision of creativity is exclusionary, restrictive, and deliberately neglectful of the efforts of women. As such, our current criteria for artistic greatness should be abandoned in favor of standards that are more likely to recognize the creative endeavors of women – standards that also recognize the social and political conditions surrounding the artist and her work.

Linda Nochlin analyzes the debate surrounding the question "Why are there no great women artists?" Nochlin holds that the question itself is problematic and rests on several grave misunderstandings about art and art history. As Nochlin sees it, artistic production is an inherently social enterprise, and our standards of artistic achievement should reflect this fact. Rather than debate, modify, or abandon our current standards of genius, Nochlin suggests that we turn our attention to the institutional aspects of artistic production in our attributions of "greatness." Using the case of the "question of the nude," Nochlin examines the educational system of the arts and provides an example of how a historical analysis of institutions of art education might be conducted.

What can we learn about an artist through his or her work? Is the goal of the artist to preserve tradition or transform it? Is it possible to understand the motivations and significance of artists from other cultures and historical periods? To what extent does the artist reflect his or her unique social milieu? The articles in the second segment of this section address these questions and probe the limits and possibilities of our interpretation of the artist and the meanings of artworks. Each selection focuses upon issues of context, tradition, cultural in-fluence, and social function. To add breadth to our inquiry, we have chosen selections that investigate the artist in the genres of writing, dance, painting, and music.

The primary goals of art criticism have been traditionally to analyze the struc-ture, internal relations, and historical significance of specific works of art. What is often left out of this equation is the relationship between the artist and the work itself. The first two essays of this part explore the relation between the artist and the work and question our assumptions about how this relation should be construed. Michel Foucault asks "What is an author?" and investigates the relationship between author and text. In an effort to expose the presuppositions and biases of contemporary literary analysis, Foucault probes the meaning of our concepts of "the work," "the author," and the function of the author's name in literary discourse. He argues that the word "author" does not simply refer to the person who wrote a text but assigns the text itself to a particular category of recognition within the history of literature.

Next W. Msosa Mwale presents a case study of the Likhuba master dancers of Malawi. Inspired by the work of Pierre Bourdieu, Mwale aims to situate both the production and the reception of art within a larger framework of social, economic, and political interests. Through an analysis of the formal structure, social setting, and performative context of Likhuba dance, he shows that the dance is an event of cultural production, one in which the master dancer strikes a dynamic balance between the preservation and transformation of tradition, as well as between the individual's unique talents and the form and function of the dance. This essay also raises questions about the identity of art works that rely on performance and frequently vary with the introduction of extemporaneous variations when they are repeated at different times; such issues obviously ex-tend to other types of performance art as well.

The final two selections present a discussion about issues of intention, inter-pretation, and aesthetic understanding. In laying out the historical and social conditions surrounding Piero della Francesca's *Baptism of Christ*, Michael Baxandall aims to determine the limits to our understanding of painters and paintings from other cultures and time periods. According to him, there is an important distinction to be made between *participants'* and *observers'* under-standings of paintings. As participants in the process of production, painters and their contemporaries understand the professional and cultural import of their works in a manner that is qualitatively different from someone who merely views the final product, especially as that product recedes into the past as time goes by. Observers, on the other hand, view the work from a perspective which allows them to take account of the historical and comparative dimensions of a painting in ways unavailable to the painter him or herself.

In the last entry, Bruno Nettl explores the relationship between ideas *about* music and musical *ideas*. As an ethnomusicologist, Nettl is primarily concerned with the ways in which the production, form, and "thinking" of music influ-ence – and are influenced by – the larger cultural context within which they are embedded. Using examples from the Blackfoot Indian and classical Persian traditions, Nettl reveals the manner in which musicians and musical ideas reflect much deeper cultural beliefs about the nature of the world and human relationships. In examining the contemporary myths about Mozart, he shows the ways in which our cultural beliefs condition and structure our ideas about music and musical composers. One such cultural belief concerns genius, and since Mozart is considered a musical genius *par excellence*, Nettl's discussion of this composer also reflects upon the notion of creative genius introduced earlier.

None of us can step outside of our cultures and examine them and their art from a neutral point of view. But the essays in this section sensitize us to questions of context and influence in our interpretation of arts and of the artists who craft them.

Jason Adsit

Genius and Creativity

---

31 From the *Critique of Judgment*

Immanuel Kant

Fine Art Is the Art of Genius

Genius is the talent (natural endowment) that gives the rule to art. Since talent is an innate productive ability of the artist and as such belongs itself to nature, we could also put it this way: *Genius* is the innate mental predisposition (*ingenium*) *through which* nature gives the rule to art.

Whatever the status of this definition may be, and whether or not it is merely arbitrary, or rather adequate to the concept that we usually connect with the word *genius* (these questions will be discussed [below]), still we can prove even now that, in terms of the meaning of the word genius adopted here, fine arts must necessarily be considered arts of *genius*.

For every art presupposes rules, which serve as the foundation on which a product, if it is to be called artistic, is thought of as possible in the first place. On the other hand, the concept of fine art does not permit a judgment about the beauty of its product to be derived from any rule whatsoever that has a *concept* as its determining basis, i.e., the judgment must not be based on a concept of the way in which the product is possible. Hence fine art cannot itself devise the rule by which it is to bring about its product. Since, however, a product can never be called art unless it is preceded by a rule, it must be nature in the subject (and through the attunement of his powers) that gives the rule to art; in other words, fine art is possible only as the product of genius.

What this shows is the following: (1) Genius is a *talent* for producing something for which no determinate rule can be given, not a predisposition consisting of a skill for something that can be learned by following some rule or other; hence the foremost property of genius must be *originality*. (2) Since nonsense too can be original, the products of genius must also be models, i.e., they must be *exemplary*; hence, though they do not themselves arise through imitation, still they must serve others for this, i.e., as a standard or rule by which to judge. (3) Genius itself cannot describe or indicate scientifically how it brings about its products, and it is rather as *nature* that it gives the rule. That is why, if an author owes a product to his genius, he himself does not know how he came by the ideas for it; nor is it in his power [*Gewalt*] to devise such products at his pleasure, or by following a plan, and to communicate [his procedure] to others in precepts that would enable them to bring about like products. (Indeed, that

Lightning Source UK Ltd.
Milton Keynes UK
UKHW052235050419
340581UK00001B/4/P